African and Caribbean Politics

From Kwame Nkrumah to the
Grenada Revolution

Manning Marable

Verso is the imprint of **New Left Books**

**British Library
Cataloguing in Publication Data**

Marable, Manning
   African and Caribbean politics from Kwame
Nkrumah to the Grenada revolution.—
(Haymarket series).
   1. Africa – Politics and government – 1960-
   2. Caribbean Area – Politics and government
   – 1945-
   I. Title   II. Series
   320.96   JQ 1872

ISBN: 978-0-86091-884-4

First published by Verso 1987
© Manning Marable 1987

Verso
6 Meard Street London W1

Typeset in Times by
PRG Graphics
Redhill, Surrey

Printed and bound by CPI Group (UK) Ltd,
Croydon, CR0 4YY

Contents

Preface	vii
Dedication	xi
1. Historical Contours of African and Caribbean Politics	1
2. Kwame Nkrumah and the Convention People's Party	88
3. Socialism from Above	150
4. Maurice Bishop and the Grenada Revolution	197
Notes	273
Index	307

Preface

Several years ago, I began to draft a manuscript entitled, *Race, Politics and Power,* which tried to examine the intricate connections between contemporary Black political movements in the USA, the Caribbean and Africa. It was admittedly an ambitious if rather unwieldy corpus, held together tenuously by several common themes. Upon the advice of my editor the text was severed, and most of the material on Afro-American politics was consolidated under the title *Black American Politics.* Since that time, I've completed considerably more research on African and Caribbean politics, and hopefully this second volume reflects my additional efforts. There is some material which discusses Black US politics, but in general the focus is outside the United States. The heart of this text comprises four general questions:

What was the specific legacy of slavery, forced labor, and colonial rule upon the evolution of Black political movements and leaders during the eighteenth, nineteenth and early twentieth centuries?

How and when were socialist and Communist parties introduced to Black colonial social formations, and what was their interaction with trade unionism and petty bourgeois nationalism in different social environments?

What have been the records of various political formations and mass movements — such as the Convention People's Party of the Gold Coast, the New Jewel Movement of Grenada, the Tanganyikan African National Union, the People's Progressive Party of Guyana, the People's National Party of Jamaica, etc., — in developing programs and transitional strategies for the construction of 'socialism'? And most crucially, what political, social and economic factors have contributed directly to the proliferation of undemocratic, authoritarian regimes in both Africa and the Caribbean in the late twentieth century?

This collection of essays does not provide a comprehensive overview of every major African or Caribbean politician or party. It does not go into substantial detail on those few liberation movements which seem to have been most successful in developing structures of revolutionary democracy; nor does it critique the contributions of the most seminal African and Caribbean revolutionary theorists: Frantz Fanon, Amilcar Cabral and C.L.R. James. In the future, I intend to undertake a more comprehensive study of these Black radical social theorists. Given these self-imposed limitations, I decided to analyze two Black societies in considerable detail.

Ghana was selected partially because it was the first sub-Saharan state after World War II to acquire nominal independence. The political achievements and contradictions of the Convention People's Party were in some ways replicated by other African parties in the 1960s. Moreover, Kwame Nkrumah was the most influential and complex figure to come to power in Africa during this period.

Grenada was selected because it was the first successful political insurrection led by Marxist-Leninists to occur in the English-speaking Caribbean. I was very familiar with the literature on the NJM, and had been invited to attend the fifth anniversary of the government. I had also spent several days talking Caribbean politics with NJM activist Vincent Noel, when both of us were guests of the PNP annual convention in Jamaica, in September 1983. Three weeks later, Noel was killed by his former 'comrades' in St. Georges, along with Maurice Bishop, Jacqueline Creft, Unison Whiteman and other revolutionaries.

Even today, it is difficult to reconcile my vision of socialism with the factors behind the tragic implosion of the NJM government, and the violent imposition of the temporary military dictatorship. The events of 1983 sparked a major debate throughout the Caribbean left, as social democrats and Marxists alike tried to explain the root causes for the party's schism. My essays on both Grenada and 'Socialism from Above' suggest that there are indeed two basic political and organizational characteristics inherent in every socialist movement and society, which may be termed 'egalitarianism' and 'statism.' What usually passes for 'socialism' is an hierarchially deformed version of statism, which emphasizes centralized decision-making and planning, extensive social engineering, the negation of political and social pluralism, and the concentration of state power within the upper levels of the ruling party's organization. Inside the Caribbean left, 'egalitarianism' is best embodied in the social thought of C.L.R. James: the advocacy of cultural pluralism, civil liberties and intellectual freedom, decentralized decision-making, the use of moral incentives, and the reduction of abolition or top-down bureaucracy and centralized authority.

Any successful socialist strategy ought to represent a dialectical synthesis of these two characteristics, based on the objective level of political consciousness and prior experiences of class struggle. Any socialist party which cannot quickly mobilize its cadre, implement political decisions with a high degree of efficiency, and marshal resources necessary to combat imperialism will not be able to hold state power for long. But any socialist or Marxist party which bans strikes, prohibits autonomous labor unions, and regularly imposes public curfews; which harasses, imprisons or executes nonviolent critics of the regime, does nothing to uproot the traditional oppression of women, and systematically suppresses workers' rights to freedom of speech, religion and assembly; and which does not foster the fullest possible participation of the masses in the reorganization of production and public decision-making has abrogated its right to rule. As C.L.R. James observed in *Modern Politics*: 'Anyone who tries to prevent you from knowing, from learning anything, is an enemy, an enemy of freedom, of equality, of democracy.'

Several segments of this book have appeared elsewhere in different form. Material from chapter two was published in *TransAfrica Forum*, vol. 5 (Summer 1986). Material from chapter four was published in the *Guardian* (US), (5 February 1986). My resourceful and energetic research assistant, Lisa Eiseman, was invaluable in finding out-of-print and obscure texts from the library. My special thanks also to Melanie Goldstein and Mary Smith for their work on the manuscript. As always, my deepest debt is to my wife, Hazel Ann, and my three children, Malaika, Sojourner, and Joshua. I have made efforts to check my compulsive workaholic habits of previous years, and as my children have grown older, I've learned to devote more time to appreciate their joy and laughter.

x *Preface*

Nevertheless, my research and political commitments still keep me away from home about two months every year. Hazel Ann remains the organizational and spiritual centre for the Marable family. Without her constant support, strength and encouragement, my various tasks as a Black scholar, political activist, husband and father would be virtually impossible to coordinate.

Finally, another debt of gratitude is required. The impetus for this study came from several important texts on comparative Black politics and social history. W.E.B. Du Bois's classic, *The Negro*, published in 1915, was perhaps the first comprehensive study of comparative political and social struggles within the African Diaspora. Du Bois's *The World and Africa* (1947) outlined the cultural and social heritage of African people, their collective struggles against the slave trade, colonial rule and economic exploitation. C.L.R. James's *History of Negro Revolt* (1938) charted the struggles of Blacks in the United States, the Caribbean and Africa, the dynamic emergence of Garveyism, labour unrest, and mass uprisings. Both scholars perceived the essential commonalities within the African Diaspora, without underestimating the peculiarities of each state and society. They were Pan-Africanists, in that their research was directly dedicated to the political liberation of all peoples of African descent. This book is hopefully a contribution to this tradition of radical Pan-Africanist scholarship.

Manning Marable, July 1986

Dedication

Throughout the recent history of Black struggle in the Caribbean and Africa, there have been countless numbers of women and men who gave of themselves completely to achieve freedom and self-determination. The legacies of Maurice Bishop, Kwame Nkrumah, Amilcar Cabral, Jacqueline Creft, Unison Whiteman, Vincent Noel, Frantz Fanon, Eduardo Mondlane, Agostinho Neto, Patrice Lumumba, and other advocates of national liberation and socialism will continue to give birth to new generations of fighters. And the current struggles now being led by Winnie and Nelson Mandela, Bishop Desmond Tutu, and the African National Congress against the tyranny of apartheid shall soon provide the material for future studies in the politics of developing an independent, democratic African state in transition to socialism.

1

Historical Contours of African and Caribbean Politics:

Colonialism, Neocolonialism, Nationalism, and Marxism

> Today the Rhodesian copper miner, living the life of three shillings a week, is but another cog in the wheels of a creaking world economy, as uneconomic in the twentieth century as a naked slave in the cotton fields of Alabama a hundred years ago. But Negro emancipation has expanded with the centuries; what was local and national in San Domingo and America is today an international urgency, entangling the future of a hundred million Africans with all the hopes and fears of Western Europe. Though dimly, the political consciousness imminent in the historical process emerges in groping and neglected Africa . . . The African bruises and breaks himself against his bars in the interests of freedoms wider than his own.
>
> C.L.R.James,
> *A History of Negro Revolt* (1938)

The general characteristic of the many political institutions and states which have dominated the life and labor of African and Caribbean working people throughout several centuries is that of brutal authoritarianism and systemic coercion. African slaves were never permitted basic human rights — freedom of speech and religion, physical mobility, political expression — since their corporeality was defined as chattel. The later colonial regimes eliminated the more odious elements of slavery, but bound the Black peasant and farmworker to new modes of exploitation. With nominal independence, in most societies, came new, unexpected methods of social control, with the elevation of parvenu, bureaucratic bourgeois strata above the Black masses. Idi Amin in Uganda, Eric Gairy of Grenada, Hastings Banda of Malawi, Jean-Bedel Bokassa of the Central African Republic, and Moise Tshombe and Mobutu Sese Seko of Zaire (Congo) represent only a short list of the neocolonial regimes which are collectively responsible for the deaths of several million Black people since 1960. Some of these authoritarian states and their leaders maintain a classical comprador relationship with international capital and Western governments. Others which have claimed adherence to some version of non-Marxist socialism — Julius Nyerere's 'Ujamaa' of Tanzania, Forbes Burnham's Guyana, Sékou Touré's Guinea, and Léopold Sédar Senghor's Senegal — have appeared to many observers as repressive, state-capitalist social formations, directed by a new bureaucratic class. And still other leaders began their political careers in close association with Communist Parties — Jomo Kenyatta of Kenya, Felix Houphouet-Boigny of the Ivory Coast and Aimé Cesairé of Martinique — but ultimately became reactionary defenders of the neocolonialist status quo.

The foundations of authoritarianism and Black neocolonialism were partially established during the long historical period of capitalist-colonial domination in the periphery. This essay cannot present a comprehensive examination of the various colonial state apparatuses, modes of popular resistance on the evolution of mass political parties and social movements throughout the Black world. But in a preliminary critique, it reviews several historical factors which were crucial in determining the repressive political character of most postcolonial states in the Caribbean and Africa. First, within the evolution of colonial social formations, there developed a heavy reliance on coercion to discipline the laboring classes. There was also a high degree of political authority which was concentrated in a small number of administrators, merchants and landlords. As modern industries developed and new social classes emerged, the elitist, coercive orientation of the colonial state and civil societies remained. Second, for many reasons, the creation of trade unions and early nationalist movements did not usually coincide with the development of large Marxist or socialist parties — indeed compared to other sectors of the periphery, the growth of the left was extremely slow. The first- and second-generation petty-bourgeois nationalists developed eclectic policital ideologies, which were used to consolidate their hegemony over mass movements. Finally, there are the different roles played by both Western imperialism and by the Soviet Union vis a vis the new nationalist leaders and movements, which directly affected the development of postcolonial states. The modern Black authoritarian state is a consequence of these as well as other historical, economic and social forces.

Historical Contours of African and Caribbean Politics 3

I

The African Diaspora is the social consequence of a series of great waves of European capitalist-colonial expansion from the sixteenth to twentieth centuries. Under the Spanish and Portuguese, millions of Africans were brought to the Americas: minimum figures of imported slaves include 3.6 million in Brazil, 702,000 in Cuba, 200,000 in Mexico, 200,000 in Columbia, 121,000 in Venezuela, and 95,000 in Peru. Dutch merchant capital was the first to transfer the Brazilian plantation system into the Caribbean in the early seventeenth century, and was soon followed by the French and British. Before the demise of the trans-Atlantic slave trade and the abolition of slavery itself, millions more Africans were transported: 864,000 to Haiti, 748,000 to Jamaica, 600,000 to the United States, 365,000 to Martinique, 364,000 to tiny Barbados, 290,000 to Guadeloupe, over 500,000 to the Guyanas, and 77,000 to Puerto Rico. Black labor-power was used in a variety of contexts — from tobacco, coffee, cotton, indigo, and cocoa production to mining — but the majority of Africans, perhaps two-thirds, were confined to sugar cane plantations.[1]

The formation of capitalist-colonial states directly paralleled the expansion of agricultural production and international commodity exchange. Sugar provides only one example. Originally a native plant of the Bengal coast, the Chinese first practiced sugar cane cultivation well before 800 A.D.; it was produced in Egypt two centuries later, and the Arabs widely used it in medical prescriptions. The Christian West encountered it only during the Crusades. Venetian entrepreneurs soon began to cultivate sugar cane in Cyprus. With the Atlantic explorations, the plant gradually was moved to the Azores, the Canary Islands, and finally to the upper Guinea coast. With the expansion of the merchant capital into the Caribbean and the Americas, sugar emerged as the dominant export crop for the European market. The Dutch transported cane to their fledgling colony in Curaçao; the French later planted it in Martinique and Guadeloupe; British penal colonists discovered that it flourished along the sea islands of Georgia. From the beginning, planters reaped handsome profits from the sale of sugar; the potential market seemed limitless. But there were certain obstacles to expanded metropolitan trade. 'Cultivation and production,' noted Fernand Braudel, 'required capital and chains of intermediaries. Where intermediaries did not exist, sales rarely went beyond the local market; this remained the case in Peru, New Spain and Cuba until the nineteenth century.' The cultivation of sugar cane on a truly profitable scale, however, demanded one essential ingredient: 'a large labor force.'[2] Africa, of course, provided that labor force, coerced and terrorized into compliance. Even British neoclassical economist Alfred Marshall admitted, 'sugar seldom came to Europe without a stain of blood.'[3]

The capitalist-colonial states during the period of mercantile expansion were authoritarian and elitist. The administrative apparatuses, which included in many instances local assemblies controlled by white planters or merchants, had limited responsibilities. These tasks involved, first, the elimination of indigenous sources of authority which represented potential threats to the colonial European populations. Through a series of brutal military invasions and the proliferation of European diseases, the Indian population of the Caribbean and much of the Americas was decimated. As Andre Gunder Frank observed, 'half a century after the Spanish arrival' in the Caribbean 'the indigenous population was all but extinct.' In Mexico and Peru the Indian population fell by 90 percent.[4] Meanwhile the state apparatuses also had to protect private property, develop the means to facilitate and expand slave production, oppress subordinate social classes, and mediate disagreements between fractions of the local creole classes and the larger interests of the crown. Thus the capitalist-colonial state was an expression of external and internal class forces. The creole planters, merchants and settlers were concerned primarily with parochial accumulation; metropolitan mercantile capitalists and the crown had broader interests, and perceived their annexes of production in a larger context of accumulation.

The legal and coercive apparatuses of the state were structured to perpetuate Black exploitation. Despite regional variations, this was the case in every capitalist-colonial social formation. Spanish officials in Mexico in 1548, for example, 'prohibited the sale of arms to Negroes and forbade public gatherings of three or more Negroes when not with their masters.' After several slave insurrections, these restrictions were tightened between 1571 and 1574. The new code required 'slaves absent from their masters for more than four days' to receive 'fifty lashes.' Those runaways absent for eight or more days were given one hundred lashes, and were forced to wear 'iron fetters tied to their feet with rope' for two additional months. Those slaves absent for more than six moths were to be executed when apprehended — but prudent masters, desiring to salvage their investments, often had this punishment reduced to simple castration.⁵ *Las Siete Partidas* sanctioned the right for a master to punish and even kill his slaves under certain conditions. The *Code Noir* of 1685 and local slave codes in the French colonies required the cutting off of a slave's ears for the crime of being absent from the fields for one month or more. Upon the second offense, the slave's hamstrings were severed.

The laws also strictly regulated the social and economic activities of Blacks and mulattoes, slave or free: In 1623, Bermuda prohibited all Blacks from selling tobacco without their owners' consent. In 1707 free Blacks in Massachusetts were ordered to render labor or service to the state for a period of weeks each year, and were also prohibited from entertaining white indentured servants in their homes. In 1726, the Pennsylvania legislature banned interracial marriages, mandated a colony-wide curfew for Blacks at 9:00 o'clock, and outlawed any meetings of Blacks larger than three persons. In 1741, South Carolina prohibited all Blacks from purchasing or consuming alcohol, banned Black public gatherings, and seized any firearms owned by free Blacks. 'In Dutch Surinam, as well as in Brazil, New York, and Saint Domingue, it was sometimes said that the condition of free Negroes was worse than that of slaves.'⁶

This system of production and exchange also had a profound impact on pre-colonial African societies. The number of slaves who arrived in the Americas, 10 to 15 million, does not include those who died during the dreaded 'Middle Passage' where the mortality rate in the eighteenth century may have averaged nearly 20 per cent. Nor does it include the millions of Africans killed in ethnic or internecine wars to furnish the captives who comprised the bulk of the slave population. The slave trade frequently upset indigenous political arrangements and social structures. Coastal chiefs 'throve and defended their power by purchasing European firearms; those in the rear, deprived of any direct link with Europeans, were reduced to impotence or involvement in the trade themselves.'⁷ As Walter Rodney observed, the longevity of the trade led to greater authoritarianism and class stratification in some African states. 'Active involvement in the Atlantic slave trade invariably meant the increase of such servile categories in the societies where they existed, and their creation where they had not previously existed. . . . By the end of the eighteenth century a sizeable proportion of the inhabitants of West Africa found themselves under some form of servitude . . . The introduction of European goods in itself brought no economic benefits, since the goods were consumed without creating growth in the economy.'⁸

Despite these common structures, the concrete historical patterns of class formation and political protest varied sharply in each of the colonial societies created during these centuries. The case of Grenada is illustrative of the complex evolution of other peripheral social formations. Native American people had settled on the island for roughly 1500 years prior to its 'discovery' by Christopher Columbus in 1498. Following an unsuccessful attempt to occupy the island by a company of London entrepreneurs in 1609, a group of two hundred French 'adventurers' seized it in 1650, and subsequently exterminated most of the Carib inhabitants.⁹ The French quickly introduced sugar cane plantations and African slave labor to the colony, following the well established pattern of labor exploitation and cane production in Brazil and Barbados. Between 1700 and 1753, the slave population increased from 525 to over 12,000. By 1763 Grenada had eighty-two sugar plantations, over one hundred sugar mills, and annual sugar exports approached 4,000 tons.¹⁰ Never slow to appreciate a profitable venture, the British seized Grenada during the Seven Years' War in 1763, and despite a brief restoration of French rule in 1779-1783, they maintained their domination for the next two centuries. As Eric Williams observed, 'up to 1773 British imports from Grenada amounted to eight times the imports from Canada, British exports to Canada were double those to Grenada.'¹¹

The new ruling class accelerated production, raising the African population to 35,000 in 1774, and transformed the colony into a major depot for the region's slave trade. By 1773, British imports from Grenada were worth more than double those of New York, Pennsylvania, or the New England colonies.¹² To guarantee its political hegemony, the British ruthlessly circumscribed the rights of the French planters. 'Churches and church property of the Roman Catholic Church in Grenada were confiscated and given to the Protestant Churches, or acquired by the Crown. Statues, altars and "Popish emblems" were ordered to the flames,' and French settlers were 'denied all political rights.' Spain offered all Catholic emigrants to nearby Trinidad (not seized by the British until 1797) thirty acres of land for each family member and fifteen acres per slave in 1783, an attractive lure which brought a large influx of French planters from Grenada. The majority of African and mulatto workers, freemen and slaves could not escape the tyranny of the British so easily.¹³

The French and Haitian revolutions radically altered the political climate of the entire Caribbean — much as the Cuban revolution would a century and a half later. In Guadeloupe, Victor Hughes seized power and created a revolutionary regime under the banner of 'Liberty, Equality, Fraternity.' In early 1795 two Grenadians, Jean Pierre la Vallette and Charles Nogues made contact with fellow radicals in Guadeloupe, and upon their return organized a general revolt against British Governor Ninian Home. The leader of the uprising was an Afro-French creole, Julien Fedon, who represented the growing middle strata of free coloreds in Grenada, numbering over 1,100. Rising against the British on 2 March 1795 Fedon and his followers seized the coastal towns of Gouyave and Grenville and captured Governor Home who was later executed along with fifty other British prisoners. In the following months hundreds of slaves deserted their plantations to join the revolutionary army. By November 1795 Fedon's forces had secured the entire island except for the beleaguered British fortress in St. George's. Two thousand British reinforcements finally arrived in 1796, and after a year of hard fighting without quarter, Fedon's guerrillas were finally subdued. Thirty-eight rebel leaders were executed, and many of Fedon's slave followers were sent in chains to Honduras. Fedon was never found, but his entire social stratum was penalized for its impudence. Most of the remaining French and free colored were either 'banished from the island,' or their 'properties were seized and given to the Crown.'[14]

Before these Grenadan events, and the great cycle of revolutionary risings of which they form one chapter, slave rebelliousness had been universal but almost always suppressed. Each capitalist-colonial society in the Caribbean during the eighteenth century experienced slave conspiracies and revolts, work slowdowns and strikes, sabotage and desertion. but, with the partial exception of the formation of maroon communities (particularly in Jamaica and Guyana), the colonial authorities never lost control and production was only intermittently disrupted. What explains the success of the slaveowners and the colonial state? In part it was a matter of 'ethics', a gulf of humanity that separated the resistance of the oppressed from the repression of their masters. Slaves desperately desired freedom and many were prepared to risk almost anything for emancipation. But as Eugene Genovese has emphasized, Africans generally did not commit acts of terrorism or crimes of a bestial nature. 'Atrocities by rebellious slaves in the United States did not occur often. Rebels killed whites but rarely tortured or mutilated them. They rarely, that is, committed against whites the outrages that whites regularly committed against them. Elsewhere in the hemisphere, where maroon wars and large-scale rebellions encouraged harsh actions, reactions, and reprisals, the level of violence and atrocity rose. But everywhere the overwhelming burden of evidence convicts the slaveholding regimes of countless crimes, including the most sadistic tortures . . . ' At the first sign of slave rebelliousness, the white planters resorted to brutality. The Spanish in sixteenth century Mexico chained Blacks and 'set wild dogs to devour them.' When an abortive slave insurrection occurred in Barbados in 1675, the whites beheaded eleven Blacks and burned six more alive. Hundreds of thousands of slaves — perhaps millions — were gangraped, dismembered, beheaded, castrated, roasted over hot coals, and broken on the wheel. Within a criminal regime, criminal behavior is normal.[15]

Thus it was taken as preordained that the masters would win and that the price of revolt was torture and death. Given the scale of repression, and the disproportion of arms and resources, it is amazing that so many slaves continued to rebel. Given the masters' control of communications and intercourse, on the other hand, it is not surprising that slave revolts, or the guerrilla warfare conducted by the maroons, remained localized and defensive; and that, as a rule, slaves did not specifically try to overthrow slavery as a socio-economic system, or to replace white power with Black state. The grandeur of the revolt in Saint Domingue that grew into the Haitian Revolution was that it was the exception to all these rules. The Haitian revolution is frequently described as being the only successful slave revolution in world history. It was that, to be sure, but much more. Saint Domingue was also the first national democratic revolution to occur within a predominately Black social formation.

Its principal leader, Toussaint L'Ouverture, was a Jacobin in ideology, a determined foe of slavery yet no opponent to capitalist production. The first stage of the revolution did not break up all the large sugar estates; it did not completely eliminate the economic power of white merchants and traders; it abolished slavery but did little to reduce the former slaves' actual physical burdens. A great revolutionary, Toussaint was nevertheless psychologically and politically incapable of building a system which would discriminate against all whites. Laws were passed guaranteeing an end to racial discrimination in employment, and thousands of Black agricultural workers were armed. Yet when exploited Black laborers, led by Toussaint's nephew Moise, led an insurrection against local whites, Toussaint and his loyal Black troops crushed the insurgents. After executing Moise, Toussaint instituted a series of severe codes designed to constrict Blacks' rights. Laborers were confined to the estates, and 'he made the managers and foremen responsible for this law under pain of imprisonment.' As C.L.R. James explains in *The Black Jacobins:* 'He prohibited the soldiers from visiting a plantation except to see their fathers or mothers, and then only for a limited period: he was now afraid of the contact between the revolutionary army and the people, an infallible sign of revolutionary degeneration.'[16]

Saint Domingue developed into a military dictatorship, in which two social classes competed for political power. State power was held by Toussaint's generals and officers in the ex-slave army, who had seized the estates of the former slaveholders. The second powerful class were the *affranchis,* or the mulatto and free Black petty bourgeoisie, who had formerly owned slaves and still controlled much commercial property. The new regime was in many ways more statist-oriented than the colonial regime. For example, Catholicism was encouraged over traditional African rites but Catholic clergy were strictly controlled. As James observes, 'the governor apportioned to each minister of religion the extent of his administration, and the clergy were not allowed under any pretext whatever to form an association in the colony.' There was absolute censorship of the press and all publications. The heads of the police department, army, and finance were directly accountable to Toussaint. The Constitution appointed him 'governor for life, with power to name his successor.'[17] The despotism of Toussaint in his approach to politics essentially mirrored the brutality of the previous slaveholding regime. The historical conditions of the Saint Domingue revolution were such that no more egalitarian set of governing principles was readily available.

For all of Toussaint's flaws, the Black revolutionary tried desperately to transcend the boundaries of race by advancing a political agenda which encouraged ethnic pluralism and racial tolerance. In contrast, his greatest general, Dessalines, not only detested whites, but made little distinctions between the handling of contradictions among the masses and the suppression of the revolution's enemies. When Toussaint appointed Dessalines military commander of Haiti's southern district, strict orders were given to implement a liberal pacification policy towards the substantial mulatto population.

Dessalines's response was to massacre hundreds of prominent colored leaders. Too late, Toussaint halted the bloody purge, declaring: 'I told him to prune the tree, not to uproot it!' Dessalines ordered his managers to whip his Black farmworkers to promote production; only Toussaint's threat to 'take away his command at the least complaint' briefly checked this policy of labor exploitation.[18]

Dessalines eventually betrayed Toussaint, turning his commander over to the French, yet he subsequently led the ex-slave army to victory over Napoleon. Haiti achieved independence, but the Black masses were not liberated from labor exploitation. Dessalines tried to restore economic order by consolidating all former estates under state authority, and 'created a special state organ, called the Administration des Domaines de l'Etat, empowered to centralise sugar production, administer and control production of agriculture in all nationalised properties, and devise a plan for the economic development of the nation.' Dessalines's program of statist controls and intervention in the private sector was in a sense Bonapartist, because it was fundamentally at odds with the interests of the dominant social classes. As sociologist Alex Dupuy notes, both the *affranchis* and the Black generals 'sought to redistribute the land amongst themselves and subjugate' the ex-slaves. Dessalines's statist agenda was 'an obstacle to the realisation of their class objectives.' In October 1806, Dessalines was assassinated, and his corpse was 'tossed into the streets, where it was destroyed by mobs.'[19]

The complex experience of Haiti prefigures much of the contradictory dynamic of the national liberation movements of our own time. On the one hand, the first generation of Black revolutionaries, fighting in the vanguard of a world democratic revolution, brought the Rights of Man to the Caribbean, overthrew slavery and created a new nation. On the other hand, to wage war for a generation and to guarantee production, they employed terror, banned free speech and reintroduced forms of coerced labor. In the visionary but politically flawed figure of Toussaint, we find the beginning of a revolutionary Caribbean tradition which was later embodied by Martí, James, Rodney and Bishop. In Toussaint's lieutenant Christophe, one can see something of Senghor or Houphouet-Boigny. And in the courageous yet brutal Dessalines, there is an intimation of Idi Amin.

Although the revolution in Saint Domingue did not result ultimately in a democratic outcome for the Haitian masses, it shook New World slavery to its foundations, promoting Black revolts throughout the hemisphere. Apart from the previously mentioned examples of Grenada and the French Antilles, major slave revolts, infected by Haiti, erupted in Bahia (Brazil) in 1807-1816, 1826-27, 1830 and 1835. Demerara experienced Black uprisings in 1803 and 1823. In Jamaica, the small-scale revolts of 1815 and 1829 were rehearsals for Samuel Sharpe's rising of Christmas, 1831, which had more than 20,000 participants. Even inside the United States, where slave rebellions were perhaps most difficult to coordinate due to the numerical domination of the whites, the revolutionary ideology of Saint Domingue found a deep resonance. The abortive slave conspiracies of Gabriel Prosser in Virginia in 1800 and Demark Vesey in 1822, and Nat Turner's revolt of 1831, were part of the broad, democratic protest currents throughout the world at that time. As Genovese notes: 'Vesey looked to Haiti as a model and for inspiration as well as for material support. His speech to his followers combined the language of the Age of Revolution, as manifested in the Declaration of Independence and the Constitution, with the biblical language of the God of Wrath. Nat Turner . . . also spoke in the accents of the Declaration of Independence and the Rights of Man.'[20] After Toussaint, Black militants everywhere would have before them the example of an independent Black state which gained its freedom by defeating European colonialists and slaveholders through protracted popular war. Nothing else could be the same again.

II

With the evolution of industrial capitalism in England and later in Western Europe, the relations between the capitalist-colonial annex states and their respective metropoles changed fundamentally. Industrial capitalists were 'more interested than their mercantile counterparts had been in finding outlets for their machine-produced products and in finding raw materials (cotton, vegetable oils, dyestuffs, etc.) to import, as well as basic foods for the populations of the growing industrial areas.' Instead of slave labor, this emerging bourgeoisie desired 'a stable labor supply for commercial agriculture and mining,' and sought the expansion of 'the use of money and exchange.'[21] Creole planters who controlled colonial legislatures opposed the abolition of the slave trade and slavery itself; in the British Parliament resistance from mercantile capitalists and landords who dominated 'rotten boroughs' blocked abolition for several decades. Nevertheless, in 1834, the British ended slavery officially throughout the empire, and slaveowners received £20 million in compensation. With manumission and the end of the 'apprenticeship period' in 1838, many Afro-American laborers withdrew to self-sufficient agriculture. In Grenada, sugar exports for 1839-1842 were only half of the amount marketed in 1831-1834. Many local planters were determined to maintain the sugar plantation economy based on coerced labor, which was as much 'a way of life to them' as a source of profits. In 1839, 164 laborers from Malta were recruited to take the places of the emancipated slaves. In 1846-1847, Grenada's planters brought over 400 Portuguese from Madeira to work. A decade later another 2,500 Indian indentured laborers were tried in the fields. None of these strategies was particularly successful, as forty-seven sugar estates halted production by the mid-1850s.[22]

Throughout the Americas local merchants and landlords relied heavily on indentured labor to maintain plantation production. In Peru, Chinese laborers from Hong Kong and Macao first arrived in 1849. Over the next twenty-five years, 90,000 to 150,000 Chinese indentured laborers were 'contracted' to work for eight-year-terms in coastal plantations, on railroad construction or in mining. In Brazil roughly 200,000 Japanese immigrants were brought in after Emancipation, while thousands of Italian immigrants labored on the coffee plantations, where they were 'treated almost as harshly as the Africans.'[23] In the Caribbean, post-emancipation sugar production shifted to Cuba, Trinidad and British Guiana. Slavery continued to exist in Cuba until 1886; sugar cane exports from the island soared from 41,000 metric tons in 1802 to over 610,000 metric tons in 1859. To insure a stable labor force, Cuban planters brought in 142,000 Chinese indentured workers from 1847 to 1874. Thousands of Mexican peasants and over 40,000 laborers from the Canary Islands were also shipped into Cuba.

In British Guiana, African ex-slaves initiated what was termed the 'village movement' in order to assert their social and economic independence. Pooling their money, Black farmers purchased their own small estates and initiated 25 'communal villages' with title to over 9,000 acres of land. White planters first turned to Chinese and Portuguese indentured servants, but soon after their contracts expired, 'these groups moved away from the estates and into the retail trade as shopkeepers in the villages set up by the former slaves and into other businesses.' Beginning in 1844, the landlords turned to Indian labor, and by the beginning of World War I nearly 240,000 Indian indentured workers had been imported to Guiana. Bound to the sugar estates by contract and coercion, the Indians 'were regarded as "Coolies" and as economically subservient."[24] Consequently, the continued demand for labor created the basis for a Caribbean social structure (rural proletariat, middle strata and land-owning peasantry) that was crisscrossed by complex cultural and ethnic differentiations: Hinduism, Islam, Afro-Christianity, Confucianism, and Catholicism in religion; Indian, African, Chinese, Spanish, Portuguese, English and French in language or origin. Class identity was so mediated by cultural and ethnic factors, that coherent, mass resistance to capital was made extremely difficult.

The demise of the sugar plantation as the mainstay of Caribbean capitalist production occurred in the mid-to-late nineteenth centuries. Given the severe depletion of the soil on some estates, older sugar plantations found it difficult to compete against the sugar producers in Mauritius and India. But the biggest blow to West Indian planters came with the development of the sugar beet industry in Europe. Between 1850 and 1895 the share of Caribbean cane imports as a percentage of all sugar imports (beet and cane) dropped from 85 percent to 10 percent. Jamaica's annual sugar production fell from 72,000 metric tons in 1828 to barely 20,000 metric tons in 1894. Sugar expansion in Trinidad and British Guiana peaked somewhat later in the 1880s, but production and profits had begun to fall there as well by the early 1890s. For over a half century, white planters tried various means to restore profit margins. Newly freed Black workers' wages were slashed in half as a means of reducing variable capital costs in production, but this resulted inevitably in labor unrest. In the Windward Islands Black workers laid down their tools and left to work their own agricultural plots. There was a series of strikes from Trinidad to St. Kitts.

Many planters turned to other agricultural commodities. The Spanish had been the first to cultivate cocoa in the Americas, as early as the 1530s in Mexico, but a large consumer market for cocoa did not develop in England or the United States until the mid-1800s. With their indentured labor force, the creole class moved from sugar to cocoa on many estates. The cocoa boom began first in Trinidad, where exports grew from 2,160 tons produced annually between 1850-1854 to 26,000 tons in 1910-1914. By the end of World War I, cocoa comprised over 40 percent of Trinidad's total exports, and one-sixth of all agricultural property on the island was covered with cocoa trees.

Grenada experienced a similar agricultural transformation, which in turn created new forms of class relations. Cocoa and nutmeg gradually replaced sugar as the principal export crops, and a form of sharecropping, the 'metayer' system, secured a stable farm labor supply to the planter class. The planter-peasant relationship which existed for the next century 'was essentially the same as the slave-master relationship, minus the physical coercion.' The overwhelming majority of landowners were small peasants who held plots of two to five acres each. A much smaller group of colored and white middle strata owned farms of 10 to 100 acres worked by Black laborers. At the top of society was the landed gentry, a tiny group of wealthy families who maintained estates of 100 to 1,000 acres. With the upper merchant class of St. George's, this planter elite continued to dominate the entire social order. The fundamental class contradiction within Grenada was the conflict between this ruling elite and the agro-proletariat. 'The peasants had led the diversification of the economy into tree crops; they had also begun to modernize the society by establishing independent rural communities that were not part of the archaic plantation system. The peasants had become the most dynamic social force in the colony – yet they remained a social underclass, deprived of all political and economic power.'[25]

The state apparatuses of Caribbean peripheral capitalist societies also changed in the wake of transformed production relations. The British imposed Crown Colony government in Trinidad and British Guiana, allowing for far greater control over their political economies. Small executive committees were set to advise British governors on policy matters, but absolute veto power was held by the governor and the Colonial Office. The British Government accelerated the change from legislative government to Crown Colony by withholding loan guarantees from colonies which retained creole assemblies. By 1866 Jamaica agreed to accept Crown Colony status, along with Montserrat, the Virgin Islands, and Dominica. In the early 1870s British Honduras and Tobago followed; only Barbados retained the old legislative model until 1900. Again using Grenada as a model, one can observe the absence of elementary democratic rights for Black agricultural workers and peasants throughout this new phase of colonial state development. Prior to the imposition of Crown Colony rule, less than one percent of Grenada's adult population had the electoral franchise. In 1850, for instance, the 26-member Grenada Assembly was selected from an electorate of 99 persons. From 1875 to 1925, the franchise was completely abolished. As late as 1944, of the 27,000 adults in

Grenada, barely four thousand were qualified to vote for the local legislature.[26]

Although the responsibilities and operations of these capitalist-colonial states were enlarged in the nineteenth century, they remained rigidly authoritarian. 'The ruling groups were by-and-large singleminded in their use of the state machinery to buttress their authority and consolidate the dominance of the plantation-based cash-crop economy.' The state actively retarded the rise of 'both the "free" labor system and the peasantry.'[27] Governments allotted more funds to mass literacy and educational programs, but usually chose to finance denominational schools rather than establish public institutions. In Trinidad by 1898, for instance, there were 57 government primary schools and 147 denominational schools, which were 'assisted by increasingly generous subsidies.' The only secondary schools were Queen's Royal College, founded in 1870 for 'the sons of civil servants' and for only 'a few exceptionally promising primary-school graduates "from the lower classes" '; and the Roman Catholic St. Mary's College. University-level training was nonexistent, except in Great Britain. These schools served a critical function in the perpetuation of British cultural, social and political values among nonwhites. C.L.R. James, who was a Queen's Royal College graduate and teacher, observed in *Beyond a Boundary* that 'the National Question did not exist' for his generation. 'It was only long years after that I understood the limitation on spirit, vision and self-respect which was imposed on us by the fact that our masters, our curriculum, our code of morals, *everything* began from the basis that Britain was the source of all light and leading, and our business was to admire, wonder, imitate, learn; our criterion of success was to have succeeded in approaching that distant ideal — to attain it was, of course, impossible.'[28]

The Anglican and Catholic churches also exercised considerable political and social authority, which buttressed the state power of the creole ruling class. In British Guiana, for example, most of the colonial functionaries were Anglican, while the Portuguese petty entrepreneurs, civil servants and retail merchants were Catholic. Thus the Catholic Church 'wielded considerable political influence within the Civil Service and in local government' and had a strong 'influence on certain sections of Guyanese opinion.' Both religious institutions closely cooperated with the state to suppress social discontent and to perpetuate the ideological prerogatives of the dominant class.

Finally, with the decline in the police powers of individual plantation masters, the post-emancipation colonial states filled the gap by greatly expanding their judicial systems, police forces and general coercive powers in order to 'ensure internal stability'. Indentured laborers were particularly subject to close state supervision. 'Laws were passed on such matters as payment for work, the number of work days per year and hours of work per day, punishments for nonfulfillment of work obligations, etc.'[29] Similarly, in the ideological and cultural spheres, state institutions perpetuated the dogma of white racism, to justify and rationalize the exploitation of Indian and Black Labor. This in turn reinforced the gender oppression of rural and poor women as well as promoting color stratification in nearly all cultural and social activities. James's remarks on Trinidad in the 1920s are particularly instructive. Cricket was the most popular sport, and 'the various first-class clubs represented the different social strata in the island within clearly defined boundaries.' Queen's Park Club was 'white and often wealthy,' but contained a few 'members of the old well-established mulatto families.' Second in prestige was Shamrock, 'the club of the old Catholic families.' Maple was the 'club of the brown-skinned middle class'; and Shannon attracted 'the Black lower-middle class'; and Stingo 'were the plebeians . . . totally Black and no social status whatever.' These social levels were not absolute. A 'Portuguese of local birth' was not considered white 'unless very wealthy,' while the Black educated middle strata could rise in social rank by keeping 'company with people lighter in complexion . . .'[30]

A similar color/class dynamic existed in Grenada. M.G. Smith estimated that the island's 'creole elite' comprised about five percent of the total population. After the reestablishment of electoral privileges in the 1920s, only the elite could vote. It controlled the largest estates and businesses on the island, and maintained its own set of social 'standards.' 'Elite Creole males,' Smith noted, 'especially take pride in their reputations as sportsmen and gamesters, and gamble freely on horses or cards in socially appropriate conditions, mainly at one another's homes in the evenings. Gambling in clubs and public places is sharply disapproved, but most of all, gambling with people of lower status.' Social clubs of the elite preserved their cultural distance from the masses. St. George's Club, founded in 1888, was known as 'the most expensive and exclusive in the island'; the club maintained a strict rule that no 'women and dogs' were to be admitted. For their sexual pleasures,

Historical Contours of African and Caribbean Politics 17

however, creole planters and merchant elite frequently visited the quarters of the urban and rural poor, demanding the daughters of the peasantry for their own entertainment. Smith described 'the extramarital unions of elite males and folk women' as casual and customary. Frequently 'the father may not even see his child, although contributing the legally required minimum maintenance to avoid undue publicity.' Children by elite women 'enjoy social recognition and full status equivalence with their fathers; at best, unlawful children enjoy a partial paternity. Relations between these two sets of children, when they know one another, are accordingly marked by sharp cleavages of status . . . ' Consequently, many if not most elite males usually had 'two families, one lawful and domestic, the other unlawful, extradomestic, and usually clandestine.'[31]

Despite sporadic outbreaks of Black and Indian labor unrest, the social conditions for a sustained and coherent regionwide movement against capitalist-colonialism did not then exist in the Caribbean. Even in particular states where the proletarianization of rural workers and the beginnings of an urban working class were more advanced, the labor force was usually split along religious and ethnic lines. Consequently for three generations — between the 1840s and the 1920s – many Black intellectuals who otherwise might have provided leadership to mass movements instead left the Caribbean. There are many examples: Edward Wilmot Blyden, born in the Virgin Islands in 1832, who later became president of Liberia College and Liberia's ambassador to Great Britain; Trinidadian Henry Sylvester Williams, born in 1869, educated in North America and England, and the coordinator of the first Pan-African Conference held in London in 1900; Jamaican Black nationalist Marcus Garvey, born in 1887, whose Universal Negro Improvement Association (UNIA), founded in 1914, achieved its greatest successes among Black workers in the United States; Jamaican journalist W.A. Domingo, born in 1889, who briefly edited Garvey's *Negro World* newspaper, and who helped to establish the pro-independence Jamaican Progressive League in New York City in 1936; Cyril V. Briggs, born in Nevis, in the British Leeward Islands in 1887, who founded the revolutionary nationalist formation, the African Blood Brotherhood (ABB) and became the leading Black figure in the Communist Party of the United States (CPUSA) in the 1920s; C.L.R.James, born in 1901, whose historical, literary and theoretical works were written largely in Great Britain in the 1930s and subsequently in the US in 1938-1952; and Trinidadian Malcolm

Nurse (George Padmore), who was perhaps the most influential Black Communist of the early 1930s, and who later was the central theoretician of the Pan-Africanist movement in the 1940s and 1950s.[32]

Culturally fragmented, and shorn of many of their most brilliant natural leaders, the labor and nationalist movements of the Caribbean struggled through difficult birth processes in the last decade of the nineteenth century – their emergence often delayed to the eve of World War I.

It was not until 1897 that the Trinidad Workingmen's Association (TWA) was formed by a druggist, Alfred Richards. But the TWA's initial effort to mobilize a dockworkers' strike in 1902 was ruthlessly crushed. In Jamaica in the same period bricklayers, carpenters, and cigar makers began to organize while Bain Alves stirred the dockworkers and Garvey mobilized the printers. Unitarian minister Egbert Ethelred Brown founded the Jamaica League in 1914 to foster cooperative stores and small industries for Blacks. Brown was also instrumental in the creation of the Progressive Negro Association and the Liberal Association in 1916-1917, which had 'three aims: to foster racial pride; to improve the economic, social, intellectual, and moral conditions of Blacks in Jamaica; and to secure rights for all Blacks.'[33] In British Guiana, militant dockworkers were led by Hubert Nathaniel Critchlow. Also in Guiana two important regional movements were founded: James B. Yearwood's Universal Loyal Negro Association and Randolph Smith's Negro Progress Convention. These early organizations expressed their goals frequently within the context of the existing political economy and state structure. In those few instances where they manifested an anti-capitalist orientation, the dominant political thrust was toward social democracy and incremental, moderate reform. The British Labour Party established fraternal ties with the TWA after 1908, and postwar TWA leader Arthur Cipriani was one of the first Caribbean labor activists to identify himself as a socialist.

Modern anti-colonialism came to Grenada in the 1890s, with the appearance of Afro-Irish journalist William Galway Donovan's *Federalist and Grenada People* newspaper. More influential was Donovan's protegé, Theophilus Albert Marryshow, who at the age of twenty-one helped to establish the Grenada Literary and Debating Society in 1908. Eight years later, Marryshow and attorney C.F.P. Renwick started the liberal anticolonialist publication *West Indian,* which demanded an expanded suffrage and the creation of an independent federation of West Indian states. After the creation of a limited franchise and legislative council in 1925 — in which only 3.25 percent of all adults were eligible to vote — Marryshow was elected to office, and 'he used the floor of the Legislature to deliver caustic oratory denouncing the Governor and the imperial regime.'[34] Influenced by the British Labour Party, Marryshow initiated in 1930 the 'Grenada Workingmen and Women Association,' a broad but ideologically uneven association which acted as both a proto-labor union and political rights lobby. The Association's mobilization of more than ten thousand protesters in the streets of St. George's in October 1931, attacking the legislature's recent tax hike, was the first proletarian and farmers' movement in Grenadian history, and forced the repeal of the tax ordinance.

However, this was the highpoint of Marryshow's political effectiveness. The Association soon began to disintegrate. Marryshow attempted to consolidate the movement by launching the Grenada Labour Party, but in several years it also disappeared. Marryshow's failure was rooted in both subjective and objective factors. Politically, Marryshow had no analysis of class struggle, and never developed a true trade union. He appealed more to liberal sectors of the creole elite, and failed to mobilize the agro-proletariat consistently. The mercantile entrepreneurs, landlords and the government maintained their 'paternalistic' influence over the subordinate classes. As Simon Rottenberg has commented, the grenadian employers 'created a father image of themselves and believe that they know best what is good for their people; workers are children, irresponsible, indolent, and prodigal . . . '[35] Discontented laborers who sought socioeconomic advancement usually left the island for Trinidad's oilfields, or for the UK or USA. For example, in 1934-1939 approximately 4,000 Grenadians went to Trinidad, and in 1941-1944 another 8,300 departed. Although Grenadians like Tubal Uriah 'Buzz' Butler were instrumental in starting powerful trade unions outside of their island, Grenada's first real union was not created until 1946.[36]

In summary, as Crown Colony government gradually ended in the early twentieth century, the leadership of the Caribbean laboring classes — the agro-proletariat, small peasantry and urban laborers — was often diffused and theoretically inconsistent. The very organizational weakness of the Caribbean proletariat allowed liberal and nationalist members of the petty bourgeoisie to assume leadership of the social and anti-colonial revolts. Domingo's father, who was Spanish, 'owned and operated a large fleet of hansom cabs in Kingston'; Cipriani was the son of a well-to-do French Creole family, and an officer of the British West Indian Regiment during World War I; Henry Sylvester Williams completed his university studies in London; James's grandfather had been the first Black engineer on the government railroad, his father was a respected school teacher, and James himself won his coveted scholarship to Queen's Royal College at the tender age of nine; and Nurse graduated from Trinidad's private Pamphylian High School, and completed further studies at Columbia, Howard and Fisk Universities.[37] Social class position does not always dictate class consciousness and political orientation. On the eve of the Great Depression, fractions of the non-European petty bourgeoisie had identified with the proto-independence, trade unionist, and Black nationalist movements. Nevertheless, a substantial economic and social distance existed between many of these early leaders and intellectuals and the classes whose interests they presumed to represent.

III

The triangular connections between capitalist Europe, Africa and the Caribbean were not severed with the abolition of the transatlantic slave trade. Although social historians sometimes mark the beginning of the imperialists' partitioning of Africa with the Congress of Berlin in 1884-1885, European capitalists and colonial officers had been extensively involved with the continent for over half a century. France seized Algeria in 1830; and the British began their long occupation of Egypt in 1882. In the Maghreb, the European settler population of merchants and landlords increased from barely one thousand in 1830 to over 10,000 in French Morocco in 1911, 128,000 in Tunisia by 1906, and 752,000 in Algeria in 1911. In the Senegambia region, the French had established St, Louis in the seventeenth century, and by the 1870s the trading center had grown to a population of 16,000. In 1883 the French secured their economic and political interests along the upper Niger, with the founding of Bamako. The British obtained a treaty with the Fante state in 1844, which established their initial claim to the Gold Coast region. After purchasing Dutch and Danish forts along the coast, the British defeated the powerful Ashanti confederation in 1873-1874, securing their local hegemony. In Nigeria, the British established an 'Oil Rivers Protectorate,' and in 1861 Lagos was made a Crown Colony. In the Congo basin, Leopold II of Belgium's commercial agency, Comité d'Études du Haut Congo, had begun to

Historical Contours of African and Caribbean Politics 21

establish mercantile centers by the late 1870s. Within the span of thirty years, West African societies began to be firmly integrated as the annexes of Western capitalism. Urbanization occurred rapidly: Lagos had 75,000 residents by 1914, Dakar had 25,000, and Accra, 20,000 inhabitants. The boundaries drawn by European-held territories were based on political and economic expediency, and made little sense within the context of local language and ethnic groups. The Masai were divided between German Tanganyika and British-controlled Kenya; the Akan were split between the Ivory Coast and the Gold Coast; the Fulani, Malinke, Ewe, Ovimbundu and hundreds of other ethnic groups were splintered between two, three or more capitalist-colonial regimes.

Excluding South Africa, the regions of sub-Saharan Africa which first experienced intensive European 'development' were the Gold Coast, Senegal, and German Togo. Samir Amin and other political economists have described this social and economic restructuring as constituting the *économie de traite*. Key features included 'the organization of a dominant trade monopoly' through colonial import-export firms; the 'taxation of the peasants in money terms, which forced them to produce whatever the monopolists offered to buy'; the establishment of European plantations, utilizing local and migrant laborers; the buttressing of indigenous social strata which cooperated with the new regimes; and the creation of an administrative apparatus of coercion to secure labor supplies whenever necessary. One social dimension of the *économie de traite* was 'kulakization,' the inevitable development of 'a class of native planters of rural origin; the quasi-exclusive appropriation of the soil by these planters and the employment of wage labor.'[38] Local states and ethnic groups which collaborated with the Europeans, or which had by accident established early trading relations with the colonialists, frequently tended to become junior partners in the dynamic of imperialist exploitation of neighboring peoples.

Although the British had been long interested in the Akan-speaking region because of gold — as early as 1750 the government had allocated £13,000 to set up the 'African Company of Merchants' to promote a steady supply of the Gold Coast's precious metal — cocoa was the greatest wealth of the colony. A Gold Coast goldsmith, Tetteh Kwashie, had introduced cocoa in 1879, but the real boom began after the turn of the century. The average cocoa tonnage exported to the European market soared from 2,261 tons in 1900-04 to 167,653 tons in 1920-24 and 263,000 tons, valued at £4.5 million in 1938. Much of the crop was produced by independent

Asante farmers in the Ashanti region, who had become economically dependent on the cocoa trade. Following the explosion in cocoa production, non-agricultural sectors began to be exploited by European capitalists. Gold mining firms accelerated production and by the late 1940s the state's seven companies were producing about 450,000 ounces of gold annually. Diamond mining was initiated by several firms, and by the early 1950s annual production exceeded one million carats. Only one manganese mine was established in the country, located in the southwest. But the mine, owned by African Manganese Company, 'a wholly owned British subsidiary of the American Union Carbide corporation,' was claimed to be 'the largest unit manganese operation in the world.' Production of manganese reached a peak of 710,700 tons by 1953-1954.[39] As Samir Amin writes, the Gold Coast had become 'the richest British colony in Black Africa.' From 1914 to 1934, 'exports and the production of non-traditional activities increased 4.1 times; imported products rose as a proportion of total consumption from 15 to 28 percent; capital formation increased 23 times, and the accumulation of monetary resources 10 times. Ghana therefore started the century with the average per capita income for the majority of the present-day French-speaking states ($70 at 1960 values); and by 1925-30 had reached a level comparable with that of the Ivory Coast just before 1960.'[40] But little of this vast wealth trickled down to the peasants and workers who had produced it.

The state apparatuses instituted a severe form of authoritarian control. Too much has been made by African historians of the distinctions between French 'direct rule' vs. British 'indirect rule' in sub-Saharan societies. In practice, the systems utilized similar coercive methods, and largely eliminated any democratic or popular access to political authority by the African masses. Using French Indochina as a model, the Afrique Occidentale Française federation was established in 1895, followed fifteen years later by Afrique Equatoriale Française. A Governor-General was appointed for both federations, and coastal colonies were administered by civilian authorities, and their subordinates, who received regular instructions from Paris. After 1925, each colony was ruled by a Lieutenant-Governor, who 'was advised by a council known as the Conseil d'Administration, except in Senegal. This council was composed of appointed senior civil servants, and, in the Ivory Coast, Dahomey, Guinea, and Sudan, included unofficial members chosen by the colony's Chamber of Commerce and by a restricted African electorate consisting of chiefs, licensed traders, property owners, and administrative officers of five years' standing.'[41] The British imposed Crown Colony government, and created legislative councils comprised largely of civil servants. Unofficial members of these advisory councils were selected from representatives of financial, trading and shipping firms, as well as from the plantation owners. Africans were subject to 'native law,' and all Europeans retained their rights. In both instances, the capitalist-colonial state seemingly stood above all competing social classes, in the classical Bonapartist fashion. Power was concentrated in the governor's office; and the European rulers were in constant, fundamental conflict with almost the entire population.

The political subordination of African peasants and workers was most evident in the settler states, which included Southern Rhodesia, Kenya, Mozambique and Angola. European immigration was vigorously promoted: in Southern Rhodesia, the white population reached 158,000 by 1953; in Kenya, more than 20,000 European merchants, administrators and landlords had settled by 1920; in Mozambique, the white settler classes increased from 18,000 in 1928 to 52,000 in 1951; and Angola's European population increased from 9,000 in 1900 to nearly 90,000 in 1950.

To foster the development of white-owned farms, the African population was forcibly removed from vast territories. In Southern Rhodesia, for example, white settlers had expropriated over 22.3 million acres by 1915, an amount which they more than doubled by 1930. A series of 'hut taxes' and rents were imposed on Africans between 1908 and 1912 to ensure the cheap labor required by white planters.[42] Colonial governments undertook to block the rise of competitive nonwhite petty-bourgeois strata, and to promote European agricultural and commercial development. In Kenya and Tanganyika, the Colonial Office vetoed attempts by Asian entrepreneurs to establish textile factories. Colonial authorities in Kenya strictly limited the licenses of small indigenous traders dealing in agricultural commodities. As Nicola Swainson observes, a 'multitude of rules' prevented Africans from 'anything but minimal levels of borrowing, limited litigation to collect debts, attachment of property for the payment of debts, prior sale of crops to raise advance cash, selling of insurance policies to Africans and restrictions on collecting money by African associations.' But white settlers readily obtained credits through commercial banks to finance their crops in advance. Thus by 1932, European settler areas were responsible for 76 percent of all exports from Kenya; mainly coffee, sisal and maize.[43]

With the maturation of the capitalist-colonial system, larger multinationals and regional capitalist firms became more prominent. In East Africa, the British East Africa Corporation, founded in 1906, began to invest in a wide spectrum of commodities. By the late 1910s, 'it owned or managed estates cultivating sisal and wattle and operated oil mills and cotton ginneries. It also held many agencies for the import and distribution of manufactured goods into East Africa.' Mitchell Cotts, a South African shipping and merchant firm, had branch offices in Mombasa, Nairobi and Kitale, and 'by 1932, it had established itself as the sole contractor for the supply of South African coal to the Kenya and Uganda railways and supplied over 100,000 tons in 1932.' Mitchell Cotts also controlled 95 percent of Kenya's wheat crop, and owned maize and coffee mills in Kitale by 1928.[44] In southern Africa, the dominant firm was Anglo-American Corporation, Ltd., incorporated in 1917. Its chief holdings were gold, asbestos, uranium, iron and coal mines in South Africa; but it was also involved through associated firms and subsidiaries in hydroelectric power and copper mining in the Rhodesias; forestry, transportation, communications and real estate throughout the Congo, Angola, Mozambique, and much of East and West Africa. Tanganyika Concessions, formed in 1899, controlled two gold mines in Tanganyika, held a 'mineral concession of 60,000 square miles' in Katanga, a coal concession of 2,500 square miles in Northern Rhodesia, and also constructed the main railway from Angola's Lobito Bay to the Congo border.[45] Five trusts controlled 70 percent of the Belgian Congo's economy; the largest, Société Générale de Belgique, had extensive holdings in mining, oil production, and finance.

Since this entire apparatus of production and exploitation was solely geared to export, it had the effect of distorting the internal class structure of African communities. Samir Amin notes that in pre-colonial West Africa, 'the internal trade in cola and salt, the exchanges between livestock breeders and farmers, the disposal of exported commodities and the dissemination of imported commodities, constituted a dense and integrated network, dominated by African merchants.' The colonial capitalists and the state 'destroyed the internal African trade and then reduced the African traders to the role of subordinate primary collectors, when it did not purely and simply do away with them, altogether.'[46] An agro-proletariat was created through taxation and mass physical relocations. Legal restrictions were placed on the small but growing urban and commercial labor force.[47]

Similarly, the colonial infrastructure was exclusively designed to facilitate economic exploitation, not to promote national integration or local development. In the Gold Coast, the first railroad, constructed after 1901, linked the gold fields to the port city of Sekondi; a decade later the railway was extended from Kumasi to Accra. By 1926 about 5,000 miles of dirt or hardtop road connected agricultural and mining centers to the coast. But after this infrastructure was in place, construction was virtually halted: total railway mileage in the entire country, at 457 miles in 1926-1927, was only slightly less than the 1946-47 total of 536 miles. In the three major cities — Accra (133,000 population in 1948), Kumasi (77,700), and Sekondi-Takoradi (43,700) — 'little effort had gone into sanitation and housing despite the increased (urban) migration.'[48]

The hegemonic ideology of the African capitalist-colonial states, whether British, French, German, Belgian or Portuguese, was white racism. Although the French claimed to support cultural assimilation, African laborers and agriculturalists experienced only cultural imperialism and rigid class and ethnic subordination. Ibrahima B. Kaké relates that in French Africa: 'Both the white and Black communities coexisted; the town was their only means of contact. And yet, the structure of these colonial towns, such as Medina in Dakar, Treichville in Abidjan, Potopoto in Brazzaville, symbolized segregation . . . assimilation hardly touched the mass of Africans.' The colonial educational institutions perpetuated racial inequality. 'In the French colonies, the authorities, in keeping with their avowed hostility toward any element of the African culture, formally prohibited the use of African languages in schools.'[49] In Southern Rhodesia, government expenditures for white students were seven times that for Africans. In 1930, the state collected eight times the amount of taxes from Africans than was spent for African education. The first African government secondary school in Southern Rhodesia was not started until 1949. In the Portuguese colonies, the state provided limited funding for several thousand small elementary-level schools run by missionaries. However, instruction was in an alien language, and 'much of the school day was devoted to religious education, with only a smattering of Portuguese-language training, reading, writing, and elementary mathematics.' In 1950, the estimated illiteracy rate of Angola was 97 percent; Mozambique, 97.8 percent; and Guinea-Bissau, 98.9 percent.[50]

One of the few exceptions to this pattern occurred in the Gold

Coast, where the absence of a white settler class led commercial and industrial firms to rely on Western-educated Africans as minor managers, clerks, and even consumers. The government, the largest single source of employment by 1946, also needed several thousand Black workers who possessed at least an elementary level, or 'Standard VII' education. Gold Coast officials increased educational expenditures from £54,442 in 1919 to £270,000 in 1938; Achimota College was initiated in 1925. By December 1948, 237,026 youth (ages 5-11) were enrolled in government and mission schools at Standards I-III. Another 49,662 students were in Standards IV-VII; 6,490 attended high schools, and 457 were in teachers' training courses.[51]

But these educational advancements in the Gold Coast did nothing to obscure the rigid racial stratification which characterized colonial culture, social and economic relations. In *Africa Must Unite*, Kwame Nkrumah reflected that Ghanaians born after independence would 'find it difficult to believe that there was a time when Africans could not walk in certain parts of every town, unless they had business there as servants.' Africans were trained 'to accept the view that we were an inferior people,' to 'bow in servility' before the European. The policy of racial inferiority informed the organization of healthcare and social services. Accra's Ridge Hospital 'was reserved for whites,' while Korle Bu Hospital for African patients 'was always overcrowded.' Seven hospitals served the white population of seven thousand, while only 36 hospitals were reserved for over four million Africans. Nkrumah continued:

> Under the British there was no poultry farming to speak of; there was no proper dairy farming, and the ordinary Gold Coast family never saw a glass of fresh milk in its life. There was no raising of beef cattle. There were no industrial crops . . . (Roads) were relatively few before 1951. Farmers found it difficult to get their produce to market, because of the lack of feeder roads from farm to main highways. Few of our villages had any regular transport to a main road or station . . . We have wide savannahs in the north, ideal with the right irrigation for the growing of cotton. Yet for many years we spent millions of pounds importing richly-patterned cloths from abroad . . . Even though malnutrition figures as a basic cause of a number of the country's diseases, and was certainly a contributory factor in low productivity, no attempt was made to initiate a (fishing industry) . . . The administrators . . . were either too lethargic or too uninterested to take action. It may be that they were reluctant to do anything which might interfere with the import of agricultural products at monopoly prices.[52]

Historical Contours of African and Caribbean Politics 27

The color line extended into all aspects of society. A small number of petty bourgeois, Western-educated Africans found places on the colonial Legislative Council after 1920, but no genuine elections with general suffrage were considered possible or even desirable. Sir Alan Burns, governor from 1941-1946 called for the revision of the colonial constitution to increase the number of elected representatives to eighteen, and to allow the gradual advancement of some Africans into the colonial bureaucracy. But neither racial equality nor democracy were on the immediate agenda: institutional racism was to be preserved in both public and private sectors. In 1949, barely a fifth of the administrative employees of the United Africa Company (UAC), one of the largest merchandising firms in the nation, were Africans. Africans were usually hired by the UAC only as skilled laborers (1,108 in 1949), unskilled laborers (3,508) and so-called casual laborers (2,471). Only 25 Africans worked as staff for the Consolidated African Selection Trust diamond-mining firm in 1938, and less than 10 more were hired over the next fifteen years. In the public sector, the same situation existed. In 1922, 27 Africans held 'European appointments' in the civil service; by 1946, their numbers had moved up to 89, only 6 percent of the total, and none in senior executive posts.[53] In short, racial stratification was as rigid in the colonial Gold Coast as in the Jim Crow USA of the 1940s, and only somewhat better than the racial system in South Africa before the electoral victory of the Nationalists in 1948.

As in the Caribbean, the imposition of colonial rule encountered bitter resistance at every stage of its development. When the British South Africa Company overthrew the traditional authority of Mashonaland chiefs, imposed a 'hut tax' and initiated 'widespread forced labor' in the 1890s, the Mashona mounted a major revolt.[54] Thousands of Africans were brutally murdered, and the Mashona spiritual leader Nehanda was executed in 1898. But 450 whites were killed in combat, 10 percent of the settler population. In 1905 the Maji-Maji rebellion against the Germans began in southern Tanganyika, and only after the deaths of 75,000 Africans by war and forced starvation was order restored in 1907. In 1915, minister John Chilembwe led an uprising against the British in Nyasaland. He had no illusions about the possibility of overthrowing the British, and told his followers: 'You are to go and strike and blow and then die . . . You must not think that with that blow you are going to defeat white men and then become Kings of your own country.'[55] The Portuguese also had a difficult struggle securing their concessions in Angola. From the 1850s through the 1880s, Portuguese settlers paid a regular tribute to one African ethnic group to buy civil peace. From 1904 to 1914 the Cuamato and Cuanhama successfully fought Portuguese troops, and the Ovambo smashed the Portuguese near the current Namibian border. It was only after World War I that the Portuguese began to assert administrative authority in the interior of the country. Like their French counterparts, Portuguese officials were said to spend 'their time collecting taxes and African mistresses.'[56]

With increased industrial and commercial development, the small African proletariat began to assert itself politically. Clements Kadalie's Industrial and Commercial Workers' Union (ICU), founded in South Africa in 1919, quickly became the most powerful African mass formation in the country. Despite its brief career, the ICU reached thousands of urban and rural laborers, gaining supporters even as far as Nyasaland. 'Kadalie aroused the African workers, taught them awareness of their economic bondage, and revealed the power that lay in unity,' observed Bernard Magubane. Yet Kadalie's lack of political radicalism — which permitted him to become a spokesman for Hertzog's racist Nationalist Party in 1923 — disoriented and soon dispersed the ICU.[57]

The pace of unionization was slow throughout the continent. The legal right to organize was given in French North Africa in 1932 and in French West Africa five years later. However, French colonialists confined union membership only to Africans who had graduated from elementary school, and who were also fluent in French. The literacy restrictions were not ended until 1944. In the Belgian Congo, no African unions were permitted until 1946. Trade unionization was also retarded in British colonial Africa. Nigerian laborers started the first legal union in 1940; however, by the end of 1942, sixty-two unions existed with a total membership of twenty-one thousand. Nyasaland's first union, the Transport and Allied Workers' Union, was organized in 1949. And Uganda's initial trade union was registered only in 1952.

But no matter whether African laborers were 'legally' organized or not, worker militancy increased during this period. In 1936, Mozambique experienced a major stevedores' strike. Copperbelt miners staged huge strikes in Northern Rhodesia in 1935 and 1940. In the Gold Coast, striking railroad workers won a pay rise in 1940. Nigerian unions achieved a 100 percent boost in their minimum wage rate in 1942; three years later, a Nigerian general strike paralyzed Lagos for 44 days. Societies which experienced the most extensive penetration of European industrial and commercial capital tended to have the largest African unions. For example, unions grew quickly in Senegal among clerks, civil servants and industrial workers. According to Y.M. Ivanov: 'After 1945 they exerted steady pressure on the administration and private employers to force increases in wages that were in line with rising prices. Senegal was the scene of more well-organized strikes during this period than any other area in West Africa . . . '[58] The Gold Coast's Trades Union Congress (TUC) contained 56 unions totaling 18,000 members in 1949 — but the TUC was also accurately described as being at best 'weak, ephemeral, badly organized, and lacking both funds and authority.'[59]

This combination of factors — a small industrial working class, the predominance of the agro-proletariat and peasantry, the late and relatively weak development of unions, widespread illiteracy among the masses, and a cultural-ideological context of white supremacy — ensured that the Western-educated, African petty bourgeoisie largely monopolized the leadership of the nascent movements for self-determination and national independence. As in the dynamics of trade-union development, this elite initially emerged in those states which had the most intense European contacts. In 1889, Gold Coast African elites created the Fanti National Political Society, which called for an end to 'the demoralizing effects of certain European influences' and the 'encroachments into their nationality.'[60] That same year, mulatto minister C.C. Reindorf published his study, *History of the Gold Coast and Asante*.

This strata's leading representative, however, was J.E. Casely-Hayford. Born in 1866, and trained in law at Cambridge and London, Casely-Hayford was an early advocate of Gold Coast nationalism. In 1897, Casely-Hayford helped to establish the Aborigines' Rights Protection Society, a coalition of the urban African middle class and prominent chiefs. His major theoretical work, *Ethiopia Unbound* (1911), attacked the British for destroying the African's ethnic groups, 'alienating his land, appropriating his goods and sapping the foundations of his authority and institutions.'[61] In 1920, Casely-Hayford was instrumental in coordinating the founding conference of the National Congress of British West Africa in Accra. Meanwhile, in South Africa, a group of Western-educated African teachers, entrepreneurs, lawyers and clergy formed the African National Congress (ANC) in Bloemfontein in 1912. The ANC's first president, John Langalibalele Dube, had been educated at Oberlin College in Ohio, was a Congregationalist minister, principal of Natal's Zulu Christian Industrial School, and publisher of the *Ilanga lase Natal* newspaper. In 1913 Dube led an ANC delegation to the UK to protest South Africa's Natives Land Act.[62] Ten years later, Zulu Anglican teacher Abraham Twala initiated the Rhodesian Bantu Voters' Association. Twala advised his supporters, 'experience has taught us that our salvation does not lie in Downing Street . . .'[63] One striking feature of these early nationalist organizations was their attempt to bridge all ethnic boundaries. As Magubane comments: 'from the day of the inauguration of the ANC, Xhosas, Zulus, Sothos, and other African peoples would begin to develop a loyalty of a new type. The nationalism of the African people as expressed in the ANC was an ideological commitment to the pursuit of a new purpose: political emancipation.'[64]

Many of the African intellectuals and the leaders of these formations were extremely conservative in economic and political outlook. Sierra Leonean physician James Africanus Horton, born in 1835, was the author of *West African Countries and Peoples* (1868), which condemned Western racism and defended Africans' rights. Yet in his 'Letters on the Political Condition of the Gold Coast' (1870), he declared that the independent Ashanti nation was ruled in a 'very unsatisfactory and undefined manner.' Even under British rule, 'it will certainly take another hundred years to infuse only the germ of civilization amongst them and to enlighten them in the true principles of a civilized Government.'[65] In 1897, Dube and John Chilembwe lectured together in the USA in a series of fundraising efforts for their respective educational and religious institutions. But Dube not only vigorously opposed Chilembwe's violent revolt; he urged the African elites to develop private enterprises to dominate the South African 'native market.' He organized the Bantu Business League of Natal, based on Booker T. Washington's National Negro Business League in the USA.[66] Similarly after joining the Gold Coast's legislative council, Casely-Hayford muted his nationalistic demands: 'Our fundamental policy is to maintain strictly inviolate the connection of the British West African dependencies with the British Empire.'[67]

The most influential African politician of the early twentieth century, Blaise Diagne, embodied the conservative nationalism and petty bourgeois aspirations of Dube, Casely-Hayford and others of his generation. Born in Senegal in 1872, Diagne became a customs officer and consummated his position in elite society by marrying a Frenchwoman. Economic circumstances soon created the opportunity for Diagne to launch a career in politics. With the entry of large French monopolies from Marseilles and Bordeaux in the 1890s, the creole merchant bourgeoisie was 'ruined.'[68] The creole elite and the métis (mulattoes) had dominated local politics, and Senegal had the right to elect a representative to the French Chamber of Deputies. In the 1914 election, Diagne won by mobilizing an eclectic coalition of clerks, teachers, and workers. As a deputy during World War I, Diagne became an intimate of Clemenceau. Appointed Commissaire-Général for all of French West Africa, he supervised the deployment of 680,000 African soldiers and 238,000 laborers to the Western Front. In 1919, Diagne reluctantly agreed to chair the Pan-African Congress in Paris, organized by the Afro-American intellectual and civil rights leader W.E. Burghardt Du Bois. His cooperation with the more radical Du Bois ended in the 1921 Pan-African Congresses held in London, Brussels and Paris, when Diagne tried to ratify resolutions praising French and Belgian colonial rule. Before his death in 1934, Diagne was bitterly condemned by many of his former supporters as a traitor. Diagne's characteristic reply was: 'We Frenchmen of Africa wish to remain French, for France has given us every liberty and accepted us without reservation.'[69]

The major political associations throughout Africa in the 1920s and 1930s were politically to the left of Diagne, but expressed their anti-colonialist positions in gradualist terms. Herbert Macaulay's Nigerian National Democratic Party won elections for Lagos's three seats on Nigeria's legislative council in 1923-1938, but confined its agitation to legalistic maneuvers reminiscent of Dube and Casely-Hayford. Attorney Lamine Guèye succeeded Diagne as Senegal's major African politician. In 1936 Guèye founded a moderate socialist party, but he continued to articulate the narrow demands and class interests of the assimilated citoyens, the mulatto and African middle strata. In 1934 the first African National Congress of Southern Rhodesia was established by Aaron Jacha, but it soon collapsed. A second attempt to revive this Congress was led by the Reverend Thomas Samkange in 1945, but its 'indecisiveness . . . left the main thrust of nationalist militancy firmly in the hands of the trade unionists.'[70] In Tanganyika, the urban-based Tanganyika African Association had established nine branches by 1939, but its principal focus was social welfare and economic advancement, not radical nationalism. At the outbreak of World War II, it was difficult to find militant mass movements which uncompromisingly advocated the immediate end of European colonialism in the continent. The hesitancy, reformism and accommodationism of the majority of Africa's political and intellectual leaders, combined with the slow development of an African proletariat and a class-conscious rural peasantry, helped the colonialists to extend their dominance for another twenty years.

IV

The rise of Marxism and mass social democratic parties in Europe in the late nineteenth century had no direct impact upon the struggles of Black workers and peasants in the periphery for many decades. For the majority of European working-class leaders, the particular economic and political problems of colonized peoples were of no special consequence. There were exceptions, but generally most of the socialists and early trade-union leaders had acquired a profound antipathy towards nonwhites and shared a belief in European cultural and political superiority which was little different from that of the ruling classes. This was even occasionally true for the founders of historical materialism. Marx's famous and pithy quotation, 'labour with a white skin cannot emancipate itself where labour with a black skin is branded,' characterizes the generally anti-racist and egalitarian orientation of his entire work. But there were also lapses. In one work Engels referred to the Germans as 'a highly gifted Aryan branch' of humanity, an 'energetic stock' who had the 'physical and intellectual power to subdue, absorb, and assimilate its ancient eastern neighbors'; in another, Marx described the Mexican people as 'les derniers de hommes.' In Marx's correspondence with Engels in June, 1853, he compares Jamaicans and Afro-American slaves, arguing that the former 'always consisted of newly imported barbarians,' whereas Black Americans were 'becoming a native product, more or less Yankee-fied, English speaking, etc., and therefore fit for emancipation.'[71]

First and second generation white Marxists usually adhered to a simplistic, reductionist interpretation of racism and colonial exploitation. This was particularly true in the United States where white socialists were forced to confront a large, indigenous Black population. In theoretical terms, racial inequality was seen as only one minor aspect of the more fundamental question of class exploitation. This is not to suggest, by any means, that all white socialists capitulated to racism. The early Marxist leader Joseph Weydemeyer denounced 'most emphatically both black and white slavery'; the New York Communist Club of the 1850s attacked slavery and 'expelled any member who manifested the slightest sympathy for the Southern point of view.'[72] A half century later, Socialist leader Eugene V. Debs refused to speak before any racially segregated audiences, and insisted that the party would 'deny its philosophy and repudiate its teachings if, on account of race consideration, it sought to exclude any human being from political and economic freedom.' Left historian Albert Fried has praised the leader's egalitarian views, while emphasizing that Debs and 'probably most socialists' of the era 'reduced the Negro problem to a class problem. They assumed that equality would prevail in America the moment capitalism ceased to exist.'[73]

Crude economic determinism was a principal motif in the attempts by the early socialist movement to come to grips with the race question. In large part, white American socialists either considered race an irrelevant factor or they reflected the 'scientific' (sic) racism that suffused Progressive thought in the early twentieth century. Daniel DeLeon was a prime example of the former case. While sympathizing with the struggles of Afro-Americans he nevertheless perceived race as a secondary question, if not simply as obscurantism. Thus when white supremacist state constitutions voided Black voting rights in the 1890s, De Leon claimed: 'the tanglefoot Suffrage legislation while aimed at the Negro ostensibly as a Negro, in fact aims at him as a wage slave.' De Leon rejected moves by leftists to demonstrate against racist legislation, because 'it was a waste of time for socialists to explore the differences between whites and blacks' as to their relative oppression.[74] The rightist and centrist wings of the Socialist Party wholeheartedly capitulated to white supremacy. Examples are numerous. Socialists in the South had several 'whites only' branches, and argued that 'socialism would bring complete segregation: blacks and whites should not live in the same areas or even work in the same factories.' Victor Berger, right-wing Socialist Party boss, frequently claimed that 'negroes and mulattoes constitute a lower race.' Centrist leader Morris Hillquit and editor Hermann Schlueter called for stricter immigration laws to exclude 'workingmen of inferior races — Chinese, Negroes, etc.'[75]

There were two outstanding exceptions, from radically different political orientations, to the general white racist drift of early socialist thought. On one hand, the Industrial Workers of the World, founded in 1905, tried to mobilize all the most oppressive sectors of the American working class in a unified struggle against capital. The 'wobblies' recruited many Black activists — R.T. Sims, Benjamin Harrison Fletcher, Alonzo Richards and so on —

organized thousands of Black longshoremen and workers in the lumber industry. But as Marxist historian Philip S. Foner notes: 'Despite its policy of integrated activity, the IWW never succeeded in recruiting the great masses of Black workers. The vast majority of Blacks in the South were sharecroppers and tenant farmers . . . By the time Blacks began entering Northern industries in considerable numbers, after 1915, the IWW . . . was in the process of being savagely destroyed.'[76] A second group of racial egalitarians on the left — including pioneer social worker Jane Addams, journalist William English Walling, Mary White Ovington, and Socialist Party leader Charles Edward Russell — joined with Black intellectuals led by W.E.B. Du Bois to found the National Association for the Advancement of Colored People (NAACP) in 1909. This socialist tendency was far more conservative than Debs or De Leon, and in many respects paralleled British Fabians in their emphasis on gradualistic, moderate social change. Walling and Russell became social chauvinists during World War I, and under their influence so did Du Bois.[77] Their seminal role in promoting the movement for civil rights did not lead to any creative synthesis between Marxism and the antiracist.

A different but equally important barrier which slowed the introduction of socialist ideologies and organizations in the Black periphery was the uneven and very complex evolution of Marxism in Europe. The major socialist party in Europe with a strongly Marxist heritage prior to 1914 was the German Social Democratic Party. Although imperial Germany established several African colonies after the Congress of Berlin in 1884-85, the actual political weight given to colonial issues by most socialists was minor. German Social Democrats generally believed that socialism would develop first in industrially-advanced, Western capitalist states, not in the colonies of Asia and Africa. To his credit, however, Marx believed that certain non-capitalist societies, such as Russia, could 'make the leap into socialism from her particularly backward pre-capitalist conditions.' But even Marx was convinced that such a 'leap' could only be successful if it was followed closely by a successful social revolution in the West.

In France and Great Britain, the two major imperialist powers in Africa and the Caribbean, the Marxist intellectual and political tradition was curiously weak. Proudhonism and Blanquism were more influential among the French workers. France's only Marxist party in the late 1800s, the Parti Ouvrier Français, comprised a fraction of all socialist parliamentary deputies. The traditional political ideology of the radical petty bourgeoisie, Jacobinism, retarded the assimilation of orthodox Marxism. As Perry Anderson has observed: 'No significant contribution to the great Marxist debates of the pre-1914 epoch was made in France. To all intents and purposes, *Captial* was a closed book to the French Socialist Party . . . The victory of the Entente in 1918, upholding the dominance of the French bourgeoisie and sparing the French working class the ordeal of defeat, further delayed the conditions for the growth of Marxism as a real force in the country.'[78]

In England, revolutionary Marxism was retarded by several factors. Among sectors of the radicalized intelligentsia and, somewhat later, within the national leadership of the British Labour Party, the dominant tendency was Fabianism. Profoundly middle class in orientation and hierarchical in approach, Fabianism accepted the legitimacy of the parliamentary system and sought only to extend gradual, democratic reforms within the state and economy. There was also the tradiion of 'ethical socialism,' promulgated in the writings of Keir Hardie, Robert Blatchford and others, which stressed social justice and peaceful political change. Hardie's small Independent Labour Party disavowed class struggle and promoted evolutionary methods. H.M.Hyndman's Social Democratic Federation, formed in the 1880s, espoused neo-Chartist ideas, and at best, a very popular and rudimentary version of Marxism. British labor leaders were often inclined towards economism, the achievement of higher wages and better working conditions, relegating political demands for empowerment and workers' control to a subordinate or nonexistent position. Moreover the general cultural terrain in Britain predisposed the working class to imperialistic chauvinism and jingoism. Consequently, the small number of radical Black intellectuals and early labor leaders who were able to study or travel in their colonial metropoles seldom encountered social theories, political formations or social movements which were receptive or relevant to their immediate concerns.

It was in Spanish-speaking peripheral societies that radical versions of socialism made the greatest advances in the nineteenth and early twentieth centuries. Curiously enough, Spain produced no major Marxist theoretician. The Spanish working class and peasantry was particularly militant, yet in 1914 only one Social Democrat was a member of the Cortes. Spanish radicalism usually took the form of anarchism and syndicalism: the radical anarchist *El Provenir* newspaper was established in Corunna in 1845; the anarchistic Spanish Alliance of Social Democracy and the Spanish Federation to the First Socialist International were formed in 1869; and in the early 1880s, revolutionary anarchists created 'Los

Desheridados,' which paralleled the Russian Narodniks.[79]

Similar formations subsequently developed throughout Latin America. The first socialist political party in the region, Chile's Democratic Party, was started in 1887, and was able to elect a member to the Chamber of Deputies seven years later. Chile's Socialist Labour Party 'altered its program to conform to that of the Comintern' in 1919, and two years later it became a Communist Party. In Argentina, a small reform movement inspired by utopian socialist writer Jose Estaban Echevarría was begun in the 1840s-1850s. A section of the First International was formed in Buenos Aires in 1872; a socialist newspaper, *El Trabajador,* was also founded in 1872; and *Capital* was translated into Spanish and circulated there in 1895. Argentina's Socialist Party was founded in 1896. Several years later, anarcho-syndicalists mobilized the Federación Obrera Regional Argentina, and socialists initiated the Unión Central de Trabajadores; by 1920, the newly-formed International Socialist Party had joined the Third International. In Uruguay, a First International section was initiated in 1874; a 'Karl Marx Study Center' was founded in Montevideo in 1904, and Uruguay's Socialist Party, organized in 1910, aligned with the Second International. In Peru, anarcho-syndicalists established the Artisans Unions in 1884; four decades later, under the leadership of José Carlos Mariátequi, Peru's General Confederation of Workers and the Socialist Party of Peru emerged. In Paraguay, a Communist Party was started in 1928. A utopian socialist workers' federation began in Mexico in 1872; Marx's writings first appeared in Mexico in 1883; and according to Sheldon B. Liss, 'prior to the 1910 revolution the anarchist version of Marxism represented the major ideological expression of the Mexican working classes.' Even Trotskyism acquired support among certain sectors of the Mexican radical intelligentsia and the working classes during the 1930s and 1940s.[81]

Only after the Bolshevik Revolution of 1917 did Marxism really begin to be assimilated across the Black periphery of Africa and the Caribbean. Not even the rigid censorship maintained by colonial authorities could retard the interest of some Black intellectuals, nationalists and workers in the new Soviet state. Certain themes in Leninism clearly distinguished it from traditional European social democracy, at least from the vantage point of many Black radicals in the early twentieth century. Lenin was, firstly, a revolutionary Marxist *politician*, in that he advanced 'the systematic construction of a Marxist political theory of class struggle, at the organizational and tactical level . . . The scale of his accomplishment on this plane transformed the whole architecture of historical materialism, permanently.'⁸¹ Lenin repeatedly condemned the economism and reformism of the liberal social democrats and ethical socialists, while simultaneously criticizing the Blanquism and anarchistic politics of radical populists and libertarian socialists. Lenin also insisted that the political catalyst essential in building the Russian revolutionary movement was a highly centralized vanguard party, an organization comprised solely of 'people who will devote themselves exclusively to Social-Democratic activities.' Party members should be active in leading mass organizations, but the party itself should be organizationally distinct. The party would function on the principle of 'democratic centralism.' Party leaders' decisions were binding on all members, but full 'freedom of discussion' and the rights of minorities were recognized at all levels of the party.

Lenin's thought contained a strong antielitist, egalitarian component, which was missing from much of European socialism, particularly Fabianism and the hierarchical, trade unionist, left. Lenin's *State and Revolution*, written in 1917, best expressed this element of his political ideology. For Lenin, the state was 'a special organisation of force . . . an organisation of violence for the suppression of some class.' The ultimate objective of Marxists was to 'smash' the bourgeois state. In the initial phases of proletarian rule after the revolution, there would remain 'for a time not only bourgeois right but even the bourgeois State without the bourgeoisie.' The task of workers and peasants, led by the party, was to 'organize large-scale production on the basis of what capitalism has already created, relying on our own experience . . . ' Every safeguard should be taken to block the growth of new political bureaucracies and elites: 'we will reduce the role of the State officials to that of simply carrying out our instructions as responsible, revocable, modestly paid 'foremen and accountants' . . . '⁸²

Finally, the implicitly antiracist and anticolonial perspective of Marx's work was greatly expanded and enriched by Lenin. In his 1914 essay, 'The Right of Nations to Self-Determination,' Lenin called upon Marxists to promote 'day-by-day agitation and propaganda against all state and national privileges, and for the right, the equal right of all nations, to their national state.' He cautioned that 'the working class should be the last to make a fetish of the national question, since the development of capitalism does not necessarily awaken *all* nations to independent life. But to brush aside the mass national movements once they have started, and to refuse to support what is progressive in them means, in effect, pandering to *nationalistic* prejudices . . .'[83] In his 1916 book, *Imperialism, the Highest Stage of Capitalism*, Lenin explained the connections between imperialist domination in the periphery and the eruption of World War I: 'the more capitalism is developed, the more strongly the shortage of raw materials is felt, the more intense the competition and hunt for sources of raw materials throughout the world, the more desperate the struggle for the acquisition of colonies.' Lenin's analysis of imperialism was valuable for several reasons. It explained that the superexploitation of Asian, African and Latin American peasants and workers generated a huge surplus which was used in part 'to bribe the upper strata of the proletariat, and therefore foster, give shape to, and strengthen opportunism . . . Imperialism has the tendency to create privileged sectors . . . and to detach them from the broad masses of the proletariat.' It also placed greater attention on the oppression of nonwhite workers, the ethnic and racial stratification of the international proletariat, and the manipulation of national chauvinism and racism to rationalize and perpetuate imperialist exploitation.[84]

The theoretical and political achievement of Lenin was substantial, but it should be placed within its historical context. Leninism emerged precisely because of the militant struggles of the Russian working class leading up to the abortive revolution of 1905-1906; indeed Lenin's Marxism was the most advanced expression of this militancy. His singular greatness was that he always took seriously the nexus between theory and practical action: 'Correct revolutionary theory assumes final shape only in close connection with the practical activity of a truly mass and truly revolutionary movement.' However, the political economy and social class structure of Russia combined with its absolutist state created a context for mass revolutionary movement which was unique in Europe. In practical terms, the specific political strategy and organizations which were necessary in the Russian environment were not directly applicable to the West. Lenin occasionally recognized this, particularly in *Left-Wing Communism*, but the most famous formulation of the dilemma was made by Antonio Gramsci: 'In Russia the State was everything, civil society was primordial and gelatinous; in the West, there was a proper relation between State and civil society, and when the State trembled a sturdy structure of civil society was revealed. The state was only an outer ditch, behind which there stood a powerful system of fortresses and earthworks . . . '[85] However, the economic, political, and social characteristics of peripheral capitalist-colonial social formations more closely corresponded with those of autocratic Russia than the bourgeois democratic West. Thus the Leninist vanguard party model, with its capability for mass organizing as well as clandestine activity, seemed particularly suited to colonial conditions.

At the Second Congress of the Communist International (Comintern) in July 1920, Lenin noted critically that 'it would be utopian to believe that proletarian parties' could be developed in colonial states, pursuing 'communist tactics and a communist policy, without establishing defined relations with the peasant movement and without giving it effective support.' To avoid isolation from the masses, Lenin advised Communists to 'support bourgeois-liberation movements in the colonies only when they are genuinely revolutionary and when their exponents do not hinder our work of educating and organizing in a revolutionary spirit the peasantry and the masses of the exploited.'[86] This strategy required both the preservation of the organizational independence of Marxist-Leninists, and a policy of firm cooperation with non-Marxists in efforts to overthrow colonial regimes.

During the 1920s and early 1930s, Communist parties were established in dozens of colonial societies. In 1920, Communist organizations were initiated in Shanghai and other Chinese cities, and in July 1921 the Chinese Communist Party was officially established. A small Indonesia Party began to agitate effectively against Dutch colonialism, but was forced underground after official repression in 1926. The Vietnamese Communist Party was founded in 1930. Korean Communists were organized in 1926, and assumed an active role throughout the region against Japanese imperialism. They participated in the Canton Commune of 1927; they also created the 'only foreign contingent on the Long March; they accounted for perhaps as much as half the entire Japanese Communist Party during the toughest years.' In India, Calcutta radicals had expressed an interest in starting a section of the First International in 1871; in 1912 a biography of Karl Marx had appeared in an Indian language; and by the 1930s there were 'a large number of groups, including the Communist Party of India,' which drew their 'direct source of inspiration' from Marxism. In May, 1934, the India Congress Socialist Party was founded. Marxist-Leninists were also active in the Middle East. The Communist Party of Iraq was formed in 1934, and by the early 1940s Egyptian Communists had cadre in the working class and some support from the radical nationalist intelligentsia. Even fissures within the Soviet Union's politburo were felt in the periphery. In 1929, Chinese Marxists sympathetic with

Trotsky initiated their own 'Left Opposition' section.[87]

Compared to the diffusion of Marxism-Leninism in Asia and the Middle East, its organizational development in Africa and the Caribbean was extremely slow. One of the earliest Soviet experts on Africa was Mikhail Pavlovich, a former anti-Tzarist exile in Paris who had developed close ties with Indian, Persian and Turkish militants during his years abroad. Under the direction of the Commissariat of Nationalities, then directed by Joseph Stalin, Pavlovich established the All-Russian Scientific Association of Oriental Studies in 1922. For Pavlovich, the 'Orient' was not simply the Asian continent, but 'the entire colonial world, a world of oppressed peoples not only in Asia, but in Africa and South America as well.' Pavlovich also believed that the oppressed colonial world included 'the Black population of the United States . . . ' The goal of the Association was to produce 'scientific knowledge on the East to the broad popular masses, and at the same time [assist] Soviet power in establishing a correct policy with respect to the peoples of the Orient.' Pavlovich emphasized the revolutionary potential of the Black masses, although he was not entirely unaffected by European ethno-centrism: 'the vitality of the Black race guarantees that in spite of all the barriers created by the European dominators . . . [Africans] will eventually rise from their semisavage state . . . ' For nearly a decade, the Association published research articles on Africa in its journal, *Novyi Vostok (New East)*. One Association member, I.L. Popov-Lenskii, published a substantial analysis on South African peasantry in 1928. Gradually, Black activitists were recruited to study in Moscow. From 1926 until 1930 Harry Haywood, a young Afro-American Communist, lived in the Soviet Union; and the first African students enrolled at the Communist University of the Toilers of the East. One of the African students trained in Moscow was a young Kenyan nationalist, Jomo Kenyatta.[88]

Despite these hopeful beginnings, efforts to attract significant numbers of Blacks into the ranks of the Bolsheviks were rarely successful. The first Communist Party located in the western hemisphere to make serious efforts to recruit Black members was in the United States: During the early 1920s, most Afro-American radicals already belonged to Black nationalist formations, such as Jamaican nationalist Marcus Garvey's Universal Negro Improvement Association. To Garvey's left stood revolutionary nationalist Cyril Briggs, who led several thousand Black activists in the African Blood Brotherhood (ABB). The American Communist Party

(CPUSA) and individual communist leaders initially made overtures to both groups. Rose Pastor Stokes spoke before the UNIA's convention in 1921, and asked the Garveyites to 'endorse the international communist movement.' In 1922-1923 about one dozen leaders of the ABB joined the CPUSA. Several radical Black intellectuals subsequently gravitated toward Communism. Chief among them was the militant Black poet Claude McKay. Invited to attended the 1922 Comintern congress, McKay was thrilled to 'stand before the gigantic achievement of the Russian Revolution.' But he was also deeply distrubed and disillusioned by the sectarian polemics of his white American comrades: 'I listened to the American delegates deliberately telling lies about conditions in America, and I was disgusted.' McKay refused to corroborate the assertion that 'in five years we will have the American revolution.'[90]

The Afro-American radicals observed other contradictions in the political behavior of white Marxists, which cooled their interest in the Communist movement. For several years after Briggs became a Communist, the ABB nevertheless maintained its organizational independence. By 1927, ten years after the Bolshevik Revolution, only about two dozen Blacks had joined the Communists — because the Party had little to offer them beyond sterile rhetoric. The Comintern's 1929 report on the 'Negro Question in the USA.' noted that many white Party members had 'yielded' to 'white chauvinism': 'In Seattle, Washington, several comrades objected to the presence of Negro members at party dances. In Norfolk, Virginia, white communists refused to admit Negroes to their meetings. And in Detroit they drove their Negro comrades from a party social given to aid the miners during the 1928 strike.' Even Briggs, the Party's most important Black activist, was expelled along with several ABB veterans in 1939 on the grounds of his 'Negro nationalist way of thinking.'[91]

In Africa itself, the only Communist formation to emerge was in South Africa. When the Communist Party of South Africa (CPSA) was formed in Capetown in July, 1921, its first manifesto 'appealed mainly to the white working man.' All of the members of its executive body were white. One early Party leader, Ivon Jones, boldly declared: 'The African revolution will be led by white workers.'[91] In the early 1920s, the Party 'dismissed the ANC as a petty-bourgeois organization,' and in 1924 it supported an 'alliance of racist white labor and Afrikaner nationalism that defeated the South African Party, which had ruled South Africa since 1910. Thus, it rejected the African organizations, which, it said, were not engaged in a revolutionary struggle against capitalism.'[92] Only in the late 1920s did the Communists begin to make serious inroads in the Black working class. Communists organized African laborers in the Laundry Workers Union and the Clothing Workers Union. In 1928, five African unions representing 10,000 workers were brought together under the South African Federation of Non-European Trade Unions, and the following year this federation affiliated with the Red International of Labour Unions. Despite these gains, less than 1,500 Africans actually joined the South African Communist Party.[93]

At the Sixth Comintern Congress in 1928, the leadership mandated a fundamental change in the Communist approach towards the Black masses. Henceforth, Afro-Americans were defined as an oppressed nation which deserved the right to 'national self-determination,' including the freedom to secede from the US as a separate territory. This 'Black belt nation thesis' rigidly drew no differences between the struggles against European colonialism in Africa and the Caribbean, and the American Negro's struggle against institutional racism and legal segregation within an advanced capitalist social formation. This shift in policy was in keeping with the Comintern's 'Third Period' line, which rejected cooperation with liberal democratic and socialist leaders, and anticipated a general breakdown of world capitalism, culminating in worldwide revolution.[94] This ultra-left political line had a direct impact on African studies inside the Soviet Union. Communist bureaucrats B. Zusmanovich and Ivan I. Potekhin crudely applied the Third Period thesis to African affairs, and halted the social science research of many Soviet Africanists in favor of revolutionary phraseology. The All-Russian Scientific Association of Oriental Studies was closed in 1930, 'some of its members were severely persecuted and most of them became jobless during the thirties.'[95] James Ford was brought from the USA in the summer of 1928 to edit the *Negro Worker*, a journal of the Communist Trade Union International (Profintern). Ford also helped to organize a Profintern-sponsored conference of the International Trade Union Committee of Negro Workers in Hamburg. The most prominent Black Communist during the Third Period was George Padmore, who was named director of the Profintern's Negro Bureau. Replacing Ford as editor of the *Black Workers*, Padmore soon organized an elaborate network of 4,000 anti-colonialist insurgents and Party members throughout the colonial world. In 1931 Padmore produced his own ultra-left version of international Black labor struggles, *The Life and Struggles of Negro Toilers*.[96]

The results of the Third Period line were at best mixed. In South Africa, the CPSA initiated the African Federation of Trade Unions in 1931. But internal controversy over the 'Black Republic' thesis led to a series of expulsions of many gifted and dedicated Party trade unionists. According to former Communist leader Eddie Roux, 'it seemed to the man in the street that the Communist Party was committing suicide.' The party's newspaper, *Umsebenzi*, became 'virtually unreadable' and declined in circulation. For several years, the impetus for workers' struggles had to bypass the CPSA. Trotskyist activist Max Gordon reorganized the African Laundry Workers Union in 1935, and later was pivotal in starting other unions. Ex-CPSA member Gana Makabeni led the African Clothing Workers Union.[97]

Inside the USA, the Communists recruited some Black supporters through their League of Struggle for Negro Rights, started in 1930. Afro-American struggles were also supported by the CPUSA through such formations as Unemployed Councils and the Sharecroppers' Union. But the Black Belt Nation thesis won few converts inside the Black community and Black membership remained unstable, with high turnover rates. In 1936, the CPUSA had only 3,895 Black members. The Party's chief difficulty with many Blacks through the mid-1930s was its hostile relationship with the NAACP and the traditional, petty-bourgeois Black leadership. The NAACP's magazine, the *Crisis*, was termed 'a Social Fascist journal.' Du Bois became the subject of venomous attack. In 1931, Padmore delivered this typical broadside: 'Du Bois, the ideological leader of the middle-class Negro Intellectuals, is trying to take away the lead of the revolutionary movement by playing with 'left phrases' . . . What stupidity! What demagogy! [The NAACP has] no program to lead the masses out of their misery.' Only in the Popular Front phases of the CPUSA, in 1935-39 and 1941-45 did the Party really attract significant numbers of Black intellectuals and labor leaders.[98]

Occasionally the Communists were able to influence or recruit Black leaders of mass organizations. Following Gumede's election as president of the ANC, for instance, he toured the Soviet Union in 1927. Upon his return to South Africa, Gumede announced: 'I have been to the new Jerusalem . . . The Bantu has been a Communist from time immemorial. We are disorganized, that's all.' Gumede's turn to the left was vigorously opposed by Dube, A.B. Zuma and other ANC leaders. In 1930, Gumede was purged from the ANC presidency.[99] The absence of Marxist parties, in Black colonial areas permitted the continued growth of national democratic, non-Marxist, protest movements. The largest of these nationalist currents was Marcus Garvey's UNIA. At its height, the UNIA claimed several million members, and had established 11 branches in Jamaica, 52 branches in Cuba, 30 in Trinidad and Tobago, 4 in British Honduras, and dozens of active branches in South Africa, Nigeria, South West Africa, Kenya, Sierra Leone, and the Gold Coast. Harry Thuku, Kenya's pioneer nationalist of the 1920s, was directly influenced by Garvey; Paul Panda Farnana, secretary-general of the Union Congolaise de Bruxelles, echoed 'Garvey's ideas on Africa and the Black world.' In some instances, Black former Communists established their own independent political groups and networks. For example, a young Sudanese teacher, Tiemoko Kouyate Garan, joined the Ligue Universelle pour la Defense de la Race Noire and the French Communist Party in the late 1920s. After breaking with the Communists, Kouyate initiated his own Paris newspaper, *Le Cri des Nègres*, and was a key figure in coordinating African students' activities in France. Kouyate was executed by Germans during the occupation of France in World War II.[100]

The greatest Black heretic from the Communist movement was, of course, Padmore. In August 1933, Padmore resigned his posts in the Communist Party, charging that the Comintern was preparing to abandon its anti-colonialist activities in order to reach a rapprochement with France and Britain against Nazi Germany. Black Communists minced no words to condemn their fallen spokesman. Harry Haywood attacked Padmore for descending into the 'swamp of counter-revolutionary petty-bourgeois nationalism.' In February 1934 he was expelled from the Comintern. Moving to London, Padmore established a modest political base among Africans and West Indians. His International African Service Bureau coordinated correspondence between African nationalists, trade unionists, editors and intellectuals throughout British Africa. C.L.R. James, Padmore's boyhood friend, briefly served as editor of the Bureau's journal, *International African Opinion.* As James recalls: 'Padmore covered the waterfront, everywhere and everybody. [He] periodically would go to France and it was very curious, he sent me to see a man called Kouyate and also to meet the Trotskyists.'[101] Perhaps Padmore's brightest lieutenant was Jomo Kenyatta. It is difficult to overemphasize Padmore's central political and ideological role in the emergence of modern nationalism in

British colonial Africa and to a lesser extent in the British West Indies.

Padmore continued to respect the Soviet Union's internal policies 'in the sphere of inter-racial relations,' and never fully abandoned historical materialism as a method of social analysis. But he rejected the Leninist vanguard party as a model for national liberation in the colonial periphery. Padmore, James, and Kenyatta were all members of a left social democratic group, the Independent Labour Party, which identified itself as Marxist but also non-Communist. James observes that there was a fundamental 'line of antagonism and conflict' between his politics and Communism. In Pan-Africanism, Padmore believed he had found a means to advance the political and economic interests of the colonized masses which rejected both Western capitalism and Soviet Communism.[102]

In the French territories, most anti-colonialists were initially not antagonistic to Communism, but nationalist intellectuals tended to express themselves in cultural rather than political terms. Indirectly influenced by the 'Harlem Renaissance', West Indian students published *La Revue du monde noir* in 1931 in Paris, followed the next year by *Légitime Defense*. A nucleus of cultural nationalists, led by Léopold Sédar Senghor of Senegal, Aimé Césaire of Martinque and writer Léon Damas formed the basis of the Négritude literary movement. Négritude, for Senghor, was 'the cultural heritage, the values and particularly the spirit of Negro-African civilization.' Its objective was to revive a 'Negro-African culture into the realities of the twentieth century.'[103] Given the cultural imperialism of assimilationism and the systemic assault on indigenous African cultures, a reaction of this type from Western-trained Black intellectuals was probably inevitable. By 1941, Césaire had returned to teach in Martinique, and established the journal *Tropique*, which popularized the Négritude concept throughout the Caribbean.

Compared to the Pan-Africanism of James and Padmore, the inconsistencies of Négritude were profound. Negritude was ahistorical, in that it sought to recreate a romanicized African and Caribbean past which had little basis in social reality. Padmore had little patience for such fantasies. As James relates: 'George [Padmore] never passed any remarks about the African character — never once did I hear him speak of the African personality . . . or the difference between Africans and Europeans. George kept his eyes on the political issues all the time.'[104] Négritude was also a form of metaphysical idealism, because it denied the centrality of social class and class struggles in the anti-colonialist movements. A tendency of the Négritude movement, however, joined the French Communist Party. Césaire also identified with the left, but retained critical reservations. As a youth, he had been influenced by Garveyism, and he was a reader of Kouyate's *Le Cri des Nègres*. Césaire condemned Martinican Communists 'for forgetting our Negro characteristics. They acted like Communists, which was all right, but they acted like abstract Communists. I maintained that the political question could not do away with our condition as Negroes. We are Negroes, with a great number of historical peculiarities.'[105]

French West African and Caribbean politicians of the 1940s developed ties with the French left, but seldom developed mass organizations which could in any way be termed Marxist. Senghor, Lamine Guèye and Yacine Diallo of Guinea were elected to the French National Assembly in 1946 as members of the Section Française de L'Internationale Ouvrière, which was aligned with the French Socialists. French Communists had begun to recruit African intellectuals and workers during World War II through the Groupes d'Etudes Communistes, which were established in West African capital cities and major towns. What resulted in the immediate postwar period was the Rassemblement Démocratique Africain (RDA), aligned with the French Communist Party. From the beginning, the French government tried to suppress the growth of the RDA and harrassed its leaders. Under pressure from the socialist Minister of Colonies, Marius Moutet, Sourou Migan Apithy of Dahomey and Dabo Sissoko of Soudan broke with the RDA.

But was the RDA a Marxist-Leninist federation? Its central founder, Felix Houphouet-Boigny, was 'a Catholic Baoulé chief and a physician, a graduate of Jules Carde, the Dakar colonial medical school.' Houphouet-Boigny had established the Ivory Coast's first political party in 1944, the Syndicat Africain Agricole, which lobbied to protect the interests of wealthy African planters. Houphouet-Boigny's sole act in behalf of African peasants occurred in 1946 when he secured a bill through the French Assembly abolishing forced labor in overseas territories. Despite the support provided by the French Communist Party to the RDA, Houphouet-Boigny was never a Marxist, or even a socialist. His singular political goal for the Ivory Coast was that of an 'inegalitarian, capitalist society closely associated with the former colonial power.' Even the left wing of the RDA was heavily influenced by the Négritude belief in an 'African Personality' and rejected a materialist analysis of

African societies. The RDA's leftist leader in Guinea, Sékou Touré, echoed Césaire and Senghor: 'Africa is essentially communaucratic. Collective living and social solidarity give African customs a depth of humanism which many people might envy. Because of these qualities, an individual in Africa cannot conceive of the organization of his life outside of the family, village or clan. The voice of African people is faceless.'[106]

The ideological basis for non-Marxist (and also anti-Marxist) nationalism was therefore set by the late 1940s. Césaire was elected to the French National Assembly in 1946; one of his campaign workers was a young war veteran, Frantz Fanon. Césaire acknowledged his socialist orientation, but continued to distance himself from Marxism. 'Marx is all right, but we need to complete Marx,' Césaire claimed. Colonized masses had to place 'Communism and Marxism at the service of Black people.'[107]

Outside the African Diaspora, but within peripheral social formations, other varieties of radical nationalism which eclectically employed Marxism had already emerged. Perhaps the initial manifestation of this occurred in Indonesia in the figure of Sukarno. The concept of 'Marhaenism,' which was perceived as 'Marxism applied on Indonesian soil,' was distinctly anti-imperialist and anti-colonialist. As early as 1933, Sukarno wrote that the Indonesian 'chariot of history' should not follow the course 'leading to the world of Indonesian capitalism and the world of a bourgeois Indonesia.' Yet Marhaenism was in all respects ideologically closer to Russian Narodism or populism than to Marxism.[109] In India, a similar tendency of left nationalism was expressed by Jayaprakash Narayan, a founder of the Congress Socialist Party in the 1930s. Deeply influenced by his relationship with Gandhi, Narayan ultimately developed the concept of the 'Sarvodaya' society, a co-operative, egalitarian form of social development which was divorced from electoral politics.[109]. The earliest model of 'Arab Socialism' emerged during World War II. Sorbonne-trained Michel Aflaq and Salah-al-Din Bitar established the Baathist movement in 1943 in Damascus. The Baathists' initial party documents argued that there was no 'contradiction' between Arab 'nationalists and socialists,' since the anti-colonialist movement could not succeed without a socialist reconstruction of society. But the Baathists firmly rejected the theory of class struggle as alien to their societies, and Aflaq refused to bind 'the Arab destiny to the destiny of another state, namely Russia.'[110] These initial forms of revolutionary nationalism would be repeated in the African Diaspora two decades later under the rubric of 'African Socialism.'

V

The final quarter century of direct capitalist-colonial rule in the Caribbean and Africa was marked by major economic and political transitions. Perhaps the most striking single feature of late colonialism was the unprecedented expansion of the state apparatus and bureaucracy. Clive Thomas observes: 'Those who controlled the local state were forced to abandon their laissez-faire ideology and to encourage the state to play an increasingly active part in providing the basis for a 'modern' economy. This period thus saw the role of the state as an institution of economic reproduction increased while its earlier and cruder emphasis on the development of a repressive apparatus decreased concomitantly.[111] Public monopsonies were created in Africa for the purchase and export of agricultural commodities. In theory, these state monopsonies were initiated to transfer funds to the planned development of the agricultural community, and to stabilize domestic prices. But in practice, the marketing boards' reserves were often diverted by colonial governments during the 1940s. 'In effect,' notes Robert H. Bates, 'this action compelled indigenous African farmers to subsidize the acquisition of war materials by their imperial overlords and the reconstruction of the homelands of their colonizers.' With the rapid rise of commodity prices in the 1950s, marketing boards became the 'wealthiest and economically most significant single units in their respective economies.' By the end of the 1950s, these agencies controlled 60 percent of all raw cotton exports from colonial Africa, 65 percent of all tea exports, 80 percent of coffee exports, and 90 percent of palm kernel exports.[112]

Colonial states played aggressive roles in expanding cash-crop economies. In Kenya, for example, the British government gave grants and loans for the establishment of African-owned farms under individual land titles. Marketing boards provided expertise and capital for rural commodity production. By 1962, about 300,000 new African farms had been formed within eight years, encompassing 2.4 million acres. Revenue by African petty capitalist farmers rose 'from virtually nothing to £4 million on the eve of independence.'[113] In social class terms, the colonialists were successfully creating a strata of stable rural capitalists and landholders who were tied directly to the state and the existing economy.

The late capitalist-colonial states also promoted the expansion of direct foreign investments and the growth of mining and light industries in many areas. At an international level, postwar capitalism had moved from concentrating investments in raw materials and plantation production to manufacturing and extractive industries, a transition which required huge increases in capital exports to the periphery. Nicola Swainson observes that 'in the period from 1946 to 1950, the net flow of private long-term capital from the traditional capital-exporting countries (Britain, USA, France and Germany) averaged 1.8 billion dollars per annum. In the following decade it rose to 2.9 billion dollars per annum, reaching a peak of 3.6 billion dollars in 1958.'[114] Direct private US investments in Africa increased from $110 million in 1945 to $789 million in 1958. Official US estimates for gross profits on capital investments in Africa for the period were between $1.2 to $1.5 billion. Most of this new investment was concentrated in light chemicals, goods fabrication, assembly and packaging, and mining. The flight of industrialists and manufacturers to the periphery was dictated by the existence of low paid labor forces, the absence of strong unions, weak and decentralized local capitalists who were unable 'to compete with foreign monopolies,' and the omnipresence of authoritarian colonial regimes which promised to check labor unrest.[115] Many colonial states directly subsidized the entry of these new firms. Again, using Kenya as an example, colonial grants to new private capital 'rose from £0.4 million in 1946 to £9.5 million in 1956 and private capital imports from £6.2 million to £21.2 million in 1953.'[116]

It is crucial to note that this pattern of expanded capital investment in the colonial periphery was highly uneven in both temporality and spatial distribution. Thus in the Caribbean a significant influx of new investment in mining and light industry had occurred as early as the 1920s, while in Africa this generally did not happen until the 1940s. In the Dutch Antilles, for example, Royal Dutch Shell began oil refining operations in 1918 in Curaçao, while later in Aruba the British Equatorial Oil Company opened what was reputably the largest refinery in the world during the 1930s, producing 250,000 barrels per day. The oil industry also became a central feature of Trinidad's economy, annual oil production sharply increasing from 2 million barrels in 1920 to 17 million barrels by the late 1930s.

Meanwhile in Surinam, British Guiana and Jamaica, foreign capital developed vast bauxite mining operations. The aluminium monopolies collaborated to suppress local wages and the general price of bauxite exports, thus ensuring high profits. As Philip Reno observes: 'From 1938 to 1959, the general U.S. price level rose by 138 percent. During these years, the price of the bauxite produced in the United States doubled. Yet the price of bauxite imported from Surinam and British Guiana was almost the same in 1959 as it had been in 1938. That the companies were holding the price of imported bauxite at a dead level did not prevent them from raising the price of aluminium, which went up by 78 percent between 1948 and 1959.'[117] Thus a new version of economic dependency and labor exploitation was established, extending into the postcolonial period. By 1975, bauxite and alumina represented 59.6 percent of Jamaica's total exports; bauxite comprised 17 percent of Guyana's GDP and 30 percent of the GDP in Surinam. Conversely, the agricultural sector had declined to only 20 percent of Guyana's GDP, and only 9 percent of the GDP of Jamaica.[118]

The social consequences of these new extractive and manufacturing industries were immediate and profound. First, thousands of agricultural workers and small subsistence farmers left the countryside to obtain wage employment. Villages were transformed into working-class towns, and in some instances, the entire composition of a local society was radically changed. Curaçao's population, for instance, expanded from 43,000 in 1915 to over 90,000 in 1938, while Aruba's soared from 8,000 to 40,000. Between 1943 and 1960, Jamaica's national population increased 30 percent, but the Kingston metropolitan area increased by nearly 90 percent. The search for wage employment directly contributed to mass migrations outside of the Caribbean. Between 1947 and 1962, at least one-tenth of the entire Caribbean population emigrated to the US, UK, or Europe.[119] The new centers of industrial production created new local markets for consumer goods, which permitted the expansion of the indigenous entrepreneurial classes and comprador elites. And in the cities, for the first time, a substantial strata of unemployed or marginally employed workers began to develop. In jamaica, for example, about 25 percent of the labor force was unemployed as of 1943. Over one third of all Barbadians were regularly or periodically unemployed annually.[120]

A similar tendency toward high, structural unemployment occurred in African cities. In 1929, an 'Association of Work Seekers' was initiated in Lagos, followed five years later by the 'Association of Disabled and Hungry Workers,' which appealed to 'the King and Government' to provide every worker with a minimum subsidy 'to prevent pestilence.' In the postwar period the number of jobless Africans increased. In Northern Rhodesia's copperbelt district as many as 40 percent of all workers were regularly unemployed. In Kenya, a government commission declared in 1955 that 'no evidence of unemployment as that is commonly understood' existed in the country — yet later estimates placed Nairobi's unemployment rate at about 15 percent. Samir Amin also suggests that 'in the Maghreb and West Africa the unemployed accounted in and around 1965 for between 15 and 20 percent of the urban labor force.' The non-agricultural sectors were simply unable to absorb the huge numbers of potential wage workers who had flocked to the cities.[121]

The creation of an industrial and urban proletariat, despite its relatively small size in comparison to the rural population, had a direct impact on all national independence movements. As the Great Depression hit the Caribbean, government-sponsored work programs were cut, private sector wages were slashed severely, and unemployment increased substantially. Labor unrest was inevitable. Workers in St. Lucia organized a coal strike; laborers in the sugar fields of British Guiana and St. Kitts went on strike. In 1933, Trinidadian petroleum workers led by Cipriani staged demonstrations, and forced the colonial government to ratify a modest minimum wage bill. Three years later, more radical oilworkers mobilized by 'Buzz' Butler created the British Empire Workers' and Citizens' Home Rule Party. In June, 1937, Butler's call for a general strike culminated in massive resistance and civil disturbances throughout Trinidad. A protege of Butler, Clement Payne, was instrumental in organizing workers' associations in Barbados. When the colonial authorities seized Payne, spontaneous rioting erupted in Bridgetown, leaving 60 casualties and over 500 imprisoned. In Jamaica, even more violent working-class uprisings broke out in 1938. In just one Kingston demonstration, on 20 May 1938, police killed 6 people, wounded 200, and arrested an additional 700.

Rising working-class militancy was soon consolidated into new political and trade-union organizations. In Barbados, the Barbados Workers' Union and the Progressive League were created; in Jamaica, Allen George Coombs's Jamaica Workers' Trade Union, and subsequently the Bustamante Industrial Trades Union, founded by charismatic leader Alexander Bustamante, and in British Guiana, the Man-Power Citizens Association was started among sugarcane laborers in 1937 by Ayube Edun, followed in 1941 by the Guianese Trade Union Council. In Africa a parallel development of labor militancy occurred later, after the end of World War II: the outstanding single example being the 160-day strike of railway workers in French West Africa in 1947-1948.[120]

Pressured from below, the colonial state apparatuses were slowly expanded to permit greater democratic access to workers, peasants and the nationalistic middle strata. This was not done out of an abstract commitment to popular democracy. As Ivar Oxaal comments, the 'great divide' in Caribbean political history 'came in the Thirties when it became clear that the old system of elite control was no longer workable and could no longer assure social stability. The British, it seems fair to say, were not inflexibly committed to the principle of Crown Colony rule per se; what they became most concerned with was a modus vivendi by which their paramount economic interests — in Trinidad, petroleum, sugar and finance — could be best safeguarded.'[123]

In Jamaica, universal suffrage was achieved in 1944, and a new House of Representatives containing 32 seats was created. Yet popularly elected officials were not permitted to wield full responsibility for government agencies. It was not until 1953 that Jamaica had a ministerial system in which Bustamante became chief minister, and the British maintained firm authority over the police and internal security forces until 1959. In Barbados, the electoral franchise was expanded from 6,000 to 30,000 voters in the 1940s; property qualifications were voided and universal suffrage was introduced in 1951. In British Guiana, legal restrictions on voting were reduced in 1947, and the electorate increased to 60,000, more than five times the number of voters in 1935. With the advance of universal suffrage by the 1953 elections, 130 Guianese candidates contested 24 legislative seats. Trinidad received universal suffrage in 1945, and in 1950 the five elected members of the legislative council were granted limited ministerial authorities. By the elections of September 1956, eighty-nine candidates representing eight different parties fought for 24 council positions.

Limited democratic reforms within the framework of colonialism were also extended to much of Africa after World War II. In 1945, all French African colonies were permitted to elect two representatives to the Constituent Assembly in Paris. The majority of these deputies and senators were drawn from the more nationalistic Black and mulatto middle strata. The legal system of forced labor was belatedly abolished, and territorial assemblies were formed. Under the *loi cadre* of 1956, universal suffrage was mandated, and the local powers of territorial assemblies were greatly increased. Neverthe-

Historical Contours of African and Caribbean Politics 53

less, authoritarian power to override local demands remained with the French high commissioner. A similar process occurred in British colonial Africa. Sierra Leone's legislative council was enlarged, and in 1951 direct elections were held. In Uganda, Africans were first nominated to the legislative council in 1945, and the first direct elections were staged in 1956.

Electoral reforms were granted more cautiously in states with substantial numbers of white settlers. In Kenya, for instance, local whites had won seats on the colony's executive council in 1937, but Africans were not represented until 1954. Six Africans finally won election to the legislative council in 1957; three years later, an African majority was seated on the legislative council. In Tanganyika, the British devised a crudely racist electoral scheme in the 1959 legislative council races: of thirty seats, only ten were allotted to Africans, and ten each were reserved for the small white and Asian minorities. In Northern Rhodesia, the legislative council of 1958 allowed the election of 14 whites and only eight Africans. The new 1957 constitution of Southern Rhodesia increased the state's assembly to 59 members — but 44 seats were strictly reserved for whites, and 8 of the Africans' seats could be selected only by European settlers' votes. No African nationalists or trade-union militants were elected.

Belgian colonialism moved even more slowly toward token African representation. In 1957, the Belgian Congo permitted urban communal elections, and the initiation of town councils based on universal suffrage. But national elections for the Congolese assembly did not occur until May 1960, barely weeks before the granting of independence. In Portuguese colonial Africa, however, no concession was granted for political participation, and indeed the regimes became increasingly repressive. The Portuguese security police, the infamous PIDE, suppressed indigenous dissent; the colonial press was rigidly censored; individuals 'suspected of subversive activities' frequently disappeared 'without trial or the knowledge of their families.' Any possibility for incremental reform within the colonial system was closed in 1961 when all Africans were made 'Portuguese citizens' by fiat.[124]

These reforms within the governmental structure of capitalist-colonialism permitted the rise of nationalist mass parties. Several characteristics of these formations were common to nearly the entire African Diaspora. First, many of these parties were formed directly or indirectly out of trade-union movements, or at least drew their primary electoral base from the urban working class or from militant agricultural laborers in rural areas. This was especially the case in the Caribbean, where 'democratic socialist' and 'conservative' parties alike often had extensive trade-union connections. In Jamaica, the Bustamante Industrial Trade Union was the base of the conservative Jamaican Labour Party; the Trades Union Congress, and later the National Workers' Union, were the core of the People's National Party, which was led by Bustamante's cousin, liberal socialist Norman Manley. In Trinidad, the major politician of the early 1950s was Portuguese leader Albert Gomes. Initially elected to the legislative council as the candidate of the socialist United Front, Gomes 'had begun his career as a trade unionist.'[125] In Barbados, the Workers' Union created the Barbados Labour Party with Grantley Adams as party leader in 1944. A decade later, the opposition Democratic Labour Party was formed by Errol Barrow, with its base primarily in the Transport and General Workers' Union. In British Guiana, Cheddi and Janet Jagan formed the anti-colonialist Political Affairs Committee in 1946. But the small organization of radicals did not acquire a mass constituency until it worked extensively with the Guiana Industrial Workers Union, mobilizing laborers on the sugar estates.

In British colonial Africa, some parallel examples included the Sierra Leone All People's Congress, formed by Siaka Stevens, the general-secretary of the country's mineworkers' union; Joshua Nkomo, a leading trade unionist who in 1957 became the President of Southern Rhodesia's African National Congress, and in later 1961, head of the Zimbabwe African People's Union (ZAPU); and Rashidi Kawawa, leader of the Tanganyika Federation of Labour, who was appointed minister for local government and housing in 1960, and later serving as deputy prime minister. The outstanding trade unionist from the French African colonies was Sékou Touré. In 1946, Touré joined Madeira Keita and Ray Autra to found the Parti Democratique de Guinea (PDG), a section of the Rassemblement Democratique Africaine (RDA). Due to French repression, the PDG was soundly defeated in the elections to the French National assembly in 1951. However, Toure's base as head of the Guinean branch of the Confederation General des Travailleurs (CGT) provided the political foundations for the PDG's future growth. When the CGT led a two-month strike in 1953 which resulted in a 20 percent raise for African workers, the direct beneficiary was the PDG.

It is no exaggeration to suggest that modern *nationalist* consciousness throughout much of Africa and the Caribbean was prefigured by *trade-union* consciousness and organization. The history of Tanganyika's dockworkers provides a good example. The first recorded strike in the country involved only 250 wharf workers, and lasted for only two days, in 1937. That same year, in August, 32 casual laborers in Dar es Salaam started the 'African Labour Union.' Although this formation survived less than one year, it marked the beginning of genuine working-class consciousness. After two abortive dock strikes, in July 1939, and August 1943, the foundations were set for a massive general strike in September 1947. Historian John Iliffe terms the 1947 strike 'the most widespread protest in Tanzanian history between the end of the Maji Maji rising and the formation of TANU.'[126] Despite arrests and harassment of workers by police, Dar es Salaam was entirely shut down. Two thousand railroad workers struck in solidarity with the dockworkers, joined by sisal laborers as well as African teachers at two government schools. As a result, the dockworkers won a 40 to 50 percent pay rise, and many other private firms were forced to elevate their workers' wages. A Dockworkers' and Stevedores' Union was started in late 1947, but was abolished by a colonial high court in mid-1950. Nevertheless, the dockworkers had established an activist model of anti-colonialist struggle, which directly contributed to the founding of the Tanganyikan African National Union in July 1954.

A second general point concerns the role of ethnicism within the nationalist movements. Caribbean political parties made earnest attempts to be multiracial and multiclass in composition and electoral appeal. In Trinidad, for instance, Eric Williams's People's National Movement (PNM), which won the island's 1956 elections, received its primary support from Black middle-class and working-class urban areas. Yet the PNM ticket included a 'Christianized Hindu' and a Muslim leader.[127] The Jagans' People's Progressive Party (PPP) in British Guiana developed a carefully balanced leadership: Afro-Guianese attorney Forbes Burnham was named party chairman, Chinese-Guianese Clinton Wong became senior vice-chairman, Afro-Guianese trade unionist Sydney King became assistant secretary, and Cheddi Jagan, of Indian-Guianese background, was party leader. In the 1953 elections, the PPP received 18 out of 24 seats in the legislative assembly, and 51 percent of the popular vote. 'Significant racial cooperation characterized the PPP campaign,' comments historian Thomas J. Spinner. 'Black Georgetown awarded all five seats to the PPP, which also won all eight seats in the East Indian sugar belt. It was a triumph for the Guianese working class.'[128]

In Senegal, Senghor's Bloc Démocratique Sénégalais (BDS), founded in 1948, was never a proletarian or peasants' party, despite Senghor's populist rhetoric. But it deliberately campaigned against ethnic divisions. Second-in-command of the party was a young Murid economist, Mamadou Dia. The BDS courted various class and ethnic blocs 'with specific promises: the veterans by higher pensions, the chiefs by higher salaries and security of status, and the various regional and ethnic groups by places on the party executive. The BDS became a catch-all coalition held together by patronage . . . '[129] In Nigeria over one hundred ethnic and civic associations joined forces in 1944 to create the National Council of Nigeria and the Cameroons (NCNC), led by journalist Nnamdi Azikiwe. Although the NCNC was dominated by Ibo politicians from eastern Nigeria, it did attempt to project a multiethnic front against British colonialism.

In Kenya, the core of the nationalist movement was formed by the Kenya African Union, established in 1944 largely by the Kikuyu ethnic group, and led by Jomo Kenyatta. But Kenyan nationalism could not seriously challenge the British authorities until it incorporated other major ethnic constituencies as well as the Nairobi and Mombasa proletariats. The Kenya Independence Movement, and later the Kenya African National Union (KANU), included the nation's largest ethnic blocs, the Kikuyu and the Luo, plus smaller groups such as the Kamba, Kisli, and Meru. Significantly, when Kenyatta was imprisoned during the Mau Mau uprising of the 1950s, the leadership of the nationalist movement was assumed by two non-Kikuyus: Tom Mboya, a Luo, who was general secretary of the Kenya Federation of Registered Trade Unions; and Luo politician Oginga Odinga.

A third characteristic of many mass nationalist parties of the postwar period was their domination at the leadership level by professionals or intellectuals from the indigenous petty bourgeoisie. There were some obvious exceptions — Ahmadou Ahidjo, the first President of the Cameroon Republic and party leader of Union Camerounaise, had begun his political life as a telephone operator. But in general, these 'exceptions' tended to occur when the Western-educated elites were extremely small, and where nationalist movements developed relatively late. The first or second-generation intelligentsia in the Caribbean invariably surfaced at the head of postwar nationalism. In Trinidad, three members of the first PNM cabinet, including Williams, were winners of the coveted 'Island Scholarship' for advanced studies in Britain. Cheddi Jagan had been born in a sugarcane workers' family, but graduated from Queen's College in Georgetown, and in 1942 received a degree in dentistry from Northwestern University. Forbes Burnham, from a middle class Black Guianese background, received his law degree with honors in the UK in 1947. Norman Manley, Grantley Adams, and Errol Barrow were all attorneys who had worked closely with workers' movements prior to their respective entry into electoral politics.

In West Africa, there was of course Senghor, who had established his reputation as a Négritude poet prior to his participation in Senegalese politics; Milton Margai, a physician and colonial official whose Sierre Leone People's Party came to power in 1951; and Nmamdi Azikiwe, who had received his college education in the United States before becoming a successful entrepreneur in the 1930s and 1940s. In East and Southern Africa, the list would include Kenneth Kaunda of Northern Rhodesia, the son of a Nyasa minister and a school instructor; Hastings Banda of Nyasaland, a graduate of Meharry Medical School in Tennessee; Julius Nyerere of Tanganyika, a Catholic schoolteacher trained at Edinburgh University, who in 1956 resigned his position to work fulltime as leader of the Tanganyika African National Union; and Robert Mugabe of Southern Rhodesia, a graduate of Fort Hare University College in South Africa, who would later 'obtain six university degrees, three of them, a Master's and Bachelor's in Law and a Bachelor's in Public Administration, during eleven years in prison and under detention.'[130]

Another stratum of radical nationalist leaders was formed by their experiences in petty entrepreneurial activity. Bustamante, for example, ran a small financial loan operation in Kingston shortly before his entry into politics in the 1930s. In Kenya, Oginga Odinga had started the 'Luo Thrift and Trading Corporation' in 1948. Odinga's nationalist consciousness first developed in the marketplace, as he later complained: 'Far from encouraging African economic ventures, the government seemed set on producing obstacles . . . we could not raise loans from banks because in African areas communal land ownership prevented individual land title which could be offered as security and banks would accept no other security . . . '[131]

A fourth feature of this rising generation of nationalists was their inclination toward ideological ecleticism, 'moral suasion,' and/or a reluctance to identify social class struggle as a fundamental feature within peripheral societies. This tendency was particularly profound among young politicians in many British colonial territories, where the impact of Marxist-Leninist thought was relatively weak or marginal. Robert Mugabe, for example, admits that during the early and mid-1950s he had 'read Marxist literature,' but that 'the most important political influence' on his life at the time 'was Mahatma Gandhi.'[132] Other nationalists, including chief Obafemi of Nigeria, Tanganyika's Julius Nyerere, and Kenyan trade unionist Tom Mboya, were influenced heavily by Gandhi's nonviolence and passive resistance strategy. Kenneth Kaunda's Zambia African National Congress employed a mass campaign of civil disobedience in Northern Rhodesia in 1961. Even Eric Williams, who had been tutored by C.L.R. James as a youth, and who would later come under the direct influence of Padmore, took his initial steps toward 'nationalist politics' by regularly attending meetings of Indian nationalist students at Oxford.[133] Meanwhile Jagan's PPP proclaimed its identification with 'the theory of Scientific Socialism,' but in fact borrowed its name from the Progressive Party in the USA, led by liberal Democrat Henry Wallace, and from Manley's People's National Party of Jamaica, which was hardly Marxist.[134] And even in those instances where Black politicians became close to Communist parties, the relationship often tended to be as superficial as that of Césaire before World War II. Burnham, to take only one example, had become 'closely associated with the left wing and communist movements' during his studies in Britain. He also had attended political conferences in Eastern Europe; and upon his return to British Guiana, he became president of a militant union of Black dockworkers. Yet Burnham's rhetoric remained laced with 'biblical jargon,' and he professed little interest in Marxist theory.[135]

Finally, most of the postwar nationalist movements had a strong messianic dimension. Charismatic leaders were elevated above the party's internal apparatus, and nondemocratic and even authoritarian constraints usually checked working-class members' demands and interests. This seems to be the case across the ideological spectrum, with rare exceptions. On the left, Jagan's PPP adopted a highly centralized party structure in April 1951. Local party cells, containing a minimum of twelve members, sent delegates to the party congress, which in turn elected national leaders. Despite its democratic intent, the structure 'gave tremendous power and prestige to party officers.'¹³⁶ In the center, Eric Williams's PNM 'was intended' to be a 'democratically-organized' party, and Padmore and James worked with Williams to draft the PNM's initial constitution in 1955. But after its 1956 electoral victory, PNM's parliamentary leadership became increasing isolated from the lower echelon party workers. Special party caucuses or committees tended 'to evaporate into thin air.' Williams himself operated behind 'a fairly tight-knit coterie of admirers.' Within several years, admission to PNM membership 'was contingent upon obtaining the personal endorsement and sponsorship of an already trusted party member . . . Every party member was expected to be personally loyal to Dr. Williams, and the development of an organized point of view within the party contrary to his current thinking tended to be viewed as presumptive evidence of disloyalty.' Williams increasingly saw himself as Trinidad's benevolent dictator, and the 'superstructure of political patronage was built on party loyalty,' observed Winston Mahabir. 'Reputations and careers were threatened or destroyed on the basis of disloyalties, real or imagined.'¹³⁷

Meanwhile, on the right, there was the example of Houphouet-Boigny's Parti Démocratique de la Côte d'Ivoire (PCDI). In the Ivory Coast's local elections of 1956, the PCDI carried all sixty seats. But Houphouet-Boigny personally selected all candidates, and his coterie of assistants directly dictated the party's conservative political line. As one PCDI leader observed: 'The people are amorphous, they cannot study problems such as questions of economic development. We need a system in which the alternatives are debated by an elite.' By the early 1960s, 'popular participation in elections had become a farce,' comments political scientist John Cartwright. 'Auxiliary organizations such as youth movements and the labour unions were also brought under tight control.' If PCDI lieutenants seemed too 'independent,' they were arrested or dropped from the ruling elite. In 1963, Interior Minister Jean-Baptiste Mockey was arrested and tried for 'plotting' against Houphouet-Boigny, who later admitted that the charge against his former colleague was a 'frame-up.'¹³⁸

Elitism also developed within nonelectoral, national liberation movements, Joshua Nkomo's autocratic behavior inside ZAPU was already legendary in the 1960s. When the Zimbabwean leader was Nkrumah's guest in Ghana, for instance, he immediately demanded a personal automobile in order to 'move in style.' Piqued perhaps by Mugabe's growing political prestige, Nkomo told him to 'go to Dar es Salaam to discuss setting up a government-in-exile.' When Mugabe arrived, 'Nyerere professed to have no knowledge of the plan to set up a government-in-exile.' Nkomo consistently made crucial political decisions without consult ZAPU's executive committee, and in 1963 he 'suspended' Mugabe, Ndabaningi Sithole, and other radical nationalists for criticizing his own erratic behavior. Nkomo's endless vacillations and nascent authoritarianism, more than the historic ethnic divisions between the Shona and Ndebele, led to the secession of the Zimbabwe African National Union (ZANU) in August 1963, led by Mugabe and Sithole.

In Angola, the situation was even worse. Holden Roberto's Union of the Populations of Angola (UPA), the forerunner of the National Front for the Liberation of Angola, was a tightly controlled outfit, characterized by nepotism and ethnicism. Sixteen of the 19 seats on the UPA's original steering committee in 1961 were controlled by members of the Bakongo group. Seven of the 19 members were also Roberto's relatives. Financed from the beginning by the US Central Intelligence Agency, UPA leaders transferred large amounts of money into personal bank accounts.[139]

By allowing minimal electoral reforms within the system, the colonialists found that they had unwillingly opened a pandora's box of nationalism in the periphery. Mass parties and trade unions emerged which they could not easily manipulate. Strategically, colonial offices attempted to protect European investments and property, while reinforcing more conservative tendencies within the various nationalist movements. They also recognized the potential weaknesses of mass democratic blocs, and tried to exploit them. In nearly every peripheral society, there was an absence of ethnic and cultural homogeneity. Even in a small country the size of Ghana, there were many traditional language groups and historic ethnic rivalries which predated the imposition of colonial rule. In many states, if a nationalist leader tried 'to address a substantial proportion of his people, the chances are good he will need at least one interpreter and maybe more.'[140] The 'government language' (English, French, Portuguese, etc.) and the local 'lingua franca' (e.g., Kiswahili in East Africa) frequently created barriers for mass access into political movements, which were usually dominated by urban, indigenous elites and to some extent, by labor leaders.

Another crucial factor was the relatively small size of the urban proletariat, and its ethnic composition within a given country. In Trinidad and British Guiana, for instance, over half of the Black population lived in urban areas, compared to only 27 percent of East Indians in Trinidad and 13 percent of all Guianese East Indians.[141] This meant that many workers' associations and unions reflected specific ethnic groups, and not others. Similarly, certain ethnic groups tended to be overrepresented within the colonial civil service, petty entrepreneurial private sector, and the security forces. These class divisions together with the sociocultural diversity of the working class and peasantry in the periphery provided colonialists with the means to use ethnicism to retard the nationalist movements.

Thus the French and British both manipulated and inflamed ethnic tensions, while persecuting nationalist formations. In the Ivory Coast, for example, the French subsidized several ethnic parties to oppose Houphouet-Boigny's RDA/PDCI. Colonial administrators used 'pressure, political blackmail, harassment, intimidation . . . and finally firing civil servants who were members of the RDA.'[142] Most of the PDCI's leaders were jailed in 1947-51, and Houphouet-Boigny escaped imprisonment only because of parliamentary immunity. Only when the PDCI broke with the French Communists was the colonial repression halted.

In Guinea, the French tried to promote local ethnic associations into political parties, in an attempt to check Touré's PDG. In the 1954 election, the names of thousands of voters in pro-PDG constituencies were deleted from the rolls, and voting cards were issued in a discriminatory manner to assist anti-Touré organizations. This blatant manipulation of ethnicism quickly backfired, as the PDG subsequently developed a firm policy of nonethnicism. Party officials were deliberately located outside of their traditional home regions, in order to build a broad sense of nationalist solidarity. Through the CGT, thousands of Guinean laborers had already developed a trade-union consciousness that was the basis for their anti-ethnocentric and anti-colonialist outlook.

Touré was of Mandinka origins, but his chief associates were not. Sayfaulaye Diallo, the son of a Fula chief, served as Touré's principal deputy; and PDG national leader B. Camar represented the Susu ethnic minority. Political economist Aguibou Y. Yansane explains: 'At the onset, the PDG membership was made of the urban wage workers, a minor segment of Guinea's population; this segment enjoyed the advantage of having broken traditional links, and were therefore a progressive and emancipating force . . . The PDG program was based on four principles. (1) The peasant class, the social base of the PDG, must be free to work to produce and sell its goods and services; (2) women are equal and should be active participants in the decision-making process; (3) labor unions are to work . . . for African unity and for world-wide working class interests; and (4) the African personality is to be encouraged, through the development of African folklore and language . . . The PDG cadres included bureaucrats from the civil service and from the private sector . . . school teachers, nurses, intellectuals, clerks, world war veterans.'[143] The PDG's counter-strategy of non-ethnic nationalism succeeded. In the 1956 municipal elections, Touré was elected mayor of Conakry, whose electorate was largely comprised of Susu-speakers. The following year the PDG won 54 of 60 seats in the territorial assembly elections. Once in office, the PDG abolished the legal powers of the traditional ethnic chiefs, and required the election of all village councils.

The British were more effective in promoting the rise of ethnic-based parties. In Nigeria, Azikiwe's NCNC was challenged in the early 1950s by two explicitly ethnic formations: Chief Awolowo's Action Group, which was based among the Yoruba of western Nigeria, and the Northern People's Congress (NPC), led by Muslim politician Ahmadu Bello. Sir John Macpherson, Governor of Nigeria, escalated ethnic rivalries with the initiation of a new constitution in 1951. The state was divided into three regions, with regional assemblies controlling their respective tax revenues. The national House of Representatives, in turn, was elected from the three regional assemblies. A national council of ministers was comprised of four leaders from each region, and six additional British appointees. This unwieldy state apparatus ensured that no single nationalist party could develop strong electoral support throughout the entire country. The Macpherson Constitution also encouraged ethnic minorities to create their own regional microparties — such as the non-Muslim United Middle Belt Congress, which was started in the predominantly Muslim North. Predictably in 1954, the Action Group won the western regional elections, the NPC carried the north, and the NCNC triumphed in the east. No single nationalist party with a significant cross section of urban workers and peasants of many ethnic backgrounds would ever emerge in Nigeria.

In British East Africa, with the important exception of Tanganyika, a similar dynamic occurred. In Uganda, the first political parties formed in the early 1950s represented Western-educated elites: The Democratic Party (DP) led by Catholic middle strata from the powerful Buganda ethnic group; and the Protestant-oriented Uganda National Congress (UNC). Both organizations were soon superseded by two very different movements. Milton Obote, a graduate of Kampala's Makerere University, led a fraction of former UNC radical nationalists to create the Uganda People's Congress (UPC) by 1960. The UPC was an amalgam of middle class, urban elites and various small ethnic minorities which favored a strong central government after independence, and the reduction of the political power of the Buganda. Edward Mutesa, the king of the Buganda, inspired the 'Kabaka Yekka' ('King Only') party in 1961, which called for a conservative, federalist state in Uganda and the preservation of political privileges won by the Buganda elites under British rule. In order to secure independence, Obote's UPC and the traditionalist Kabaka Yekka united temporarily, winning the 1962 elections. But Obote's non-Ganda majority gradually eroded the political influence of the Kabaka and other traditional chiefs. Finally in 1966, Obote purged the government of his opponents, and ordered the army to occupy the kingdom of Buganda. The Kabaka Yekka was destroyed; later, all traditional kingship positions of the Ankole and other ethnic sub-states were also eliminated.

In the Caribbean, ethnicism often took the form of political conflicts between East Indian and Black elites, who mobilized their respective ethnic proletarian and peasant communities. In Trinidad, the PNM's major opposition in the mid-1950s was the People's Democratic Party, which drew its primary electoral support from East Indians in the island's sugar district. The PNM's opposition came together into a united front for the December 1961 elections behind Rudranath Capildeo's Democratic Labour Party (DLP). Capildeo's background roughly paralleled that of Williams. A graduate of Queen's Royal College, he obtained his Ph.D. in mathematics at the University of London. During the war Capildeo had become a leader of Communist university students, and was admittedly 'enthralled' by Stalin. But upon his return to Trinidad, he was more than prepared to lead a demogogic campaign against 'the new black tyranny.' The DLP was an incoherent bloc of creole businessmen, the East Indian middle strata and workers who opposed both the domination of the Black middle class within the local state apparatus, and the development of a British West Indian Federation.

When it became apparent that the PNM would win the election Capildeo exhorted his followers: 'Smash the voting machines! Arm yourselves with weapons and prepare to take over the government of this country!' The demand for ethnic and petty bourgeois 'armed struggle' collapsed, as the DLP received only one third of the legislative seats, clearly winning only the predominantly East Indian rural constituencies. Oxxal observes: 'the Trinidad two-party system emerged in a form which strongly tended to parallel the island's ethnic structure. Vertical ethnic and status group consciousness and conflict took precedence over horizontal class conflict of the type which had characterized the ideology of Cipriani, Butler and the earlier socialist radicals. Both parties rested heavily on the charismatic appeal of their respective men of knowledge; neither was initially based directly on strong support from the major trade unions.'[144]

The transition from class to racial politics was more devastating in British Guiana. The April 1953 elections which brought the People's Progressive Party to power led to an immediate confrontation between the nationalists and the British colonial authorities. The PPP called for increased taxes on the sugar industry, workers' compensation laws, education reform, and the right for sugar workers to select their own labor union — hardly a Marxist-Leninist agenda. But British Governor Alfred Savage, terrified by rural labor unrest and the 'deterioration of parliamentary life' under the PPP, concluded that gunboat diplomacy was in order. Savage was convinced that the PPP was 'trying to use the machinery of democracy to destroy democracy and substitute rule by one party on the Communist model.' The constitution of British Guiana was suspended on 9 October 1953, and British troops occupied the nation. The democratically-elected PPP ministers were sacked; all public meetings were banned, and police raided Jagan's home to confiscate his personal papers. Cheddi Jagan was later sentenced to six months' imprisonment at hard labor, and Janet Jagan was jailed for holding a political meeting.

The British strategy was to split the PPP, either along ideological or racial lines. Thus in 1954, a royal commission headed by senior colonial bureaucrat James Robertson surveyed the Guianese situation, and issued a report which deliberately attempted to 'exacerbate racial discord between Africans and East Indians,' as well as to divide Marxists and social democrats within the PPP. The Robertson Commission report condemned the masses of Guianese voters as 'politically immature'; it characterized the Jagans as 'communists,' but praised Burnham as a moderate 'democratic socialist.'[145]

Burnham's personal ambition, his strong base within Georgetown's Black working class, and pressure from both the creole business community and the British authorities, produced a split within the PPP in early 1955. Initially, the schism was not along strictly racial lines. J.P.Lachhmansingh, head of the predominantly East Indian Guiana Industrial Workers Union, supported Burnham; key Black Marxists, including school teacher Sydney King, Ashton Chase, Rory Westmaas and Martin Carter, backed Jagan. But when the British finally permitted local elections in 1957, and again in 1961, the PPP and Burnham's People's National Congress (PNC) descended down the slippery path of racial chauvinism. In 1957, the PPP carried nine of the fourteen legislative seats, but none in predominantly Black constituencies. East Indian workers were encourage to 'Apan Jhaat' — 'vote for your own kind.' Sydney King, recently purged from the PPP, ran as an independent without Burnham's support: but the 'Marxist' PPP endorsed an affluent East Indian businessman against the Black radical, and King was defeated. In 1961, the PPP again defeated the PNC, but by only 3,000 popular votes. Both parties still attempted to present a multiethnic slate. The PPP candidates included 14 East Indians, 14 Africans, 3 Chinese, 3 Portuguese, 2 American Indians, and one Englishman; the PNC nominated 24 Africans, 6 East Indians, 3 Portuguese, one Chinese and one American Indian. But at the level of popular political culture, neither party made substantial efforts to transcend narrow racialist appeals. At some post-election celebrations, for instance, East Indians were heard chanting 'we are on top.'[146]

The dilemma for young Black Guianese radicals was that the nationalist politics 'were fundamentally dictated, not by any class position but by the ongoing race conflict.' Walter Rodney, born in British Guiana in 1942, later observed: 'I recall very well, as late as 1961, being very confused on the question of whether one went for the PPP or the PNC. As I listed the pros and cons, I said, well the PPP says its a Marxist party but it's not operating that way and it has Indian races. On the other side, the PNC didn't even claim to be Marxist or even a serious socialist party. Yet it had the Africans. And for those of us Africans who were struggling for some clarity, struggling to take a progressive position, it was extremely difficult. Many who had joined the PPP as the better of a bad choice actually had to leave the party. And ultimately, because of those racial questions, a generation of us have actually stayed clear of those two dominant political parties.'[147]

The racial and ethnic bifurcation of mass electoral politics under late capitalist-colonialism was not a universal phenomenon. Moreover, important distinctions also must be made between some African social formations which experienced the growth of ethnic parties and the racialist politics of both Trinidad and British Guiana. In African societies, many of the traditional ethnic communities 'did not necessarily have any conflicting interests in production,' as Rodney noted. But in parts of the West Indies, 'the Indians were introduced into the society specifically to counter and break the development of Black working class movements after slavery.'[148]

However, as African independence was achieved, 'the pitfalls of national consciousness,' in Frantz Fanon's words, became more obvious. 'The national middle class which takes over power at the end of the colonial regime is an underdeveloped middle class. It has practically no economic power, and in any case it is in no way commensurate with the bourgeoisie of the mother country which it hopes to replace.' National chauvinism became a means to create conditions suitable for capital accumulation, as non-national traders and entrepreneurs — who had entered local markets during the previous regime — were attacked. Fanon termed the anti-Dahoman and anti-Votaic disturbances in the Ivory Coast 'racial riots . . . From nationalism we have passed to ultra-nationalism, to chauvinism, and finally to racism. These foreigners are called to leave; their shops are burned, their street stalls are wrecked, and in fact the government of the Ivory Coast commands them to go . . . we observe a falling back toward old tribal attitudes, and, furious and sick at heart, we perceive that race feeling in its most exacerbated form is triumphing.'[149]

The development of racialist politics in 1950-1960 tended to occur in states which had one or more characteristics: (1) where several dominant ethnic groups possessed hierarchical, traditional political structures, which in turn exercised local hegemony over other smaller ethnic communities (e.g., the Buganda in Uganda, the Ibo, Yoruba and Hausa in Nigeria, the Kongo, Lunda, Luba and other groups in the Belgian Congo); (2) where the transitional colonial state apparatus, designed in theory to lead to full 'independence,' permitted or encouraged the growth of regional or local formations, led by traditional chiefs, rural entrepreneurs or ethnic-oriented urban leaders (e.g., Joseph Kasavubu's Alliance des Ba-Kongo in Léopoldville, Moise Tshombe's Confédération des Associations Tribales du Katanga in Elisabethville, and the Kabaka Yekka party of Buganda); and (3) where trade unions and other multiethnic workers' associations were particularly weak, or exercised marginal influence over the broader nationalist movement. The colonial administrators in the Caribbean and Africa (with the important exceptions of the Portuguese and Southern Rhodesians) were prepared to divest themselves of the day-to-day operations of their peripheral state apparatuses by the end of the 1950s. But they had no desire to leave behind Marxist or mass socialist parties in positions of state authority. Ethnicism and racialism were important weapons to guarantee continued social divisions within their former colonies.

VI

The various nationalist movements which achieved independence in the 1950s and early 1960s inherited a number of thorny problems. Although Hamza Alavi's influential 1972 essay on 'The State in Post-Colonial Societies' focuses on Pakistan and Bangladesh, many of his insights are directly applicable to Africa and the Caribbean. First, the colonial state bureaucracy and coercive apparatuses were ' "over-developed" in relation to the "structure" in the colony.' All indigenous social classes, from the nascent urban petty bourgeoisie to rural pre-capitalist agriculturalists, were dominated and constrained by the colonial regime. None exercised state power; and indeed, state power itself was external to the social formation. Second, the capitalist-colonial state apparatus exercised a 'relatively autonomous economic role, which is not paralleled in the classical bourgeois state.' Through bureaucratic structures such as the marketing boards, the capitalist-colonial regime directed production and trade. 'The state in the post-colonial society,' observes Alavi, 'directly appropriates a very large part of the economic surplus and deploys it in bureaucratically directed economic activity in the name of promoting economic development.'[150]

Indeed a substantial fraction of the nationalist leadership recognized that control of the state apparatus would provide access to a surplus that could be utilized for personal consumption and long-term accumulation. Julius Nyerere candidly admitted this: 'many of the leaders of the independence struggle saw things in these terms. They were not against capitalism; they simply wanted its fruits, and saw independence as the means to that end. Indeed, many of the most active fighters in the independence movement were motivated – consciously or unconsciously – by the belief that only with independence could they attain that ideal of individual wealth which their education or their experience in the modern sector had established as a worthwhile goal.'[151]

Another factor which influenced the subsequent evolution of post-colonial states was the absence of a single class in a position of ideological and cultural hegemony. The artificial geographical borders imposed by colonial rule, traditional and recent grievances between religious and ethnic communities, and the competition between rural petty entrepreneurs and farmers and the urban elites, created an environment of social and political fluidity and uncertainty. The petty-bourgeois nationalists who occupied administrative and bureaucratic positions on the eve of independence were not a coherent, stable 'ruling class' in any conventional sense of the term. In her study of Tanzanian politics, for example, Micheala von Freyhold observes: ' "Petty bourgeoisie" has a double meaning: it refers to small capitalists on one hand and all those who look to the bourgeoisie as their model on the other. As long as the educated stratum to which we refer is directly employed by colonialists or a national bourgeoisie it is necessarily a petty bourgeoisie in the second sense. In the absence of such direct employers the educated stratum can choose whether it wants to remain subservient to those by whom it has been created.'[152]

Some critics of neocolonialism, such as Frantz Fanon, described the African leaders of these postcolonial states simply as parasitic clients or 'intermediaries' between the metropolitan capitalists and the oppressed masses. Such a critique is much too rigid on several grounds. The African petty bourgeois politicians who occupied the state apparatuses exercised at best semi-autonomous state power, but nevertheless acquired the ability to control major economic and political decisions, within a circumscribed range of options. Moreover, since in the majority of cases, the new political elite lacked a substantial material base of its own within the local political economy, it sometimes did not have a coherent set of policies towards domestic or international capital. It was a 'bureaucratic bourgeois stratum,' a class-in-formation — not a 'class.' Ideologically, this stratum frequently assimilated the authoritarian style of the former colonial bureaucrats, but under specific conditions, fractions could also advance egalitarian and democratic agendas, which at least rhetorically were consistent with the anti-colonialist agitation of the 1940s and 1950s. The petty bourgeois class-in-formation could move to the left or to the right, even occasionally in both directions.

In the majority of post-colonial states, however, the administra-

Historical Contours of African and Caribbean Politics 69

tive apparatuses gave greater leverage to the authoritarian and Bonapartist impulse of the bureaucratic bourgeois stratum. Nationalist politicians in the French African colonies, for instance, seem to have been influenced by the failure of the *regime d'assemblee* symbolized by the collapse of the Third and Fourth Republics. The Gaullist Constitution of the 1958 Fifth Republic gave supreme authority to the Preseident, greatly curtailing the powers of the parliament. Many former French colonies — Senegal, Tunisia, Madagascar, Mauritania, Gabon, Guinea, Ivory Coast, and Niger — adopted similar constitutions providing for strong executives elected by universal suffrage. In former British territories, the executive systems were more diverse. Tanzanians used the method of direct elections for the presidency; in Kenya, the president was chosen by the House of Representatives; in Zambia, the National Assembly elected the president. Other states created dual executive parliamentary systems, with a weak president as nominal head of state and a powerful prime minister. In this category fell Sierra Leone, Nigeria, Uganda, Somalia, and Gambia.

Despite their range of constitutional variation, most postcolonial regimes had several basic similarities which directly reflected their colonial governmental predecessors. First, all chief executives were granted extraordinary powers by their respective constitutions. African presidents generally exercised control over all military and most civil appointments. Many constitutions gave their heads of state the authority to issue decrees or ordinances having the effect of law. In several states, including Gabon, Mali and Chad the dissolution of the parliament or national assembly did not require the automatic resignation of the head of state or his cabinet. Moreover most African presidents could reinforce their power through plebiscites. As Bereket Selassie observes, 'the institution of the referendum, while on the face of it democratic, could be used to defeat democratic ends.'[153]

African chief executives were usually granted other autocratic powers as well. In the former British colonies, presidents named the Chief Justices and all other superior court judges. Many presidents had the power to declare a 'state of public emergency.' suspending civil and political liberties. Selassie suggests, 'if the colonial executive held autocratic power on behalf, and in the interest, of a metropolitan power, it was not unnatural for those African leaders who grew up under such a system to demand the same kind of power . . . ' Nevertheless, the inevitable political by-product of a powerful executive system was the tendency towards 'a single party and the dominance of a single person over others and this in turn creates a tendency for loyalties to single figures rather than to the party structure.'[154]

Despite differences in ideology this tendency was marked throughout postcolonial Africa. For Sékou Touré, nation-building was identical with the calls for ideological uniformity, a one party-state, and loyalty to his personal leadership. 'Each one must consider himself as a "part", an element indissociable from a "whole" and subject to the laws and exigencies of this "whole",' Touré asserted in 1959. 'This discipline to which we freely submit . . . is indeed dictatorship.'[155] In Kenya, the opposition party, the Kenya African Democratic Union, began to disintegrate within months after independence. By 1967, Kenya scrapped its constitution, abolished the Senate, and invested President Jomo Kenyatta with near-dictatorial powers. In neighboring Tanganyika, Nyerere was at first a strong proponent of a two-party system. Speaking in defense of a possible anti-TANU opposition party in 1961, Nyerere declared: 'I would be the first to defend its rights.' Several years later, Nyerere announced that the Tanganyikan state would not tolerate a second party. 'Our Union has neither the long tradition of nationhood, or the strong physical means of a national security, which older countries take for granted,' *Mwalimu* argued. ' . . . A handful of individuals can still put our nation in jeopardy, and reduce to ashes the efforts of millions.'[156]

Once in charge of the administrative apparatuses, the bureaucratic bourgeois stratum could promote its parochial economic interests, or those of its prime constituencies within the petty bourgeoisie. Most of these Black elites targeted the removal of expatriates from the civil service, and the reallocation of public-sector administrative posts to member of their own racial fraction. Administrative salaries and expense accounts were expanded to meet spiraling class expectations. As political scientists Ali A. Mazrui and Michael Tidy observe: 'In Senegal, for example, 47.2 percent of the 1964-5 budget was spent on administrative salaries alone; the comparable figure for the Central African Republic was 58 percent and that for Dahomey was 64.9 percent.'[157]

A similar situation occurred in Kenya after independence. 'If Kenya started *uhuru* without an African elite she is now rapidly acquiring one,' commented Oginga Odinga in 1967. 'Ministers and top civil servants compete with one another to buy more farms, acquire more directorships and own bigger cars and grander houses.' Between 1963 and 1966, the salaries of Kenyan members of

Historical Contours of African and Caribbean Politics   71

parliament were doubled, to £1200 annually. Junior ministers received £2260 per year, and President Kenyatta was granted a tax-free annual stipend of £15,000. Odinga noted, 'in six months an M.P. receives more money than the average peasant earns in half a life-time. This salary scale reflects nothing like the true economic standards of the country, and can only encourage the emergence of a governing group that is almost as remote from the mass of the people as were the former colonial administrators.'[158] A corrupt, swollen state bureaucracy, protected by the armed forces, seemingly stood above virtually every social class, yet representing the interests of none — neocolonial state power was in many respects a parody of colonialism.

Most post-colonial regimes quickly moved to silence working-class opponents, suppressing strikes and labor unrest in the public and private sectors. To this end, the more politically moderate to conservative states found a helping hand from the United States. In 1949, the American Federation of Labor, the Congress of Industrial Organizations, and the US State Department formed the International Confederation of Free Trade Unions (ICFTU), a conservative, pro-capitalist alternative to the leftist World Federation of Trade Unions (WFTU). Twelve years later, the AFL-CIO, the US government and the CIA established the more overtly anticommunist American Institute for Free Labor development (AIFLD). Both organizations played aggressive roles in promoting US corporate and foreign policy interests in tandem with the concerns of neocolonial parties and regimes.

In the Caribbean, the ICFTU was supported initially by Grantley Adams and Norman Manley. As head of the Caribbean Labour Congress, Adams tried to purge all WFTU-affiliated unions from the Congress. Unable to achieve this, he pulled his own Barbados Workers Union out of the Congress, and established ties with the ICFTU center. Other Caribbean unions quickly followed. In Jamaica, the PNP created a new union, the National Workers Union, which promptly joined the ICFTU group. In the French Antilles, the Force Ouvriére developed ties with the AIFLD; in St. Vincent, the AIFLD created the island's largest union, the Commercial Technical and Allied Workers Union; and in Grenada, AIFLD established close relations with the Seamen and Waterfront Workers Union. The AIFLD was staffed by anti-Communist activists, with ample funds to coopt local rank-and-file leaders. Between 1962 and 1983 AIFLD indoctrination centres in Guyana, Barbados and Jamaica trained over twenty thousand trade-union leaders from the English-speaking Caribbean. The AIFLD provides material incentives to affiliated unions only, such as housing, labor community centres, and medical clinics. More importantly, it aggressively 'seeks to break or bypass progressive unions and to force dissenters out of AIFLD unions.'[159]

Because of the historic role of Communists in the development of trade unions throughout French-speaking Africa, the ICFTU had less success. In Algeria, however, the Union Générale des Travailleurs Algérien was affiliated with the ICFTU in the 1950s, during the Algerian war for independence. The Organisation Voltaïque des Syndicats Libres of Upper Volta was also briefly associated with the ICFTU. In English-speaking Africa, however, the ICFTU became more influential. Ghana's Trades Union Congress (TUC) was an affiliate of the ICFTU, and Nkrumah's close political associate, TUC general secretary John Tettegah, was a member of the ICFTU's executive board. The Kenyan Federation of Labour was headed by Tom Mboya, who also served on the ICFTU's executive board. As in the Caribbean, the ICFTU discouraged the growth of progressive African labor unions of a socialist orientation. In Portuguese-controlled Angola, one of the few unions permitted to exist before the revolution was ICFTU-affiliated Ligue Générale des Travailleurs de l'Angola. A former ICFTU official with CIA connections, Irving Brown, served briefly as Holden Roberto's adviser on trade-union matters, helping to channel funds to Roberto's group. In Ethiopia, Americans also played a major role in the development of the Confederation of Ethiopian Labour Unions (CELU), established in 1963. CELU consisted primarily of urban, white collar employees in the public sector. In 1964, a CIA-financed project was started, the African-American Labour Centre. The Centre trained about one thousand CELU leaders and members during its decade of operations.[160]

American imperialism also attempted to buttress neocolonial states by cultivating and promoting materialist values and favorable perceptions of capitalism within indigenous cultures. This ideological warfare can be best observed in the media. As of 1970, fifteen African states lacked daily newspapers. In the entire continent, according to Stewart Smith, 'there were some 200 newspapers, fewer than 40 national radio stations (plus 10 stations serving racist or colonial regimes). There were about 6 million radio sets (over one-half in Arab-speaking countries), and 20 television stations.' The US Information Agency (USIA) has traditionally taken advantage of underdeveloped indigeneous media to emplace its own propaganda. It publishes its journal *American Outlook* in Kinshasa and Accra, and distributes free copies of *Life, Newsweek* and *Ebony* magazines in most countries. A teletype wire service provides free copy to the African press, while USIA 'reading rooms' in over 30 African cities, are often the largest libraries. Voice of America broadcast stations have been located in Kinshasa, Addis Ababa, Monrovia, and Tangier since the early 1970s.[161]

Most major radio stations and newspapers in the Caribbean are privately owned by large corporations or bourgeois families. The only daily newspaper in Martinique and Guadeloupe, *France-Antilles,* is owned by Robert Hersant, an ultra-conservative who controls a chain of rightwing newspapers in France. In Jamaica, the country's only daily is the *Daily Gleaner,* controlled by the island's powerful Ashenheim family, which also holds interests in cement, steel, sugar, insurance, real estate, tourism and manufacturing. The Barbados *Advocate* and the Trinidad *Guardian* are owned by the McEnearney-Alstons conglomerate; the Trinidad *Express* is controlled by the Neals and Massy Corporation. As Catherine Sunshine observes, the major Caribbean dailies 'support capitalism and middle class consumerism; they are anticommunist; and they rarely challenge the principle of US hegemony in the region or the world. All the major papers supported the US invasion of Grenada, even in Trinidad where the government opposed it . . . ' Television stations also promote capitalist ideology and American cultural values. About three-fourths of all television programming in the English-speaking Caribbean originates outside the region, primarily in North America and Britain.'[162]

This 'cultural imperialism' has helped legitimate neo-colonial policies in many newly-independent states. But another factor which has also promoted the trend toward authoritarianism has been the inherently unstable position of the military in such countries. During colonialism, as previously illustrated, the police and army functioned as coercive forces which guaranteed civil order and, more basically, the continued unequal distribution of wealth and power. Nominally, they were 'outside' of politics, but their specific function was profoundly political and economic — to preserve the status quo. The achievement of formal independence in Africa and the 'Africanization' of the upper level officers' corps radically changed the situation. The army and police forces now acquired the potential for becoming an antagonistic political power vis a vis the bureaucratic bourgeois stratum and ruling party. The military had served as a vehicle for thousand of ambitious rural youth, a means to escape the poverty of the countryside. Subordinated ethnic groups often viewed military service as a path for class advancement, at the expense of indigenous urban elites who dominate the civil service, government posts, and white collar positions in the private sector. The fragility and highly volatile character of most neocolonial regimes contributes to their vulnerability to coups d'etat. In *Dark Days in Ghana,* written immediately after his overthrow, Nkrumah reflected: 'Fragmented into so many separate states, many of them weak and economically non-viable, coups d'etat have been relatively easy to arrange in Africa. All that has been needed was a small force of disciplined men to seize the key points of the capital city and to arrest the existing political leadership.'[163]

'Tribalism' or ethnicism has been viewed by many political observers as the key to the political instability — coups and civil wars — that has wracked Africa over the last generation. Examples of apparent 'tribal conflict' between the military and governmental ruling elites are many. For instance, the Togo coup of 1963, in which President Sylvanus Olympio was murdered, was led by a group of former French army sergeants primarily from northern Togo's Kabre ethnic group. Olympio, a southerner, had refused to admit Kabre veterans into the army. The January 1966 coup in Nigeria was led primarily by Ibo officers against Northern Muslim politicians; the July 1966 counter-coup witnessed the torture and execution of Ibo officers and leaders by Northern junior officers and sergeants. The January 1971 coup in Uganda seemingly split the armed forces on ethnic lines; the Kakwa, Madi and Lugbara groups generally supported army chief Idi Amin, while most of the Acholi and Langi remained loyal to deposed President Obote.

It would be a mistake to relegate all ethnic conflict to a subordinate function of social class antagonisms; ethnicity informs the development of class consciousness, discourse and culture, and fundamentally influences political behavior. But it would be a greater error to suggest that 'tribalism' is the *decisive* variable in post-colonial politics, or that the coups in the instances outlined above have as their basic source of impetus ethnic competition. Ethnicism can become a form of 'clientelism writ large,' a means for rival fractions of the aspiring petty bourgeoisie to create loyal blocs or constituencies within the peasantry and proletariat in their struggles to maximize their political and economic power.[164]

The fundamental, motivating factor in virtually every putsch is the failure of government to redress chronic political and economic crisis. This represents a collapse of political legitimacy, and more profoundly, a crisis of ideological hegemony of the dominant, local ruling classes over other contending social classes. The prime source for coups d'etat is found neither in ethnicism nor in the armed forces, but within society itself. In most pro-capitalist, pro-Western regimes, moreoever, the state may lack an active, mass party or political base among sizeable sectors of the working and peasant classes. Such regimes usually fail to provide reasonable institutional means for the transfer of state authority from one segment of the petty bourgeoise to another. In these instances, the only significant power bloc which is not completely subordinated to the ruling party is the military. Coups generally assume two types: the 'classical' putsch, where a segment of officers and units initiate a military action against a regime; and the less frequent occasions in which the entire general staff orders the army and police to overthrow civil authority. In both cases, the army's officers ultimately become a military bureaucratic caste, as they consolidate their positions. But lacking a coherent political ideology, the new regime must either permit one of the existing, privileged groups or class fractions to help manage the state apparatus. Or in instances where the officers have political affinities on the left, they must initiate new mass formations and political reforms to acquire popular legitimacy within the working class and peasantry.

Few career military officers in peripheral capitalist societies perceive themselves as 'neutral observers' of political and civil society. As part of the coercive wing of the bureaucratic bourgeois stratum, they are not immune to the prerequisites of power. As public administrators, they become more cynical as graft and incompetency are institutionalized within the executive branch and parliament. For example, long before Olusegun Obasanjo served as Nigeria's army commander and head of state (1976-1979), he had developed a bitter contempt for his country's political officials. In his opinion, the Nigerian election of 1964, which foreshadowed the military coups of 1966 and the Nigerian Civil War, was 'neither free nor fair. All devices imaginable' were used by the various 'ruling, parties in the Regions to eliminate opponents.' The barracks bureaucrat comes to the conclusion that political democracy must be 'suspended' in order to 'save' the state. Obasanjo argues that the army's primary function in African societies is to be 'an instrument of modernization in the socioeconomic and security context . . . ' However, if civil authorities are unable to maintain 'political stability,' the basic 'task of military leadership in a pluralistic society like Nigeria may then become difficult.'[165]

Many African officers in post-colonial states were among the most ideologically indoctrinated fraction of the indigenous petty bourgeoisie. Their grievances against civilian authorities grew partially from their residual belief in the supposed 'benefits' of European rule. Colonel A.A. Afrifa, a chief organizer of the 1966 Ghanaian coup, expressed his allegiance to neocolonialism without qualification: 'The Army and the Police are the custodians of the nation's Constitution . . . We will stand against anything undemocratic. I believe that all men are born free. Democracy based on the freedom of the individual is more acceptable than any form of totalitarianism . . . I am a great defender of the British way of life, its legal system, the Magna Charta, the Petition of Rights and the Bill of Rights . . . One of the reasons for my bitterness against Kwame Nkrumah's rule was that he paid only lip-service to our membership in the [British] Commonwealth . . . African Unity . . . is impossible to achieve within our life-time. Organization of African Unity or no Organization of African Unity, I will claim my citizenship of Ghana and of the [British] Commonwealth in any part of the world. I have been trained in the United Kingdom as a soldier, and I am ever prepared to fight alongside my friends in the United Kingdom in the same way as Canadians and Australians do.'[166]

It would be incorrect to dismiss the majority of African and Caribbean petty-bourgeois leaders in postcolonial states as narrow opportunists. The antagonisms and grievances against the European oppressors during the long nightmare of colonialism could not be easily forgiven or forgotten. But their immediate models for public and private behavior did descend from the bureaucrats and officials of capitalist colonial regimes, men who had excelled in duplicity, authoritarianism, and rampant exploitation. Even during the transition from direct rule to independence, 'as the African representatives were sucked into the processes of Parliament and constitutional conferences a change came over them,' reflected Odinga. 'The more adept they became at parliamenteering the more remote they became from their own people.'

The histories of national independence struggles frequently were rewritten, placing unjustifiable credit for achievements upon those government bureaucrats, military officers or politicians who had actually played minor roles, or those who had actually been sympathetic to the colonialists. Less than one year after Kenya's formal independence, for instance, one African parliament member, Ole Tiptip, publicly denounced the central role of the Mau Mau freedom fighters who intensified the anti-colonialist struggle in the 1950s: 'I believe we obtained our independence in a very nice way at the instigation of the British Government but not through fighting in the forest!' Kenyatta soon appointed Tiptip his Assistant Minister for Commerce and Industry.[167] In mid-1966 Odinga resigned from the Vice Presidency in protest, and joined other veteran nationalists to create the Kenya People's Union (KPU), a radical populist formation in opposition to the increasingly conservative KANU. But the KPU was legally outlawed within three years, and Odinga was held in detention. Labor militancy, a critical element during the anti-colonialist movement, was also checked. In 1974, President Kenyatta went so far as to ban all strikes in the country.[168]

Not surprisingly, the majority of nationalist leaders were heavily influenced by the anti-Communist diatribes and propaganda of their former rulers, and they continued to exhibit an explicit distrust of Marxism. Former Tanzanian Vice President Abdul Mohamed Babu suggests that many nationalists 'accepted the extraordinary Western-inspired proposition that to be pro-communist was to be against independence.'[169] However, the objective circumstances of the bureaucratic bourgeois stratum's rise to power dictated an ambivalent and often convoluted advocacy of some form of 'socialism.' The definitions for socialism varied widely, depending on many factors — such as the relative strength of the local trade-union movement, the presence of Marxists or radical nationalists within the state bureaucracy, and so on. In Mali, Minister for Development Seydou Kouyate argued in 1962 that socialism could be successfully established 'in an agricultural pre-capitalist society,' because it could be advanced 'by a movement led by elements not essentially proletarian . . . ' But what of the specific programmatic content of socialism, and its theoretical orientation? For Senghor, socialism was more than anything else a set of metaphysical principles: 'it involves a merciless struggle against social dishonesty and injustice, excessively high salaries, embezzlement of public funds, illicit trading and bribery.'[170]

African and Caribbean versions of post-colonial socialism were deliberately vague on timetables for the initiation of government-sponsored cooperatives and the nationalization of foreign enterprises. In a 1958 election campaign speech in Trinidad, Eric Williams explained that socialism was 'probably some vague sort of equality' which did *not* necessarily include 'public ownership and central planning.' At best, socialism was 'distributive justice,' government intervention and limited control in the national economy — and 'if this is Socialism,' Williams noted with some satisfaction, 'we are all Socialists nowadays. Nehru calls it Socialism, the late Franklin D. Roosevelt called it democracy.' For several brief years, Williams seemed to move the PNM to the left. C.L.R. James returned from exile in Britain after a twenty-five year absence, and became editor of the Party's newspaper, *The Nation*. One associate of Williams at the time recalled that James 'was number two in the party. In fact, there were times when we thought he might be number one.'

James and Williams led a dramatic campaign to oust the US military base in Trinidad, culminating in a mass 'March in the Rain' demonstration in April 1960. Soon afterward, however, Williams stated 'Unequivocally' that 'Trinidad regarded itself as "West" of the Iron Curtain,' and for the next year James was 'entirely frozen out from the position of easy access to Williams.' American and British pressure led Williams to abandon his left rhetoric; James and other younger leftists inside the PNM were betrayed and abandoned. James' book *Modern Politics* was banned in 1962, and three years later his former pupil placed him under house arrest. Despite Williams's verbal advocacy for democratic socialism, as Oxaal relates, he 'was no revolutionary; and James, although he had curbed his radical instincts, was no bourgeois reformist.'[171]

Such has been the growing popularity of 'socialism' amongst the workers in peripheral societies that even military dictators came to mouth a 'revolutionary' rhetoric. When Amin assumed power in Uganda, for instance, he declared: 'I am one of those who believe that pure capitalism like pure communism or socialism is neither desirable nor practicable . . . the direction and impetus in the entire development of the country must be provided by the Government.' One of Amin's major criticisms of Obote, which had its grain of truth, was that the deposed leader 'always claimed that he was a great socialist and yet there were very many things that he did that showed that he was anything but a socialist.' For the Ugandan masses, socialism had unfortunately come to mean 'endless taxes,' 'high prices of basic commodities,' and official corruption which 'was so widespread that it was almost taken for granted.' I.K. Acheampong, the Ghanaian military boss who put K.A. Busia in power in 1972, also claimed some vague affinity with socialism: 'I have said that a country with our limited resources cannot leave everything to the market forces . . . we have to use state power to capture the commanding heights of the economy for Ghanaians.'[172]

Such 'socialists' had no scruples in imprisoning trade unionists, religious leaders, rural militants and Marxist intellectuals.

One of the earliest and most comprehensive official statements of state socialism to emerge in East Africa was the Kenyan government's 1965 document, 'African Socialism and its Application to Planning in Kenya.' Typically, the document expresses the bureaucratic bourgeois stratum's aversion to orthodox Marxism. 'Valid as Marx's description [of Europe] was, it bears little similarity to Kenya today. African traditions have no parallel to the European feudal society, its class distinctions, its unrestricted property rights, and its acceptance of exploitation.' Despite several generations of colonial rule, 'no class problem . . . exists today among Africans.' Class contradictions in the future could be 'prevented,' the document notes, only through the institutionalization of specific 'reforms'. The government favored the adoption of 'a wages and incomes policy that recognizes the need for differential incentives as well as an equitable distribution of income,' and the use of 'various forms of ownership – State, co-operative, corporate and individual – that are efficient for different sectors . . . ' The rights of the proletariat were recognized, but trade unions were cautioned to 'avoid abuses of union power.' Nationalization of foreign enterprises was an option to be avoided, 'since it does not always lead to additional resources for the economy as a whole . . . ' The political agency for implementing 'African Socialism,' the document insisted, was not a Leninist-style vanguard party, but the eclectic, mass-based KANU: 'Political democracy in the African tradition would not countenance a party of the elite, stern tests or discriminatory criteria for party membership . . . The State, therefore, can never become the tool of special interests, catering to the desires of a minority at the expense of the needs, of the majority. The State will represent all the people . . . '[173]

Historical conditions thus forced the African petty bourgeoisie to learn something of the language of Marxist socialism, while vigorously negating its class analysis and political content. In practice, Kenya's 'African Socialism' became a crude slogan to justify the conservative nationalists' hegemony over the state apparatus, while promoting capital accumulation by the African private sector. Nicola Swainson observes that during the 1960s and 1970s the Kenyan 'ruling class gradually consolidated an immense amount of power in the hands of the executive.' KANU was 'allowed to decline as an organization,' and after 1963, the state bourgeois stratum 'was intent on asserting full administrative control over the country which was achieved through the civil service rather than the party.' In real estate, transportation, farming and commerce, the post-colonial state passed legislation which advanced the interests of small African entrepreneurs. By 1975, almost 90 percent of all foreign-owned coffee plantation acreage had been sold back to native Kenyans. The Central Bank of Kenya restricted the amount of loans offered to non-residents, and expanded funds to African enterprises. Between 1963 and 1973, the number of privately-owned firms initiated by African businessmen increased from eighteen to over four hundred. In short, Kenyatta's 'African Socialism' simply permitted 'the African merchant class to move into large-scale capitalist production.' 'Everyone advocates "African Socialism" but in the case of most party and government leaders this has become a cloak for the practice of total capitalism,' comments Odinga. 'These politicians want to build a capitalist system in the image of Western capitalism but are too embarrassed or dishonest to call it that.'[174]

Every social class rising to power must organize the political economy and social relations partially on the basis of the personnel and institutions of the ancien regime. It must use the expertise and resources of the old system in order to advance the new order. It must copy some of the methods of labor discipline, political and social repression from those who utilized such techniques against yesterday's insurgents. This was certainly the case In Saint Domingue. To establish his regime, Toussaint borrowed many of the tools and techniques of his former masters. Again, to a lesser extent, the Bolshevik revolution faced the same dilemma. Lenin candidly admitted in 1918: ' . . . it is impossible to create or introduce socialism without learning from the organizers of the trusts. For socialism is not a figment of the imagination, but the assimilation and application by the proletarian vanguard, which has seized power, of what has been created by the trusts.'[175] The burden of colonialism limited the range of historical alternatives in both the Caribbean and Africa. In most states, as illustrated, Communist and Socialist parties developed relatively late, if at all; the trade unions did not begin to expand until the 1930s in the Caribbean, and even later in Africa. Literacy rates were low; the media was dominated by capitalists; the legal system reinforced the unequal division of wealth within every society. The urban petty bourgeois strata which emerged as the leaders of neocolonial states had little intention of sharing their privileges and authority with the proletariat. The new bureaucratic bourgeois elites had 'learned from the organizers' of the former colonial systems, and had created state apparatuses which closely approximated the old regimes.

VII

In retrospect, the central, missing element in most national independence movements in the African Diaspora — the lack of strong Marxist parties or cadre-style organizations — was decisive in pushing the Black petty bourgeoisie towards varieties of anti-Marxist 'socialism.' The more fragmented and marginal the labor movement, the less weight it exerted upon mainstream nationalists; the more abstract and isolated Black Marxist intellectuals were from the process of anti-colonial resistance, the less likely they would assume roles in the post-colonial bureaucracies. However, another contributing factor, which must be examined briefly, was the contradictory and sometimes backward role of Communist Parties in critical areas of the periphery in the 1950s and 1960s. Many revolutionary nationalists in Africa and the Caribbean who could have made the theoretical and political leap to Marxism failed to do so, partially because of the inconsistent political behavior of the Soviet Union, and the non-Leninist and even 'reactionary' policies of some Communist parties in peripheral societies.

Under Stalin, the USSR showed little interest or awareness of Africa. During World War II the Soviets established diplomatic relations with Ethiopia, and in 1945 Haile Selassie gave £10,000 to the USSR as a donation to assist its war victims. A Soviet hospital was constructed in Addis Ababa in 1947, followed by a Czech arms factory in 1953. But despite the publication of the massive Soviet encyclopedia *Narody Afriki* in 1954, few African specialists existed in the country. An African Department was established in the late 1940s in the Institute of Ethnography, but the larger and more influential Institute of Africa, which was part of the Soviet Academy of Sciences, was not formally established until 1959. Overall trade with African colonial and independent states remained low — only 12.2 million rubles worth of exports, versus imports totaling 37.1 million rubles in 1955. In the United Nations, the Soviets assumed a staunch anti-colonialist posture, winning praises from many nationalist politicians. But the small Communist parties in these countries, which looked to the Soviet Union for some political guidance, were often left floundering.

In postwar Egypt, to cite one example, the Communists were unable to establish strong organizations within the working class.

Under the Nasser regime, the Soviet bloc gradually consolidated cordial political relations. In 1955, the regime signed a Czechoslovakian arms deal, and the first Egyptian cotton was sold to the Soviets. Subsequently, Soviet-bloc economic and military assistance reached massive proportions. Yet inside Egypt, Marxists were subjected frequently to harrassment, imprisonment and even executions. Penal colonies for Communists and other leftist critics of 'Arab socialism' were established in both Syria and Egypt. In 1959, the Egyptian state-controlled media 'engaged in the crudest kind of hysterical anti-Communist campaigns.' Nasser himself accused Arab Communists of conspiring to 'break up Arab unity.' The Communist Party of Egypt was officially dissolved in 1965, and not reestablished until 1975. Nasser's successor, Anwar Sadat, purged the state bureaucracy of 'left Nasserites' who favored a closer alliance with the Soviets in 1971; two years later, all Soviet advisers were expelled from Egypt.[179]

The Communists' position toward the Algerian Revolution was at best short-sighted. When the Front de Libération Nationale (FLN) of Algeria initiated armed struggle against the French colonialists, the Algerian Communist Party, committed to incremental reforms, forthrightly denounced the FLN's actions. The French Communist Party vigorously rejected the nationalistic dimensions of the liberation struggle; and in 1956, it called for 'the existence and the permanence of the specific political, economic and cultural ties that exist between France and Algeria.' Frantz Fanon and other revolutionary nationalists bitterly condemned the Communists' position. In 1957, Fanon commented ruefully: 'In a colonial country, it used to be said, there is a community of interests between the colonized people and the working class of the colonialist country. The history of the wars of liberation waged by the colonized peoples is the history of the non-verification of this thesis.'[177]

Conversely, the Soviets took a dim view of both Fanon and the first president of independent Algeria, Ahmed Ben Bella. Soviet scholars later criticized Fanon for not devoting sufficient 'attention to the question of the liberation movement joining forces with the democratic forces and the working class of the metropolis.' Fanon was a 'metaphysician' who had 'absolutised armed methods, declaring them to be the only means of achieving true independence, and this led to significant miscalculations.' The Soviets approved of Ben Bella's support for 'Arab socialism,' but subsequently accused him of being 'unable to suggest anything that could

Historical Contours of African and Caribbean Politics 83

promote even an early elimination of the social anarchy and disorder reigning in the country . . . He was . . . rather like the Caliph of Bagdad, [who] would unexpectedly appear in some suburb or village in order to 'settle' local problems.'[178]

Such profound tensions between Arab revolutionary nationalists and the Communists could not escape the critical purview of Black nationalists. By 1960, approximately sixty percent of the Arab-speaking population was located in the African continent. While relations between many African nationalist movements and the Soviets were in many instances nonexistent, radical Arabs exerted a significant influence south of the Sahara. In the 1950s, Nasser brought hundreds of African students to Egypt on educational scholarships. 'Radio Swahili,' which promoted the cause of the Mau Mau uprising in Kenya, was based in Cairo. Fanon served briefly as the Algerian ambassador to Ghana — although Ghana's actual material and political support of the FLN during the war, it should be noted, was miniscule.

In their initial encounters with the new African leaders, the Soviets repeated their misjudgements with Arab nationalists. In 1955, Soviet Africanist expert I. Potekhin sharply criticized Nkrumah in a published essay, 'Anti-imperialist Movement in the Gold Coast Colony.' Nkrumah represented 'the interests of the local bourgeoisie,' and under his leadership the country would 'remain in the orbit of British imperialism.'[179] Subsequent events sharply refuted Potekhin's analysis. By 1961, Leonid Brezhnev visited Accra on a state visit; the following year Nkrumah was awarded the Lenin Peace Prize. This turnabout in Soviet-Ghanaian relations had less to do with the African regime's internal moves toward 'socialism', than with Nkrumah's need for Soviet economic aid and his willingness to endorse Soviet positions at the UN. The USSR shelved its principles, refraining from criticizing even the most conservative or repressive African states, so long as they did not adopt an anti-Soviet posture in foreign affairs.

Throughout the 1960s and much of the 1970s, Soviet-backed Communists suffered reversals across Africa. In Kenya, the USSR publicly supported Odinga against Kenyatta's KANU, and as a consequence, the Kenyan government voided Soviet economic projects and curtailed Soviet imports. In Sudan, local Communists backed the 1969 military coup, led by General Jaafar al Nimeiri. Some Marxists were permitted in the military's cabinet. But in February 1971, Nimeiri launched a national campaign to destroy the Sudanese Communist Party. In July the same year, Marxists led an abortive coup against the Nimeiri regime, and most of the prominent Communists were quickly arrested and executed. In Zimbabwe, the Soviets provided political and military support to ZAPU, led by Nkomo. Guerillas were trained in North Korea, Cuba, Bulgaria and the USSR. But the actual guerrilla force which was most effective in fighting the Ian Smith regime was ZANU, which was backed by the Chinese and a majority of independent African states. As David Martin and Phyllis Johnson note, 'The Russians were behaving over Zimbabwe much as the Americans had behaved over Angola . . . refusing to recognize which liberation movement was the choice of the majority of people of the country. They refused military support to ZANU for the duration of the war – the East Germans told ZANU towards the end that they regarded them as a "splinter group" that should rejoin ZAPU . . . ' When Robert Mugabe and ZANU ultimately came to power, their attitude toward the Soviets could hardly be fraternal.[180]

In Guinea, Touré broke with the CGT in 1955 and helped to establish an Afrocentric trade-union confederation. But when Guinea achieved its independence, Touré was forced to deal with the Soviets, who gave him $35 million in economic aid and arms. Two years later, however, the unpredictable Touré expelled the Soviet Union's ambassador on spurious grounds.[181] In 1962, Touré accepted $70 million in US assistance. During the remainder of the 1960s, a number of joint economic ventures with Communist countries continued — e.g., a Polish-Guinean fishing monopoly, and in 1969, a USSR-Guinean bauxite mining project — but Guinea never became a close or cordial ally of the Soviets, despite its official policy of 'socialism.'[182]

In Somalia, the Soviets became heavily involved with the military regime of Mohammed Siad Barre, which came to power in October 1969 and undertook a series of nationalizations. Siad 'called for a study of the experience of socialist countries' as providing the appropriate model for Somalia's future evolution. In January 1972, a national campaign 'for propagandizing scientific socialism' was initiated. The next year, the regime's public relations bureau initiated the monthly journal *Labour and Socialism,* in order to 'explain to the Somali people in simple and comprehensible language the principles of Marxist-Leninist doctrine.'[152] The Soviets were permitted to use Berbera, Somali's northern port, as a naval base; a large Soviet air base was constructed at Hargeisa, and a communications centre at Kismayu. Fraternal ties were severed, however, during the 1977-78 Ogaden war, as the Soviets supported the new Ethiopian regime against Somalia. 'Socialist' Somalia thus overnight became a client regime of the USA.[183]

Perhaps the strangest case of Soviet involvement in Africa occurred in Uganda. The Obote neocolonial regime, from 1962 to 1971, was generally in the orbit of Western imperialism. Israel trained Uganda's police, army and intelligence bureau; the major investors in the nation's agricultural and industrial concerns were British, Canadian and Italian corporations. Obote signed a cultural agreement with the Soviets in July 1964; the USSR initiated a spinning mill project, and provided a number of fighter planes with a training team in the late 1960s. But despite the Obote regime's 'leftward' turn in 1969-1970, relations with the Soviets were cool. When Amin seized power, he initially returned to Obote's pre-1970 neocolonialist policies. The Soviets were expelled and replaced by seven hundred Israeli military and technical advisers. Immediately, *Pravda* condemned the coup as having been orchestrated by 'internal reaction and representatives of foreign capital.' The British promised Amin £1 million worth of armoured vehicles, plus £10 million in economic aid. By mid-1972, however, Amin quietly turned to Libya and the Soviet Union, which apparently promised even more assistance. Amin destroyed much of his public credibility in the West by expelling 50,000 Asians from Uganda from September to November 1972. A British military team was also ordered out of the country. In December 1972, the British cancelled all assistance to the regime; Amin retaliated by nationalizing 41 foreign-owned firms, of which fifteen were British. Most of the remaining concerns were small-scale plantations. 'But very few of the big monopoly British investments in Uganda were included in this nationalization move.'[184]

Amin consolidated his authority by ordering the executions of several thousand soldiers suspected of retaining loyalties to Obote. The Langi and Acholi ethnic groups particularly bore the brunt of this brutal repression. The army was expanded to nearly 20,000 soldiers, and two new intelligence agencies were formed, the Public Safety Unit (PSU) and the State Research Bureau (SRB). Both employed several thousand agents and part-time informants, who terrorized Uganda's working class, peasants, and middle strata. All political parties and the parliament were outlawed, and Amin essentially ruled via decree. His Minister of Internal Affairs was empowered to imprison 'indefinitely any person suspected of being "dangerous" or of "endeavoring to excite enmity between the people of Uganda and the government." ' A new ruling strata emerged, the *mafutamingi*, for whom the mass terror of Amin's regime and the Asian petty bourgeoisie's expulsion 'provided a framework for quick enrichment.' The largest agricultual and industrial enterprises seized by the state were distributed between Amin and his chief officers.

The economic impact of Amin's chaotic and despotic regime was not difficult to imagine. Uganda's cotton exports declined by 50 percent; coffee exports dropped by one third; many of the nation's largest industries ceased to function; thousands of skilled workers, technicians, and professionals fled the country or were imprisoned. The Western media took the lead in pillorying the authoritarian regime. But Western governments and corporations had few qualms about maintaining business relations with Amin. Several British firms sold communications equipment, telephone-tapping devices, and related security apparatus to the SRB. British Leyland sold landrovers and trucks to Amin's army in 1977. Although the US closed its embassy in November, 1973, American business also continued as usual. Amin's personal jet was purchased from the Grumman Corporation in 1974, and the regime also purchased several Boeing jets. The percentage of Uganda's total coffee crop purchased by the US actually increased, from 20.6 percent in 1973 to 33.5 percent in 1976. Key SRB agents were trained by the CIA inside the United States during the mid-1970s.[185]

Although the United States became Uganda's principal trading partner during Amin's bloody rule, the Soviet Union was one of the few states which proclaimed the regime's 'progressive' orientation. In 1974, Soviet publicist O.Tsvetaev toured Kampala, and concluded that the 'economic war' had created a 'revolutionary transformation' in the country. Uganda under Amin's leadership had 'opened the road to economic and social progress.' Between 1973 and 1975, the Soviets supplied dozens of light tanks and armoured personnel carriers, as well as anti-aircraft guns, trucks, seven helicopters and a squadron of fighter jets. Seven hundred Ugandans were sent to the Soviet Union for military training, and almost 200 were stationed in Czechoslovakia. Several hundred Soviet troops were stationed in Uganda for 'on-the-spot training.' By 1977, Amin was urging the Soviet ambassador, Evgeni Moussiyko, to consider a bilateral agreement which would construct 'the most modern nuclear reactor' and the 'biggest Soviet military base on the African continent' inside Uganda. Had the USSR accepted Amin's offer, the regime might still exist. But when Amin ordered the invasion of northern Tanzania in October, 1978, the Soviets promptly pulled back. In November, Soviet pilots left for the USSR. Nyerere authorized a counterinvasion in January 1979, and Tanzanian troops reached Kampala on 10 April. The financial and military backers of Amin had disappeared and the regime rapidly collapsed.[186]

Soviet policies in these and other instances, however questionable, do not constitute 'social imperialism'. There is no real equivalence to the logic of Western imperialism, which remains fundamental in providing material and political support for the most repressive and reactionary regimes. Imperialism throughout its various historical mutations has retained, as Lenin observed, its basic 'parasitic' character.[187] Moreover there are many instances where Soviet diplomatic, military and economic assistance has been critical to the development of revolutionary movements: Guinea-Bissau, Mozambique, Angola and South Africa. The real problem of Soviet policy has been an incautious readiness to accept the self-designation of single-party regimes or 'left' juntas — especially when their foreign policies have temporarily intersected with the Soviet Union's.

This represents, on balance, an opportunistic departure from Leninist analysis based on the study of the historically specific conditions of particular non-Western societies. Too often the bureaucratic bourgeoisie have garnered Soviet support merely by mouthing 'scientific socialism' or by claiming to follow the 'non-Capitalist path', while at the same time engaged in actual repression of their own working classes and intellectuals. Such 'Bonapartist' regimes, who regularly violate the human rights of their citizens, reduce 'socialism' to a caricatural justification for brutality and state coercion. To falsely encourage such policies because they are clad in a pseudo-Marxist apologetic only reinforces the general trend towards statist authoritarianism throughout the entire neocolonial periphery.

2

Kwame Nkrumah and the Convention People's Party

Seek ye first the political kingdom, and everything else will be added unto ye.

Kwame Nkrumah

A man who has just come in from the rain and dried his body and put on dry clothes is more reluctant to go out again than another who has been indoors all the time. The trouble with our new nation . . . was that none of us had been indoors long enough to be able to say 'to hell with it.' We had all been in the rain together until yesterday. Then a handful of us – the smart and the lucky and hardly ever the best – had scrambled for the one shelter our former rulers left, and had taken it over and barricaded themselves in. And from within they sought to persuade the rest through numerous loudspeakers, that the first phase of the struggle had been won and that the next phase – the extension of our house – was even more important and called for new and original tactics; it required that all argument should cease and the whole people should speak with one voice . . .

Chinua Achebe
A Man of the People (1967)

He who makes a revolution by half digs his own grave.

Saint Just

On 21 February 1966, President Kwame Nkrumah of Ghana, the most influential African statesman of his generation, flew via Cairo to the People's Republic of China and to Vietnam, in an effort to secure peace in Southeast Asia. At 4:00 a.m. the following morning, 600 troops under the command of Colonel Emmanuel K. Kotoka and Brigade Major Akwasi A. Afrifa left the Tamale garrison in Ghana's Northern Region and proceeded swiftly south to Kumasi, the capital of Ashanti. The troops were told that they were moving to 'an unknown destination for a test exercise.' The next morning, the Accra police swiftly 'rounded up' most of Nkrumah's ministers in the nation's capital. Proceeding from Kumasi, the troops were now told that Nkrumah had 'deserted Ghana,' that 'no Government' now existed, and it was 'their duty to assume control of the country to maintain law and order.' The national radio station was quickly seized, and Kotoka announced

Kwame Nkrumah and the Convention People's Party 89

that 'the Military, in cooperation with the Ghana Police, have taken over the government of Ghana. [Nkrumah's ruling] Convention People's Party (was) disbanded . . . '[1] After two hours of bloody combat, Nkrumah's presidential residence, Flagstaff House, was taken by troops. Kotoka personally murdered a Nkrumah-loyalist, Major General Barwah, in front of his wife and children, and Barwah's seven security personnel were also killed. By midmorning hundreds of police and troops were patrolling the Accra streets with submachine guns.

Soon, signs of guarded support for the military regime were evident. Local chiefs, rural farmers, and civil servants issued public pledges of support; demonstrations praising the coup were held in Sekondi-Takoradi and Kumasi; dozens of churches held special services 'to give thanks for what had happened'; 'the Association of Kwahu Citizens' gave the regime the sum of £1,200, 'a sheep, corned beef, yams and twenty cases of sardines.' Nkrumah's impressive statue in downtown Accra was smashed, and all streets and public institutions bearing his name were changed. Estimates concerning the number of people killed in the coup vary radically, but one thing seems certain: the Convention People's Party, which had been the ruling power in the state since 1951, presented no systemic, organized mass resistance. The CPP — a nationalist party which claimed over one million paid members, 103 full-time party organizers, and 2,885 local offices in 1955 — collapsed as an organized social force a decade later.[2]

Nkrumah's explanation for the lack of serious national resistance to the coup — that 'the people of Ghana were stunned' and 'nobody outside Accra knew what had happened, or was happening' — is hardly convincing.[3] The President and a few members of his entourage were shocked perhaps, but others were not. In his 1964 study of Ghanaian politics, Dennis Austin noted that the CPP had 'lost much of its former popular base . . . ' A coup was a real 'possibility. Once having seized power in Accra, the replacement of the CPP commissioners in the regions by junior and senior officers was not likely to present any great difficulty to a determined army commander.'[4] As Austin was writing, Afrifa was actively preparing for the coup: 'from 1964 every day I considered plans for the removal of Kwame Nkrumah from power. I knew that militarily it was possible to break through his well-armed security force without bloodshed.'[5] None of the President's closest advisers in Flagstaff House wanted Nkrumah to take the trip. Over the weekend of 18 February, 'reports came in that officers were plotting a coup d'etat in Kumasi.' At the airport on 21 February, some diplomats 'wondered if he would return'; others were 'placing bets on the possibilities and time of a coup.'

The new regime's personnel was drawn, in part, from politicians who once had been leading Nkrumaists. Kwesi Lamptey of Sekondi, who in 1950 had been CPP national acting deputy chairman, was named chairman of the regime's State Gold Mining Corporation; Victor Owusu, a CPP Ashanti militant in the early 1950s, was named the new Attorney-General; another former Ashanti leader of the CPP, R.R. Amponsah, became chairman of Ghana Airways in 1967, and also served on the regime's Electoral Commission and the Political Committee. These leaders had broken with the CPP a decade or more prior to the coup, so their allegiance to reaction was not remarkable. What Nkrumah could not explain, however, was the behavior of his closest aides after the military's seizure of power. Kwaku Boateng, once Minister of the Interior and a 'radical Nkrumahist,' declared his solidarity for the coup behind prison bars, telling the new authorities that ministers had been 'reduced to gaping sycophants' under Nkrumah. Kwesi Amoako-Atta, Ghana's Finance Minister, hastily 'condemned Nkrumah's insensitivity to people's hardships.' Kofi Baako, one of the original members of the CPP Central Committee and the 'leading exponent of Nkrumahism, claimed that if someone could eavesdrop at the prison, they would know "our" attitude to Nkrumah.' Another founder of the CPP, Krobo Edusei, past Minister of Communications and Transportation and Minister of Agriculture, bitterly condemned Nkrumah's 'corruption.'[6]

Imprisonment has made many deposed leaders repudiate themselves and their past political associates. But more revealing still was the behavior of those officials who had travelled with Nkrumah to China. Oxford-educated Alex Quaison-Sackey, Ghana's past UN ambassador and in 1966, Nkrumah's Foreign Minister, quickly 'developed diarrhoea' upon first learning of the coup. Nkrumah asked Quaison-Sackey to depart to Addis Ababa, headquarters of the Organization of African Unity, 'to represent the legal government of Ghana' at a foreign ministers' conference. Quaison-Sackey agreed, and then went straight to Accra to denounce Nkrumah. Minister of trade Kwesi Armah fled in exile to London, where he had accumulated a considerable fortune during his years of public service. African Affairs Secretariat director M.F. Dei-Anang returned to Ghana to join the new regime, but 'much to his surprise,' he was imprisoned. Other defectors included Kofi Aduma

Bossman, Ambassador to the United Kingdom, and Aberdeen-trained economist F.S. Arkhurst, 'one of the shrewdest African diplomatists' at the UN, who was for a time restored to his old post.[7]

The capitulation of Nkrumah's petty-bourgeois leadership does not, by any means, indicate that the military regime ever had the majoritarian support of Ghana's working class and peasantry. Nkrumah did not exaggerate the popular resistance to the 'National Liberation Council' (NLC), as the eight police and military officers called themselves. Pro-Nkrumah leaflets were printed and distributed, and cells of CPP members did organize underground for a time. The Overseas Branch of the CPP denounced the coup, and a 'Socialist Ghana Defence Committee' was formed. Students offered some degree of protest. On 12 November 1966, about 300 Cape Coast University College students held an anti-NLC demonstration. Two weeks later another 300 students in Kikam used tree trunks to block a road to their school in a demonstration against a pro-regime Headmaster.[8]

But it was the working class which presented the greatest difficulties to the NLC. The regime purged most of the Nkrumahist leaders of the Trade Union Congress (TUC), but a base for leftwing Nkrumahism still remained within the rank-and-file. The TUC, which consisted of 17 national unions with a total membership of 700,000, had created district councils 'to help promote the social and economic interests of the workers and to secure a united front on questions or matters affecting or likely to affect their interests.' Although legal strikes were outlawed, the NLC was hit by 58 strikes in 1966-67, 37 strikes in 1968, and 51 strikes in 1969. The NLC regime responded to labor unrest by removing the compulsory membership clause from the Civil Service Act of 1960, which reduced TUC membership by half. The conservative, neocolonial government of K.A. Busia, which followed the NLC regime, actually abolished the TUC; but thousands of loyal unionists continued to pay their dues.[9] The continuing pro-Nkrumahist sentiment of the workers was illustrated during the 1972 election of the TUC secretary general. The Nkrumahist candidate for the post, John K. Tettegah, had been elected secretary general of the TUC with Nkrumah's backing in September 1954. Under Tettegah's direction, the TUC had been remodeled 'on the lines of the Israeli Histadrut.' After the 1966 coup, the Busia regime, and yet another coup in 1972, Tettegah retained a popular base of support among the workers. The new military regime, fearful that Tettegah would easily win a national labor election, ordered the 17 national union leaders to choose the new secretary general. The regime's candidate won by only one vote.[10]

Throughout its three-year reign, the NLC was under no illusions that it possessed a popular mandate to rule. After denouncing Nkrumah as 'ruthless,' 'dishonest,' a 'kind of Joshua and Father Divine and Cassius Clay rolled into one,' Afrifa ended his polemic with the following observations: 'The irony of the present situation in Ghana is that it is quite probable that President Nkrumah and the CPP would command the support of a majority of the electorate, even in genuinely free elections. It is a pity that it is not possible to test this hypothesis.'[11]

Afrifa's revelation raises one fundamental question: Why did the Ghanaian workers as a mass refuse to resist the February 1966 coup, when thousands of them retained ideological loyalties to what Nkrumah and Nkrumahism represented? The Ghanaian army had fewer than 10,000 men, and a substantial minority of the junior officers were left-wing Nkrumahists. As it was, the NLC retained a tenuous hold on the situation. In late 1966 two CPP members, one an army lieutenant, were arrested and imprisoned for plotting a 'counter-coup.' Two other Nkrumahist lieutenants were more successful in April 1967. They assassinated General Kotoka, and managed to hold the national radio station for several hours. In November 1968, the commander of the Ghana Armed Forces, Air Marshall Michael Otu, was imprisoned for planning to restore Nkrumah to power. Among some of the ruling elites, Nkrumah's restoration remained a viable if wishful option to military rule, until his death in 1972. But this does not resolve the problem of Nkrumah's lack of active support within the very class he claimed to serve. If the CPP had one-tenth of the members it claimed to have in 1966, a coup of the Afrifa-type could not have lasted a single week. A general strike would have paralyzed the handful of frightened civil servants, police commissioners and army generals who benefitted from the coup. If C.L.R. James's 1960 statement in Accra had been true — that 'the centre of the world revolutionary struggle is here in Accra, Ghana' — Nkrumah's own ministers should not have begged the military junta for mercy.[12]

The contradictions of Nkrumahism were evident to an on-the-scene observer, the venerable Pan-Africanist, Ras Makonnen. A friend of Padmore's since their college years at Howard University in Washington, D.C., Makonnen had first worked with Nkrumah in the planning of the Manchester Pan-African Congress of 1945. Coming to Ghana in 1957, he worked with Padmore's African

Affairs Centre, and remained in the country until the coup. Upon arrival, Makonnen was frankly shocked by the low level of ideological development among the leaders of the CPP. At independence, 'nobody was asking "What Is To Be Done"!' the CPP 'elite did not know the difference between a plantation and a collective farm.' The rhetoric of the CPP was 'socialist.' But watching the evolution of the regime from 1957 to 1966, Makonnen concluded that virtually none of the CPP leadership was really interested in defending the material interests of workers and peasants.

'You can't build socialism without socialists,' Makonnen wrote. The CPP bosses 'had a simple conviction, that if there were going to be any capitalist millionaires around, then they might as well be Ghanaian ones. Some of them had acted in a helpful way with sums of money when the party was just being founded, and they saw to it that once the party was in power, they got their reward.[13] The striking testimony of Soviet leader Anastas Mikoyan confirms Makonnen's analysis. Visiting Ghana in January, 1962, Mikoyan informed the work via *Tass* that Ghana under Nkrumah 'had made great progress in building socialism in the country.' But meeting with Nkrumah's cabinet privately, Mikoyan noted, perhaps with a smile, that 'none of you are socialists.' No one disagreed.[14]

To his many defenders, Nkrumah still remains 'the great internationalist, African freedom fighter, and the first man in history to make Pan-Africanism a living political reality.' To Amilcar Cabral, the greatest theoretician of African liberation, Nkrumah 'was above all the strategist of genius in the struggle against classical colonialism.' Even Afrifa described the deposed president as having 'represented the hopes and aspiration of Black people all over the world. Ghana became . . . a beacon to the millions of Black people who inhabit the African continent. Nkrumah was a man of great personal charm and warmth . . . '[15] Nine years after breaking his long political relationship with Nkrumah, James wrote, 'Kwame Nkrumah was one of the greatest political leaders of our century. We must be on guard that his years of exile do not remove from our constant study and contemplation the remarkable achievements of the great years.'[16] This is the essential paradox of Nkrumah and the CPP: that a young African intellectual could seize the imagination of the entire Ghanaian people, and for that matter, the world, in 1948-51, but fail to lead a successful social transformation of his own nation in the years that followed.

I

Francis Nkrumah was born in the small village of Nkroful, in the southwest corner of the Gold Coast, in September 1909. After eight years of elementary school training, he became a school teacher. In 1935 Nkrumah borrowed funds from a relative and travelled to the United States, enrolling at the all-Black Lincoln University, near Philadelphia. Like many other students, he worked part time at odd jobs, occasionally as a dishwasher and clerk, to pay his tuition. Through determination, he received his undergraduate degree from Lincoln in the field of philosophy in 1939, and later obtained masters degrees in philosophy and education at the University of Pennsylvania. During these formative years there was nothing particularly striking about Francis Nkrumah. His grades were good, but not outstanding. Despite his Roman Catholic background, he applied for admission to the Lincoln Theological Seminary, a Protestant school, and soon graduated as Bachelor of Sacred Theology. In the early 1940s, he travelled to New York, Philadelphia or Washington, D.C. nearly every Sunday to preach the gospel. At the University of Pennsylvania, he was instrumental in oprganizing the initial 'General Conference of Africans in America,' held in September, 1942. With fellow Gold Coast student Ako Adjei, Nkrumah founded a journal, *The African Interpreter*, which printed 'analytical and fiery articles about Mother Africa.'[17]

Nkrumah's real political education began quite by chance in 1943, when he encountered C.L.R. James in New York. Since his immigration to the United States five years before, James had been involved in many activities, including organizing Afro-American and white tenant farmers in southern Missouri. At the time, James and his small group of supporters (including Marxist Grace Lee) were operating as a dissident current inside the small Trotskyist Workers' Party of Max Shachtman.[18] For two years, James and his faction met with Nkrumah and exchanged ideas. 'Even in those years, Nkrumah was noted for his acute intelligence, his intellectual energy, the elegance of his person, the charm of his manners, and his ability to establish easy relations with any company in which he found himself.'[19] In their informal study group, James acquainted the young African with literature from the Pan-Africanist movement, as well as his own interpretation of Trotskyism. James's impact upon Nkrumah was fundamental, only to be superseded by that of Padmore later.

James directly equated British colonialism in Africa with fascism.

In his September-October 1939 polemic against World War II, he had predicted, 'If the fascists win, they will take the colonies back. If the "democracies" win, they will keep them. But whether "democracies" win, or fascists win, the Africans remain slaves in their own country.' James insisted that the Black movement in the Caribbean, USA and Africa had its own 'independent validity,' and that 'it must not be subordinated to the struggles of the workers against the bosses.' James retained a deep belief in spontaneity, and a revulsion against Stalinism. The precise forms of political transformation would be generated by the masses themselves, not imposed from above. Above all, James had a 'passionate belief in the contribution that Black people *must* make to their own liberation and *can* make to the advancement of all humanity.'[20]

Nkrumah never became a Trotskyist, and was actually more attracted to the Black nationalist ideas of Marcus Garvey than to James's variety of Marxism. Although he was 'very friendly,' James was troubled that Nkrumah 'used to talk a great deal about imperialism, Leninism and similar data, with which my friends and I were very familiar. Nkrumah used to talk a lot of nonsense about these matters.' Nevertheless, when Nkrumah decided to go to England for further study in early 1945, James promptly wrote Padmore, urging him to assist the young man. 'He is not very bright,' James added, but he was 'determined to throw the Europeans out of Africa . . .'[21]

Padmore met Nkrumah upon his arrival in London. Within a few weeks, Nkrumah enrolled at Gray's Inn to study law, and began attending lectures at the London School of Economics. But unlike his old associate Ako Adjei, who had moved to London to finish his law degree, Nkrumah had little time or inclination for studies. He attended meetings of the British Communist Party for a time, and joined the West African Students' Union. Most crucially, he immersed himself in preparations for Padmore's Fifth Pan-African Congress, which was held in October 1945, in Manchester. Through Padmore, Nkrumah met Jomo Kenyatta, South African writer Peter Abrahams and Pan-Africanist militant Ras Makonnen. Padmore and Nkrumah served as joint secretaries of the organizing committee. Nkrumah recalled later: 'We worked night and day in George's flat. We used to sit in his small kitchen, the wooden table completely covered with papers, a pot of tea which we always forgot until it had been made two or three hours and George typing at his small typewriter so fast that the papers were churned out as though they were being rolled off a printing press. We despatched hundreds and hundreds of letters to the various organizations throughout Africa and the West Indies explaining the aims of the Congress and the political tactics that should be adopted to achieve liberation in the colonies.'[22]

The Manchester Congress marked Nkrumah's arrival as a potential leader of a major current in the African independence movement. Du Bois, then seventy seven years old, participated at the sessions and drafted one of the Congress' main declarations. Du Bois was grateful for Nkrumah's extensive organizational work, but saw little in him which indicated a capacity for leadership. To the Afro-American scholar, Nkrumah seemed 'shabby, kindly, but earnest . . . I did not then dream that Nkrumah had the stamina and patience' for achieving 'freedom for the Gold Coast.'[23] But with Padmore's theoretical guidance, the young Nkrumah already comprehended that the Fifth Pan-African Congress was superior to Du Bois's earlier political efforts, beginning in 1900. 'For the first time,' Nkrumah wrote in 1957, 'the delegates who attended it were practical men and men of action and not, as was the case of the four previous conferences, merely idealists contenting themselves with writing theses but quite unable or unwilling to take any active part in dealing with the African problem.'[24]

By 1946-1947, Nkrumah — now 'Kwame' — had become, second only to Padmore, the best known figure amongst the African anti-colonialist activists living in England. He worked closely with fellow countryman, Joe Appiah, a delegate at the Manchester Congress and later president of the West African Students Union. With Padmore's help, Nkrumah drafted his own manifesto for African independence, 'Towards Colonial Freedom.' Upon receiving a copy, James noted with approval, 'In one year [Nkrumah] had learnt what had taken us so many years to learn and pare.' Impatient with some of his more conservative African student associates, Nkrumah and other militants — including Kojo Botsio, Awooner Renner and Ashie Nikoe of the Gold Coast — created the West African National Secretariat 'in order to put into action the new Pan-African nationalism.'

In March 1946, the new Secretariat published the first issue of *The New African*, which claimed as its credo, 'For Unity and Absolute Independence.' Attempts were made to establish cooperative relations with French West African intellectuals and leaders. In Paris, Nkrumah caucused with Houphouet-Boigny, Senghor, and Gueye, and tentative plans were drawn for 'a movement for the Union of West African Socialist Republics.' Within the

Secretariat, Nkrumah's closest followers created a vanguard group called 'The Circle.' Members were required to fast one day each month, maintain themselves as 'the Revolutionary Vanguard of the struggle for West African Unity and National Independence,' and to 'accept the Leadership of Kwame Nkrumah.' Although the Circle 'disintegrated' at the end of 1947, the small cadre group formed the basic pattern of the Convention People's Party's core structure years later. Circle members were committed to 'nonviolent methods' and civil disobedience, and placed no great emphasis on traditional organizing through the unions. An elite would emancipate the masses without the 'use of armed force.'[25]

An incident which nearly destroyed Nkrumah's budding career occurred sometime in 1946. Makonnen learned that Nkrumah was 'double-dealing between Pan-Africanism and communism' by attending Communist Party meetings. Such alliances with Marxist-Leninists had been outlawed by Padmore and other Pan-Africanist leaders. Makonnen also became suspicious when Nkrumah's West African National Secretariat established a separate office for its headquarters. When copies of Communist literature on colonial questions were discovered by Makonnen in Nkrumah's office, a special session of the Pan-Africanist central committee was called in Manchester, and Nkrumah was sternly 'summoned.' With Padmore, Kenyatta, and others in attendance, Makonnen 'acted the role of Vishinsky' to prosecute Nkrumah: 'Do you not realize that some of us had already gone through the communist mill, and that we knew only too well their tactics . . . Our anti-colonial movement must be unfettered. To carry the burdens of Russia on our shoulders would be a terrible thing.' Nkrumah's future role in Gold Coast politics was instantly on a narrow precipice. Padmore's hatred and loathing for Communism was scarcely less than his commitment to African independence. Nkrumah also knew that Padmore had direct ties to influential West African newspaper publisher Nnamdi ('Zik') Azikiwe, and that 'through Zik' his reputation would be finished 'in a single dispatch.' Nkrumah reeled back, apologizing for his political errors. Perhaps as a former Leninist, Padmore was more forgiving, and he accepted his protege's *mea culpa*. The episode was closed, but not forgotten.[26]

In late 1947 Ako Adjei, who had recently returned to the Gold Coast, contacted Nkrumah with an intriguing proposition. Adjei had been asked to become full-time general secretary of the United Gold Coast Convention (UGCC), the major nationalist formation in the country. Adjei declined the post, but urged the organization to hire Nkrumah. The UGCC's leaders — attorney J.B. Danquah, timber merchant A.G. Grant, and William Ofori Atta — represented the Gold Coast's affluent African petty bourgeoisie and some of the more prosperous ethnic chiefs. After some hesitation, and the receipt of £100 for sea passage from Grant, Nkrumah accepted the post. From the first, he confided in Adjei that he was fearful to 'associate myself with a movement backed almost entirely by reactionaries, middle class lawyers and merchants.' But his ideological perspective, which tended to devalue class divisions within African society, and emphasize the 'masses' as a transclass category in the anticolonial struggle, permitted him to work with Danquah and the UGCC. The members of the West African National Secretariat endorsed Nkrumah's decision to return home, as did Padmore. In November 1947 Nkrumah left London, accompanied by his friend and collaborator Kojo Botsio. However, Makonnen retained doubts about Nkrumah's ideological orientation: 'To my mind it was preferable to back the old-style nationalist in the Gold Coast . . . even though their nationalism was somewhat royalist, than to go back tarred with the communist brush.' Makonnen was fearful that 'Kwame was coming back' to the Gold Coast with 'a Communist Party card in his pocket,' and he relayed to the conservative nationalists 'my grave doubts about Kwame's present trend.'[27]

Nkrumah promptly went to work. He established an office in the small coastal town of Saltpond and began to recruit new members. His capacity for work surprised and even alarmed his more complacent colleagues. Nkrumah phoned associates in the middle of the night with new ideas; he printed membership cards and organized an efficient dues-paying structure. The 'respectable gentlemen' at the head of the UGCC were urged to initiate militant clubs throughout the entire country, not just in Accra and among the middle strata. Before these plans could be implemented, the essential 'spark' which ignited the nationalist movement took place. The key figure was not Nkrumah, however, but a sub-chief of the Ga State, Nii Kwabena Bonne III, who was outraged by the high prices of goods charged by European and Syrian entrepreneurs in Accra. From 24 January 1948, until 28 February, a nationwide boycott of consumer goods was held. On the final day of the boycott, the Ex-Servicemen's Union held a peaceful march of 2,000 in Accra which was fired upon by police. Two ex-soldiers were killed, and five other Africans were wounded. The African urban working class responded by looting European-owned shops, and some whites were stoned. After several days of unrest, twenty Africans were killed by the authorities, and 237 were injured. Using typical colonial logic, the frightened Gold Coast governor, Sir Gerald Creasy, arrested six UGCC leaders, including Danquah, Adjei and Nkrumah. Nii Bonne was not connected with the UGCC at all, and at the time of the riots, the UGCC had only 13 branches and 1,765 members. But the arrest of Nkrumah and Danquah made them national heroes, and overnight the membership in the UGCC soared among young urban workers and intellectuals. Students and teachers initiated a sympathy strike for the imprisoned nationalists, and many were expelled and fired.[28]

The brief period of imprisonment had a salutary effect upon the UGCC's leaders. They now viewed Nkrumah suspiciously: 'What kind of a man was this that they had saddled themselves with?' They castigated Nkrumah and blamed his radical rhetoric for 'their predicament.' Upon the release of the detained leaders, they reviewed the Saltpond files and Nkrumah's personal correspondence. They were especially alarmed that Nkrumah still maintained connections with the West African National Secretariat, and that he employed the Marxist-style greeting 'comrade' in his letters. In the aftermath of the disturbance, the Watson Commission, an official board of inquiry, tried to widen the breach among the nationalists. The Commission ruled that Nkrumah was 'imbued with a Communist ideology which only political expediency had blurred. (He) has never abandoned his aims for a Union of West African Soviet Socialist Republics . . . ' The Watson Commission's findings later led to the creation of the Coussey Constitutional Committee, which in October 1949, called for the creation of a new Legislative Assembly with 84 appointed and elected members.

With the growing prospects for a peaceful transition of power, the UGCC viewed Nkrumah as a liability in their negotiations with the British. On 3 September 1948 Danquah, Adjei and other leaders 'relieved' Nkrumah from his position as UGCC general secretary. But the move came too late. That same day, Nkrumah and Komla Gbedemah, a young UGCC recruit, published the first edition of the *Accra Evening News*. The uncompromisingly anti-colonialist newspaper carried the slogans: 'We prefer self-government with danger to servitude in tranquility . . . we have the right to govern ourselves.'[29]

Nkrumah rapidly established his own political base and legitimacy, without breaking directly with the UGCC. He rented a small building in Cape Coast and started 'Ghana College,' a school for students who had been expelled for their strike earlier that year. By mid-1949 Ghana College had 230 pupils, and soon more than one dozen protest academies were established. In Gbedemah's Accra home, the 'Committee on Youth Organisation' was organized as a youth section of the nationalist movement. In Kumasi, nationalist youth led by Krobo Edusei and Bediako Poku started the 'Ashanti Youth Association'; Nkrumah-supporters Kofi Baako, Saki Scheck and Kwesi Plange created the 'Ghana League of Patriots.' In early June 1949, the leaders of these youth organizations caucused in Tarkwa to determine if they should create 'a real political party.' Younger elements within the leadership led by Kofi Baako and Saki Scheck opposed a new political party; more mature nationalists in their thirties, led by Gbedemah, Botsio and Dzenkle Dzewu, urged a complete break, and called for the slogan 'Full Self-Government Now.' Nkrumah sided with Gbedemah and Botsio, and the new party was launched on 12 June 1949. Approximately 60,000 people gathered in Accra to attend the founding of the 'Convention People's Party.' 'The time has arrived,' Nkrumah announced, 'when a definite line of action must be taken if we are going to save our country from continued imperialist exploitation and oppression.'[30]

Despite the growth of mass activism, Nkrumah still retained faint hopes that a total rupture with the UGCC could be avoided. On 16 June 1949, arbitrators selected by the executive committee of the UGCC proposed a compromise: that Nkrumah be reinstated as general secretary of the UGCC, and that the CPP 'should still stand but as a political party acting as the vanguard within the UGCC.' Nkrumah accepted the proposal, but Danquah and the majority of UGCC leaders refused. A month later, a special UGCC delegates meeting was held in Saltpond. Nkrumah capitulated to their demand that the CPP 'should be dissolved,' but won the concession that a new, democratically-selected executive committee be formed. But as the negotiations were nearly ending, Nkrumah was called from the conference table. An excited crowd waited outside: ' "Resign!" they shouted, as soon as they saw me, "resign and lead us and we shall complete the struggle together!" ' Nkrumah immediately resigned from the UGCC. 'The overwhelming support I had received from the masses had prompted me to act,' he later wrote. 'This marked the final parting of the ways to right and left of Gold Coast nationalism . . . from now on the struggle was to be three-sided, made up by the reactionary intellectuals and chiefs, the British Government and the politically awakened masses with their

Kwame Nkrumah and the Convention People's Party   101

slogan of "Self-Government now." [31]

This small but critical event in Ghanaian political history has been interpreted in various ways. For C.L.R. James, it validated the spontaneity thesis of social change. 'Nkrumah did not want to split from the UGCC,' James noted. 'But the youth and thousands of others were shocked at the news . . . Nkrumah is not ashamed of the fact that at every decisive stage the mass drove him on and at this, the most decisive stage of all, roughly told him what it wanted.'[32] Basil Davidson, on the other hand, has suggested that Nkrumah's version of the incident did not tell 'the whole truth.' 'Was the call to resign prearranged, just in case the working committee went along with him?' In any event, 'the break was now complete. Either the CPP would make good its struggle for independence, or the CPP would be destroyed by failure, and Nkrumah and his colleagues along with the CPP.'[33]

Spontaneity had its limitations. James would have been the first to agree that any nationalist movement must be arduously organized and in the earliest stages of social protest the character and commitment of its leaders is absolutely decisive. The CPP's first central committee consisted of Nkrumah, vice chairman Gbedemah, secretary Botsio, journalist Saki Scheck, Krobo Edusei, Kofi Baako, Nathaniel Welbeck, Kwesi Plange, Dzenkle Dzewu, and Ashie Nikoe. Each contributed to creating a viable movement. Scheck was Nkrumah's personal secretary and handled crucial correspondence; Baako edited the CPP's *Daily Mail* newspaper in Cape Coast; Nikoe and twenty-year-old Plange were the Party's youth leaders; Edusei established support for the CPP among the Ashanti. From the beginning, one of Nkrumah's favorite slogans to his supporters was 'organization decides everything.' And they attempted to live up to his expectations. CPP secretaries went out to meet people in the villages and hamlets; old vans were borrowed or purchased and mounted with loudspeakers and used for propaganda purposes. Throughout late 1949 hundreds of CPP fundraisers were held — athletic events, parties, open rallies. By the end of the year Party secretaries were receiving small salaries, and were working on a full-time basis.

Nkrumah himself worked tirelessly, travelling thousands of miles across the country and organizing branches of the CPP in Liberia, Nigeria and the Ivory Coast amoung Gold Coast migrants. But the Party's most dedicated and loyal supporters were African women. As CPP propaganda secretaries, they travelled in hundreds of villages and towns, recruiting new members. They kept Nkrumah 'in their houses, fed him and looked after him when the police were looking to arrest him. The market women, the petty entrepreneurs in the towns, according to Bankole Timothy, formed 'the backbone of Nkrumah's mass movement . . . ' The CPP's opponents used various methods to suppress the young movement. Nkrumah and his aides were ridiculed as 'verandah boys,' 'Communists,' and 'riff-raff' by the UGCC. The British officials urged conservative civic leaders to file libel suits against the CPP press. Danquah sued the *Accra Evening News* for libel, and won damages and also the right to seize the publication. In October 1949, Gbedemah was sentenced to six months' imprisonment on libel charges.[34]

To protest the final report of the Coussey committee, the CPP organized a mass public meeting in November, the 'Ghana People's Representative Assembly,' which again endorsed the demand for 'immediate self-government,' or 'full Dominion status within the Commonwealth of Nations.' Pobee Biney, the national vice-chairman of the Trade Union Congress (TUC), mobilized thousands of laborers and served as chair of the insurgent assembly. Nkrumah's rhetorical call for 'Positive Action' or nonviolent protest provoked more radical CPP members to demand a general strike against the regime, which was set for early January 1949. Once again Nkrumah hesitated, and after a meeting with authorities agreed to call off Positive Action. But when Nkrumah pressured the TUC leaders to call off the strike, they replied that they 'no longer had any control over the wild men.' The CPP press twice denied that it had endorsed a general strike, but the rank-and-file workers refused to listen. A final strike date was set for 6 January; Nkrumah reluctantly announced that the Party would strike after midnight on 8 January.

The strike was virtually absolute. 'The economic life of the whole country came to a standstill. All employed workers stayed home and employers, including the government . . . closed down.' On 11 January, the authorities decreed a state of emergency. The CPP party headquarters 'were raided, the premises wrecked, the files taken away, the party members beaten up and gaoled.' After the strike was called off on 19 January, Nkrumah and several other key CPP leaders were imprisoned. Pobee Biney was sentenced to eight months' imprisonment 'for provoking an illegal general strike,' and Anthony Woode, acting secretary of the TUC, was jailed for one year.[35]

The authoritarian response of the regime exceeded anything anticipated by Nkrumah and his colleagues. 'Accra became the scene of persecution,' Nkrumah later recalled. 'In the streets of Accra, Syrians, Lebanese and British nationals were appointed as special constables and given truncheons to help them restore order . . . a number of people disappeared and were never accounted for . . . ' The African petty bourgeoisie relished the purge, and cried for blood. Their chief representive, Danquah, solemnly declared: 'It is my opinion that those who go against constitutional authority must expect to pay for it with their neck.'[36] Nkrumah was sentenced to serve three consecutive one-year terms in prison. Terrified, many CPP organizers standing trial on the charge of 'inciting disorder' betrayed their principles and the movement. As Chinweizu notes, 'Some said they did not know what Positive Action was; others said they knew but disliked it and even spoke against it at party executive deliberations. Some party officials even went as far as to deny that they were members of the CPP. Their general denial of responsibility was a foretaste of what would happen after Nkrumah's regime was overthrown in 1966.' Only Nkrumah and a few others proudly proclaimed their 'responsibility and dutifully went to jail.'[37]

British authorities relaxed. Although Nkrumah continued to communicate with CPP leaders — writing directives 'by the light of the street-lamps on toilet paper' — the principal spokesman for radical nationalism was behind bars for three full years. Most 'villagers did not know what was going on and many believed that the CPP was dead,' James observed. The government was now prepared to implement the new Legislative Assembly scheme, with the CPP crushed beneath the weight of capitalist-colonialism's criminal justice apparatus. Danquah and the UGCC rejoiced:
' "We told you so" was their leitmotif.'[38]

A motley collection of petty bourgeois formations sprang up, at a safe ideological distance from the CPP, to contest the new elections under the Coussey Committee's guidelines. One European, Charles Deller, initiated the 'Ghana Freedom Party' in May 1950, which called for self-government by 1 June 1953. In Kumasi, the 'People's Democratic Party' was created in June, which advocated a 'law and order' program and the protection of private property and 'native institutions.' This formation was led by Ashanti attorney Cobina Kessie, later the leader of the Moslem Association Party, and Ben Tamakloe, the secretary general of the Ex-Serviceman's Union and an activist in the 1948 Boycott. The 'Gold Coast Labour Party' was founded by newspaper manager John Tsiboe (later national treasurer of the conservative United Party) and S.H.K.

Cleland of the Obuasi Mineworkers Union. Nii Kwabena Bonne financed and ran a small group, the Liberal Party. The two largest moderate nationalist forces, which enjoyed some degree of confidence from colonial authorities, were the National Democratic Party, founded in June 1950 by two Accra lawyers, Kofi Aduma Bossman and Nii Ama Ollennu; and Danquah's UGCC. All of these groups, most of which dissolved after a brief existence, represented potential alternatives to the CPP. The British fostered the proliferation of these microparties to promote the illusion of democratic pluralism, and to splinter the base of the nationalist movement.[39]

Fortunately for the CPP, Gbedemah was released from prison in early March 1950, and the British colonial regime failed to recognize his significance in the nationalist struggle. Before his incarceration, Nkrumah authorized Gbedemah to take 'the full responsibility of running the Party.' Nkrumah later observed: 'It was no easy task for Gbedemah to keep the Party united, and it was especially difficult when so many of the members were vying with one another for leadership . . . Gbedemah managed to keep my name alive in the minds of the people and encouraged them to carry on their struggle under his guidance . . .'[40] Thirty-seven years old (three years Nkrumah's junior), Gbedemah had been both a school teacher and a petty entrepreneur before working as the CPP's main journalist. Now his task was to rebuild the party to contest the new elections. James describes Gbedemah in the historic role of 'Trotsky leading the revolution' while Lenin was in hiding after July 1917; but this characterization is inappropriate on several counts. Gbedemah was not a socialist, much less a Marxist. He did not share Nkrumah's training under James and Padmore, and had no interest in a Pan-Africanist politics which transcended the Gold Coast itself. He was a nascent, nationalistic businessman, who instictively understood that his own class would be forever subservient unless the British authorities were removed. Gbedemah seized Nkrumah as a symbol to rally the masses, and to win over sections of the urban working class and petty bourgeoisie.

This technique was not original. Several years before in Nigeria, radical nationalists used the image of Nwamdi Azikwe to promote their cause by celebrating his birthday and by 'organizing a Nigerian National Church with Azikwe its patron saint.' The remnants of the CPP followed the pattern already established by Nigeria's radical 'Zikists.' One can hardly imagine Lenin asking the Bolshevik Party to hold mass celebrations in honor of his birthday. But the CPP's constitution required party members to hold a 'national holiday' on the 'Life Chairman's Birthday,' 18 September. Gbedemah projected Nkrumah as the nation's martyr: 'Nkrumah provided the answers. If one did not know what to believe, the answer was follow Nkrumah. If one did not know quite what to hope for, the answer was follow Nkrumah.'[41]

In historical perspective, Nkrumah appears virtually irreplaceable as the leader of the anticolonial struggle in the Gold Coast. But as George Plekhanov once observed: 'Every man of talent who actually appears, every man of talent who becomes a social force, is the product of social relations . . . talented people can change only individual features of events, but not their general trend; they are themselves the product of this trend . . . ' In analyzing Nkrumah's role in African political history, there is a tendency to 'fall victim to a sort of optical illusion,' as Plekhanov termed it.[42] Nkrumah's social weight is projected in a 'magnified form'; we tend to read history backward, and credit him with the achievements of others. But during the difficult days of 1950-1951, the CPP was consolidated as a national electoral political formation by Gbedemah, not Nkrumah.

Observers on the spot fully attested to Gbedemah's crucial role. In 1955, Bankole Timothy wrote that while Nkrumah and Botsio 'were mending fishing-nets in James Fort Prison, Komla Agbeli Gbedemah kept the fire of the CPP burning. It is also to Gbedemah's credit that during Nkrumah's confinement he did not seek to take the leadership away from him, but did everything possible to stabilise the organisation of the party.' In another sense, the temporary removal of Nkrumah was actually beneficial, because it produced local leaders who were less reliant on Nkrumah's personal prestige, and who cultivated their own organic constituencies around local issues and concerns. In the Transvolta region, editor G.K. Amegbe mobilized supporters; in Ashanti, the major leaders were Krobo Edusei, attorney Victor Owusu, and R.R. Amponsah; in the crucial industrial center of Sekondi-Takoradi, Saki Scheck published the *Takoradi Times*. These men cut across traditional ethnic boundaries, and appealed to agricultural and industrial workers, small farmers, the unemployed, elements of the petty bourgeoisie, and the youth. They also recognized Gbedemah's authority: as G.K. Amegbe observed, 'With Kwame in jail, Gbedemah was in command and he really organized the party.'[43]

But what kind of party did Gbedemah and his young comrades

organize? Roger Murray suggests that the CPP did not represent a stable, petty bourgeois faction, which could express itself without hesitations or ambiguities. Its leaders and cadre 'were drawn from the petty bourgeois salariat . . . a mixed stratum which concentrated many of the political and cultural tensions of colonial society.' The CPP had no coherent economic program, beyond a self-serving desire to supplant Europeans in the civil service in favor of African employees. 'It is precisely the socially ambiguous and unstable character of this stratum,' Murray notes, 'which helps us to understand its relative autonomy and volatility in the political arena.'[44] The social composition of the CPP – a radicalized petty bourgeois leadership and strong base within the wage labouring classes — roughly paralled that of many social democratic parties.

The political style of CPP leaders — vaguely populist and egalitarian — reflected the movement's social ambiguity. The Party's earliest internal documents show that no ideological demands were made on any members. Indeed, the organizational characteristics that were most pronounced were the demands for centralized authority and regular financial donations to the CPP apparatus. Members were charged an enrollment fee of two shillings, and an annual payment of three shillings. Members could not belong to any unions or farmers' organizations 'proscribed by the Party,' and since members' 'affiliations are apt to cause divided loyalties,' Party leaders urged that 'only individual membership should be encouraged.' Power in the Party was already concentrated at the top rather than decentralized at the mass level. Only Party organizations 'and not individual members' could submit resolutions to the Annual Delegates' Conference. Individuals or entire factions could be expelled by the National Executive Committee if they were members 'of any other political party or of any organization whose policy is inconsistent with that of the Party,' or if they supported 'a candidate in opposition to the Party's official candidate.' Even before the party had achieved power, a strong tendency toward statism and hierarchicalism was evident.

Under Gbedemah's direction, the CPP won a series of stunning electoral victories. In April 1950, the Party carried seven seats in the Accra municipal races. On 1 June, it won two by-elections in Cape Coast. On 14 June, CPP Central Committee member Kwesi Plange defeated his uncle in a by-election. In the February 1951 general election the CPP simply overwhelmed Danquah's UGCC and other petty-bourgeois opponents. The CPP won 34 of a possible 38 seats, with the UGCC winning 2 seats. Through a legal technicality,

Nkrumah was permitted to run in Accra, receiving 22,780 out of 23,122 votes cast. In the municipal seats (Accra, Cape Coast, Kumasi, and Sekondi-Takoradi), the CPP won 58,585 votes to the opposition's 5,574 votes. Bitter opponents of the CPP lost their districts by incredible margins. Danquah was just barely elected; and prominent sociology professor K.A. Busia, a vocal critic of Nkrumah, was buried beneath the nationalist landslide. A close analysis of the vote reveals that roughly 95 percent of the urban electorate endorsed the CPP, while the Party carried somewhat less than four-fifths of the rural vote. Overall voter turnout was 47.2 percent in the four major municipalities, but was significantly higher in working class Sekondi-Takoradi, with 59.3 percent.

The governor had no choice except to call the CPP 'Party Leader' from his jail cell to form the new government.[45] But even upon Nkrumah's release, the 'electioneering' features of the CPP were apparent. When Nkrumah was first released from prison no CPP supporters were present, because the decision had not been announced publicly. The Party's cadre subsequently organized a mass demonstration at the prison entrance 'to demonstrate what they would have done had they known he was being released.' Photographs were taken and the story was circulated that the mass rally had actually occurred spontaneously upon Nkrumah's release. Nkrumah's initial public statement upon leaving prison was designed equally for public relations purposes: 'I desire for the Gold Coast dominion status within the Commonwealth. I am a Marxian socialist and an undenominational Christian. The places I know in Europe are London and Paris. I am no communist and have never been one. I come out of gaol and without the slightest feeling of bitterness to Britain.[46]

The achievements of the CPP in 1951 can hardly be overemphasized. Basil Davidson has correctly observed that this was Nkrumah's 'greatest hour. He had done what few thought possible, and opened a breach into the fortress of power where fewer still had looked for any great success. The news of this went out through Africa in electrifying ripples of encouragement to all who hoped for anti-colonial change.' Padmore characterized the electoral victory as that of 'the plebeian masses, the urban workers, artisans, petty traders, market women and fishermen, the clerks, the junior teachers, and the vast farming communities of the rural areas who are the makers of Gold Coast history.'[47] Throughout 1949-1951, Padmore had publicized Nkrumah's movement in the Western press, and now advised his friend to demand independence without further delay.[48] Padmore and others recognized the severe limitations confronting the CPP. Their government was to have 'no power in vital questions of foreign policy, national defence, internal security. They were not even to have any power over appointments in the civil service.' Sensitive files were soon removed from colonial offices, or 'were still regarded as being fit for British eyes alone.'[49] Under these constraints, the CPP would be unable to implement most of their programs for years to come. However, Padmore also understood that the British were, at that moment, most vulnerable to the demand for complete self-government. Sir Charles Arden-Clarke, the governor who had ruthlessly suppressed the CPP, desperately needed Nkrumah's cooperation. 'Nkrumah and his party had the mass of the people behind them and there was no other party with appreciable public support to which we could turn,' Arden-Clarke admitted in 1958. 'Without Nkrumah . . . there would no longer be any faith in the good intentions of the British Government . . . the Gold Coast would be plunged into disorders, violence and bloodshed.'[50] Between the democratic platitudes, one senses a fear of genuine social revolution, and the threat to British investments in the colony.

Nkrumah's previous political training under James and Padmore allowed him to analyze the situation with clarity: 'Two courses of action lay open to me and my party. We could boycott the existing colonial government machinery, the civil service, the police, the judiciary. Or we could co-operate with it, meanwhile strengthening the position of myself and my colleagues in the cabinet and so advance the date for full independence. In choosing the second, we did not forget, but tried to bury, past differences and sought cooperation with the existing executive machinery of government. Two major aims impelled this decision: the speeding up of Africanization, and the prevention of a breakdown of administration through a wholesale exodus of British officials . . . It was of prime importance to us, therefore, and the freedom movements in other parts of Africa, that we should be able to effect a smooth take-over of power, free from serious administrative shocks. It called for what I termed at the time 'tactical action' . . .'[51]

Others have advanced a less charitable view of the situation. The British deliberately chose the CPP over the UGCC, comments Chinweizu, not just because it was 'a better-organized party,' but also because 'the big cocoa planters, the agro-capitalist chiefs and their retainers had begun to show signs, alarming to the British, of itching to throw off the colonial restraints on their big bourgeois ambitions. The poorer CPP elements, the British calculated, would take some time in acquiring and consolidating wealth.' Ironically, the 'Oxford education, British accents and manners' of Danquah and Busia had become a liability. As a non-Marxist, mass party — devoid of ideologically-oriented cadre, dominated by young school teachers, clerks and journalists, and lacking a large trade-unionist wing — the CPP could better serve British interests in the transition period. The CPP was a 'commoners' party' which employed socialist rhetoric, without a coherent program to socialize anything inside the Gold Coast.[52] Viewing the decision from afar, James was reluctant to voice criticisms. But he knew that the CPP in victory was 'straightjacketed in a British constitution before it could take a single hesitant step ... As soon as the struggle became internal, the revolutionary impetus was lost, and constitutions are made by revolutions, not by jurists.'[53] The CPP was committed to fight for African independence through the gradualist route of British bourgeois democracy, colonial-style. Everything which occurred after February 1951 was directly or indirectly a product of that fateful decision.

II

'It is impossible to understand the development of the revolution in the Gold Coast that brought Ghana,' James wrote, 'unless you realized from the start, the man behind [it] was Padmore.'[54] During the period from 1945 through 1959, Padmore's ideas largely shaped Nkrumah's policies and tactics, and in turn, affected the course of Ghanaian political history. For several years he continued to advise Nkrumah from his modest London flat, and only came permanently to Ghana in September 1957 as 'adviser to the prime minister on African affairs.' Foreign affairs adviser A.L. Adu controlled Padmore's budget, but Padmore's office was next to Nkrumah's. Until his death in September 1959, he remained 'the one person who commanded Nkrumah's respect. When he died, there was no one Nkrumah considered as eminent as himself on African affairs.'[55] Padmore's formative experiences within the Communist movement, and his subsequent rejection of Marxism-Leninism, colored his entire approach to Pan-Africanism, political alliances with the Western and Soviet blocs, and even his understanding of domestic political developments in Ghana.

Most of Padmore's important political ideas were expressed in detail in his 1955 manifesto *Pan-Africanism or Communism*. Padmore stressed the necessity for post-colonial Africa to move toward a 'federation of regional self-governing countries,' which would later 'amalgamate into a United States of Africa.' The basic economic framework for Pan-Africanism would be 'Democratic Socialism, with state control of the basic means of production and distribution.' Within international affairs, Padmore wrote, Pan-Africanism 'rejects the unbridled system of monopoly capitalism of the West no less than the political and cultural totalitarianism of the East. It identifies itself with the neutral camp, opposed to all forms of oppression and racial chauvinism . . . ' Although Padmore claimed to represent a nonaligned position in the Cold War, his interpretation of Marxism-Leninism placed him firmly within the ideological camp of Western imperialism: '[Pan-Africanism] refuses to accept the pretentious claims of doctrinaire Communism, that it alone has the solution to all the complex racial, tribal, and socio-economic problems facing Africa. It also rejects the Communist intolerance of those who do not subscribe to its ever-changing party line even to the point of liquidating them as "enemies of the people." Democracy and brotherhood cannot be built upon intolerance and violence.' His polemics against Communism were not aimed at the African proletariat as much as US government and corporate interests, which might underwrite many of Ghana's state expenses after independence. Padmore urged the US to initiate a second 'Marshall Aid programme for Africa . . . If America, the "foremost champion and defender of the free world" is really worried about Communism taking root in Africa and wants to prevent such a calamity from taking place,' a new Marshall Plan would do so.[56]

Padmore's blanket rejection of class struggle in the postcolonial African social formations and his unambiguous pro-US orientation had certain policy implications for Ghana, domestically and internationally. First, Nkrumah's CPP must disavow any use of violence, and adhere to constitutional, nonviolent means of change. 'Political democracy as defined by politicians on the western side of the global Iron Curtain,' Padmore observed, 'means the will of the majority freely expressed through the ballot box with respect for the rights of minorities.' Watching the Mau Mau uprising in Kenya, for example, he denounced the young militants as a nihilistic 'lumpenproletariat.' 'But for the grace of God and the wisdom and foresight of the Governor of the Gold Coast, Sir Charles Arden-Clarke, that colony, too, might have gone the way of the Mau Mau,' Padmore wrote. The greatest threat to African liberation was not indigenous

Black capitalists, but Marxism-Leninism. Blacks must be 'mentally free from the dictation of Europeans, regardless of their ideology,' Padmore insisted. 'The oppressed Negro workers and peasants are regarded by Communists as "revolutionary expendables" in the global struggle of Communism against Western Capitalism.' Communist behavior was always 'cynical' and 'opportunistic.' 'Communists cannot be allowed to squander the people's sacrifices and jeopardize the limited opportunities grudgingly conceded them to plant their feet firmly on the constitutional road to independence.'

Watching the removal of the democratically-elected Jagan government in British Guiana, Padmore's curses were aimed at Jagan, and his praises toward the 'brilliant democratic socialists' led by Forbes Burnham. 'Instead of indulging in revolutionary romanticism,' Padmore observed, Jagan should have cooperated to the fullest extent with the British by demonstrating 'his party's ability to govern.' Burnham and Nkrumah, not Jagan, represented 'wise and constructive socialist leadership.' Padmore's version of Black social democracy, enacted by Nkrumah, would have certain consequences throughout his entire rule: the failure to expel British military 'advisers,' civil servants, and reactionary Africans from his administration; the failure to advance any major Pan-Africanist initiatives until after 1957; the failure to develop CPP cadre ideologically; the failure to introduce even modest socialist economic programs until after 1960.[57]

Du Bois also monitored the startling events in the Gold Coast, and praised the CPP program as a 'plan for home rule on socialist lines.'[58] But he retained reservations about Padmore's political ideas, and questioned Nkrumah's policy of 'tactical action' or cooperation with the colonial authorities. In April 1952, R.E.G. Armattoe, a Gold Coast critic of Nkrumah, wrote to Du Bois: 'Today Nkrumah has become the friend of imperialists . . . I am fully aware that George Padmore, after dragging your name and mine in the mud as communists or crypto-communists now has the effrontery to assure you that Nkrumah is a savior of our country . . . By no stretch of the human imagination can one label the CPP as a nationalist movement, although it began as such.' When questioned by Du Bois, Padmore denounced Armattoe as a 'reactionary' and an 'enemy of the people.'[59] Several years later, when Du Bois urged Padmore and Nkrumah to accelerate plans for a major Pan-African Congress in the Gold Coast, Padmore was evasive. 'We cannot do it before as we don't want to create undue alarm before we have full power in our hands.' Padmore explained, 'It is a skillful game of manoeuvering and we cannot afford at this stage of the struggle to give the imperialists any excuse to intervene as in British Guiana. They are ready to pounce the first opportunity we give them.' DuBois's reply was polite yet reserved. 'I understand the policy of you and Dr. Nkrumah, although I am a little afraid of it. The power of British and especially American capital when it once gets a foothold is tremendous.' Du Bois warned that even when 'political power is in your hands,' that the CPP might have to struggle with 'your own bourgeoisie.'[60]

Samir Amin's criticism of Padmore and Nkrumah during the 1950s remains both succinct and accurate. Padmore's thought 'may best be summed up in three terms: "Africanization of the administration"; "panafricanism"; and "anticommunism".' Following Padmore's theories, the CPP began a 'close collaboration' with Great Britain. 'In politics there was no thought of any structural reform, either in the economic system (freedom of foreign capital, close relations with the sterling area, and so on) or in the social system (the situation of agricultural workers and tenant farmers in the plantation areas). Nor was any policy formulated for industrialization or development of the public sector.'[61]

In the public and private sectors, larger numbers of educated Africans were advanced to middle-level managerial posts. In the Civil Service, the number of Africans increased from 351 in 1951 to 916 in 1954, about 36 percent of the bureaucracy's personnel. The percentage of African employees in the United African Company's management increased only slightly, from 18 percent in 1951 to 25 percent in 1957. In 1956 Barclays Bank initiated a training program for Ghanaians, sending eleven potential managers to the UK for 'special training.'[62] A small number of Ghanaian entrepreneurs were able to enter the construction and manufacturing spheres of the economy, but operated with fewer workers and with little capital. The 'economic climate' of the Gold Coast still favored British capital, and the Colonial Office knew it. The number of Barclay's branches increased from seven to 56 in 1951-1961, followed closely by the growth of the Bank of West Africa, with 11 to 41 branches in the same period. The amount of gold produced by the Ashanti Goldfields increased from 176,610 ounces in 1951 to 380,776 ounces in 1961, more importantly, the amount of gold produced per man soared, 27.3 ounces per man in 1951, 66.5 ounces per man a decade later.[63] Capitalist oppression was still the rule, despite the CPP's rhetorical commitment to 'African socialism.'

Initially, there were few indications that the CPP would essentially carry out the now-defunct UGCC's conservative economic agenda. The specific policy goals of the CPP, ratified at the Party's second annual conference in August 1951, seemed clear. On national matters, the CPP called for 'self-government now,' the removal of 'all forms of oppression' and 'the establishment of a democratic socialist society . . . where there shall be no capitalist exploitation.' Internationally, the party supported coalitions with 'nationalist democratic and socialist movements,' leading to the creation of 'a West African Federation' and 'Pan-Africanism.'[64] Nkrumah was 'Life Chairman' of the party, to be sure, but others — Gbedemah, Scheck, Edusei, Dzewu — had actually constructed an electoral force capable of garnering about nine-tenths of the popular vote. Already, clusters of supporters and aides gravitated around Gbedemah and Botsio, the two leaders viewed most capable next to Nkrumah. Their preeminence was confirmed in Nkrumah's official cabinet of March, 1952: Gbedemah became Minister of Commerce and Industry; Botsio was Minister of Education and Social Welfare. Party members perceived Nkrumah as first-among-equals, but he was no dictator. The first Party congresses and local caucuses were spirited debates, and no one, least of all Nkrumah, was exempt from criticism. 'Kwame Nkrumah is our Leader, admitted,' Party organizer Kwesi Lamptey wrote in the *Evening News*. However, 'we cannot make him a tin god or a Hitler impervious to criticism.'[65]

Dissent within the Party's lower levels almost immediately appeared after Nkrumah's decision to cooperate with the British. Awooner Renner, an attorney and a former member of the London-based West African National Secretariat, complained openly that most of the CPP's leadership was 'already getting their hands into the honeypot,' by using the state apparatus for personal gain. The colonialists were 'simply giving the CPP enough rope to hang itself.' Renner had served time in prison during the previous year, and was now 'disgusted' that the momentum had passed 'from the hands of the oppressed to the hands of the oppressors.'[66] Others agreed, yet their motives were mixed. Some criticized the beginnings of what would become a huge patronage system; others were disappointed at not sharing in the wealth; and still others condemned the slow pace of the transition to complete independence.

Nkrumah's response was to apply Padmore's line to his own social movement. A handful of dissidents were expelled or left the CPP voluntarily in late 1951. By April 1952, a major bloc was expelled, consisting of many dedicated CPP national leaders and organizers: Central Committee members Ashie Nikoe and Dzenkle Dzewu; Eastern Regional Secretary E.S. Nartey; acting general secretary H.P. Nyemetei; *Takoradi Times* editor Saki Scheck; Kwesi Lamptey, a ministerial secretary in the new government; and Party leaders Sydney Brown, Mate Kole, Kojo Nkrumah, J.G. Swaniker, and K.G. Kyem. Another round of expulsions occurred after the third Party congress in August 1952. Leaders of the left wing of the CPP — journalist Cecil Forde, TUC president Anthony Woods, lawyer Kurankyi Taylor, TUC general secretary Turkson Ocran, and J.C. de Graft Johnson — 'criticized the party leadership for having compromised over the issue of immediate self-government.' If the CPP was committed to socialism, they demanded, why had the party done nothing to support workers' democratic struggles? Nkrumah's supporters warned the left that the 'usual CPP way of tolerance, the exercise of patience' in debates of 'burning issues' had its limits. 'The minority will accept, without much ado, the decisions of the majority.'

Throughout 1953, the CPP left 'back bench members' tended to follow the lead of Anthony Woode, who frequently attacked 'the moderate position taken by Nkrumah on many issues.' Conscious of their minority status inside the party, they 'refused to submit to party discipline,' but increasingly looked to Gbedemah as a potential ally. Gbedemah's chief liability, from the vantagepoint of socialists, was that he was the most conservative major figure in the CPP on economic issues. Yet he had not succumbed to political graft or patronage — which could not be said for Botsio, Edusei, and many others. Given a simple choice between Nkrumah and Gbedemah, the left may have reasoned, the latter was preferable: less autocratic, more dedicated to party diversity and democratic debate. Had Woods and Gbedemah formed a United front against Nkrumah at this point, the 'Life Chairman' would have been in deep trouble.[67]

But the British colonialists resolved Nkrumah's problems. The suspension of British Guiana's Constitution and the forcible removal of the Jagan government in 1953 caused consternation in the Gold Coast. Nkrumah informed the CPP that only his accommodationist 'Tactical Action' policies had saved their country from a similar fate. Now it was time to clean house of all Jagan-type Marxists inside the CPP. Within weeks, Kurankyi Taylor was expelled from the party, Woods was suspended, and Ocran was ousted from the TUC, replaced by a 'moderate' Nkrumahist, J.K.

Tettegah. Another problem area was the Party's youth organization, the National Association of Socialist Youth, which had many Marxist sympathizers. One youthful militant leader, journalist Kofi Batsaa, had taken journalism courses in Prague. But Nkrumah was determined to eliminate all traces of radicalism. Speaking before the National Assembly in February 1954, Nkrumah warned that his government would fire any persons 'who have shown that their first loyalty is to an alien power, or a foreign agency which seeks to bring our country under its domination . . .' Batsaa and other CPP radicals were denied their membership cards. In his modest London residence, Padmore was overjoyed. 'Disciplinary action against Ocran, Woode and other leftists was essential 'to protect (Nkrumah's) party and Government from Communist infiltration, as well as to avoid a constitutional crisis' as in British Guiana.[68]

The mass expulsions from the CPP in 1951-1953 created the cadre necessary for popular opposition parties. Some ex-CPP leaders — Dzewu, Scheck, Lamptey, Nyemitei and Nikoe — reluctantly joined forces with Busia and the lawyer-merchant elite around Danquah to create the Ghana Congress Party in 1952. Internally divided from the beginning, it included both radical nationalists and conservatives. Among the Ewe ethnic group, a Reverend F.R. Ametowobla began to raise 'common grievances' through the Ewe Youth Association: 'the very bad state of the roads, the general poverty and illiteracy, and the enforced sale of cocoa through the Gold Coast Marketing Board' at ridiculously low prices. Awooner Renner, whom Padmore denounced as a 'prominent ideologist of Crypto-Communism,' and Ashanti lawyer Cobina Kessie organized the Moslem Association Party (MAP) in May 1954, which called for increased state-sponsored welfare programs and 'Arabic training centres' for Ghanaian Muslims. In the northern Gold Coast, the Northern People's Party (NPP) was formed in April 1954 by J.A. Braimah, Nkrumah's former Minister of Communications and Works. The NPP soon brought together most of the traditional chiefs in the area, but to build a mass following it deliberately copied the political cultural style of the CPP: 'a flag, a salute (a clenched fist), a slogan ('United We Stand' or 'Unity'), the holding of rallies . . . the use of propaganda vans, and the sale of a membership card.'[69]

The British consented to a new general election, and the results, 'they promised, would in turn lead to an all-African cabinet with responsibility to an all African-parliament.'[70] Seven national parties, including the CPP, NPP and the Ghana Congress Party, fielded candidates for the 1 June 1954 election. Under new legislature terms, the country was divided into 104 constituencies. When 81 CPP members demanded the right to seek office against the official Party candidates favorable to Nkrumah, they were promptly expelled. The CPP once again was the electoral winner, receiving 72 seats. But there was no landslide victory, despite Gbedemah's extensive labors as national campaign chairman. The CPP received 391,817 votes (55.4 percent) in all contested constituencies, vs. 314,903 votes (44.67 percent) for all opposition parties and anti-CPP independents. NPP won 15 constituency seats to only 8 for the CPP in the north; the sharpest national critic of Nkrumah, K.A. Busia, won a narrow victory over a CPP candidate; and M.K. Apaloo, another prominent conservative opponent of the CPP, was also elected. What undoubtedly saved the CPP from even greater losses was the failure of the opposition parties to unite within a single formation.

Nkrumah viewed the election results with alarm, and called for 'stiffened party discipline' under his personal control. Remaining CPP dissidents were warned that no 'affiliation to "foreign" beliefs and political associations' would be 'tolerated.' For the first time, there were hints that the CPP would not feel constrained to respect the limits of bourgeois democracy, once independence was achieved. In *Pan-Africanism or Communism*, Padmore condemned Nkrumah's opponents as 'careerist politicians,' and 'tribal backwash.' In 1954 Nkrumah vigorously protested the recognition of the leader of the NPP as 'Leader of the Opposition' in the Legislative Assembly on the questionable grounds that the nation's second largest party had only a 'regional base.' CPP newspapers also called for the 'outlawing' of MAP because of its politico-religious character.[71]

During the mid-1950s, a distinct change began to occur within the CPP. Its achievements in government, although limited, were recognized by all but its harshest critics. In the area of education, the government abolished all fees for primary education, doubling the school population in only two years. The University College at Legon was expanded, and a new technological institute was started in Kumasi. In 1953 alone, the CPP loaned over one million pounds at low interest rates to small farmers. Many other modest economic and social welfare reforms followed. Yet the farmers commonly complained, and quite correctly, that the government's Cocoa Purchasing Board was selling their produce abroad at all-time highs, and only a fraction of the wealth was remitted to them. In 1953, for instance, the Board 'sold cocoa to a value of £74 millions. But the amount paid to cocoa producers was only £28 millions.' Many believed that the CPP had 'lost its living contact with wage-earners in the towns and cocoa farmers in the country.'[72]

A share of the government revenues had begun to filter into the CPP's national and regional offices; and soon, some government ministers were accepting illegal payments from corporations and local entrpreneurs. Tommy Hutton-Mills, Nkrumah's Minister of Health and Labour, openly boasted: 'I have now left poverty behind me forever.' Civil servants, professors, and other middle strata were told bluntly that 'those who joined the Party' would be 'assured of promotion, wealth and influence.'[73] For every political movement which finally seizes state authority after a long ordeal, careerist tendencies and some degree of corruption are inevitable. Petty bourgeois elements which had been outside the party now gravitated toward it; individual members who recognized their own past sacrifices to the 'cause' frequently expected favors and privileges from the state. In the case of the CPP, Nkrumah and other leaders either ignored the growing instances of graft and clientage, or more frequently, participated in the process.

To counteract rumors and mounting evidence of Party malfeasance, the CPP hierarchy responded by increasing its political propaganda, and boosting the image of Nkrumah as the nation's savior. Loyal members chanted 'Nkrumah Never Die' at rallies, to proclaim his near-immortality and omniscience. The Party Leader was the 'Osagyefo' – 'victorious in war,' 'Oyeadeeyie' – 'One who puts things right,' the 'Man of Destiny,' the new 'Messiah,' the 'Teacher and Author of the Revolution.[74] No longer first-among-equals, Nkrumah was now elevated far above the Party. For veterans like Gbedemah, Edusei and Botsio, there was perhaps something surrealistic in these orchestrated acclamations. They had known 'Francis' Nkrumah when he, like they, had been plagued with doubts, and when he appeared willing to disband the Party for the sake of political expediency. This petty-bourgeois cult of the personality was potentially dangerous, yet they joined in the hosannas without thinking too much about the consequences.

Meanwhile an anti-Nkrumahist united front was finally consolidated in September 1954, as the 'National Liberation Movement' (NLM). The core of its originators, Busia, Danquah and Apaloo and members of the Ghana Congress Party, combined with leaders from the Ashanti Youth Association, the Asante Farmers' Union, and most of the Ashanti chiefs. In January 1955, a bloc of CPP leaders and cadre defected to the NLM, including Victor Owusu, R.R. Amponsah, and Kurankyi Taylor. The most shocking defection of all was that of Nkrumah's old friend Joe Appiah, who had served as the 'accredited representative' of the Prime Minister and the CPP in London. Appiah had finally come to condemn the party as being both 'corrupt and dictatorial.' The NLM's principal base of support was among the Ashanti traditional chiefs, small farmers, and intellectuals, and their major political demand was the creation of a decentralized federal form of government, which would benefit the NLM's major constituents. Violence erupted in Ashanti against pro-CPP members, and several hundred CPP activists fled the region. Edusei's sister was killed in the fighting. A bomb was exploded outside the Prime Minister's home in Accra, 'shaking it severely and shattering all the windows,' but no one was injured.

CPP leaders attacked the NLM as 'feudalists,' 'tribalists,' and subversives. But, in fact, such criticism was only half truth at best. The economic policies of Busia and the conservative Ghanaian intelligentsia — which Busia would later implement as leader of Ghana in 1969-72 — were only slightly to the right of Nkrumah's economic policies in 1951-1957. Some radical Pan-Africanists, such as ex-CPP member Kurankyi Taylor, joined the NLM. By mid-1955, eighteen of the 21 members of the NLM's national executive committee were former CPP members. That same year, two of the country's largest unions formed the 'Congress of Free Trade Unions,' which promptly affiliated itself to the NLM. In short, the CPP had trained, developed and then expelled the core leaders of its electoral opposition.[75]

The CPP declared that the 1954 election had provided 'a clear mandate to negotiate "self government now", and that there was no justification for calling another general election before Independence.' Carefully monitoring the rise of the NLM, the British demanded that one more general election be held, which would settle the NLM's demand for a federal form of independent government one way or another. The campaign was especially bitter, since few were certain whether the CPP would agree to become the 'loyal opposition' after an NLM victory. The CPP told the electorate once again: 'Nkrumah is honest, straight-forward, hardworking, vigilant and stainless'; 'In Africa today the sun is rising not in the East but in the West all through Kwame Nkrumah'; 'if Nkrumah fails, a great hope will die in Africa.' The NLM replied: 'CPP are thieves, rogues, traitors, double-tongued receivers of bribes, givers of bribes and gangsters . . . it is your money they want.'[76]

In the elections of July 1956, only about 50 percent of the registered electorate voted, and the CPP won its third victory. In 99 contested constituencies, the CPP received 398,141 votes (57.1 percent) to the opposition's 299,116 votes (42.9 percent). The CPP won 71 seats (67 percent) of the 104 Assembly seats. The CPP had a comfortable majority, but the election was in many respects closer than in 1954. Ex-CPP leader Victor Owusu trounced his CPP opponent, 8,984 votes to 1,354 votes; Danquah lost, but only by 600 votes out of 9,000 cast in his district; in the fifteen Ashanti districts, the CPP won only 58,597 votes (36.6 percent) to the NLM and MAP's 101,465 votes (63.4 percent); and Busia was once again elected over a CPP opponent, 4,884 votes vs. 3,125 votes. The CPP won for several reasons. In the north, it used the power of incumbency and its now ample finances to run local leaders with established constituencies. The NPP received more northern votes (77,172 to 66,641), but won only 15 to 26 seats in the region. In the Brong region of Ashanti, the CPP government had been financially generous with local projects; on election day, it received 61.3 percent of the vote in five Brong districts which were expected to go to the NLM.[77]

Second, and perhaps most critically, the CPP attracted the critical support of fractions of the petty bourgeoisie who had long opposed the Party. The two prominent examples were Ako Adjei and Tawia Adamafio. Adjei had stood as the UGCC's candidate against his former friend in the 1951 elections. For years he 'had spared no pains in writing articles full of heat and invective and in making venomous speeches against Nkrumah.' Suddenly, in 1954, Adjei approached Nkrumah and asked to join the CPP. He was rewarded after the election with the post of minister of the interior. Adamafio's 'conversion' was more complex. In the early 1950s, the former clerk turned journalist was among the CPP's bitterest opponents, denouncing Nkrumahists as 'Nazis' and 'thieves.' He led a raid on one CPP newspaper office and physically attacked the editor. In 1953, Adamafio was assistant general secretary of Busia's Ghana Congress Party. But even as an opposition polemicist, he acquired 'a reputation for blatant opportunism.' Under Padmore's direct guidance in London, Adamafio was recruited to lead the CPP-backed National Association of Socialist Student Organizations in 1955-56. By January 1960, Nkrumah (whom Adamafio had frequently attacked as a 'Hitler') made him the general secretary of the CPP. Meanwhile, Adjei was advanced to the position of Foreign Minister in 1959.

The cooptation of Adjei, Adamafio, and others served several purposes. It sowed confusion among Nkrumah's conservative opponents; it gave evidence to the broad masses that the Osagyefo 'has a forgiving spirit.'[78] But it also provided Nkrumah with new lieutenants who had been on the 'wrong side' of the barricades during the lean, early years. Their standing in the Party was directly subject to the Party Leader's wishes, since they could claim no legitimate base for themselves among rank-and-file members. Potentially, such cadre could be used against the power-brokers in the CPP — Gbedmah, particularly — whose national authority did not depend on Nkrumah.

The British granted Ghana its independence as a Commonwealth member on 6 March 1957. For Nkrumah, the triumph proved beyond doubt that the 'national revolution had been won, and without the necessity to resort to armed struggle.'[79] On the new agenda were two major items: the initiation of a Pan-Africanist foreign policy which would unify the continent, and the prompt elimination of the domestic opposition parties. Padmore had visited the Gold Coast in December, 1953, as a participant in a 'West African Nationalist Conference' held in Kumasi. The small meeting proposed the inauguration of an international congress which would 'embrace all sections of Africans and peoples of African descent.'[80] But these plans were shelved until Padmore arrived permanently in 1957. In weeks, Ghana's foreign affairs assumed Padmorian lines. In April 1958, a 'Conference of Independent African States' was held in Accra with delegates from Egypt, Liberia, Sudan, Ethiopia, Tunisia, Libya and Morocco. The participants agreed to 'co-ordinate their economic planning . . . and encourage trade among their countries; to exchange educational, cultural and scientific information; to improve communications between the African States; to assist people still under colonial rule in their struggle to be free; and to provide training and educational facilities for them.' Nkrumah subsequently led a fifteen member delegation to visit African states. In December 1958, 62 nationalist organizations caucused in Accra at the 'All-African People's Conference' to discuss strategies for liberating the entire continent. When the Republic of Guinea became independent under the leadership of Sékou Touré, Nkrumah invited Guinea and Liberia to form a 'Community of Independent African States' in July 1959. The function of the Community accord was not political, 'but an economic, cultural and social organization designed to promote African unity.'[81]

In Accra, African, West Indian and Afro-American revolutionaries were quartered at the African Affairs Center. In 1958-1959, the guest list included Hastings Banda, Kenneth Kaunda, Harry Nkumbula, and Joshua Nkomo. Du Bois visited Ghana for six weeks in 1960, and Nkrumah proposed that the Black scholar establish a scholarly research project, an 'Encyclopedia Africana,' to be produced in Accra. Du Bois agreed, returning in late 1961 to launch the project with Africanist scholar Alphaeus Hunton.[82] In this protracted campaign to establish Pan-African unity, certain prejudices of Padmore and Nkrumah influenced policies. Padmore probably never completely overcame his 'old anti-chief, anti-emperor' attitudes toward Ethiopian monarch Haile Selassie. Nkrumah held a more positive view of Selassie, but relations between the two states were hardly the best.[83]

Despite Nkrumah's renewed interest in Pan-Africanist politics, Ghana's closest 'ally' in international affairs between 1956 and 1960 was not an African country at all, but Israel. Through its cordial relations with Nkrumah, Israel was able to cultivate close ties with Nyerere, Banda, Kaunda and other African leaders, allowing it to break out of its diplomatic isolation in the Afro-Asian world. Israel managed to do all this despite the 1956 Suez crisis, its lucrative diamond business which rested on the exploitation of Black South African mine workers, and its production of thousands of weapons for Portugal's genocidal colonial wars in Mozambique, Guinea-Bissau, and Angola in the 1960s.[84] Nkrumah's friendly approach toward the Israelis was, in part, a legacy of the Pan-Africanist tradition. When Du Bois had organized the first major Pan-African Congress, held in Paris in 1919, he directly equated his efforts with Jewish Zionism. Throughout the late 1940s and 1950s, Du Bois denounced the arming of Arab countries against the young state of Israel; he spoke frequently before the American Jewish Congress, and emphasized 'the way in which African and Jewish history had been entwined for 3,000 years.' As historian Gerald Horne observes, 'throughout his career' Du Bois strongly favored Jewish Zionism, defended Israel, and 'was virtually mum about the Palestinians.'[85]

Padmore and Makonnen brought the Pan-Africanist and Zionist movements even closer together. Both saw parallels between their Pan-Africanist ventures of the 1930s and 1940s with those 'handful of Jews in the Haganah movement gaining independence militarily for Palestine,' and 'we wondered whether we could do the same.' During the Ethiopian war Makonnen directly patterned his 'Education Foundation for Ethiopian Youths' on Zionist-sponsored relief efforts for European refugees. Given their long-time sympathy for Zionism and for the plight of the Jewish people, it was not surprising that both Padmore and Makonnen urged Nkrumah to create an alliance with the Israelis. 'The feeling that Israel and Ghana had both fought their way to independence of the British in ten years made us something like comrades in arms,' Makonnen observed. 'We had seen what role the Muslims had been playing with Busia in his National Liberation Movement.'[86] Padmore disliked Nasser, whom he believed was being 'used by the Russians.' Thus in 1956, months before Ghana's formal independence, the British permitted the Israelis to establish a consulate in Accra. Egypt, the leading radical state in Africa, was not even invited to the independence celebrations. When, after independence, Padmore convened a brains trust of influential party members to analyze key issues, he also invited along Israeli diplomats.[87]

Most of the rest of the CPP leadership, with the prominent exceptions of Edusei and Adjei, fell in line with the policy of Israeli-Ghanaian friendship. Tettegah's advocacy of the Histadrut model for organizing Ghanaian labor has already been noted; more important still was the profound impact of Israel upon Kojo Botsio, who was for a decade the third most influential CPP leader, after Nkrumah and Gbedemah. Botsio and Makonnen toured Israel extensively in 1957, and the former was 'incredulous at what he had seen.' For years afterward, the Israelis termed Botsio their 'best friend in Africa;' Edusei contemptuously began calling Botsio 'Soleh Boneh' after an Israeli firm. The Israeli ambassador Ehud Avriel became a close friend of Makonnen's, and performed a variety of duties for the Nkrumah government. When Nkrumah proposed to fulfill Garvey's dream of initiating a 'Black Star Shipping Line,' which would 'break the hold which the monopoly interests' had on Ghanaian trade, he asked Avriel for help. Israel provided most of the financing and Nkrumah gratefully praised the Israelis before his parliament. When Nkrumah desired to express his Pan-Africanist politics in a book, Avriel supplied 'ghostwriter' Moshe Pearleman, who later wrote most of General Moshe Dayan's official memoirs: much of this text formed the basis for Nkrumah's *Africa Must Unite*.[88]

When the 'All-African People's Conference' was being planned, Makonnen asked Avriel to assist him in contacting any young African nationalists in the Belgian Congo and Angola. Avriel immediately left Accra, and returned with the names of several local nationalist leaders in whom he had some confidence. The first was Patrice Lumumba, who would become the independent Congo's first Prime Minister. This created some problems for Padmore, who was a firm advocate of conservative Congolese nationalist Joseph Kasavubu, leader of ABAKO. Although Ghana continued to support Kasavubu and ABAKO over Lumumba's MNC until Padmore's death, the Israelis had decided that Lumumba was the leader they preferred. Financing his trip to the Accra conference in December 1958, 'Avriel introduced Lumumba to Nkrumah.'[89] The second rising star favored by Avriel would play a more ominous role in the African liberation movement, Holden Roberto. Traveling under the name 'Joseph Gilmore' with an Algerian passport, Roberto was then leader of the Union of Angolan Peoples. After the conference, he lived and worked at the Accra African Affairs Centre for a year, until Ghanaian officials began to suspect Roberto's financial and political links with the United States. The only tangible display of Afro-Arab unity which Nkrumah expressed during these years was his unhappy marriage to an Egyptian Coptic woman.[90]

In late 1957 virtually all the anti-Nkrumahist factions and groups rallied together to form the United Party (UP). Ideologically diverse, it represented far more than the Ashanti and Northern oppositional elements who had been the strength of the old NLM/NPP coalition. Its national chairman, Tommy Hutton-Mills, had been elected with Nkrumah as Accra's CPP assemblymen in 1951 and had been a prominent Cabinet Minister; ex-CPP leaders Joe Appiah, Ashie Nikoe, and Kwesi Lamptey served on the national working committee, along with Danquah and Busia. The UP developed a powerful Women's League, and received the endorsement of the Asante Youth Association. It also received strong support from the newly created Ga Shifimo Kpee, the United Ghana Farmers' Council, and the United Africa Company Employees' Union, as well as experienced cadre from the NPP, MAP, and Togoland Congress.

The new opposition party soon managed to win a few elections. In Accra's municipal by-elections in 1959, the UP defeated the CPP in four contested wards, 3,707 to 3,292 votes. The leaders of the UP were fully prepared to defeat the government by any means — democratic or otherwise. UP general secretary R.R. Amponsah purchased military equipment in London under an assumed name, and stored the cache in French Togo. In the following months, both sides essentially abandoned any commitment to representative democracy. As Basil Davidson notes, 'From now onwards the opposition was to show itself even less willing or capable of acting as a responsible parliamentary check on the CPP machine; and the CPP machine, duly unchecked, went recklessly upon its way.'[91]

The government struck first at the traditional ethnic chiefs. In early 1958 many Ashanti chiefs were downgraded in official status, and others favoring the CPP were upgraded. The regional assemblies created by the British prior to independence, which gave access to local grievances and constituencies, were abolished. A Deportation Act was passed in August 1957, which gave the government the power to expel any non-citizen 'whose presence in Ghana is not conducive to the public good'. The Preventive Detention Act of 1958 gave the Prime Minister the legal power to incarcerate 'certain persons for up to five years without trial.' The legal justification for preventive detention was based on colonial precedent. As political scientist W. Howard Wriggins observed, 'Other states in the Commonwealth had similar emergency powers, drawn from the colonial tradition.' Nkrumah's use of the law, however, was for 'direct political effect,' that is, to intimidate, harrass and eliminate any opposition party leaders, and to coopt neutral forces in to the CPP.[92] Government agents were replaced by District Commissioners who were political supporters of Nkrumah. Chief Regional Officers were fired and replaced by CPP loyalists.

In December, 1958, Amponsah and M.K. Apaloo were briefly arrested under the Preventive Detention Act. The UP leadership began to crumble. Busia went into exile in June 1959; UP national treasurer Nancy Tsiboe resigned her post and immediately joined the CPP. The distinction between the Party and the state virtually disappeared. At the June, 1959 CPP tenth Congress, Nkrumah declared openly: 'the Convention People's Party is Ghana.' John Tettegah of the TUC spelled out the fine print: 'The CPP is Ghana and Ghana is the CPP . . . those who sit outside the ranks of the CPP forfeit their right to citizenship in the country. For it is only within the CPP that any constructive thing can be done in Ghana.'[93]

Nkrumah's decisions to leave the Commonwealth and to hold a national plebiscite to make Ghana a republic were the final steps toward consolidation of total party dictatorship over the state. The proposed republican constitution greatly increased the authority of Nkrumah as chief executive. The President was empowered to control 'the appointment, promotion, dismissal, and disciplinary control of members of the public services'; he could override the legislative powers of parliament; and his term in office was vaguely defined to continue 'until some other person assumes office,' The remnants of the UP urged a 'no' vote on the 'Nkrumah Constitution,' and selected Danquah, now 64 years old, to contest the presidency. Danquah bitterly attacked the government, but no Ghanian newspaper would publish his speeches: 'Our country has witnessed a great display of the power of the State as against the individual . . . Laws have been passed which have put the verdict of the Courts to nothingness and have elevated the power of the State . . . even to the extent of depriving the individual of his property . . . we are veering away from the liberalism of Christianity to the absolutism of Communism.'[94]

Danquah's public rallies were attacked by CPP members; some UP assemblies were cancelled when authorities revoked permits; the opposition candidate was denied the right to speak on Radio Ghana. The UP cadre fought back, organizing their own 'Action Groupers' to disrupt CPP events. But the power of the state was too great. The government announced that the new republican constitution had been approved by 88.5 percent, and that Nkrumah had defeated Danquah by 1,016,076 votes (89.1 percent) to 124,623 votes (10.9 percent). In Accra, where the election seemed reasonably honest, Nkrumah defeated Danquah, 16,804 to 9,035 votes, in a turnout of only 45 percent of registered electors. In pro-UP constituencies, however, there was clear evidence of massive fraud. In Kumasi West district, for example, the UP received 7,853 votes in a 1959 election: the same district gave Danquah only 137 votes less than nine months later.

For Makonnen, witnessing this vote-stealing was quite painful. 'My concept of the socialist world was an open world, where you fight openly for the right of a free press, and the right of collective bargaining. You legalize the Communist Party' and all other groups in order to prevent conspiracies 'in the body-politic.' Under the Nkrumah Constitution, Makonnen observed, Ghana was 'more of a closed than an open society, and there was often no correspondence between the statements of the Party and its actions.'[95] Party leaders were no longer embarrassed to admit the great distance between their rhetoric and social reality. Nathaniel Welbeck, the CPP's national propaganda secretary, declared that 'the commitment to power comes first, while the commitment to ideologies comes second.'[96]

The destruction of the opposition United Party meant that no viable checks existed to halt the growth of the CPP's patronage and graft network. Davidson terms this process 'the bureaucratic degeneration' of the CPP: 'They had acquired large houses which they filled with expensive furniture and *objets d'art* of a curious and wonderful vulgarity; and here they lived, amidst a host of lackeys, hangers-on and poor relations in an atmosphere of pomp and pretentiousness . . .'[97] Corruption became a normal method of public affairs. Party chairmen of city councils received free housing, £1800 annual salaries and an entertainment stipend of £250 annually. But this was simply the beginning. Local construction firms were expected to give funds to the party and individual leaders of government contracts; public jobs could be bought for a percentage of one's salary. The CPP, as James later admitted, had become a 'body of stooges . . . All sorts of ignoramuses, gangster-types, only had to prove their loyalty to the regime, i.e., to Nkrumah, and they could go places in the party and in the country.' The corruption and bureaucratization within the state reinforced the Nkrumahist cult of the personality.

By 1960 the chief proponent of this cult was Adamafio. Through an extensive propaganda campaign, public buildings and streets were renamed for the Party Leader. 'There were the Kwame Nkrumah Markets, the Kwame Nkrumah University, the Kwame Nkrumah Leadership Training Camps . . . Hymns were sung in praise of Nkrumah; and meetings began with such songs as "If you follow him, he will make you fishers of men." ' Adamafio's purple prose reached extremes in an essay printed in the Accra *Evening News* in May 1960: 'We all are at best a small star shining only through the grace of Kwame Nkrumah, our Political Central Sun and Author of the Ghanaian Revolution. We must learn from Kwame Nkrumah's supreme modesty, humility, and simplicity of life.' The primary objective of Adamafio and his supporters was to isolate and discredit the party factions led by Gbedemah and Botsio. His success was almost complete. By early 1961, he was named minister plenipotentiary and ambassador extraordinary. Any access to Nkrumah became 'almost impossible without his intervention.' Nkrumah's profile was soon printed on the nation's currency and stamps.[98]

The 'dual degeneration of the Parliament and of the Party' had several immediate social consequences. The small middle strata, those who had opposed Nkrumah since the late 1940s, withdrew from public life. As James comments, 'The ablest, the most qualified, and the intellectuals of finest character turned their backs on Nkrumah. Some of them, an astonishing number, went abroad and took jobs elsewhere. Those who stayed at home either devoted themselves to their professions, such as law and medicine, or did their work in the government, drew their pay and let Nkrumah govern or misgovern as he pleased.'⁹⁹ The Ghanaian working class, despite the Party's expulsions of the left and key trade-union activists in 1953-54, retained much of its original solidarity with the government. But as the political power of the parliamentary opposition declined in the late 1950s, the organized workers represented to the regime a potential alternative opposition. In fact, wage labourers were hardly unaware that they shouldered the burden of the costs of official corruption. In Sekondi-Takoradi, for example, the National Housing Corporation built two new housing estates designed for 'lower-paid workers.' The apartments in fact were allocated for the sexual trysts of party bigshots and Accra-based MPs and their girlfriends.

The first All-African Regional Trade Union Conference was held in Accra in January 1957. Under Tettegah's direction, labour representatives voted to establish an African Regional Organization which was linked to the ICFTU — a decision which was in accord with the Padmorian, pro-West orientation of the government. Nkrumah addressed the conference, promising that his government would give 'all the support which it can to the establishment and maintenance of independent and free trade unions in [Ghana]'¹⁰⁰ In January 1958, at the TUC annual convention, Tettegah proposed that the sixty-four unions then affiliated with the TUC should be regrouped into twenty-four national industrial unions. Theoretically, each new union would continue to enjoy complete autonomy in collective bargaining; however the TUC's executive committee, comprised of CPP bureaucrats, would direct the Congress's overall policy. To sweeten the proposal, the Nkrumah government gave the TUC a grant of £25,000 for 'organizational work.' Several months later, the regime abruptly approved the Industrial Relations Act of 1958, which vitiated trade union democracy. The act gave the government the authority to freeze TUC funds if unions' actions were 'not conducive to the public good'; it outlawed strikes by teachers and all public sector employees; it barred strikes by unions which were uncertified by the state as official collective bargaining agencies; and empowered the minister of labour to dissolve any union at a moment's notice.

Most of the workers reluctantly accepted these terms, but a vocal minority did not. The Railway Workers union and employees in the United Africa Company union denounced the new law, and withdrew from the TUC. Forty-nine strikes broke out in 1958-59; fifty, in 1959-60. Younger, urban workers tended to be the vanguard of anti-Nkrumahist sentiment. Ten to fifteen percent of Ghana's male wage-labour force was unemployed by 1960, and over two-fifths of the unemployed lived in urban areas. Unemployment was highest among both male and female workers aged 15 to 29. The Industrial Relations Act was changed in 1960, and the dissident unions were forced back into the TUC. But increasingly there were signs of another crisis on the social horizon; not from above, as in the abortive maneuverings of the UP, but from below.[101]

The one person who possessed the political acumen to intervene at this moment was C.L.R. James. He had visited Ghana briefly in 1957 and returned to Accra in July 1960. He recognized at once that 'Ghana, from being the finest jewel in the crown of Africa, was obviously in a state of impending crisis.' In a lecture before CPP leaders, James praised the Pan-Africanist vision of Nkrumahism as 'a beacon light in the political development of the modern world.' True to his Trotskyist intellectual orientation, James also supported Ghana's general foreign policies and its refusal to 'submit itself or support the two monstrous blocs of imperialism which today hang over the world . . . ' Then James offered a series of cautious criticisms of the CPP's evolution since 1949. No colonial society could ever achieve 'complete socialism immediately,' and capitalist production would have to exist for years. But the establishment of 'a socialist pattern of society' absolutely required the building 'of a completely socialist party.' The state of Ghana had to set the standard for the private sector's treatment of workers. 'It is not only a question of wages,' James argued, 'it is a question of the human conditions and human relations of the labor movement . . . ' Labor could not be treated the way it was 'in the early days of your nationhood.'

James urged the CPP leadership to criticize bribery and corruption, to set 'a high standard of morality for itself. It must scrutinize with the utmost vigilance and severity not only the actions of the government but the actions of itself, because that is the only way it will have the moral authority to being the government back if it shifts from the line.' Nkrumah learned about James's lecture, and asked that it be published and circulated. Sending a copy to his former student, James later noted: 'Nkrumah was very acute and, knowing my general political ideas well, he must have recognized far more than anyone else what I was saying; without fanfare I had not modified the perils that I saw ahead . . . my audience understood what I was talking about.' James's speech was never published in Ghana.[102]

III

After a decade in power, Nkrumah had become intolerant of private and public criticism. Yet his personal and political degeneracy had not yet reached the point where he was incapable of recognizing many of the failures and contradictions inside his own regime. The Osagyefo's pro-Western foreign policies, and especially the capitalist-orientation of his domestic programs, had only led to a dead-end. The regime's chief economic policy makers, led by Gbedemah, had 'listened to the most cautious and "respectable" advice, and had regularly taken it,' comments Basil Davidson. 'They had rigorously curbed inflation at the expense of the working people. They had fully "met their obligations" in the way of allowing foreigners to bring their capital into Ghana and take it out again as profits.' The net result, of course, was that 'the country was running only in order to stay in the same place.' The other major problem, now growing by scandalous proportions were the continuous reports of vast corruption. One particularly embarrassing story concerned Krobo Edusei's wife, who had purchased a 'golden bed' to add to 'her sense of comfort and prestige.'[103] His earlier political education under James provided Nkrumah with a vaguely Marxist critique of the situation. The CPP and the state would have to move to the left, if it hoped to maintain its traditional base among the workers. This meant, in effect, a radical re-evaluation of the nation's foreign and domestic policies. It would also require the elimination of Party leaders such as Gbedemah, Botsio and Edusei who were either too conservative in their fiscal policies, or who had been fatally compromised by their graft and personal excesses.

There was another supplemental benefit to be gained by shifting the politics of the state toward the left. The old-guard CPP veterans had never really accepted Nkrumah's complete preeminence, his vulgar cult of the personality. They had used this as a tactical maneuver in electoral campaigning, as part of their opportunistic appeal to the illiterate and rural voters. Nkrumah knew that their removal from public affairs would only reinforce his own personal domination over the Party and state. With the decline and near-disintegration of the UP, the forces aligned with Gbedemah were potentially a conservative opposition bloc. Sometime in late 1960 and early 1961, Nkrumah must have come to these conclusions. But the bureaucratic trappings of power had, unfortunately, distorted his ability to advance an egalitarian and democratic socialist agenda. The Osagyefo's 'socialism' was both mechancial and autocratic; it would be launched not from below, but from above. Its theoretical basis came not from historical materialism, but from an idealist or neo-Hegelian desire to promote 'the revival and development of the "African Personality",' which transcended the class struggle.[104]

On the morning of 8 April 1961, Nkrumah announced a war against the Party's 'bureaucratic and professional bourgeoisie' in what widely became known as the 'Dawn Broadcast.' The President attacked the 'degrading tendency' of Party members 'to create agents for collecting money,' warning that such behavior 'must be crushed in the most ruthless manner.' He ordered civil servants to 'eliminate all tendencies toward red tape-ism, bureaucracy and waste.' Nkrumah condemned trade-union officials for their 'loose talk and reprehensible statements which do no good either to the party, to the Government or to the nation. This is not the time for unbridled militant trade unionism in our country.' But Nkrumah reserved his strongest censure for the Party's hierarchy. Members of the National Assembly and ministers would no longer be permitted to 'own a business or be involved in anyone else's business, Ghanaian or foreign.' No Minister, 'member of a Government corporation or institution,' or Government employee was permitted henceforth to make any 'public statement affecting Government policy . . . unless that statement has first had Presidential or cabinet approval.' A strict 'limit' was to be imposed 'on property acquisitions by Ministers, party officials and Ministerial Secretaries.'[105]

The 'Dawn Broadcast,' whose authorship has been attributed to Adamafio, created a popular base for the semi-purge of the old guard. The Accra *Evening News* immediately attacked Botsio for not endorsing 'a socialist economic policy.' Gbedemah was condemned for owning a large poultry farm. Other ministers and Party officials fell under polemical attack in the Party-owned media. In early May, Nkrumah assumed the General Secretary's position in the CPP; Adamafio was named Minister of State for Presidential Affairs, a position formerly held by Gbedemah; and longtime Nkrumah-loyalist Kofi Baako was appointed Minister of State for Parliamentary Affairs. Gbedemah was demoted to Minister of

Health, although Botsio was permitted to retain his position as Minister of Agriculture. Nkrumah privately requested the police to 'prepare dossiers on all his ministers and Party functionaries, detailing the extent of their holdings.' These events created confusion and tremendous hostility among the CPP's ruling elite toward both Adamafio and Nkrumah. Botsio's private property 'included a mansion with a private chapel,' but he soon retreated from public life without challenging Nkrumah's decision. Gbedemah refused to retreat, perhaps recognizing his stronger constituency within the Party. He subsequently offered to sell his entire poultry farm to the state, and to divest from any questionable holdings. Nkrumah refused to negotiate with him.[106]

The semi-purge of April-May 1961 'did no more than tinker with the problem' of gross corruption and income inequality within Ghanaian society.[107] When the regime ordered a five percent compulsory reduction in workers' wages and a regressive property tax on all homes of two rooms or more in July 1961, the disagreements between the ruling party and the working class became an antagonistic schism. The center of anti-Nkrumahist, working-class sentiment was in Sekondi-Takoradi, and the movement's leader was CPP veteran Pobee Biney. Richard D. Jeffries describes Biney's political ideology, which was widely 'expressed at union mass meetings and at nationalist rallies he organized in Sekondi . . . [as] "African nationalist." ' Biney and his proletarian supporters were militantly anti-colonialist, and were strongly opposed to the UGCC/UP petty bourgeoisie. But they were also critical of Marxism-Leninism, or at least the Soviet variety; Biney later condemned Left Nkrumahism's collaboration with the USSR, and deplored 'that Soviet"ism" nonsense which has nothing to teach us about Socialism.' Jeffries notes, 'Biney's emphasis on the vanguard role of the organised, enlightened workers in leading the Ghanaian people to achieve their independence involved the corollary that they should continue to act thereafter as defenders of the Nationalist Movement's aims, checking degenerative tendencies in the party-become-government.' From the vantagepoint of Sekondi-Takoradi's proletariat, the CPP ruling elite had become 'revisionist'; it had broken with the nationalist workers 'who had remained faithful to the original ideals of the movement . . . '[108]

In September 1961, thousands of harbor and railroad workers staged a seventeen-day strike against the regime, popularly supported by nearly the entire Sekondi-Takoradi population. Workers criticized not only the new tax, but all of the social ills addressed by

James the previous year — the vast wage inequalities between government officials and workers, the lack of genuine worker control in their workplaces, the excessive wealth and conspicuous consumption of politicians. St. Clair Drake and L.C. Lacy observe that 'the Government saw its very existence implicitly challenged' by the Sekondi-Takoradi proletariat. Strike leaders declared that 'if Parliament did not give way to the demands of the people, they would disband that body by force.' Nkrumah, Adjei and Adamafio were out of the country on a lengthy tour of the Soviet Union and East Europe. Although neither Botsio nor Gbedemah were technically in charge of law enforcement, Nkrumah expected them to direct the suppression of the strike. But his former lieutenants were unable, and also perhaps unwilling to do so. Panic paralyzed the government bureaucrats and Party officials. The remnants of the United Party in the National Assembly, led by ex-CPP official Victor Owusu, openly attacked the 'members of the new Ghanaian aristocracy and their hangers-on . . . ' Labor unrest quickly spread to Kumasi. African market women joined the strikers by providing food and other essentials. Even some soldiers sent to discipline Sekondi-Takoradi's labourers became sympathetic to the strike. Socialism-from-below threatened to overturn the statist regime.[109]

Adamafio was sent back to Ghana by Nkrumah to break the strike and to restore order. Radio Ghana placed a news embargo on any information relating to labor unrest; police and soldiers were ordered to arrest and beat labor leaders and workers. All insurgents held responsible for the strike were prohibited from ever holding union office in the future. When Nkrumah returned, he described the general strike as the product of a sinister 'neo-colonialist conspiracy.' But he turned his anger against both the old guard bureaucrats, whose inaction had nearly toppled the regime, and the few remaining leaders of the opposition. Joe Appiah, Victor Owusu, and Danquah were promptly arrested and jailed without charges; also imprisoned were several UP journalists, nineteen labor leaders, and five Sekondi-Takoradi market-women. The strike also gave Nkrumah the pretext to complete his purge of the Party's chief leaders. Six cabinet ministers, including Botsio and Gbedemah, were ordered to resign. Six others, including Edusei, were asked to 'surrender excess property' to the state. The regime simultaneously proposed two bills before the National Assembly: 'the first imposed a fine of £500 or three years' imprisonment, or both, on anyone summarily convicted of publishing defamatory or insulting matter which might bring the President into hatred, ridicule or contempt.

The second created a Special Criminal Division of the High Court to hear cases of treason, sedition, rioting and unlawful assembly, from which there would be no appeal.'[110]

The final confrontation between Gbedemah and Nkrumah's regime occurred on the floor of the National Assembly, as he denounced the introduction of the second bill. Gbedemah began by attacking the 1958 Preventive Detention Act, which had just been used to suppress civil liberties during the recent strike: 'How many people are languishing in jail today, detained under this Act? If we are to learn from experience, the Bill when passed into law would soon show that the liberty of the subject is extinguished forever. Today, there are many people whose hearts are filled with fear – fear even to express their convictions. When we pass this Bill and it goes on to the Statute Book, the low flickering flames of freedom will be forever extinguished. We may be pulled out of bed to face the firing squad after a summary trial and conviction . . . there will be many persons ready to face the squad, but it will not be the freedom for which we were imprisoned and which we struggled for.'[111]

Gbedemah's failure was that of the Ghanaian liberal petty bourgeoisie. He had not opposed the elimination of parliamentary democracy, the silencing of nonviolent critics, or the suppression of trade-union democracy. He had been prepared to support an increasingly authoritarian regime, so long as his personal interests were protected. Pathetically and tragically, he tried to warn Adamafio, Adjei and other 'left Nkrumahists' that they, too, would become expendable: 'Today, we may think that all is well, it is not my turn, it is my brother's turn, but your turn will come sooner than later.'[112] Finishing his speech, Gbedemah fled the country before the police arrested him.

The Sekondi-Takoradi strike and the fall of Gbedemah marked the highpoint of what Samir Amin terms 'Nkrumahite Socialism.'[113] Few of the pre-1951 leadership of the CPP remained — the most prominent was Kofi Baako, who became Nkrumah's Minister of Information and a principal ideologist of 'Nkrumahism.'[114] The vast majority of the new leadership had played insignificant roles in the Positive Action campaign; some were former members of the NLM or UP, like Adamafio, or were too junior to have been involved one way or another in nationalist politics. For instance, Kofi Batsa, a former United Party official, was appointed by Nkrumah to edit *The Spark*, the CPP's 'Marxist' theoretical journal. The major figures of 'left Nkrumahism' included: Deputy

Minister of the Interior H.S.T. Provencal, CPP executive secretary Coffie Crabbe; Interior Minister Kwaku Boateng; Tettegah; Adjei; and most prominently, Adamafio. All aggressively promoted the Nkrumahist cult. Adamafio's 1961 pamphlet, 'A Portrait of the Osagyefo Dr. Kwame Nkrumah,' for example, declared that their leader's name 'is a breath of hope and means freedom, brotherhood and racial equality . . . Kwame Nkrumah is our father, teacher, our brother, our friend, indeed our very lives . . . (He) is greater even than the air we breathe, for he made us as surely as he made Ghana.'[115]

Left Nkrumahists had begun to influence Ghanaian foreign policies months before the demise of Gbedemah. Only a year after Padmore's death, Adamafio and Tettegah met with Krushchev, and negotiated a long-term credit of 160 million rubles for Ghana, which also involved the establishment of manufacturing and fishing industries. In 1962, Adamafio urged Nkrumah to 'make Ghana a formal Soviet ally in the manner of Cuba.' Ghanaian policies soon shifted almost completely from the USA toward the USSR. Under Adjei's direction, trade with Egypt nearly doubled between 1961 and 1962. Nkrumah, who had once been nearly as hostile toward Nasser as Padmore, now denounced Israel as a 'neo-colonialist' state, and announced his plan for the creation of 'a separate state for Arab refugees from Palestine'; Soviet ambassador Georgi Rodionov replaced Avriel as Accra's most influential foreign ambassador. To be sure, other international factors, particularly the Congo crisis, the assassination of Lumumba, and the US-directed 'Bay of Pigs' invasion of Cuba, also pushed Nkrumah to the left. What is important, however, to recognize, is that these left Nkrumahists had absolutely no ideological commitment to socialism as it related to the political empowerment of the Ghanaian working class. At the peak of his power, Adamafio explained that Nkrumahist socialism could never be finitely defined: 'we are very anxious to get a Bible of Nkrumahism [but] we do not want to tie the hands of our Leader in a way that when he acts he will be accused of going against his own principles.'[116]

A type of statist, bureaucratic deformed socialism was initiated in 1961, with the nationalization of five gold mines which produced less than half of the nation's total output. The State Mining Corporation did not run the mines directly, but functioned as a holding company for all of the shares taken over. Barclays Bank and the Bank of West Africa branches were no longer permitted to forward surplus funds to London, and were forced to lend solely inside

Ghana. Still, in 1963 about half of all banking business was done by expatriate firms. A new 'Seven Year Plan' was introduced for 1963-1970, calling for major increases in government spending in heavy industry and agriculture. By February 1966, 150 of the projected 600 new industrial projects were completed. To finance these ambitious projects, the state was forced to borrow funds from abroad. As Samir Amin observed, 'Interest and depreciation on the national debt took up a growing proportion of fiscal revenue: 17 percent at the fall of the regime, compared with 4 percent in 1960.'[117]

These policies followed a 'left' model of socioeconomic development; but they faltered due to the ideological hostility from the civil service, which remained largely British-trained and anti-Nkrumah, and from the failure to involve workers themselves at all levels of planning. The percentage of public-sector workers quickly soared: in late 1963, 39 percent of all industrial workers were employed in state-owned firms, and by the end of 1964, almost 70 percent of all wage earners were public employees.[118] But the left Nkrumahists had substituted for genuine workers' democracy and collective planning a swollen state bureaucracy still riddled with corruption.

On 1 August 1962 Nkrumah narrowly survived an assassination attempt in the northern village of Kulungugu. He immediately suspected that his closest associates were responsible. Four weeks later, a bomb was exploded outside Nkrumah's residence, killing one young girl and injuring 63 people. Adamafio, Adjei and Coffie Crabbe were arrested, and the state-controlled press campaigned for their prompt execution. For the old-guard CPP and many workers, there was a measure of revenge in their acclaim for the left's downfall. Laborers had not forgotten that Adamafio had described Sekondo-Takoradi strikers as 'despicable rats' during the previous year. Krobo Edusei declared before a CPP protest rally that 'the arch-traitors' should be taken 'to Accra's Black Star Square to be publicly tried and shot.' Adamafio was blamed for every problem plaguing the regime. The 'wages of sin (are) death,' Edusei cried; Adamafio 'must pay for his deeds.' Some junior members of the Adamafio-Adjei group managed to save themselves by hastily condemning their former patrons. Nkrumah was forced, moreover, to restore several CPP leaders to their bureaucratic posts. Edusei was named Minister of Agriculture, and Botsio became Foreign Minister. But as Davidson correctly observes: 'these men took office as instruments of his policy, and merely did what they were told. Before, they had been his companions. Now they were only his employees.'[119]

In August 1963, Adamafio, Crabbe and Adjei came to trial. The state's case against them was at best circumstantial. The Chief Justice, Arku Korsah, acquitted the defendants on 9 December 1963. But Nkrumah refused to accept this decision, especially given that Korsah had belonged to the old UGCC elite. The President demanded that the National Assembly overturn the acquittals, and he dismissed the Chief Justice. The legislature dutifully declared on 25 December that Kirsah's ruling was 'null and void.' Adjei, Adamafio and Crabbe received the death penalty, although Nkrumah commuted their sentences to life imprisonment.

Nkrumah's oldest friends were shocked by this most recent fiasco. C.L.R. James explained: 'You can poison a Chief Justice, [but] you cannot dismiss him for a decision from the Bench.' When Nkrumah failed to reply to his urgent inquiries, James openly broke off their relations. He had realized at once that Nkrumah and 'Africa had crossed a Rubicon': 'The very structure, judicial, political and moral, of the state is at one stroke destroyed, and there is automatically placed on the agenda a violent restoration of some sort of legal connection between government and population. By this single act, Nkrumah prepared the population of Ghana for the morals of the Mafia. Those learned societies which passed resolutions disapproving of his act should have known that Nkrumah could have said the most admirable things about the rule of law. It wasn't that he did not know. What was important was that he knew all the arguments against such a step and its inevitable consequences . . . A prime minister who has not got people around him who can tell him that is living on borrowed time. If he hasn't got such people around him, it is his misfortune and his fault. Worse still it is the misfortune of the people over whom he rules.'[129]

The fall of Adamafio and other left Nkrumahists did not impede the continuation of the turn toward bureaucratic 'socialism.' But Nkrumah never again permitted another potential rival from within the Party to acquire the status of Gbedemah or Adamafio. Even in the 1950s, he had already shown a preference to recruit non-Ghanaian advisers. During the capitalist-phase of Nkrumahism, the key figure in economic policy was W. Arthur Lewis, a West Indian who promoted private-sector investments by multinationals. In the 1960s, as Nkrumah became more isolated from the Ghanaian intelligentsia and from his own Party leaders, he had no choice except to appoint non-Ghanaians. A short list of foreign assistants and bureaucrats would include: Joseph Bognor, a Hungarian economist who advised the regime in 1962; Sir Patrick Fitz-Gerald, a Unilever corporation executive and self-proclaimed 'imperialist' who ran the largest state-owned enterprise; H.M. Basner, a former radical senator in South Africa, who served as the regime's journalist and occasional speechwriter; left Laborite Geoffrey Bing, Nkrumah's Attorney General and liaison with the European left; Sir John Howard, head of Parkison Howard, Ltd., and advisor on construction projects; Nigerian intellectual Sam G. Ikoku, who provided constructive criticism on an informal basis; Major General Edward Spears, an adviser on international trade and mining; and Sir Robert Jackson, an Australian, who was Nkrumah's main adviser on the Volta River Dam Project.

One obvious benefit of relying on foreign advisors was that they lacked any political constituency within the Party or society. Nkrumah could accept or reject their suggestions, depending on his own intuitions or mood. As for the 'official' members of his Cabinet, their actual powers were greatly reduced. Some were 'assigned errands for the President and functioned as watchdogs for the political machine.' None could ever forget their personal and political vulnerability. The National Assembly had become meaningless and impotent, a remnant of a colonial past. Decay spread throughout the Party at all levels. As Davidson comments: 'Asked to embrace non-capitalist policies, eventually socialist policies, its leaders were lost in disbelief or in confusion. Active political work among ordinary members had practically ceased . . . So little democracy did it have that its central committee was no longer elected; and the names of its members were not even allowed to be made public.'[121]

The Ghanaian state was no longer simply an authoritarian statist regime, dominated by a deformed, populist-social democratic style party. By severing all meaningful ties with its traditional class constituencies, eliminating virtually all elements of democratic discourse and destroying its original leaders, the state had become 'Bonapartist.' The classic definition of the term was advanced by Marx in the *Eighteenth Brumaire of Louis Bonaparte:* 'This executive power with its enormous bureaucratic and military organization, with its ingenious state machinery, embracing wide strata, with a host of officials . . . this appalling parasitic body, which enmeshes the body of French society like a net and chokes all its pores . . . ' In the Bonapartist state, 'the executive power, in contrast to the legislative power, expresses the heteronomy of a nation, in contrast to its autonomy . . . The struggle seems to be settled in such a way that all classes, equally impotent and equally mute, fall on their knees before the rifle butt.' The leader of the regime tries to 'appear as the benefactor of all classes,' but the state bureaucracy ruthlessly subordinates almost every social class.[122]

Antonio Gramsci also developed the concept in his *Prison Notebooks*. In any Bonapartist regime, Gramsci observed: 'The government in fact operated as a "party." It set itself over and above the parties, not so as to harmonise their interests and activities within the permanent framework of the life and interests of the nation and State, but so as to disintegrate them, to detach them from the broad masses . . . Hence, scarcity of State and government personnel; squalor of parliamentary life; ease with which the parties can be disintegrated, by corruption and absorption of the few individuals who are indispensible. Hence, squalor of cultural life . . . instead of serious politics, ephemeral quarrels and personal clashes . . . Thus the bureaucracy became estranged from the country, and via its administrative positions became a true political party, the worst of all, because the bureaucratic hierarchy replaced the intellectual and political hierarchy. The bureaucracy became precisely the State/Bonapartist party.'[123]

In Ghana, the state and nation were no longer identified with the CPP, but with Nkrumah alone, as the Bonapartist 'benefactor.' As the *Ghanaian Times* constantly reminded citizens, 'Ghana is unquestionably Kwame Nkrumah.'[124] The Nkrumahism personality cult reached maniacal proportions. A paradoxical sense of intellectual inferiority drove the Osagyefo to rewrite the histories of his own social movement. In his initial autobiography, published in 1957, Nkrumah had few reservations in crediting Gbedemah, Botsio and many others for their decisive contributions toward Ghanaian independence. Even with his opponents he tried to be fair: Dzenkle Dzewu was mentioned as 'a staunch supporter who later defected,' and Busia's scholarly sociological research on the Ashanti was cited objectively. But with the publication of *Africa Must Unite* in 1963, Nkrumah projected himself as the sole originator, strategist and organizer of the CPP. 'I had spearheaded a mass movement,' Nkrumah emphasized. Botsio, Gbedemah, Adamafio and other Party leaders were not mentioned once, even critically. 'I ardently desired' to give 'liberal democracy every chance,' he claimed; but his parliamentary opposition had consisted of 'unscrupulous politicians' who used 'demagogic appeals' to arouse 'emotions rather than reason.' Senegalese radical Habib Niang was commissioned to write *Consciencism*, which was followed in 1965 by *Neo-Colonialism: the Last Stage of Imperialism.* Despite their Marxian elements, Nkrumah's academic works reveal a metaphysical adherence to the 'African Personality' which transcends class stratification and conflict. 'Posing as an authority on all sorts of historical and philosophical subjects, [Nkrumah] began to publish book after book,' James noted sadly in 1966. 'Years ago I ceased to read them.'[125]

It was only in the mid-sixties that the partial fruits of Nkrumahite socialism began to become evident. Despite its depotism, the regime delivered services and provided an improvement in the quality of life for many Ghanaians. The state's 'Program of Work and Happiness' initiated in 1962 proclaimed as its 'fundamental objective' the development 'of a socialist state devoted to the welfare of the masses.' There was a noticeable expansion of hospitals and rural health clinics throughout the country. Five new mental hospitals, four urban polyclinics and six district hospitals were being prepared for construction at the time of the coup. A concerted effort was made in the industrial sector: the state constructed a major steelworks plant, two sugar refineries, two cocoa refineries, a meat processing plant, a glass factory and other industrial enterprises within several short years. A state-owned atomic reactor was planned for Kwabinya; a gold refinery at Tarkwa and cement, rubber and shoe factories were being developed in Kumasi.

Rural agricultural production also increased. Cocoa production nationwide jumped from 264,000 tons in 1956-1957 to 590,000 tons in 1963-64. But many state-owned cooperatives and projects lost money due to mismanagement and inept planning. In early 1965, the regime admitted that the State Mining Corporation, the State Farms Corporation and Ghana Airways had lost a total of £13.6 million. But there were some exceptions. The Timber Marketing Board's foreign exchange earnings increased from £5.7 million in 1962 to £8 million in 1964, and during these years the Board granted £2 million in loans to local cooperatives. But perhaps the greatest achievement was in education. Textbooks were free for all students, and all schooling was without charge. Over 1.2 million Ghanaian youth attended primary, middle and secondary schools by 1963. The total number of teacher training school and university students increased from 2,100 in 1951 to 8,000 in 1963, with projected enrollments of 26,000 by 1970.[126]

Despite the regime's internal corruption and bureaucratic deformities, the masses of working people and small farmers recognized that Nkrumahism represented a qualitative improvement over

British colonialism. The old regime had never been democratic; the British had done little to promote educational, social welfare and economic reforms beyond their own direct needs to maintain a level of efficient social control and material exploitation. Judged by the standards of the colonial past, the accomplishments were substantial. But weighed against the democratic visions and egalitarian promises of the early days, the regime's failures seemed monumental. From the practical perspective of the Ghanaian proletariat, moreover, many of the massive state projects seemed irrational and illogical. The Volta Dam, a project promoted by Western capitalist interests, was 'tragic because there was no need for it.' argued Makonnen. Only 1,600 jobs were created when the project was finished, at a cost of £75 million.

During the regime's left turn, Makonnen protested the appointment of Fitz-Gerald as head of the Ghana National Trading Corporation (GNTC). 'This made it clear that Ghana was interested in state capitalism and not socialism. Otherwise what are you doing appointing one of the oldest United Africa hands as the manager of your nationalized sector?' Fitz-Gerald was never comfortable with the state's extensive economic relations with Communist states on ideological grounds, yet he raised a series of practical issues for which left Nkrumahist planners had no answers. Ghanaian contractors and builders refused to use Soviet cement, and the supplies hardened on the docks. Soviet cameras were 'unsalable,' Fitz-Gerald complained, because 'they had no English instructions.' The Soviets proposed that the GNTC purchase Soviet-built automobiles, but made no provisions for spare parts. A Ghanaian planning commission in 1962 noted that a Soviet contract for a prefabricated panel factory did not 'even show the total cost to [the] Ghana Government of signing it.' The chronic breakdown of Soviet equipment and machinery became a major problem. 'We had socialist talk without socialist planning,' Makonnen recalled, 'the worst of both worlds.' Left Nkrumahists who shouted loudest 'about socialism were more steeped in capitalism than the West where capitalism had undergone some reform at least . . . But all that socialism meant to the ordinary people was "funny Russian sardines, instead of the good old British brands that we knew." ' Even the director of Nkrumah's 'Ideological College' at Winneba, Kodwo Addison, 'was no socialist.'[127]

The vast distance between the rhetorical and political reality of 'Nkrumahist-Bonapartism' was also manifested in Ghana's foreign policies. In the 1950s, 'Nkrumah had been a popular symbol of

African liberation,' observed W.Scott Thompson. But by the time the Organization of African Unity was established in 1963, few leaders 'took him seriously.'[128] There were several reasons for this. Radical nationalists, well aware of the deteriorating political conditions for Ghana's proletariat, questioned Nkrumah's leftist credentials. Ghana's criticisms of the developing East African Federation alienated Nyerere, who finally denounced Nkrumah's policies as 'attempts to rationalize absurdity.' Ghana's initial membership in the British Commonwealth (which then still included South Africa) called into question Nkrumah's commitment in fighting apartheid. Ghana repeatedly failed to provide funds to UN-sponsored or OAU-directed programs to support African freedom fighters. The ANC, after several years of lobbying efforts, finally dismissed Nkrumah as hopeless.

Conservatives despised Nkrumah for different reasons. The Ivory Coast was angered by Nkrumah's financial support of the Sanwi rebels in their country. Houphouet-Boigny was so hostile to Nkrumah that he succeeded in adding a clause to the OAU charter which condemned 'political assassination as well as subversive activities on the part of neighbouring states.' Senegal reduced its total 1965 exports to Ghana to the value of £120, as Senghor bitterly attacked Nkrumah's 'Pan-African Government' schemes. Banda referred to Nkrumah as an 'idiot' before his own puppet parliament; Nigerian leader Nnamdi Azikiwe deplored the death of Danquah 'in a detention camp barely eight years after his country had become free from foreign domination.' Even Nkrumah's closest African associate, Touré, attacked his 'ally' before the UN General Assembly, telling delegates that Africa had no need for 'philosophical formulas or doctrinal theories; it needs honest cooperation . . . One of the major obstacles to [unity] has been the widespread conception that it had to be formed around a single state or a single man.'

Nkrumah isolated himself further by initiating or financing dissident groups, assassination attempts and various schemes against other African bureaucratic elites. In Nigeria, for example, Tettegah's TUC funnelled money to underwrite the Nigerian dock workers' strike in 1963, and the Ghanaian regime 'dispatched arms and ammunition' to certain political factions during Nigeria's 1964 elections. In late 1965, with East German secret intelligence assistance, a new 'Special African Service' was established which would 'report directly to Nkrumah.'[129] The great irony of the situation was that Nkrumah's call for Pan-Africanist unity was essentially correct.

'The international system isolated Nkrumah on the continent,' Samir Amin argues. 'His pan-Africanism was labelled "aggressive" by his neighbours, although in fact only such a policy would have made it possible to begin solving the real problems of development.'[139]

Symptomatic of Nkrumah's alienation from African leaders were his strained relations with many Black Americans living in Ghana. One instance occurred in May, 1964, when Black nationalist Malcolm X came to the country. Nominally, he was treated as a visiting dignitary. Malcolm's schedule included breakfast meetings with Makonnen, and political discussions at the Accra embassies of Algeria, China, Mali and Nigeria. Kofi Baako held a private party in Malcolm's honor, and the Chinese ambassador, Huang Hua, gave a state dinner for him. Malcolm lectured at the Kwame Nkrumah Ideological Institute at Winneba, and was permitted to present a speech before the Parliament. Malcolm wrote later in his autobiography, 'the highest single honor' he had experienced 'in all of Black Africa' was an 'audience' with Nkrumah: 'We discussed the unity of Africans and peoples of African descent. We agreed that Pan-Africanism was the key also to the problems of those of African heritage. I could feel the warm, likeable and very down-to-earth qualities of Dr. Nkrumah. I promised faithfully that when I returned to the United States, I would relay to Afro-Americans his personal warm regards.'[131]

Within hours after Malcolm X left Ghana, an essay critical of the Afro-American militant appeared in the state-owned *Ghanaian Times*, written by Nkrumah aide H.M. Basner. The article essentially attacked Malcolm's 'ignorance' in failing to admit the fundamental 'economic motivations and the class function of all racial oppression.' Basner warned that unless Malcolm X repudiated his errors, 'his politics can only be of service to the American imperialists . . . Nothing suits the capitalists more than that Governor [George] Wallace [of Alabama] and Malcolm X should be at each other's throats because one is white and the other Black . . . ' One week later, Basner was urging univeristy students to reject the politics of Malcolm X, declaring that Nkrumah and other African revolutionaries understand 'that it is the lust for profit and not racial differences which makes the white man behave in colonial Africa as he does.' The Afro-American colony in Accra was 'caught by surprise.' As Leslie Lacy explained: 'We know how Basner felt privately about Malcolm's views,' but his attacks 'had appeared in a Black, revolutionary, government-controlled newspaper . . . No criticism, however objective, could have appeared attacking Nkrumah.' Black Americans were not alone in their outrage. University students 'already hated Basner' and 'now had another reason to want him out of what they considered a confused political culture.'[132] Other students probably recognized that the problem was not with Basner, but with his political master.

Nkrumah never understood that his capricious and authoritarian behavior made legions of silent enemies, who waited for an opportunity to strike back. On 2 January 1964 a policeman attempted to assassinate Nkrumah. Following this incident, the Police Commissioner and nine police officers were dismissed and several critics of the regime were imprisoned. The same month, Nkrumah staged a national referendum on his policies. According to the regime, nearly 93 percent of the Ghanaian electorate voted, and the masses gave Nkrumah an astonishing majority: 2,773,920 votes in favor vs. 2,452 opposed. Rigged elections under bourgeois democracies, fascist and one-party regimes were nothing new. But for most of the Ghanaian working class and peasantry, the referendum shattered even the fragile facade of democratic relations between themselves and the state. Some observers thought that Nkrumah could have won an honest election, even in 1964, perhaps by a margin of about 55 percent of the electorate. But sooner or later, Nkrumah would have to be held accountable, despite the positive social and economic reforms which had been initiated from above.[133]

The decline of world cocoa prices catalyzed the final crisis of the regime. The Seven Year Plan had assumed that the price of cocoa would be approximately £200 per ton from 1963-1970. Economic leverage from the UK and USA artificaly lowered cocoa prices, which fell from £208 per ton in 1963 to about £140 per ton in 1965. The Americans stockpiled several hundred thousand tons of cocoa as part of a coordinated effort to destabilize Nkrumah's state. The decline in cocoa revenues increased the regime's reliance on foreign loans to maintain its massive state projects. In July 1963, Ghana's outstanding credits and loans already exceeded £92 million. The regime continued to borrow heavily: £3.4 million from France for a cotton mill, £6.9 million from the Netherlands for eight merchant ships, £19 million from the British contractor Parkinson Howard; £15 million in credits from Stahl-Union of West Germany.[134]

Left Nkrumahism had tried to do too much, too quickly, without developing a sufficient cadre of socialists who could implement programs with some degree of efficiency. Nkrumah recognized this, yet he felt reasonably secure. There were no coherently organized political groups capable of challenging his authority in the National Assembly, the Party, or in the streets. The only potential threat left was the military and police. Once again, there is sad irony here, for the very men Nkrumah advanced into the state's agencies of coercion during the 'Africanization' of the colonial apparatus were those who would topple their patron. For years a British officer, Major-General H.T. Alexander, had been Nkrumah's chief of staff. Those Africans who took the place of Alexander and other British officers still had the 'Sandhurst' mentality. Nkrumah's Deputy Chief of Defence, Major-General Joseph Ankrah, had been the camp commandant of the Gold Coast District in 1947, and had been trained in the Officer Cadet School in Britain. Colonel Emmanuel Kotoka had been a company Sergeant-Major in the British West African Frontier Force during the Positive Action campaign. Nkrumah's Deputy Commissioner of Police, Bawa Andani Yakubu, had enlisted in the Ghana Police Service in February 1945. John Harley, Nkrumah's Police Commissioner, had been a police officer since 1940; and Afrifa was trained as an army officer at Sandhurst Royal Military Academy in 1958-1960.[135]

The Ghanaian officers corps was firmly loyal to British tradition, and hostile to left Nkrumahism and its growing political and economic ties with the Soviet bloc. They had imprisoned the regime's critics, restored order in Sekondi-Takoradi, and buttressed the Osaygefo's authority. Publicly they praised Nkrumah; privately they viewed him as a 'lunatic' or worse. For Afrifa, the President's reversal of the Adamafio-Adjei decision was a 'disgrace. The constitution itself was perverted, parliament was a mockery, the judiciary had lost its independence and the executive had become autocratic. I became Kwame Nkrumah's bitterest enemy.'[136] But even in the mid-1960s, a coup might have been averted. Popular defense committees, modeled after Cuba's 'Committees for the Defense of the Revolution,' could have armed the workers and peasantry, ideologically and militarily. State industrial projects could have promoted workers' criticisms, direction and input. But Nkrumah still feared his industrial working class, preferring to place his trust in British-trained military officers and constables, securing their allegiance with promotions and graft. When the CPP finally fell, the workers in turn failed to support Nkrumah and Nkrumahism. After the bitter experience of Sekondi-Takoradi, after the rigged elections and the deliberate dismantling of the Party, they could have acted no other way.

IV

The NLC coup represented a victory both for Western capitalism and the 'old establishment — the old elites of chiefs, professional men, wealthy traders, senior civil servants who lost political power to Nkrumah's new coalition at independence.'[137] Local capitalists were overjoyed: Major-General Edward Spears, Chairman of Ashanti Goldfields, was among the first to congratulate the NLC. Within weeks, left Nkrumahist economic policies gave way to a renaissance of CPP policies of 1951-1959. State-controlled firms, including the Diamond Mining Corporation, Black Star Shipping Line, Ghana Airways, the Timber Products Corporation and the National Steel Works, were sold to private corporations and investors. In March 1966, the International Monetary Fund provided a stand-by credit line of £13 million to the new regime. Over 2,500 Soviet and Chinese advisers were expelled. Although the world price of cocoa had nearly doubled by mid-1968, the actual material benefits did not filter down to Ghanaian working people. The regime's annual rate of economic growth averaged one percent in 1966-68, and by mid-1967 nearly one-quarter of the wage labor force was unemployed.[138]

In August 1969 the NLC, then led by Afrifa, permitted national elections. Ethnicism and ideological interests both played roles in the regime's decision. Afrifa, an Ashanti conservative, favored handing over the reigns of state authority to Busia, whose primary ethnic base was the Ashanti Brong-Ahafo region. A new constitution was formed, providing for a weak Presidency, a Prime Minister with strong executive powers, and a 140-member legislature. Five political parties were formed, and a total of 480 candidates campaigned for the legislature. The major contenders were the Progress Party, led by Busia, and Gbedemah's National Alliance of Liberals. Many foreign observers predicted that Gbedmah would be elected as the new Prime Minister. His party waged a strong 'grassroots election campaign' similar to the electoral mobilizations he had directed in the 1950s. But the Liberals were defeated at the polls, winning only 29 seats to Busia's 105 seats. Busia's Progress Party won all 35 seats in the Ashanti and Brong-Ahafo regions, which were the core of the NLM/UP opposition to Nkrumah a decade before. The urban petty bourgeoisie, intellectuals, bureaucrats, and prominently the military, actively supported Busia. Yet Gbedemah might have won by appealing directly to the former supporters of the CPP — the trade unionists, urban workers, the unemployed and small farmers. He refused to do so. The polemical thrust of his whole campaign was 'firmly anti-Nkrumah,' and some believed that 'his party's failure was partly due to its inability to attract votes from CPP elements.' The government was turned over to Busia in September, 1969, and 'the military men who feared a return to the former regime were able to sleep more easily at night.'[139]

The conservative Busia regime remained in power barely two and one-half years, and set a public record for authoritarianism which transcended Nkrumah's regime considerably. Busia was unashamedly neo-colonialist in outlook, and spared no pains to crush any opposition, real or imaginary. The regime made it illegal 'to revive the Convention People's Party of Nkrumah, or to display a photograph or effigy of the ex-President, or shout any of the slogans of his party.' It 'disqualified' Gbedemah from his elected seat in Parliament. In its foreign agenda, the regime courted Western investment, loyally supported the US at the United Nations, and even flirted with 'a policy of dialogue with South Africa.'

But what truly worried the Busia government was the threat of populist, 'left-Nkrumahism' from the working class. In 1971, the regime abolished the TUC's check-off system, whereby union dues were automatically deducted from workers' wages. Police were ordered to raid TUC offices, and all union assets were frozen. Perhaps Busia's most significant errors were his attacks on two prime constituencies which had helped elevate him to power. The middle stratum was dismayed when the government refused to comply with new Constitutional provisions requiring all ministers to declare their personal assets. Bureaucratic corruption and clientage was revived, but now only the officials of the Progress Party and a section of the petty bourgeoisie benefited. Busia slashed the wages and housing privileges of civil servants, and in 1970 he fired 568 public employees. One official legally challenged the regime's right to dismiss him, and the Supreme Court ruled in his favor. Busia overruled the high court, just as Nkrumah had done in 1963. 'No court can enforce any decision that seeks to compel the Government to employ or re-employ anyone,' asserted this defender of liberal democracy. The military also received a rude surprise when Busia authorized deep reductions in wages and supplies. The regime's decision to devalue Ghana's currency by 44 percent, as demanded by the IMF, eroded any popular support Busia may have retained. In January 1972 the military easily overthrew Busia, naming Colonel Ignatius Kutu Acheampong head of state.[140]

The National Redemption Council (NRC) of Acheampong carried out a type of 'military Nkrumahism.' It instinctively distrusted the workers' movement, and used coercive means to check labour militancy. But it rehabilitated most of the former bureaucrats in the old CPP government, and imprisoned 1300 state officials and members of Busia's Progress Party. A new system of patronage and graft quickly emerged, in which officers were placed over state-owned corporations and received numerous 'tax-free allowances' as well as their military pay. The CPP was not revived, but some of the Party's former leaders received prominent positions in the state apparatus: Gbedemah and Botsio became 'roving ambassadors' for the NRC; Kwesi Amoaka-Atta, the governor of the Bank of Ghana under Nkrumah, was named chief economic consultant; journalist Kofi Badu was the 'NRC spokesman' for the press; and in 1977, Geoffrey Bing, former Attorney General, returned to advise the NRC on the drafting of a new Constitution. The NRC resurrected Nkrumah's Pan-Africanist foreign policy by denouncing apartheid, imperialism and neo-colonialism, and it reduced the position of foreign investments in the economy. The personality cult of Nkrumahism was not permitted, yet Acheampong deliberately tried to identify himself with the late President's image: 'I think [Nkrumah] was a great man . . . In his lifetime he waged a relentless war against colonialism and racism, and even after his death his spirit will, no doubt, continue to inspire the valiant fighters against these twin enemies of Africa . . . [Nkrumah was] a worthy son of Africa.'[141]

There is little evidence that Nkrumah ever seriously analyzed the real factors behind his fall from power. He always believed that the coup was the work of 'a clique of army and police traitors, supported by neocolonialists and certain reactionary elements within Ghana.' His enemies had 'turned back the processes of socialist revolution in Ghana, and so betrayed the African people in their struggle for total liberation and unification.' Seeking exile in Guinea he lived in a 'secluded villa by the sea' and pondered his plight. At first, he issued proclamations and empty threats: the imperialist 'agents and stooges' could never 'destroy the socialist gains we have achieved. For no reason other than their morbid ambition, inordinate and selfish desire for power, certain officers had rebelled against him. But over time, he began to reassess his enforced retirement from the historical stage. Perhaps his political philosophy, his comprehension of social forces, had been incorrect. His 1966 essay ' "African Socialism" Revisited' marks a partial shift away from his 'African Personality' thesis towards historical materialism. He criticized Senghor's cultural version of socialism as 'metaphysics,' and suggested that 'the view that the traditional African society was a classless society imbued with the spirit of humanisim' was undoubtedly a 'facile simplification.' In 1970 he revised *Consciencism* to include his new 'conclusions on the various processes of the African Revolution, the nature of the struggle which lies ahead, and the practical implementation of our socialist revolutionary objectives.'

Toward the last years of his life, Nkrumah called for the creation of African revolutionary parties, based on an alliance of the peasantry, rural proletariat wage workers, and the revolutionary intelligentsia. However, he now overcompensated for the gradualism and reformist policies of his earlier career. Nkrumah condemned as 'sham independence' the achievement of political self-rule, as in Ghana in 1957, and advocated 'genuine independence, the product of a mass political movement or an armed liberation struggle . . . Socialist revolution is impossible without the use of force. Revolutionary violence is a fundamental law in revolutionary struggles.'[142] In his enforced isolation from the actual national liberation struggles across Africa, Nkrumah substituted a mechanical, quasi-Fanonist analysis for Marxism.

Some of the most provocative criticisms of Nkrumah's post-coup writings have come from Soviet scholars. 'Despite the extreme diversity of conditions and tasks of the democratic, revolutionary movement in various countries and parts of Africa,' Soviet theorists noted, 'Nkrumah recommended all to use his universal method – armed struggle, which was an exaggeration of the role of armed struggle, its fetishisation, and a reaction to his own defeat.' The Soviets criticized Nkrumah's rejection of 'the tactics of a united anti-imperialist front,' and his Fanon-like condemnation of the entire African bourgeoisie as 'a counter-revolutionary force.' Finally, Soviet scholars sharply condemned Nkrumah's traditional goal of Pan-Africanist unification as 'misguided,' 'harmful,' and 'quite unrealistic, ignoring completely both the total absence of the conditions for such an organisation and the essential heterogeneity of the African revolutionary movements . . . '[143]

Nkrumah died on 27 April 1972 in Bucharest, Rumania. The body was returned to Ghana, accompanied by Botsio. The NRC regime held a major state funeral, and flags throughout the nation were lowered to half-mast. The legacy of Nkrumah still perplexes his critics. Samin Amin suggests that Nkrumah attempted to 'fight the landed trading class by means of the urban bureaucracy, instead of looking for genuine organized popular support. Nkrumah's mistake was not to go far enough.'[144] But C.L.R. James points correctly to Nkrumah's fundamental failure — an inability to comprehend the centrality of democracy to the dynamics of national liberation. Without a thorough commitment to popular democracy, workers' participation, and complete freedom within the framework of socialist construction, the road to Bonapartism is short indeed. As James observes: 'Nkrumah's great political error was this. He believed that the question of democracy was a matter between him and Danquah and Busia and Appiah and such. He never understood that democracy was a matter in which the official leaders and an opposition were on trial before the mass of the population. It is not a question of conflict between rivals for power, as so many who shout 'democracy' believe . . . Nkrumah was very energetic. But, overwhelmed with work, Nkrumah depended more upon the party and less and less upon Parliament. But here his shallow concept of democracy found him out.'[145]

3

Socialism From Above

Social Democracy, Military and Civil Bonapartism In Africa and the Caribbean

> Nationalization with an antidemocratic state structure and an increasing managerial bureaucracy under the control of the ruling party has put the political rulers in a position analogous to that of the former expatriate owners. Their use of state resources, privileges and facilities stamp them as a bourgeoisie of a new type, occupying with increased license the gap left by foreign business . . . Control of the state gives the new rulers the juridical base from which they seize the social surplus to divert it not only to personal consumption, but to private accumulation with the aim of building indigenous capitalism.
>
> Working People's Alliance
> Guyana, 1979

> It is good that the cook will be taught to govern the state; but what will there be if a Commissar is placed over the cook? Then he will never learn to govern the state.
>
> Nikolai Bukharin,
> 1918

In recent years, many socialists have argued that transitions to socialism cannot be successful within peripheral social formations. Extreme structuralists have insisted that the construction of socialist societies in Africa and Latin America must await 'the demise of the dominance of the world-capitalist system,' and that any effort of 'a single state to make the transition is doomed by the compromises it necessarily has to make for its survival.' Some leftists identified with the Trotskyist political tradition have written that 'only an internationalized revolution can create the conditions for a [peripheral] socialist transition.'[1] And some democratic socialists take the position that there are 'two Marxian preconditions for socialism — a productive economy and a conscious working class'; hence virtually all peripheral states are by definition devoid of 'the material preconditions for a just society.' One prominent American socialist declared in 1972: 'The peasants and the urban poor are not a substitute for the proletariat; the economy of a backward nation does not provide the material basis for socialism. The best and most enthusiastic will in the world cannot transcend these cruel limitations . . . Socialist faith is not a substitute for the proletariat.'[2]

This essay takes the opposite view. National liberation movements in societies that have experienced both capitalist exploitation and imperialist domination have frequently acquired a socialist political perspective. The beginning stages of a transition to socialism depend upon three principal variables. First, the internal struggle for state power — that is, the control over the administrative bureaucracy, police, army, courts, etc. — must be decided in favor of those parties or social forces which favor the ultimate abolition of the private ownership of the central means of production, and the democratic empowerment of working people and peasants in politics and the economy. Second, a substantial segment of the proletariat and peasantry — preferably a clear majority — must no longer perceive the old regime as legitimate, and must actively endorse policies favorable to a socialist transition. Before this can occur, the old ruling class and its political representatives in the state apparatus must lose their hegemony over the other classes. Elements within the local political culture must be sympathetic to socialist ideas and the insurgent movement's programme. The third variable is the 'international conjuncture.'[3] External political conditions should favor, on the whole, a transition to socialism. The absence of any of these factors can and has led to the defeat of socialist movements in the periphery.

This scenario raises several important theoretical and strategic questions. Does the seizure of state power have to be led by a traditional Marxist-Leninist or Communist party? To date, this has not occurred anywhere in the Caribbean or Africa. In Cuba, the Popular Socialist (Communist) Party appears to have been almost more of an impediment to the revolutionary movement than a key actor. During the 1940s, the PSP briefly collaborated with dictator Fulgencio Batista. The Party knew nothing about Castro's plans to attack Santiago's Moncada barracks on 26 July 1953. After Moncada, the PSP spared little invective in denouncing Castro's 'putschist methods,' which were only 'peculiar to bourgeois factions.' As the guerrilla movement escalated in the late 1950s, the

PSP reevaluated its position towards Castro, but retained its mistrust. PSP militant Carlos Rafael Rodrigues joined the rebels, but noted subsequently that Castro was 'not an ideological comrade' due to 'prejudices built upon a lifetime of exposure to anticommunism.'[4] In the early years of the revolution, the PSP dominated the united political formation of Marxists and progressives, the Integrated Revolutionary Organizations (ORI). Under PSP leader Anibal Escalante, the ORI fell into dogmatism and sectarianism: new leadership posts were given disproportionately to former PSP members, and a bureaucratic, 'patronage-dispensing machine' rapidly emerged. Only through Castro's direct intervention in 1962 was the ORI's sectarianism reversed. Six years later, Escalante was found guilty of plotting against the government in a 'pro-Soviet' conspiracy. When the new Communist Party of Cuba was finally formed in 1965, only about one fourth of the Central Committee members were veterans of the former PSP. No former Communist was a member of the secretariat or politburo.[5]

In Guinea-Bissau, revolutionaries were confronted with a situation where, at least according to some Western socialists' standards, a national liberation movement culminating in a socialist transition was simply impossible. The overwhelming majority of the population consisted of peasants, frequently engaged in pre-capitalist modes of production. The traditional chiefs and artisans were closely tied to the Portuguese authorities. Most of the small, urban African petty bourgeoisie was either heavily committed and compromised with colonialism, or was politically neutral. And the tiny African wage-earning working class had acquired 'an extremely petty bourgeois mentality' and was inclined to simply 'defend the little they had already acquired.' For Amilcar Cabral, the solution was to build a core of dedicated revolutionists, recruiting cadre from the radicalized petty bourgeoisie, the peasantry, and the 'declasses' — the young, unemployed labourers recently arrived from the rural areas. The African Party for the Independence of Guinea-Bissau and Cape Verde (PAIGC) trained approximately one thousand cadres at its party school in Conakry, and established a country-wide network to wage political and military conflict against the Portuguese colonial system. 'For a revolution to take place,' Cabral observed in 1964, 'depends on the nature of the party (and its size), the character of the struggle which led up to liberation, whether there was an armed struggle, what the nature of this armed struggle was and how it developed and, of course, on the nature of the state.' Cabral added: 'We are not a Communist party or a Marxist-Leninist party but the people now leading the peasants in the struggle are . . . connected with the urban wage-earning group. When I hear that only the proletariat can lead the struggle am I supposed to think we have made a mistake? All I can say is that at the moment our struggle is going well.'[6]

Another important question is whether the transition to socialism in the third world can ever be initiated through electoral means. The example of Chile continues to be debated on the left. Chile's 1833 Constitution had existed for nearly a century, and its 1925 Constitution was still in force when Salvador Allende was elected president in 1970 as the candidate of Unidad Popular, a coalition of left parties. Moreover Chile's political culture was based on a deeply entrenched tradition of parliamentarism and civil liberties. True, the Communist Party had been outlawed by the state in 1925-35 and 1948-58. But until the early 1970s, the last signficant Chilean political assassination had occurred in 1837. Chilean socialists and communists alike therefore concluded that a transitional strategy towards socialism could be realized through established, legal norms. Whatever valid criticisms one can make of the Allende government's tenure, one should at least recognize that its intention was to take policy measures which would promote the peaceful transition toward a democratic, socialist society. In his discussions with Regis Debray, Allende firmly placed himself in the radical tradition of Sandino. He argued that socialist transformation would necessarily assume different forms: ' . . . in the guerrilla *foco* or in urban insurrection; it may be the people's war and it may be an insurgence through the polling booths; it depends on the content it is given.'[7] One of the left's central errors was to assume that the Chilean capitalist class and military would permit the government to undermine their interests without resorting to a violent struggle. In the face of radical legislation, the traditional 'partnership' between the state and dominant classes, which is characteristic of bourgeois democracies, broke down. As Ralph Miliband observed: 'Chile had know class struggle within a bourgeois democratic framework for decades: that was its tradition. With the coming to the Presidency of Allende, the conservative forces progressively turned class struggle into class war . . . as far as the conservative forces are concerned, electoral percentages, however high they may be, do not confer legitimacy upon a government which appears to them to be bent on policies they deem to be actually or potentially disastrous.'[8]

The quest for a general theory of socialist transformation in peripheral states led Soviet scholars in the 1950s to develop the 'non-capitalist path' thesis. The successes of the first wave of national liberation movements coincided with a general shift within the USSR's foreign policies toward increased awareness and involvement in African affairs. Soviet scholars suggested that the newly independent states might seek socialist developmental lines without experiencing social revolutions. In I. Andreyev's *The Non-Capitalist Way*, for example, the author argued that *both* the national bourgeoisie and working classes in peripheral societies are at odds with the established interests of imperialism. Consequently, peripheral Marxists should engage in long-range alliances with the national bourgeoisie, in forming a 'non-capitalist' social order. 'The non-capitalist way is not socialist development proper,' Andreyev noted, 'but a specific period of creating the material, social and cultural conditions for transition to socialist development — a pre-socialist stage, when the nation-democratic state follows a socialism-oriented policy at the democratic, that is, anti-imperialist and anti-feudal stage of the revolution.'[9] The major characteristics of a 'non-capitalist'-oriented state were a firm oppposition to Western foreign policies; a general nonaligned position which was sympathetic to existing socialist states; and a powerful state apparatus which controlled local economic development.

There are many obvious theoretical and practical problems with this 'non-capitalist road' thesis. Some Marxist theorists, notably Fitzroy Ambursley and Robin Cohen, have protested that 'the theory of non-capitalist development has no real basis in the writings of Marx, Engels and Lenin . . . the real origins of official communist 'stagism' as required by the theory . . . are the neo-Menshevik theses advanced by Stalin during the 1920s.' Ambursley and Cohen argue that the thesis 'mystifies the objective nature of the process it describes with vague talk of "bypassing the capitalist stage." '[10] The theory of non-capitalist development is virtually silent on the question of building working-class institutions, or in suggesting tactics and strategies to increase the political power of the proletariat vis a vis the national bourgeoisie. Nor does it systematically develop the distinct differences between peripheral states with long-established bourgeois democratic institutions versus states dominated by military regimes. Perhaps the most concise critique of the thesis was made by C.Y.Thomas in 1978. Thomas observed that the gradualistic non-capitalist strategy applied by the Unidad Popular forces in Chile had reaped disaster. In general, the non-capitalist path thesis overestimates the patriotic and anti-imperialist characteristics of the peripheral national bourgeoisie. It fails to address the specific economic measures and programs such states should take as underestimating the pivotal role of workers' parties in leading a democratic transition to socialism. It also ignores the international conjuncture, the role of US imperialism in promoting counter-revolutionary groups inside such societies, and the ability of western capitalism to conduct campaigns of economic disruption. Most crucially, Thomas noted, the theory minimizes the pivotal role of democratic rights in the very definition of socialism: 'Anyone who has read Marx must know that the concept "dictatorship of the proletariat" refers to the sociological domination of the working class. This domination does not mean any such trite and superficial political notion as authoritarian and tyrannical government . . .'[11]

Criticisms of the non-capitalist development thesis, combined with political reversals suffered by the Soviets in Egypt, Indonesia, Mali, Sudan, Ghana and other peripheral states, led to a rethinking of the entire strategy. In the mid-1970s, Soviet scholars researching national liberation movements developed the theory of 'socialist orientation.' Whereas in the 1960s the Soviets had tended to address only the external pressures of imperialist destabilization which could upset the transition to socialism in non-capitalist-oriented regimes, they now examined peripheral states more closely, recognizing internal contradictions that could lead to a reversal of the social developmental process.

Karen Brutents's two-volume study, *National Liberation Revolutions Today* (1977), made a distinction between 'national liberation' which represents the earlier movements abolishing colonial oppression, and 'national-democratic revolution,' which embodies those social forces which favor 'anti-capitalist transformations, paving the way for transition to socialist reconstruction. In contrast to national liberation revolutions of the past, national-democratic revolutions are not carried out primarily in the interests of the bourgeoisie or the exploiting classes as a whole, and their social orientation cuts across the aspirations of these classes.' Brutents characterized the national-democratic forces as only a *'tendency* making headway — or suffering defeat — in conflict with the other, contending tendency backed by domestic and external class forces seeking to confine these revolutions to a bourgeois or bourgeois-democratic framework.' Many governing third world parties often exhibit *both* tendencies. Under the 'reformist' category, Brutents placed

Kenyatta's KANU, the Indian National Congress prior to 1969, and Senghor's Union Progressiste Sénégalaise (UPS); in the national-democratic camp were Nyerere's TANU, Nkrumah's defunct CPP, Touré's Party Democratique de Guinée (PDG), Algeria's FLN, and the Iraqi Baath party. But unlike some earlier Soviet scholars, she emphasized the acute ideological and political fluidity within these formations: 'In actual life, the dividing line between the reformist and the revolutionary wing does not run only *between* the various parties, but equally *within* them . . . there are [also] important differences within the conservative-reformist (as within the revolutionary democratic) trend, because of the different condition of the local bourgeoisie and the acuteness of its contradictions with imperialism, and the concrete balance of strength between the bourgeois and the petty-bourgeois advocates of these theories.'[12]

Brutents and other Soviet researchers continued to criticize pro-Western and capitalist-oriented national bourgeois elements, particularly the 'bureaucratic bourgeoisie.' 'The privileged bureaucratic section most frequently has a peculiar parasitic philosophy, looks to the joys of the present and by its plunderous activity in a sense even hampers capitalist development,' Brutents commented. In the 'second phase' or post-independence period, the national bourgeoisie as a whole 'ceases to play the role of motive force of the national liberation revolution, which is why it cannot be its leader.' And yet, Brutents added numerous qualifications to these cutting remarks. Her sharp criticisms of the bureaucratic bourgeoisie 'applied mostly' to its upper sections, since 'party functionaries,' civil servants, and minor administrators often could be anti-imperialist. The urban petty bourgeoisie was 'even more inclined than the peasantry to strike up rebellious attitudes.' And even the army, under certain circumstances, could 'act in the role of revolutionary force.' Thus in 'the socialist-oriented countries,' whether dominated by the 'progressive' armed forces or by various combinations of reformist national bourgeoisie, petty bourgeois and proletarian fractions, 'the national state serves as an instrument of resolute anti-imperialist struggle and deep-going social transformations in the interests of the masses.'

The practical implications of this line of analysis were major. Within peripheral societies, Communists should initiate strategic united fronts with the national 'patriotic' bourgeoisie. Other social classes represented within these fronts would include the proletariat, peasantry, urban intelligentsia, and the petty bourgeoisie. 'Unity of action can be achieved only through constant efforts,'

Brutents emphasized. 'Communists want to consolidate anti-imperialist alliances and make them lasting.'[13] States of 'socialist orientation' have specific socioeconomic and political characteristics. As outlined by Anatoly Dinkevich, these include: 'liberation from capitalist monopoly domination', expanded public sector ownership and the curtailment of the socioeconomic power of the local bourgeoisie; democratic agricultural and land reforms, including 'a cooperative movement launched on democratic principles'; 'a democratized state machine, the involvement of representatives of the working people in government, and the granting of genuinely democratic rights and freedoms to the peoples'; the establishment of literacy campaigns and public education; and the legal 'establishment of a vanguard party of scientific socialism.' Other criteria are state control of all media and general support of the Soviet bloc in foreign affairs.[14]

The Soviet theories of non-capitalist development and socialist orientation, as well as the failures of 'focoist' guerilla movements in the Congo, Peru, Guatemala, Bolivia and other countries in the 1960s, affected the thinking of many Marxist parties throughout the periphery. Cuba provides an excellent example. In 1966, at the Tri-continental Conference held in Cuba, Fidel Castro endorsed guerilla warfare, implicitly rejecting the 'revisionist,' reformist strategies of some Communist parties: 'The struggle on this continent, in almost every country will take the most violent forms, and as we know this fact, the only correct course is to prepare for it.' Nine years later, when Cuba hosted the Conference of Communist Parties of Latin America and the Caribbean, the gradualist theory of the non-capitalist path and the building of revolutionary democratic united fronts became the new regional orthodoxy. In early April 1975, a conference of Arab Communist parties similarly announced: 'One of the most important phenomena in the Arab national liberation movement is the emergence of parties . . . which in class terms, belong to the petty bourgeoisie, but have raised themselves to the position of revolutionary democracy.'[15]

This basic shift on questions of multiclass political alliances in the transition to socialism within the periphery was as significant in many respects as the Popular Front line which emerged from the Seventh Comintern Congress in 1935. But as in the implementation of Popular Frontism, there were certain ambiguities. A state of 'socialist orientation' might indeed permit Communists to participate in reform programs which dispossessed reactionary elements, greatly increased literacy and public health, initiated land reform, broadened the national trade union movement, and so on. But the hegemonic, non-Marxist-Leninist forces within the so-called democratic anti-imperialist front which actually exercised control over the state apparatus might also use these statist initiatives to empower themselves as a new bureaucratic-bourgeois stratum. As Fred Halliday and Maxine Molyneux have pointed out, the non-capitalist path of development in Iraq, Egypt, Somalia and the Sudan 'concealed a process of class formation that laid the basis for a new acceptance of capitalism, with the necessary changes in internal social structure and international alignment.' Even the nationalization of industry and banking establishments may simply 'secure the conditions for the development of national capitalism.'[16] Moreover, the taxonomy of states of 'socialist orientation' varied from year to year, and depending upon who was classifying the regimes. Brutents praised Tanzanian 'revolutionary democracy' for its agricultural and peasant policies, which were a 'moving force in the construction of the new society . . . ' Brutents also cited Siad Barre of Somalia, Algerian leader Houari Boumediene, Syrian President Hafez Assad, Marien Nguoabi of the Parti Congolaise du Travail, Touré, Nyerere, and Nkrumah as among the leading 'revolutionary democrats' who favored 'the principle of a mixed economy . . . at least during the transition period, [a] combination of a public (i.e., state and cooperative) with a private sector.' In every instance, revolutionary democratic regimes 'advance the slogan of building socialism.'[17]

In the late 1970s, Soviet leaders reached something of a revised consensus in constructing their 'socialist orientation' list. Somalia was deleted, Afghanistan, Nicaragua, and Grenada were added; the other non-capitalist regimes were Benin, Burma, Libya, Angola, Tanzania, Mozambique, Guinea-Bissau, Cape Verde, Congo, Malagasy, Guinea, Ethiopia, São Tome, Algeria, Syria, and South Yemen. Because of the Soviets' long-standing ties with Jagan's PPP, the Communists weren't certain whether to designate the Guyanese regime of Forbes Burnham as 'socialist oriented.' However, as Ambursely and Cohen note, 'at least three Caribbean proponents of official communist orthodoxy' have accorded the title of socialist orientation to the PNP government of Michael Manley in Jamaica (1972;1980), and even Burnham's PNC regime.[18] Despite Burnham's anti-communist and anti-Castro rhetoric of the 1960s, diplomatic relations were established between Cuba and Guyana in 1972. Three years later, Burnham was given Cuba's pretigious Jose Martí Award.[19]

Of course, any categorization of socialist peripheral and semi-peripheral states is a difficult matter. Yugoslavia and Zimbabwe, among several other countries, share many of the characteristics of 'socialist-oriented' states, but usually aren't cited. Perhaps a more accurate method of differentiation would be to arrange these states into four overlapping groups, which deliberately exclude those states which are specifically dominated by Marxist-Leninist parties. The first category consists of 'social democratic' governments, in which the ruling party has a rhetorical and, to some extent, programmatic commitment to a liberal reformist agenda.[20] Politically, these states (e.g., Jamaica under Michael Manley and Senegal) have parliamentary systems and a multiparty elections. The parties reject insurrectionism and are committed to the postcolonial institutional arrangements of the state. Although they respect constitutional procedures, they will employ authoritarian means and systemic violence to ensure their electoral control. A mixed economy exists, but the interests of multi-national corporations and the conservative national bourgeoisie predominate. In effect, a sometimes uneasy partnership exists between capitalism and the ruling party.

The second and third general categories of leftist regimes are 'state capitalist' governments — civil and military. For half a century, there has been an extensive theoretical debate among Marxists over this controversial term. Specifically, I am *not* referring to the various arguments of Milovan Djilas, Tony Cliff, Charles Bettelheim, Max Schachtman, and many others over the years who have attacked 'bureaucratically-deformed' socialist states, or denounced Stalinist 'state capitalist' states in which the ruling party and public officials constitute a 'new class.' In peripheral societies, there is tremendous ideological and social fluidity within the state bureaucratic stratum. Within almost every regime, there are multiple ethnic, national minority, cultural and political differences, which frequently lead to conflicting and competing blocs within single parties, and shifting clientage or patronage systems of rewards to various segments within the petty bourgeoisie and bourgeoisie. There is often simultaneously *public* accumulation in the form of state-directed programs, and *private* accumulation both within the existing private sector and also among party bureaucrats who use their positions or authority within the state to enrich themselves. Given the political weakness of the wage-earning proletariat, its current inability to become a hegemonic class, the bureaucracy undoubtedly serves, to some extent, a progressive role. The regime expands the cooperative and state-owned sector, carries out land reform, education and health improvements, and sometimes expands the trade-union movement. But it does this generally within a mono-organizational framework. Most — but not all — state capitalist regimes are one-party governments. Democratic rights, freedom of the press, free speech, etc. are severely curtailed. Trade unions are controlled by party-selected bureaucrats, and authoritarian means are frequently used to smother proletarian and peasant dissent.

In *civilian-directed* state-capitalist regimes, the party is dominant. It acquired state power through anti-colonialist agitation and mobilization, but usually not through protracted guerrilla warfare. Some of these regimes were initially pro-Western, favorable to continued multinational exploitation, and anti-Communist (e.g., Ghana, Tanzania, Guyana). Others assumed a more pro-Soviet foreign policy, and initiated the post-colonial period with a series of statist reforms (e.g., Guinea, Mali). But, in both cases, the ruling party's administration was merged with that of the state apparatus; the government's agencies were soon used to finance the growth and social control of the parties. Political authority was greatly centralized, and the lower-to-middle levels of the party itself atrophied. In *military-directed* state capitalist regimes, coups d'etat were usually utilized to replace unpopular or politically discredited regimes (e.g., Ghana under Jerry Rawlings, Nasser's Egypt, Somalia and Ethiopia); although in the instance of Grenada's short-lived Revolutionary Military Council, a coup was launched against a relatively popular and successful prime minister.

In both civil and military state-capitalist regimes, government policies promote the development of new social groups and classes, and depending upon local and international factors, the 'non-capitalist' regimes can create new forms of traditional capitalism, and embrace imperialism. Somalia and Egypt are certainly two notable examples. Both the civilian and military variants of state-capitalist regimes are potentially Bonapartist, especially if a deliberate demobilization of the masses occurs, and the state's political base deteriorates to the point that the upper levels of the bureaucracy and the army are the only direct beneficiaries of the government. It is at this point that the state appears to be detached from civil society, and coercion becomes the only method of social control.

Finally, there are the 'revolutionary democracies.' They are also directed by a hegemonic party, usually organized roughly along

Marxist-Leninist lines. They achieved power outside of the parliamentary process, either through guerrilla warfare or political insurrections with the overwhelming support of the population (e.g., Nicaragua, Grenada, Guinea-Bissau, Mozambique, Angola). The party controls the state apparatus, but a healthy degree of political and social pluralism exists. Although public-sector corruption exists, there are clear sanctions against the abuses of authority. Mass organizations (e.g., women, youth, workers, farmers) are encouraged, and to some extent have a degree of autonomy in action from the party *per se*. Economically, there is a growing public sector, but private investment is not forbidden. The military is specifically subordinate to the party, and mass civil defense formations are developed. Within the revolutionary democracies there are, of course, many possible contradictions: an authoritarian tendency toward statist abuses ('commandism', privileges within the party's elite) as well as an egalitarian 'substitutionist' tendency, which builds a populist-style leadership cult and substitutes the party's bureaucratic decision-making for the more time-consuming process of popular discussion and mass participation. Revolutionary democracies uniformly have a difficulty distinguishing between critics of public policies who stand, nevertheless, in solidarity with the revolution, and those critics who are the vanguard of imperialism. The inability to preserve the democratic right to dissent *within* the institutional boundaries of a new society can lead to the political isolation of the party from its mass base. The Bonapartist danger here is the degeneration of the party itself; the democratic dictatorship of the workers and peasants becomes the dictatorship of the party apparatus over and above society.

All attempts of social categorization are to some degree arbitrary and schematic. Zimbabwe, for instance, has many characteristics of revolutionary democracies like Nicaragua, together with some of the fairly grim traits found in Touré's Guinea and Nkrumah's Ghana. What makes any kind of classification difficult is that in every left-oriented peripheral society, social class struggle continues. Some states may successfully develop internal economic structures which are 'socialist,' but evolve statist, authoritarian political institutions which eliminate genuine freedom for working people and suppress all manifestations of legitimate dissent. Others may retreat from state-ownership, and return to free market economies; and still others may make the transition towards socialism and proletarian democracy. The class struggle within each society is pivotal in determining the future evolution of the state.

I

Jamaica is one of the few peripheral capitalist societies which has maintained a two-party electoral system approximating those found in the West. The two major parties, the Jamaica Labour Party (JLP) and the People's National Party (PNP) were founded by the island's leading national politicians, Alexander Bustamante, the conservative head of the Bustamante Industrial Trade Union (BITU), and nationalist barrister Norman Manley. Between 1944 and 1972, both parties developed partisan multiclass constituencies which provided stable electoral bases from which national elections were contested. The JLP drew its support from the rural peasantry, trade unionists in the BITU, the marginal petty bourgeoisie, and decisively, from most of the national bourgeoisie and virtually all capitalists. Parochial in social outlook and conservative in political ideology, the JLP seemed more preferable to the capitalists than the Fabian-socialist-oriented PNP. Manley's party attracted the bulk of the educated, affluent petty bourgeoisie and considerable labor support, but was not as strong as the JLP in rural areas. Because it advocated a more progressive version of nationalism than the JLP, and favored modern statist reforms, it also attracted a small but articulate Marxian left wing. After their initial period of organization, both parties consistently controlled dependable electoral blocs. In the five national elections between 1949 and 1967, the JLP won 3 elections, gaining an average of 45.3 percent of the popular vote in all five contests; the PNP won only 2 national elections, but received a slightly higher popular vote average of 49.5 percent.[21]

Despite their continuous verbal joustings, the JLP and the PNP were remarkably similar in most respects. Both parties were controlled internally by 'maximum party bosses' (Bustamante and Manley), who exercised authority through networks of multiple patrons, brokers and clients. As political scientist Carl Stone comments: 'The top leadership . . . including the party leaders, the parliamentarians, and the principal party officials, are essentially patrons or political bosses. The middle-level leadership of party organizers and local government officials are primarily brokers or intermediaries who provide the points of contact and communication in the spoils system of benefits distribution, promising rewards or actually allocating them . . . Individual survival and mobility up the ladder of power depends on careful cultivation of the goodwill of the party boss or leader, which demands unquestioning personal loyalty.'[22]

Socialism from Above 163

On policy issues, both parties also displayed more continuity than conflict. The JLP minimized popular mass participation in non-electoral politics, while the PNP generally encouraged it; the PNP advocated increased state intervention along Keynesian lines, while the JLP favored private sector initiatives for growth and somewhat limited state involvement. But both parties supported education and literacy programs, state-financed housing for low income workers, and social welfare expansion. 'Both party governments,' Stone observes, 'have promoted import substitution via the local manufacturing sector, heavy reliance on North American loan financing for infrastructural development and public expenditure, government ownership of utilities and some productive enterprises.'[23] Both formations were willing to permit the British colonial regime 'to dictate the pace of decolonialization,' so formal independence was not achieved until 1962. Perhaps the most significant differences between the parties emerged in the late sixties, when the ruling JLP government inclined toward state authoritarianism. In October 1968, the regime banned the entry into the country of Pan-Africanist scholar Walter Rodney, who held a post at the University of the West Indies. This precipitated the 'Black Power Riots', and the state responded by banning all Black Power and socialist literature and increasing its repression against leftists.[24]

Michael Manley became the PNP's 'maximum leader' after his father's death in 1969, and was elected Prime Minister in 1972. Little in his prior history indicated much sympathy for Marxism or the left in general. Manley's successful campaign employed the political cultural symbols and populist discourse designed to appeal to the urban poor and working class — e.g., 'Power to the People.' Reggae music and a populist style were complemented by a traditionally liberal PNP policy agenda which disavowed any kinship with radical socialism. The result was a major PNP triumph: 56.1 percent of the popular vote, and 36 parliamentary seats to the JLP's 17 seats. The PNP measured very small gains in rural peasant and very poor working class communities, but in larger urban centers with large percentages of petty bourgeois and working-class voters, it won by substantial majorities. Thus in Kingston, St. Andrew and Montego Bay, Jamaica's three largest metropolitan areas, the PNP's majorities over the JLP were respectively 8 percent, 24 percent, and 43 percent; while in Kingston's more affluent petty-bourgeois areas, it received 75 to 80 percent of the popular vote.

Predictably, the PNP's first two years in office brought only a more liberal version of the JLP's policies. On one hand, some of the island's most prominent capitalists received senior appointments in the state bureaucracy. On the other hand, foreign-owned telephone, bus and electric companies were nationalized with compensation, and a modest rural reform ('Project Land Lease') was launched. Despite the elevation of former Black Powerites D.K. Duncan and Paul Miller to government posts, radicals were clearly in the minority. Many Jamaican Black nationalists who had gravitated toward Marxism continued to condemn the PNP government as a liberal bourgeois, neo-colonialist regime. A number of them formed the Workers' Liberation League in 1974, which was led by Black Communist Trevor Munroe. A caustic critic of Manley, Munroe denounced any overtures toward cooperation with the PNP: 'This call, far from hastening revolutionary social and political change, amounts to strengthening the national bourgeoisie, dragging out and prolonging the agony of the people. It is a call to give up revolution and take the path of reform, since any alliance with the bourgeoisie can only be on the basis of the bourgeoisie, the basis of reform.'[25]

Severe oil price increases and escalating inflation rates in 1973-74 led to a PNP 'left turn'. A domestic austerity program was approved, as the nation's oil import costs jumped from $150 million in 1973 to $1180 million in 1974. A production levy was placed on all Jamaican bauxite, increasing the tax rate by 480 percent. Revenue from this levy increased the state's earnings from $125 million to over £1170 million. Social programs were expanded and further reforms initiated including a poor people's 'self help' housing project, the generation of jobs for the chronically unemployed through the 'Pioneer Corps,' public legal aid clinics, and free university education. In late 1974, the PNP announced a detailed party programme of 'Democratic Socialism,' which still advocated a multi-class alliance, but within a context of growth in public services, cooperatives and related statist reforms. Jamaica's foreign policy also shifted considerably to the left. Manley visited Cuba in 1975, and the Marxist state began to provide educational and economic assistance to Jamaica. The PNP expressed its complete solidarity with the popular revolutionary movements in southern Africa, the MPLA and FRELIMO.[26] As a result, Manley became something of a charismatic, international symbol of third world militancy and nonaligned socialism — although his 'leftist' identity was actually more akin to that of his Mexian counterpart, Luis Echeverría, than to Fidel Castro.[27]

But Washington was not prepared to sit back and watch Jamaica 'turn to Communism'; the Ford administration was convinced that Manley's populist-styled democratic socialism was fundamentally dangerous to US interests. US aluminium corporations cut their bauxite imports from Jamaica by 30 percent. The US Agency for International Development rejected the PNP's request for food. American travel agents informed clients that Jamaica was 'unsafe' and tourist receipts declined by 23 percent in only two years. Meanwhile US government assistance to Jamaica fell from US $13.2 million in 1974 to US $2.2 million in 1976. All of this had the effect of pushing Jamaica's national bourgeoisie toward openly hostile relations with the reformist state. At least $1200 million was smuggled out of the island during 1975-76 by the bourgeoisie and affluent middle strata. Some JLP leaders established a liaison with the CIA, possibly to prepare conditions for a coup d'etat. JLP lieutenants shipped arms into the country; in July 1976 JLP member Peter Whittingham was 'arrested on suspicion of involvement in the political violence.' At least seven CIA officers and four key 'collaborators' were working out of the US embassy in Kingston in efforts to destabilize the government.[28]

The political crisis of 1975-1976 produced basic changes inside the Jamaican left. Manley was no longer ridiculed and dismissed as a petty-bourgeois populist, but viewed as a major spokesperson of the non-capitalist periphery. The Marxist tendency within the PNP became a more significant force inside the party. D.K. Duncan became general secretary, in command of 50,000 party activists and organizers. A socialist youth wing of the PNP expanded rapidly. To the left of the PNP, Jamaican Marxists were forced to reevaluate their positions. Munroe's WLL was directly influenced by the Communists' non-capitalist path thesis, as well as the new political line of the 1975 Havana conference, which urged cooperation with the liberal reformist national bourgeoisie. The League, which was soon renamed the Workers' Party of Jamaica (WPJ), announced a new policy of 'critical support' for the PNP.[29]

The active role of the left, and especially the mobilization skills of Duncan, were an important factor in the PNP's parliamentary victory in December 1976. The massive voter turnout was 872,000, 84 percent of the electorate. The PNP received 56.9 percent of the popular vote, and 47 out of 60 parliamentary seats, the largest popular mandate any Jamaican party had received since 1944. A closer analysis of the 1976 election, however, reveals a sharp reduction of PNP support among its traditional patrons in the petty bourgeoisie and 'better-off' working class. Two constituencies with large concentrations of petty-bourgeois voters switched from the PNP to JLP. High income neighborhoods in Kingston and St. Andrew voted for the JLP by over 70 percent. Where the PNP achieved its greatest gains were among youth, the unemployed, and low-income workers. For the first time, the two-party system seemingly assumed a more finite class-oriented realignment, with the JLP representing the upper to middle strata, and the PNP speaking mainly for the poor and working masses. Leftist PNP leaders became convinced that the victory 'signalled the beginnings of a one-party PNP monopoly based on solid socialist mass support.'[30]

The first months of the PNP's second term witnessed the acceleration of democratic-socialist reforms. Manley rejected the IMF's proposals for massive concessions and refused its credit line. The government established the State Trading Corporation to control external trade, nationalized Barclay's Bank, and instituted higher tax rates on the national bourgeoisie. The left pressed for even more substantial changes. Some called for a new Jamaican Constitution modelled on the Cuban constitution. Others agitated for further nationalizations and a revised legislative and executive political structure which would be more accountable to the masses. Marxist political economist Norman Girvan was named chief technical director of the National Planning Agency, and supervised the drafting of a 'People's Plan' as an alternative to the IMF loan programme. Girvan writes: 'The People's Plan . . . envisaged rejection of IMF loans, some modest changes in the structure and organization of production, especially by developing community economic organizations, and further diversification of trade and financial relations towards socialist, social-democratic, and non-aligned countries.'[31] The Jamaican national bourgeoisie feared that another 'Cuba' was now a distinct possibility, and some fled to the USA. Thousands of workers were laid off by businesses cutting back in production. The PNP reached its political moment of truth by mid-April 1977. It could either press forward a fully socialist reorganization of society, which simultaneously would have probably meant the purge of the PNP's extreme right wing, or it could retreat from the brink, and return to its gradualist 1972-73 policies.

Manley retreated. Girvan suggests that the Prime Minister 'made the political judgement that his Government could not have managed the dislocation in jobs and supplies in the urban areas that doing without the IMF money would have entailed.'[32] The rising star of the PNP's anti-Communist right wing, P.J. Patterson, had already been appointed to the foreign ministry, and he made overtures to the Washington for 'friendly relations.' Manley accepted the IMF's harsh terms, slashed social services spending, froze wages, and devaluated the Jamaican dollar by almost 40 percent. This represented a more austere economic programme than the JLP had ever initiated. As Jamaican workers' living standards rapidly deteriorated, the PNP shifted back to the right to regain its old support among the petty bourgeoisie. Duncan was pressured to resign as general secretary; conservatives like Eric Bell (Finance Minister) were elevated into leading positions. The PNP's return to conservative populism reduced its standing in all opinion polls. According to Carl Stone, the PNP's popularity fell from 48 percent vs. 37 percent for the JLP in October 1976, to a 32 to 28 percent plurality for the JLP by June 1978. Significantly, the percentage of Jamaicans polled who were 'non-party and anti-party' jumped during this period from 15 to 40 percent. Stone notes, 'Mass alienation towards the regime quickly replaced the euphoric populism that surrounded the 1976 election victory . . . Cynicism and hopelessness replaced vibrant populist optimism . . . '[33] Anti-Communist rhetoric inside the PNP's ranks was permitted again. In early 1978 speaking before the Jamaican parliament, Eric Bell warned: 'if any member of the People's National Party is a communist and avowed to be a communist then they are entitled to be expelled.'[34]

The PNP left could have broken from Manley at this point, establishing itself as a viable, mass third party, perhaps in conjunction with Munroe's WPJ. This did not occur. Some leftists still believed that the party would eventually return to the left before its credibility disintegrated among workers. Although Stone estimated that about 30 percent of PNP's electorate 'gave support to the Marxist-Leninist route,' this bloc was not aggressively organized against Manley. At the same time, the WPJ was accommodating itself to the PNP's conservatism. The Marxists organized a national campaign against IMF concessions, but opportunistically refused to attack the PNP leadership for its capitulation. WPJ theorist Cecil Nelson justified the party's conciliatory tactics by arguing against any leftist criticism of Manley. 'Any opposition by a left, not strong enough to lead this opposition, is going to end up in the strengthening of reaction.' Even Castro, during his 1977 Jamaican visit, expressed some support for the PNP's pragmatic policies and criticized 'ultra-leftism.'[35]

The political currents shifted again in 1979-1980, as the Carter administration adopted a more reactionary approach to Caribbean policy matters. In October 1979, Carter authorized the formation of a Caribbean Joint Task Force to 'ensure the ability of troubled peoples to resist social turmoil and possible communist domination.' Six months later, the State Department promoted the formation of the Caribbean-Central American Action Committee, an organization of large corporations with regionwide investments. At least fifteen CIA operatives were inside Jamaica by early 1980; and in June of that year, an American 'right-wing fanatic,' Charles Johnson, tried to initiate an unsuccessful coup against the PNP. Political violence escalated between JLP and PNP supporters, with 350 people killed between February and June 1980.[36]

As national elections approached, the heavy cost of the PNP's second-term U-turn became self-evident, even to Manley. A return to a left-oriented strategy was ordered. Discussions with the IMF were broken off, and Duncan was renamed PNP general secretary. Bell resigned as finance minister and was replaced by a leftist. But the PNP's hasty manoeuver was too little and too late. Unemployment stood at 27 percent on election day; the working class was disillusioned and demobilized. The JLP's slick election campaign was run by a New York public relations firm. The fiercely anti-socialist newspaper *Daily Gleaner* informed voters that a JLP administration would receive substantial funds from abroad. One JLP popular slogan promised to 'Make money jingle in your pocket.' Through a mixture of propaganda and armed terrorism, combined with the programatic bankruptcy of the PNP, the conservative JLP won nearly 59 percent of the vote and 52 of 60 parliamentary seats.[37]

Since 1980, the JLP and its leader, Prime Minister Edward Seaga, have taken decisive steps to consolidate a pro-capitalist, authoritarian state. In the first place, Jamaica has become more closely integrated into regional US-dominated networks. Through President Ronald Reagan's Caribbean Basin Initiative, Seaga received US $50 million. Another US $4 million was spent to equip the Jamaica Defense Force; Jamaican soldiers were sent to Puerto Rico in 1980, 1982, and 1983 for special training. Reagan vowed to make Seaga's regime America's principal surrogate in the Carribean: 'Free enterprise Jamaica, not Marxist Cuba, should serve as a model for Central America in the struggle to overcome poverty and move towards democracy.'[38] Moreover, Manley's defeat was the signal to capitalism that fiscal and political conditions for investment were again favorable. In April 1981, the IMF gave the JLP regime a loan of US $698 million on very generous terms, while the US Congress granted Jamaica 'most favored nation' status.

Despite these and other benefits, the popularity of Seaga's regime began to plummet after mid-1982. The PNP social welfare programs were slashed, while official unemployment rates remained at approximately 25 percent. Economic austerity reduced the real wages of workers, while inflation placed the cost of everyday household items and food beyond the reach of thousands of poor people. The economic crisis deepened in 1983, when Seaga devalued the Jamaican dollar by 43 percent. Three years later, the official exchange rate stood at an incredible ratio of J$5.50: US$1.00. In early 1985, when the regime hiked gasoline prices, thousands of poor and working class people staged a two-day riot. After six years in office, the JLP's popularity in public polls was only 20 percent. The popular mandate for 'Jamaican Reaganomics' had been destroyed.[39]

After the PNP's electoral debacle of 1980, Fitzroy Ambursely predicted that Manley's defeat buried any hope for a renaissance of Jamaican social democracy: 'When the Jamaican masses do make another lurch to the left, it will not be under the banner of "Democratic Socialism." Bourgeois nationalist-populism has had its day in Jamaica.'[40] This statement seems premature for several reasons. The PNP shifted back to the right in 1981-1984, eliminating Duncan as general secretary again, and placing considerable distance between themselves and the WPJ. It noticeably reduced its level of street activism and worker political mobilization. But not until the collapse of the JLP regime's economic policies did substantial sections of the middle class return to the PNP's ranks after an eight year hiatus. P.J. Patterson dominated the proceedings at the PNP's 1984 convention, while Manley seemed confined to the honorific post of charismatic senior statesman. From my vantage-point, Duncan and the PNP left appeared isolated and largely ineffectual.

At the next parliamentary elections, a rejuvenated but ideologically neutered PNP should handily defeat the JLP. But at this point, it does not appear likely that the left will be in ascendancy. The WPJ continues to moderate its public image, going so far in the mid-1980s as to make friendly overtures to religious organizations. Although the WPJ has recently crept upwards to 5-10 percent in public opinion polls, it has a very long path to tread before it can seriously compete for power within the bourgeois democratic electoral system. Carl Stone points out that a vast majority of Jamaicans including a majority of 'democratic socialists', still have negative reactions to Communism.[41] The complexity of Jamaican political culture lends itself to multiclass alliances, and Westminster parliamentarianism is so deeply established that the left would have a difficult time achieving a majority to pursue radical transformation of the state apparatus.

For these reasons perhaps, the Cubans have expressed their strong opposition to any premature split on ideological grounds within the PNP. But a schism of some sort appears inevitable, possibly within the next decade, as the next PNP government will probably fail miserably to resolve the island's structural socioeconomic problems.[42] Girvan has criticized the PNP's recent official programme for not mentioning socialism 'as an objective in the economic programme as such.' Girvan continues: 'There is also a notable absence of policies of income redistribution and major new or expanded social programmes . . . The PNP's programme, then, recognizing the constraints of the present material base, seems to aim merely at managing the existing situation as best it can, while attempting to alleviate some of the worst effects of austerity on the poor.'[43]

Manley might not disagree at all with Girvan's main point. The PNP is not designed to *transform* society, but to *manage* an unequal social order with a degree of compassion for the poor. But inevitably this strategy will run its course. Jamaica's workers and unemployed will have to be convinced for themselves that liberal paternalism is meaningless. Duncan observed in 1985: 'My view on the PNP's real economic policy is that it's a watered down, more humane version of Seaga's economic policy. [The PNP] has returned to what it was originally, a party of reform and not a party that transforms . . . A Social Democratic party capable of mild reforms which definitely cannot meet the aspirations of the people.'[44]

II

The once-celebrated 'non-capitalist' path in Guyana has produced a draconian regime, under the authoritarian rule of Forbes Burnham and the People's National Congress (PNC). The beginnings of the Burnham dictatorship go back to 1962-1964, when the destabilization efforts of the CIA, the British government and conservative forces inside Guyana undermined the pre-independence Marxist government of Cheddi Jagan. In the December 1964 elections, Jagan's People's Progressive Party (PPP) received 45.8 percent of the vote, an increase over its electoral percentage in 1961. But the British imposed a new proportional representation system on the country. Under the new rules, the PNC, which had received only 40.5 percent, and a minor conservative party, the United Force (UF), formed an unsteady center-right government. After independence was granted in May 1966, the PNC-UF coalition government pursued conservative domestic and international policies. The head of the UF, Peter D'Aguiar, served as Finance Minister and developed a neocolonial economic strategy. Rice exports to Cuba, which comprise an important share of Guyana's agricultural trade, were halted to express support for the US trade embargo against the Castro government. The dominant political characteristic of the regime even at this early stage was widespread corruption and clientage. Thomas J. Spinner notes that in one instance, 'the director of audits was unable to produce proper vouchers for almost G$20 million of government expenditures. The PNC even thrust the party faithful into the supposedly impartial civil service, judicial, and police service commissions.'[45] But the government's graft, although conducted at a vast level, was not atypical of other neo-colonialist, capitalist regimes in the periphery. The ambitious leaders of the PNC did not yet exercise full control over the state apparatus.

The December 1968 Guyanese elections represented the first decisive step towards authoritarianism. Officially, the PNC achieved an absolute majority, 55.8 percent of the popular vote, and 30 legislative seats, to the PPP's 36.5 percent (19 seats) and UF's 7.4 percent (4 seats). However in a truly democratic contest, the PPP would have won a majority with little difficulty. But the PNC's total included 34,000 votes cast by Guyanese living overseas. Another 19,000 'proxy' votes were cast, almost all favoring the PNC. Polling places in PPP constituencies closed early, or were not opened at all. Some Guyanese went to vote and were informed 'that a proxy had already been exercised for them.'

Burnham's 'victory' permitted him to control the state apparatus without a coalition partner, and, even more importantly, to initiate a purge of rival PNC leaders. As Reynold Burrowes notes, virtually all the members of the PNC-UF cabinet 'had a political base of his or her own.'[46] Burnham's techniques virtually duplicated those of Nkrumah. Several months before the 1968 election, Burnham convinced one UF and two PPP members of parliament to defect to the PNC. In late 1968, legislation was narrowly passed giving the leader of each political party the power to select any individual members to serve in the legislature after elections. This greatly reduced the political independence of all party representatives, and essentially severed any direct elective relationship between the voters and parliamentary members. And in early 1969, a number of prominent PNC leaders were dropped from the parliament by Burnham, and promptly replaced by more youthful non-entities. As they owed their new positions to the PNC party leader, the new legislators were in no position to challenge him.

Burnham's 'turn to the left' occurred in 1970, predating Manley's conversion to socialism by four years. In Guyana's case, a 'noncapitalist' orientation for development was the logical consequence of local political culture. The majority of Guyanese workers belonged to unions whose leaders claimed some identity with Marxism. Furthermore, as Clive Thomas comments, the 'PNC's need to use the state to transform itself into a national class meant that it had to adopt a popular socialist rhetoric if this process was to be made acceptable to the masses.' Like Manley, in a somewhat different context, Burnham's rhetoric was cast in a populist discourse. In August 1969, Burnham outlined his decision to create a 'cooperative socialist republic' to PNC members: 'Our basic proposition is this: the organization of our human and material resources through the cooperative movement, with government providing financial assistance, management, training and administrative direction.' Such a commonwealth would permit 'the small man to own large and substantial business enterprises . . .'[47]

In the span of several years, the regime nationalized 32 corporations, including three utilities and four financial institutions. In 1971 the Demerara Bauxite Company was bought for US $107 million. Five years later, with the purchase of eight large sugar companies and other firms, the state directly owned or controlled roughly 80 percent of the national economy. The new parastatals were run by the Guyana State Corporation, whose chairman was of course Burnham. The direct control of these enterprises permitted private accumulation by PNC officials to grow at a rapid rate, under the nominal guise of socialism. An opportunistic, parasitic clique of politicians was quickly making the transition to becoming a bureaucratic bourgeoisie.

Accompanying Burnham's 'left turn' were new foreign policy initiatives. In December 1970 diplomatic relations were established with the Soviet Union. Guyana became involved in the nonaligned nations movement, and Burnham publicly pledged to donate US $50,000 per year to assist 'the freedom fighters in Southern African.' In August 1972, Guyana hosted the Caribbean Festival of

Creative Arts, which permitted the regime to appear progressive on questions of regional political culture. To the festival participants, Burnham attempted a crude imitation of C.L.R. James: 'This festival is an attempt on the part of the people of the Caribbean to identify themselves, their history, their strains, their habits, their way of life. That, no man can take from us, no bomber, no war ship.'[48]

Burnham began to attract some support from prominent West Indian and Afro-American intellectuals, who accepted at face value the leftist pronouncements of the Guyanese state. Afro-American novelist/actor Julian Mayfield, who had previously worked as an aide to Nkrumah, moved to Guyana in 1971. Evidently Mayfield was impressed, because he wrote a stirring defense of Burnham in the US publication, the *Black Scholar*, in 1973. 'Forbes Burnham is the head of the political establishment in his country, and it is puerile to make anything evil out of that,' Mayfield declared. ' . . . Not a single other West Indian leader has offered sanctuary to Black political refugees. Only Forbes Burnham has done it.' Mayfield agreed with local critics of Jagan and the PPP: ' . . . Jagan's Marxist cover really [hides] an East Indian racist . . . Burnham was first and last an African of considerable political genius who must also be a national leader if he were to unite the entire country.' When Burnham was interviewed by Black American poet, Marvin X, in 1972, he emphasized his solidarity with Black Power and racial pride: 'Our Government favors the emancipation of the Black man wherever he may be . . . we welcome Black Americans with the skills, the interest in helping us develop the country . . . Here the Black man is a full man. There ain't no white boss 'round here, in social terms, political terms, or economic terms . . . '[49]

In conjunction with this Black nationalist and socialist rhetoric, the regime gradually extended its patronage network to several thousand people, rewarding loyal subjects who faithfully supported the PNC from below. After another fraudulent election in July 1973, in which the PNC claimed 37 legislative seats to the PPP's 14 seats, Burnham 'took a number of steps to ensure the survival of his party in office without a popular base.' In November 1974, Burnham announced fundamental changes in the relationship between the ruling party and the state apparatus, which would permit the PNC to become 'the major national institution.' The party and state were merged into a new united institution called the Office of the General Secretary of the PNC and the Ministry of National Development. Under this new state body, the PNC was given full use of all state resources and public funds. In 1975, a ten percent 'levy' was placed on the wages of all public sector employees and armed forces, which was given to the PNC. The party/state used these resources to place its cadre in charge of all types of organizations within civil society. The PNC dominated the Guyana Teachers' Association, the Mineworkers' Union, and the Public Service Union. In order to control delegate conferences of Guyana's trade unions, the party/state created 'phony' unions with nonexistent memberships, such as the Government Employees' Union and the Public Employees' Unions.[50]

Throughout the early and mid-1970s, the political position of Jagan and the PPP was exceedingly difficult. The PNC had begun to call itself a 'Marxist-Leninist party'; leaders of nonaligned and socialist states such as Castro and Nyerere expressed fraternal greetings and solidarity with Burnham. The 1975 regional conference of Communist parties, held in Havana, had urged unity with 'revolutionary democrats' pursuing a non-capitalist path towards socialism. Jagan shifted theoretical gears and tried to apply the new line to Guyanese conditions. Speaking before the PPP annual conference in August 1975, the veteran Marxist urged his party to use a 'more flexible approach' towards the PNC, because the PPP had 'no monopoly on socialism.' Jagan was now prepared to work with Burnham in 'building socialism in Guyana . . . Our political line should be changed from non-cooperation and civil resistance to critical support.' For several years, the PPP pursued the will-o'-the-wisp of coalition government — but over a decade after Burnham might have accepted the offer. In August 1977, Jagan called for a 'National Patriotic Front Government, including all parties and groups which are progressive [and] anti-imperialistic . . . '[51] The proposal called for a power sharing arrangement between the PNC, PPP and other small progressive formations. A new cabinet would be selected from members of both parties; the nationalizations initiated in the early 1970s would be expanded to include insurance companies and all financial institutions; human rights would be protected, and all future elections would be conducted fairly and democratically.

The PPP's coalition initiative was flawed, however, for several reasons. Although a majority of PPP stalwarts dutifully supported the coalition proposal, some were confused and disoriented. Why had the PPP suffered in the political wilderness, when the PNC was an acceptable partner in the construction of socialism? A few leading PPP members carried Jagan's argument to what they believed to be its logical conclusion: they resigned from the PPP and embraced the PNC. Ranji Chandisingh, the party's chief Marxist theoretician, left the PPP in 1976. He later charged that Jagan and his former comrades 'were less interested in socialism and the unity and well-being of the Guyanese people than in furthering their ambitions for personal power and prestige.' Chandisingh was convinced that 'the PNC had demonstrated its commitment to socialist transformation and development in deeds, not merely in words . . .'[52]

The PNC had every reason to reject Jagan's attempt at diplomacy. The party's hierarchs already dominated the state apparatus; several hundred PNC middle level members would probably be demoted or lose their positions in a power-sharing situation. The PNC elite was on the verge of becoming an authentic statist bourgeoisie, and Jagan's talk of multiracial reconciliation was simply ignored. Burham informed his bureaucratic lieutenants that unity was out of the question: 'the Bolsheviks had not compromised with the Mensheviks.' In retaliation, PPP sugar workers staged a massive strike, which lasted 135 days. As production came to a halt, Burnham brought 'scabs' from Georgetown to work in the fields. Even PNC supporters were expected to 'spend a few hours each day cutting cane.' Burnham's regime finally broke the strike, but at a heavy cost to both sides. Many sugar workers never recovered their jobs, and others were jailed. But Burnham's popularity among thousands of Black laborers disintegrated. By 1978, the regime's actual social base had eroded to negligible proportions: A Bonapartist state.[53]

The regime's major constituency had become the agencies of coercion. All members of Guyana's fire departments, militia, police departments, and the Guyana Defense Force were now required to swear a loyalty oath to the PNC. Security forces increased at staggering rates. In 1964, there were two thousand police and soldiers; thirteen years later, there were more than twenty thousand. A fascist-style militarization of civil society occurred. The People's Militia was expanded; new armed units included the Young Socialist Movement and the Women's Revolutionary Socialist Movement. Military expenditures soared from G $8.8 million in 1973 to G $48.7 million in 1976. By the mid-1970s, at least one of every 35 Guyanese citizens was 'a member of one or other military or para-military group . . . Besides providing the ruling party with a formidable means of deterring opposition, incorporating large numbers of urban unemployed into the military also ensured that they did not themselves become a focus of opposition to the government.'[54]

The regime also relied indirectly on the bizarre and disruptive presence of several religious cults inside Guyana. Two notorious examples were the House of Israel and the Rev. Jim Jones's People's Temple. The former established a core of followers among Georgetown's Black unemployed, who were used to disrupt PPP public meetings. Jones meanwhile was allowd to bring firearms and drugs into the interior, where he had his followers established 'the Jonestown experiment in cooperative socialism.' PNC officials accepted bribes from Jones, and permitted him full independence running his own authoritarian rural village. When over nine hundred residents of Jonestown were discovered as murder and suicide victims in November 1978, the PNC government succinctly responded: '(it's) essentially an American problem. We're just unfortunate that they came.'[55]

A major recurring problem of most statist, authoritarian social formations like Guyana is the deterioration of production capacity and living standards for the working class. The bureaucratic bourgeoisie's vast corruption, incompetency, and coercion leads to the emigration of thousands of skilled labourers, technicians and professionals. About 90,000 Guyanese migrated between 1970 and 1980. Sugar production declined from 369,000 tons in 1971 to 285,000 tons nine years later. Alumina production declined from 312,000 tons in 1970 to 211,000 tons; dried bauxite production fell from 2.3 tons to 1.6 tons in the 1970s. To finance the nationalization schemes, the Burnham regime was forced to incur massive debt, which in turn limited state expenditures for necessary social services. Clive Thomas notes: 'The public debt, which stood at G $267 million in 1970, had risen to G $673 million in 1974, and to G $1.3 billion in 1976; at the end of 1981 it was over G $3.1 billion.' The regime tried to cope with the crisis by printing money. 'Between 1973 and 1975 the money supply doubled and between 1975 and 1977 it grew by a further 38 percent.' But consequently the inflation rate also increased by at least 70 percent between 1975 and 1980; real per capita income declined by 15 percent, and the unemployment rate reached 40 percent. Thomas continues: 'All the major public services: electricity, pure water supply, public transport, postal services, telephones, and sanitation have deteriorated so much as to constitute major bottlenecks in the production process. Thus electricity 'outages' occur for several hours daily in the main production and residential areas. Public transport is so poor that workers' representatives claim that as many as four hours per day on average have to be spent on commuting to and from work.'[56] The state's response to public criticism was to destroy freedom of speech and all democratic rights to media access. Guyana Broadcasting Service was owned by the state, and in the late 1970s the British-owned Radio Demerara was also purchased by Burnham. The PPP's newspaper was virtually forced out of business, and in 1974 the state bought the *Graphic* daily newspaper.

The failure of the PPP to provide a powerful left opposition to Burnham's Bonapartist regime created a political space for various smaller formations. Most of these organizations' leaders were former members of either the PPP or PNC. Ascria [Association for Social and Cultural Relations with Independent Africa] had been founded by Eusi Kwayana (Sydney King) in 1964. Kwayana had served briefly as the PNC's general secretary, and in the late 1960s was head of Guyana's Marketing Board. Breaking with Burnham over the party's massive corruption and authoritarian practices, Kwayana and his supporters in Ascria developed a constituency among more progressive Afro-Guyanese. The Indian Political Revolutionary Associations (IPRA) was led by an attorney, Moses Bhagwan, who had been expelled from the PPP in 1965 for 'excessive revolutionary zeal.'[57] The Working People's Vanguard Party (WPVP) was headed by Brindley Benn, Jagan's former Minister of Natural Resources and Deputy Premier in the early 1960s. Benn had been purged from the PPP in 1966.[58] Another small revolutionary group formed in 1969, Ratoon, was largely comprised of intellectuals at the University of Guyana, including Marxist political economist Clive Thomas. These four organizations merged in late 1974 to create the Working People's Alliance (WPA). In the coalition's initial public statement, the Alliance promised to build a truly multiracial mass movement against the PNC, which would create a national 'program of justice through democratic socialism.'[59]

The outstanding revolutionary intellectual of the WPA was Walter Rodney. In both theoretical and political terms, Rodney was a descendent of C.L.R. James, a proponent of Pan-Africanism, Marxism, and popular democracy.[60] Best known for his classic study *How Europe Underdeveloped Africa*, Rodney had been hired as professor of history at the University of Guyana, but Burnham blocked the appointment. Rodney and Thomas developed a critique of the PNC government which departed significantly from the non-capitalist road thesis of the PPP. They argued that what the PNC had created was not 'socialism' but a 'dictatorship of the petty bourgeoisie,' a social class which was using its state control over the economy in an attempt to transform itself into a full-fledged bourgeoisie.' Rodney was convinced, notes Trevor A. Campbell, that 'despite anti-imperialist slogans and fancy pronouncements about socialism . . . the old state built up under colonial and neocolonial conditions had not been smashed, and the oppressive internal class structure had not been fundamentally altered. Rodney was aware that the struggle against neocolonialism would be as difficult, and perhaps more complex, than that against direct colonialism.'[61]

Rodney undertook various political assignments for the WPA, believing very strongly that all members had to illustrate their dedication to the democratic struggle. When sociologist James Petras questioned Rodney's safety inside Guyana, and the capacity of the PNC regime to commit political murder, Rodney replied: 'There's only one way to bring about basic changes in Guyana or any Third World country, and that's by working with the people in the country. I have to run the same risks as everyone else.'[62] In well-attended public addresses in Guyana, Rodney repeatedly ridiculed the government, referring to Burnham as 'fat boy' or 'King Kong.' By 1978, according to Reynold Burrowes, Rodney 'had succeeded in antagonizing the government more than any other politician had.' Rodney frequently promised that a WPA-led government would act as a 'firing squad' to prosecute corrupt bureaucrats and party officials. 'His words must have caused many a government minister to shiver.'[63]

Burnham's reponse to the WPA's challenge was increased repression. In 1978, the PNC passed a new constitution which gave Burnham virtual dictatorial powers. The regime actively sought the physical elimination of WPA activists and supporters. In July 1979, five WPA leaders including Rodney were arrested and charged with burning a government building. In the previous year, Moses Bhagwan was viciously beaten by a PNC gang, and suffered a fractured hand; Martin Carter, Guyana's most prominent poet and ex-PNC supporter was severely assaulted by Burnham's agents. WPA members' homes were bombed, and in November 1979 WPA activist, Ohene Koana, was slain by police.

Burnham's bloody suppression of the independent left was, of course, appreciated by the US government. A number of Burnham's police officers began to be retrained at the CIA-financed International Police Academy in Washington, D.C., including the chief of the Guyana Defence Force. The US increased its aid to the Burnham government from US $2 million in 1976 to almost US $25 million in 1978. The Carter administration viewed Guyana in the same political league as Somalia and Communist

China, a nominal socialist regime which outlawed democratic rights at home and was willing to become a junior partner with US imperialism. Even during Burnham's flirtation with the Cubans, Washington recognized the opportunistic nature of the regime. In 1977, Assistant Secretary of State for Inter-American Affairs, Terrence Todman, observed: 'Guyana is seeking a different path to social and economic development, one with which we have no quarrel and which we have no reason to fear.' Two years later, the US ambassador to Guyana stated that differences between the two governments were not critical: 'The important thing is of course the existence of a bond of friendship and mutual respect of both sides which can prevent such differences from becoming acrimonious and harmful.'[64]

The WPA began to make preliminary plans for armed struggle, in the face of their inability to obtain any democratic concessions from Burnham. But what form would this struggle take, given the PNC's domination of the military and police, its vastly superior firepower? Speaking to Sam Silkin, a British member of Parliament, Rodney expressed his abhorrence of violence, but also asked, 'at what stage is a people justified in taking up arms against its oppressive government?'

But Burnham was not perplexed by matters of political philosophy or ethics, when his power was being threatened. On the night of 13 June 1980, Rodney was killed by an antipersonnel bomb that had been planted inside a walkie-talkie device. Rodney's probable murderer, Gregory Smith, was a former member of the Guyana Defence Force, and had been ordered to join the WPA as a 'disaffected' Burnhamite. Three days after Rodney's death Smith was flown out of Guyana. Burnham had hoped that Rodney's murder would go unnoticed in the Caribbean, but he was wrong. Manley attacked the murder as 'a wanton and brutal action and an assault against humanity'; Maurice Bishop, Prime Minister of Grenada, declared that 'only imperialism and reaction can benefit from this murder'; Castro termed the killing 'barbaric' and sent Cuban officials to Rodney's funeral.[65] More than 25,000 Guyanese — Indians, Blacks, Chinese and whites — participated in the vast funeral procession. George Lamming observed: 'It was a people's funeral. Earlier in the day, thousands of Guyanese had walked a distance of over twelve miles behind the murdered body of this young historian. He was not the first victim of political murder in Guyana, but the radical nature of his commitment as a teacher and activist, the startling promise that his life symbolized, made of his death something of a novel tragedy. Directive had gone out to government employees that they should avoid this occasion; yet no one could recall, in the entire history of the country, so large and faithful a gathering assembled to reflect on the horror that had been inflicted on the nation. For Guyana had become a land of horrors. The question was whether it would survive this official crucifixion.'[66]

Nevertheless, Burnham's regime survived. In December 1980 the PNC conducted another orchestrated election and, to no one's surprise, achieved another landslide victory. The WPA boycotted the election; on the other hand, Jagan and the PPP participated, refusing to confront the fact that their participation in a corrupt process helped to legitimate the dictatorship. It was a perverse partnership which Burnham recognized. Speaking before the national assembly in 1980, he declared: 'As long as the People's Progressive Party exists, the PNC will be automatically entrenched by its ally, the PPP . . . Some people make very good bridesmaids but never brides; still, they should be part of the matrimonial entourage on terms to be decided by the bride.'[67]

Upon Burnham's long overdue demise in 1985, the PNC selected the vice president for economic planning, Desmond Hoyte, as their new leader. But conditions continued to deteriorate. Food shortages worsened in 1982-83, and thousands of workers depended solely on supplies from the black market. In 1984 the regime devalued its currency by 25 percent, as demanded by the IMF. Medical facilities in Guyanese hospitals virtually 'collapsed,' notes Thomas Spinner. 'The water supply in the capital was permanently brown and smelly. Shortages of teachers and books placed Guyanese students at the lowest educational level among the Caribbean countries.'[68]

Why did the WPA fail to remove the PNC state capitalist dictatorship? I am not referring to the obvious difficulties involved in this maneuver: the development of countervailing forces strong enough to divide or defeat the PNC's military and police. Nor is it a question of social and political hegemony, since the PNC has forfeited any remaining shreds of legitimacy to 90 percent of the population. The broader issue is, in part, a question of revolutionary strategy and tactics in the politics of a neocolonialist state. C.L.R. James suggested in 1981 that one of Rodney's primary weaknesses was that he 'had not studied the taking of power.' No one doubts that 'Burnham is a catastrophe for Guyana,' James observed. 'But that is not enough.' Any social insurrection requires at minimum three elements: 'Firstly, there must be a clash, a revolutionary upsurge of the people. Then, secondly, there must be a turning point, when the activity of the advanced ranks is at its height; and thirdly, the enemy must be vacillating.' James argues that these precise conditions did not converge in Guyana during the 1970s. The Guyanese proletariat detested Burnham, yet most of the workers weren't prepared to mount a 'revolutionary upsurge' against the state. The PNC was besieged, but it never lost its confidence that it could control the protracted crisis. The armed forces did not split from the bureaucratic administration. 'Walter was expecting a civil war,' James states, 'but the people of Guyana were not ready for civil war.' Tactically, the WPA also should not have permitted Rodney to engage in any activities which potentially risked his life. The events leading to Rodney's assassination represent 'a political mistake. It was not a mistake in personal judgement. It was because [Rodney] was doing all sorts of things to show [WPA members] that a revolutionary is prepared to do anything. And that was not the way.' James emphasizes, 'It is the business of a political organization to protect its leaders . . . '[69] All revolutionary parties must learn 'how to retreat' and 'how to work legally in the most reactionary of parliaments,' Lenin also observed. 'We must not regard what is obsolete to us as something obsolete to a class, to the masses . . . You must soberly follow the actual state of the class-consciousness and preparedness of the entire class (not only of its communist vanguard) . . . '[70]

In September 1981 the WPA concluded that violent social revolution was not yet on the agenda. Calling for renewed civil disobedience campaigns, the party stated that Guyanese working people could not endorse 'armed struggle' until 'all peaceful means have been used and set aside.'[71] By 1984 the WPA became an associate member of the Socialist International, and distanced itself from the PPP. The WPA's leaders insist that party members do not juxtapose 'Leninism as against social democracy,' but desire to build a party 'most suited to meet the needs of the struggle against dictatorship.' The WPA remains fully committed to 'political pluralism, tolerance of internal dissent, free pluralist elections, press freedom, and open party debate.'[72] There is an obvious pitfall in the WPA's decision to engage in a nonviolent 'war of position' against the PNC regime. The grossly distorted features of the Burnhamite apparatus make a return to bourgeois democracy seemingly desirable. But should state capitalism under a bureaucratic bourgeoisie be replaced by liberal capitalism directed by Caribbean Fabian socialists, possibly repeating the errors of Manley and the PNP in Jamaica?

The WPA's long-term task is to develop a synthesis of revolutionary democratic principles and Marxian organizational forms within the party, structures that promote free discussion and debate, while simultaneously organizing the masses against the regime. It does not seem likely that a Cuban-style guerilla strategy would be successful in removing the PNC regime; so the WPA needs to continue to develop strategic alliances with all democratic, anti-PNC social forces. Certainly a desirable relationship would be a united front between the PPP and WPA, but regrettably, Jagan's party has forgotten that the duty of revolutionaries is to make revolution. Because of the country's political ordeal under Burnham, the authentic Guyanese socialism of the future will undoubtedly reflect Rodney's democratic and egalitarian orientation. 'In the context of historically determined under-development there can be no development to socialism that is not based on justice,' writes Clive Thomas. 'Political democracy and socialism are therefore not counterposed as far as working-class interests are concerned. They are counterposed by the propagandists of the ruling class only in order to bolster its claims to hegemony.'[73]

III

The closest African parallel to the regime of Forbes Burnham was the authoritarian state capitalism of Sékou Touré in Guinea. Like the PNC, the Partí Démocratique de Guinée (PDG) quickly developed the 'paramountcy principle' within several years after acquiring formal independence. Technically, the Constitution provided for the existence of legal opposition parties, but by the early 1960s, the PDG was the only functioning national political formation. In 1962, one half of Guinea's adult population held membership in the party. The PDG developed mass organizations for women — the Comité National des Femmes — and for youth — Jeunesse de La Révolution Démocratique Africaine. Twenty-six-thousand PDG cells were established in villages and rural areas. However, in 1964-65 Touré and other PDG hierarchs decided to drastically reduce the size of the party, eliminating thousands of workers and agriculturalists from the process of political decision-making. The number of party committees in Conakry, the capital, was reduced to fifty, with a membership ceiling of thirty thousand. Criteria for party membership became much more rigid. A new party structure called the Pouvoir Révolutionaire Local (PRL) was initiated which established party cadre 'brigades' in education, public works, communication, production, marketing and health. The PRLs 'assured the PDG control over labour unions, youth, women's organizations and state enterprises.'[74] The autonomy and power of Guinean trade unions vis-a-vis the state was consequently greatly diminished. As E.J. Berg and J. Butler observed in 1964, Guinea's labour unions had been 'taken over' by the PDG, 'the labour movement, if not completely subordinated to the party, is at least pliable and responsive to party pressures.'[75]

The upper levels of the PDG used their access to state funds for personal capital accumulation even in the early 1960s; according to John Cartwright, 'observers remarked on the luxury villas built by high government and party officials, both for their own enjoyment and to rent out for hard currency to foreign missions.'[76] There was also a growing personality cult, largely fashioned after Nkrumah's. Touré was the 'Guide Supreme de la Revolution.' 'In every field, from agriculture to philosophy to soccer, he was portrayed as an expert. More than twenty volumes of his speeches and reflections upon Guinean and African development were published and made compulsory reading . . . No major decision could be taken without his approval.'[77]

The PDG's hegemony over Guinean working people was secured, as in Burnham's PNC, by the military. In 1966 eight thousand party members were mobilized in 'civic brigades' to help the army monitor the security of the towns, ports, airports, banks and oil reserves, as well as to check the growth of prostitution and black-marketeers.[78] The Guinean army was 'completely integrated into civilian administrative structures,' notes Olatunde Odetola.[79] To ensure his personal authority within the party-state bureaucracy, Touré ordered political trials and purges of all real or suspected rivals. When Guinean entrepreneurs and petty bourgeois leaders initiated the Parti de l'Unité Nationale de Guinée in 1966, the PDG quickly suppressed the small formation. The abortive party's leader was subsequently arrested and sentenced to death. In 1969 Touré ordered the arrest and execution of his defense minister, Fodeba Keita, and anti-Touré politician Diawadou Barry on charges of collaborating with 'French, Ivorien, and Senegalese agents to overthrow the regime.'

After a 1970 invasion by Portuguese and Guinean exiles was successfully thwarted by Touré's military, he exploited the emergency to eliminate other internal critics. In a series of show trials, ninety-one death sentences were ordered. Victims were often lynched in public. In July 1971, eight army officers were executed. That same year, Touré arrested Diallo Alpha Abdoulaye, his former foreign secretary and UN representative. He was brutally tortured by electric shock, and ordered to sign a 'confession' linking him to a conspiracy involving the CIA, the British Secret Service, and even the Nazis. He was subsequently imprisoned without trial for ten years.[89] In 1976, Touré authorized the arrest and torture of other PDG leaders; the next year, his militia murdered several market women who had demonstrated against government policies in front of the presidential palace. 'By 1977, very few of Sekou Touré's close political associates had survived unscathed,' comments John Cartwright. 'Of the 71 ministers and secretaries of state he had appointed, nine had been shot or hanged; eight had died in detention; 18 were doing hard labour for life, and another 20 had served prison terms . . . five had escaped abroad; and only eleven had avoided condemnation.'[81]

The regime's economy was structured along heavily centralized, top-down lines. Immediately after independence, the government challenged the economic domination of French export-import establishments by founding a parastatal that took over most of the nation's external trade. The role of the state within the economy was tremendously expanded. Samir Amin estimates the state expenditure increased from 7 billion Guinean francs in 1959 to 16 billion in 1969; 'The growth rate of this expenditure (8.5 percent a year) was certainly higher than that of the material base of the economy.'[82] Initially there was a series of economic mobilization projects termed 'investissement humaine,' in which workers 'voluntarily' built schools, hospitals and other human service-oriented institutions. However, the real purpose of investissement humaine was to exploit unpaid labour-power in the construction of private homes for party bureaucrats and government buildings. Land reform policies were similarly designed. In 1959 all land was declared to be 'in the public domain.' Two years later, the regime ordered landowners to begin cultivation on unused properties, or face confiscation. 'In practice, this meant that the local Party chairman or his relatives gained preferred access to the land.'[83]

Rural cooperatives and collectivization projects also yielded discouraging results. The Centre de Modernisation Rurale (CMR) was started, which used state funds to provide agricultural supplies and equipment to rural collectives. The Centre National de Production

(CNPA) established seven state-owned farms and 16 'national production centres.' Nearly five hundred rural cooperatives with 60,000 participants had also been created by 1962. But inefficient planning, rampant state corruption, inadequate supplies and the lack of technical assistance led to the rural sector's near-collapse. Both the CMRs and CNPAs soon dissolved. Coffee production fell nearly 50 percent between 1963 and 1975; millet production dropped from 146,000 metric tons in 1963 to only 65,000 metric tons in 1972; rice production rose slightly, 350,000 metric tons in 1964 to 400,000 metric tons a decade later. Overall population growth (2.8 to 3 percent per year) consistently outstripped food supply growth (2.3 percent average annually). 'As a result,' Yansané notes, 'the importation of 60,000 tons of rice cost the Guinean Treasury 15 to 25 million US dollars in the early 1970s.'[84] As in Burnham's nationalization programme, Touré proceeded cautiously with Western capitalists. The French-owned Bauxites de Midi was nationalized in 1961, but other bauxite companies concluded state partnership deals with the PDG, usually giving Guinea 49 percent ownership. One large bauxite mine remained privately held until 1973, when the PDG agreed to 49 percent ownership and 63 percent of all profits from the company.

In social as well as economic terms, Guinean state capitalism failed to produce meaningful improvements in the lives of workers and peasants. Touré and his party made no special effort to increase the political power of women, or to address their specific needs. Helen Ware notes that at least 90 percent of all Guinean women above the age of 15 were illiterate as of 1965. In 1970, 32 percent of Guinea's primary school students and only 19 percent of all secondary school students, were females. Polygyny remained a flourishing institution, with 160 married women to every 100 married men. About 75 percent of all Guinean women still lived in polygynous unions.'[85]

Over two decades, at least 500,000 Guineans emigrated from their country, while from exile both liberal and leftist critics tried to alert progressive world opinion to the consequences of Guinea's authoritarian social system. Claude Rivière observed: 'To set up a cannery without products to can, a textile factory that lacks cotton supplies, a cigarette factory without sufficient locally grown tobacco . . . all these were gambles taken by utopian idealists . . .'
To his left, Samir Amin added: 'Since the growth in numbers of employees was much faster than that of the product, the potential unemployment implied by urban growth seems to have been largely

absorbed by over-manning in government and the nationalized industries . . . [Growth] was uneven, giving practically no benefits to the peasants, and changing the social structure very little after independence . . . The public sector became bureaucratic and inefficient; this led to continual inflation which aggravated social imbalances and was only partially contained by an increase in foreign indebtedness . . . '[86]

Touré's international political reputation, however, was maintained by his rhetorical commitment to the non-capitalist developmental thesis and to militant Pan-Africanism. In 1967, Touré's essay in *World Marxist Review* defined 'socialism' as a 'definite stage of historical development which is followed by communism.'[87] In the *Black Scholar*, Touré condemned 'the monstrosity and the cruelty of capitalism and imperialism against Africa . . . with the gun, with fire and with blood, imperialism . . . has sworn to bury the Guinean Revolution.'[88] Inside the USA, many Black nationalists viewed Touré as an esteemed freedom fighter, second only in prestige to Nkrumah. Stokely Carmichael, former leader of the Student Non-violent Coordinating Committee and a principal advocate of 'Black Power,' renamed himself Kwame Toure. His small group of militant Pan-Africanists, the 'All-African People's Revolutionary Party,' looked to 'socialist Guinea' as the appropriate model for African social transformation.

The Soviets viewed developments inside Guinea with a degree of reserve, given the expulsion of their ambassador from the country in 1961. But as Guinea's exports to the USA fell sharply, from nearly GF 3 billion in 1965 down to GF 350 million in 1972, the Soviet Union's economic assistance once again became decisive. Guinea's exports to the USSR climbed steadily, from GF 310 million in 1964 to over GF 2 billion in 1972.[89] Soviet scholars now classified Guinea as a state of 'socialist orientation,' but had problems with the metaphysical dimensions of Touré's political thought. Brutents criticized Guinean leaders as well as other African 'revolutionary democrats,' for lacking a traditional class analysis. Touré and others tended 'to substitute or confuse social analysis with purely political analysis of the conflicting forces in the class struggle.' Brutents cautioned, 'such an approach to classes and class contradictions naturally has serious political and theoretical consequences . . . in the conception of socialist security.' However, Brutents also added that the PDG stood 'closer to the method of scientific socialism' than some other Third World political parties.[90]

Soviet scholar Nikolai Kosukhin, head of the USSR Academy of Science's African Institute, praised Guinea's advances in education and mass political organization. 'Revolutionary-democratic power is striving to involve each person in active industrious and social life, to help him make the fullest use of his rights.' As partial evidence of Guinea's revolutionary democratic credentials, Kosukhin cited the progressive slogans of the PDG: 'The people make the revolution for itself'; 'Democratic Guinea will never recognize foreign rule.'[91] The Cubans had already established a small mission in Conakry by 1966, and within several years they provided security advisers to Touré. Party and state delegations from the German Democratic Republic, the French Communist Party, and the Italian Communist Party visited Guinea and attended PDG conferences. Guinean official Mamouna Touré singled out the special 'contribution of the French Communist Party to the political organization and ideological education of [PDG] Party activists.'[92]

As Guinea's economy drifted deeper into chaos, however, the unstable statist bureaucracy began to rethink its left orientation. Touré once again looked to Washington and multinational capitalism. In 1973, the regime opened a new bauxite mine in cooperation with a US corporation. A year later, during Jamaica's battle with the bauxite owners, the multinationals turned to Guinea for increased production. By greatly speeding up the production process, Guinea's bauxite exports soared from 3.1 million metric tons in 1973 to 10.8 million metric tons in 1976. Since Jamaica earned 64 percent of its export income from alumina and bauxite, and its production was cut by one-third, Guinea's actions directly aided in the economic destabilization of Manley's PNP government.[93] During the Angolan civil war of 1975-76, the Cuban government asked Conakry for landing rights for their air transports to send troops, medical supplies, and other materials to aid the MPLA. Unexpectedly Touré refused the request, and Cuban troops had to be routed to Angola via Guyana.[94]

Washington appreciated Touré's act of solidarity with imperialism, but was not convinced that the regime had moved sufficiently toward the right. Thus in 1978, the regime eliminated many statist regulations over the economy. Guinean entrepreneurs once reviled as 'renegades' were encouraged to initiate small enterprises. Touré cultivated friendly relations with his former archenemy, Houphouet-Boigny, and developed new ties with Saudi Arabia. Conversely, Guinea initiated aggressive acts against neighboring progressive states. In 1980, as Basil Davidson explains, Touré's government 'quietly signed an agreement with Texas Oil which conceded to that corporation's off-shore prospecting rights in the territorial waters of what was now the Republic of Guinea-Bissau. To this the government of Guinea-Bissau reacted sharply, rejecting both the claim and the Texas Oil licence.'[95]

In 1982, Touré came to the United States on a state visit. President Reagan received him with cordiality, and, later, in a session with financial and corporate executives in New York, Touré promised 'an absolute guarantee of all foreign investments and a very high rate of return on investment' in Guinea. During the visit, when Guinean exiles charged that Touré's regime 'practices tyranny and torture on a daily basis,' the Reagan administration responded: 'While we have expressed concern over the Sékou Touré Government's performance with regard to human rights, we have noted the progress he has made in this area.'[96]

Two years later, the 62-year old president died in a Cleveland clinic. Only days after his state funeral, the Guinean military seized power. Opposition groups based in Abidjan, Dakar, Paris, and inside Conakry, were too disorganized and too weak to provide a viable alternative. Throughout his career, Touré had maintained a special political relationship with Nkrumah. Both had relied on Soviet and US aid at various times; both had come to power via popular mobilizations of workers, peasants and liberal nationalistic petty bourgeoisie; both had eliminated their respective nation's democratic rights and political freedoms. When the military finally moved against both regimes, neither the CPP nor the PDG waged meaningful resistance. Socialism was an illusion in both African societies.[97]

IV

Nearly a decade ago, Befekadu Zegeye wrote a perceptive essay entitled 'On the Nature of "Leftist Juntas." ' Focusing on military governments which 'claim socialist and revolutionary ideals,' such as Algeria, Iraq and Ethiopia, Zegeye argued that western leftists tended 'to accept these pseudo-socialist regimes at face value, providing unqualified support instead of much-needed criticism.' Leftwing juntas tended to develop from tactical alliances between military officers and bureaucrats who were 'dissatisfied with the neocolonial arrangement, since they do not directly or substantially benefit from the expertise or investments of the continued foreign presence in their countries.' The comprador class and neocolonial

Socialism from Above 189

parties are overthrown, and a form of state capitalism or 'corporate state, complete with capitalist social relations' is established. The peripheral corporate state run by the military may carry out leftist programmes, such as nationalizations, agricultural reform, and centralized economic planning. 'In this way,' Zegeye argues, 'a corporate state can begin to build up its strength without threatening its newly groomed ruling class.' Although many left juntas maintain traditional market economies, they usually like to call themselves 'socialist' in order to placate domestic left groups and to acquire support from the Soviet bloc and progressive states. Left military regimes also advance anti-imperialist foreign policies but they strictly limit democratic rights for their own working classes; 'The masses have no hand whatever in the shaping of the corporate state — which, once constituted, holds total power and dominates every aspect of society . . . All forms of political opposition, in fact, are suppressed. A constant campaign is waged to eliminate any authentic domestic radical movement, since the juntas regard the left as a greater danger to their authority than any other force.'[98]

Zegeye probably underestimates the fluidity of competing social forces even inside left military Bonapartist states. The activity of Marxist parties or militant trade unions within such regimes especially at early stages of the regimes' development, may directly affect the political composition and orientation of these states. However, he is correct to stress that the main political features of 'left juntas' — the banning of opposition parties, nonexistent legal rights and civil liberties, heavy use of political coercion and systemic terror reproduce many of the worst features of authoritarian states in general.

The Ethiopian revolution has posed a particularly complex model of reform and repression, generating a substantial body of critical studies, some of which generally concur with Zegeye's thesis.[99] In many ways, however, the social revolution in Ethiopia had special characteristics which set it apart from other African postcolonial states.[100] A more representative case of a left, populist military regime, which is also trumpeted in some quarters as 'non-capitalist,' is Ghana in the 1980s. To analyze the current regime of Flight Lieutenant Jerry Rawlings, it is essential to recall briefly the chaotic political events of 1979. On 15 May that year, Rawlings and a group of airforce men were arrested for attempting to overthrow the regime of General Frederick Akuffo, who in turn had displaced General Acheampong the previous year.[101] During Rawlings's court martial, another group of junior officers and enlisted men suc-

190

cessfully seized power, and installed the charismatic Rawlings as chairman of their 'Armed Forces Revolutionary Council' (AFRC). Jan Pieterse observed, 'The months that followed were probably the most dynamic in Ghana's history as a nation.' Senior officers who had profited from corruption were 'imprisoned by their men and shaved bald.' People's courts were organized throughout the country to 'mete out revolutionary justice.'[102] Three former military heads of state — Generals Akuffo, Acheampong, and the leader of the anti-Nkrumah coup, Afrifa — were executed for acquiring illegal fortunes.

If the 1979 'revolution' was essentially a military coup d'état it did spark popular energies and encourage attacks on privilege. Rawlings articulated militantly populist and vaguely moralistic demands. The rebellion was 'in the interests of the common man', he insisted. The target of the uprising was not a particular social class, however, but a form of public and private-sector corrupt practices, termed 'Kalabule.' Merchants who sold overpriced goods were beaten in the streets and their stores were demolished; officers and politicians guilty of 'kalabule' usually received long prison sentences; tax defaulters were ordered to remit back dues, or face 'revolutionary justice.'

Although AFRC was tremendously popular, there were divisions within its fourteen-member ruling body. Populists like Rawlings desired only a 'thorough housecleaning' of the existing system, and were prepared after several months to return state authority to the politicians. Rawlings was essentially devoid of a class analysis, and refused to take any position on the question of capitalist or socialist development: 'No matter the quantity of money that's going to be pumped into this country or systems devised, the success or failure of this system depends on one thing: integrity, accountability, a certain degree of honesty.' Although AFRC gained the popularity of working people in urban and industrial areas, its links with rural regions were very weak, and it made no systemic changes within the Ghanaian political economy. Workers were told to attack the 'kalabule' practices of their managers, but not to 'take justice into their own hands' or to seize the factories. A minority faction of AFRC was 'anti-capitalist' and desired more fundamental institutional changes. However, Rawlings voluntarily relinquished power in September 1979.[103]

Under the new civilian government of President Hilla Limann, 'kalabule' was firmly reestablished within the state and private sectors, and inflation in 1981 exceeded 300 percent. The class struggle between the bureaucratic bourgeoisie and workers intensified. In June 1980, Joachim A. Kwei, the national secretary of the Ghana Industry Holding Corporation Workers Union, led four thousand workers in a demonstration which stormed the parliament building. Ex-AFRC leaders Rawlings and Joseph Nunoo-Mensah were dismissed from the military. As a civilian, Rawlings and his populist supporters established the 'June 4th Movement,' whose key organizer was a socialist, Chris Bukari Atim, a former leader of the National Union of Ghana Students (NUGS). Also opposing the Limann regime were the more leftish popular forces of the New Democratic Movement and the African Youth Command, as well as rank-and-file activists from the Trades Union Congress.

On 31 December 1981, Rawlings and other democratic forces easily toppled the Limann government, outlawed his Peoples National Party and abolished the Westminster parliamentary system. As Kwarteng Mensah observed a year later 'the December action cannot be classified as a coup d'état in the contemporary African sense . . . As a popular intervention of the lowest and oppressed strata of the military it seeks to secure the fundamental conditions for a general democratisation of Ghanaian society by involving the broad masses in the national decision-making process through their own institutions, to consolidate on the gains of foreign capital on the economy and creating a culturally resilient and socially egalitarian nation.'[104]

Six days after the coup/insurrection, Rawlings informed the nation that the masses should 'take over the destiny of this country . . . making possible what has been denied to you all these years.' The leaders of the Provisional National Defence Council (PNDC), the effective national government, included Rawlings, Joseph Nunoo-Mensah, Chris Atim of the 'June 4th Movement,' the Reverend Kwabena Damua (a former detainee of Nkrumah, and an advocate for Accra's unemployed and poor people), the left-leaning Sergeant Alolga Akata-Pore, and trade unionist Joachim Kwei. The PNDC was much more politically advanced than AFRC, and it sought to restructure Ghanaian society from the bottom up. A progressive Federation of Ghanaian Women was created to advocate women's economic and political rights. TUC rank-and-file leaders finally removed their bureaucratic leaders, and in at least one case, 'kalabule' executives were kidnapped. Students shut down the universities and were organized into brigades to cultivate subsistence crops and to help process the cocoa supply for export. The decisive figure to emerge from the PNDC at this point was Atim. He initiated the concept of People's Defence Committees (PDC), which were organized in workplaces and neighborhood levels. The PDCs quickly became popular vehicles to promote worker self-management and mass solidarity with the new regime. Although Rawlings remained the PNDC's most popular representative, Atim's stature as an uncompromising left tribune grew rapidly. As Atim declared before a mass workers' rally in March 1982: 'We can't allow multinational companies to continue to oppress and treat Ghanaian workers as sub-human beings to enable them to make their huge profits.'[105]

Throughout 1982 and 1983, elements of the national and petty bourgeoisie, with support from Washington, waged a continuous struggle against the left populist regime. One of the Ghanaian right wing's chief leaders was Victor Owusu, the former opponent of Nkrumah and an unsuccessful presidential candidate in the 1979 elections. Evidence suggests that US embassy officials in Accra were responsible for assisting anti-PNDC groups and Owusu to mount several unsuccessful coups. After a third abortive coup effort on 19 June 1983, the PNDC arrested several prominent lawyers, journalists and businessmen, including Owusu aide Mike Adjei, for 'calling for return to civilian rule.' Owusu's conservative Popular Front Party was outlawed. But other forms of dissent continued. Rural farmers and entrepreneurs reduced agricultural production, and farmworkers were laid off. The amount of produce which arrived in urban areas fell sharply. By mid-1983, food prices in Accra's marketplace 'reached astronomical prices, with one yam — sufficient for one family meal — costing around two weeks' wages for the ordinary labourer.'[106] Petty-bourgeois associations, including the Ghana Bar Association and the Association of Registered Professional Bodies, called for a national strike. Ghana's Christian Council circulated a document demanding the abolition of the PNDC and the creation of a 'national government' comprised of 'senior groups' such as religious leaders, university and 'professional bodies' — in short, the identical groups which had formed K.A. Busia's conservative regime in 1969-72.[107] In retaliation, Rawlings ordered the arrest of many professional and business leaders without trial. In some instances, pro-PNDC activists from the Workers' Defense Committees (WDC) dispersed middle-class protests.

However there was also a concurrent ideological struggle inside the PNDC which led increasingly to sharp conflicts between pro-Rawlings forces. To some extent, the internal dissension was roughly along Marxist versus populist lines, but even that does not adequately describe the compexity of issues at stake. The Ghanaian left in early 1982 seemed to represent the most coherent and best organized of all the pro-PNDC forces. Individual leftist leaders included Chris Atim, PNDC member Alolga Akata-Pore, Kwame Karikari, director-general of the state-owned Ghana Broadcasting Company, Yaw Akrasi-Sarpong, secretary for the PDC/WDCs, John Ndebugre; leftist intellectual Mawuse Dake, and professor Fui Tsikata at the University of Ghana, who was referred to as 'one of Rawlings's Marxist mentors.' Nearly all of these activists and intellectuals had reached political maturity after the fall of Nkrumah, and few had any direct relationship with the old CPP regime. They recognized the positive features as well as the contradictions in 'Nkrumahite socialism,' and sought to advance a socialist perspective and orientation for the broad populist-oriented mass movement. Numerous organizations with mass constituencies generally favored the left's policy positions, including much of the TUC's rank and file, NUGS, the Kwame Nkrumah Revolutionary Guards, the New Democratic Movement, the African Youth Command, and many youth and workers who had joined the PDCs and the WDCs.

In short, the Ghanaian left was far stronger than it had ever been within the Convention People's Party. Leftists favored an explicitly anti-imperialist foreign policy, and closer relations with socialist, Soviet bloc and nonaligned states. In March 1982, for instance, Atim led a PNDC delegation to the USSR and Eastern European countries, and established terms for credits toward economic and social projects. Six hundred Ghanaian students were sent to study in Cuban schools in 1982-83, and the Castro Government sent technical teams to restore several Ghanaian sugar plants. The left faction desired more centralized controls over the economy, and criticised the government's increasing tendency to resort to arrests and imprisonment without trial. Marxists demanded greater accountability of the regime to the working class, and complete freedom of speech and political expression for left and democratic formations.

On the other side, the so-called 'pragmatic' elements closer to Rawlings, represented chiefly by Finance Minister Kwesi Botchway, resisted a radical transformation of Ghana's foreign and domestic policies. Something of a war of attrition broke out between the two groups in mid-1982, with Rawlings drawn gradually toward the right. One by one, nearly all of the original

PNDC members were eliminated. An early casualty was Atim, who fled into exile in late 1982. Akata-Pore was arrested and imprisoned for allegedly mounting 'two attempts at mutiny or insurrection against Rawlings' in October and November 1982.[108] Joachim Kwei was executed in 1983; Rev. Kwabena Damua was permitted to resign in 1982. Mawuse Dake was dismissed from his post in the PDC after allegedly making critical remarks about Rawlings. Other leftists were purged from the PDC's upper levels in late 1983, and the formation 'was reorganised, its powers and authority considerably reduced.'[109] Several of Rawlings's ex-colleagues organized anti-PNDC formations. Major Boake Djan, the second-in-command in the AFRC, chaired a London-based opposition front, the Campaign for Democracy in Ghana. A small colony of anti-Rawlings politicians and leaders, left and right, developed in neighboring Togo. Another purge of leftists occurred in November 1984, when Ahwoi and Ndebugre were demoted to low level government posts, Karikari was dismissed from Ghana Broadcasting Company, and Kwame Dwemoh-Kesse, the leftist secretary for local government, was also removed.[110]

The 'pragmatists' were not opposed to aid from socialist countries. Financial Secretary Botchway led a delegation to the Soviet Union in August 1984, and the Soviets agreed to give Ghana a US $8.4 million grant for gold mining and cement factory development, and for starting a new bauxite project.[111] What they opposed were the populist and democratic initiatives taken by the PNDC left which alienated the professionals, business sectors and petty bourgeois classes. They opposed class struggle against the national bourgeoisie, and advocated essentially a strategic alliance with them at the expense of workers' rights and interests. They endorsed partial nationalizations with compensation and other statist economic initiatives, but questioned workers' self management.

Like Nkrumah, the PNDC rightists were also prepared to use authoritarian means to silence any opposition from left or right. Rawlings led the ideological retreat, pledging to put an end to the 'populist nonsense' which had characterized the PNDC government in 1982. Technocrats and administrators from previous neocolonial military regimes were brought back into the upper levels of the state apparatus. In several instances, generals and officers from the corrupt Acheampong and Akuffo regimes were rescued from obscurity and reinstated in leading positions. Ghana came to terms with the IMF, while the World Bank lent the regime US $40 million for its timber industry. In 1984, the International Finance Corporation reached an agreement with the partially state-owned Ashanti Goldfields to spend US $120 million on gold production. Exiled Ghanaian businessmen now had second thoughts about Rawlings, and some began to return. In late 1984, the first 'positive' articles about Ghana began to appear in the US press. The Reagan administration began to ship food supplies to the regime, and provided some military training to Ghanaian troops. According to the *New York Times*, the Reagan administration gave Rawlings's 'domestic economic policies (high) marks . . . Washington also has proposed some development aid, although not as much as Mr. Rawlings would like.'[112]

By 1985-86, the Rawlings regime had lost most of its credibility with the Ghanaian working class. In January, 1985, TUC organizers demanded a 'realistic living wage' above the PNDC's meager minimum wage rate of US $1.40 per day. The regime could not accept the workers' legitimate grievances 'without upsetting the carefully-calculated IMF tables of price and wage relativities.' Thus the Ghana Broadcasing station accused the TUC of becoming an 'undemocratic institution,' and charged that it had launched 'a campaign of condemnation' against the state's 'economic recovery' programme.[113] The National Union of Ghanaian Students (NUGS) had turned against Rawlings in 1983, and was instrumental in leading mass demonstrations against the regime. Journalist Kwame Karikari, Marxist intellectual Fui Tsikata and other progressives drafted a public manifesto challenging the state's conservative economic policies and austerity compromises with the IMF. Matters came sharply to a head in April 1986, when the government ordered the detention without charges of four leading leftists, including the general secretary of the Kwame Nkrumah Revolutionary Guards and a major activist in the New Democratic Movement. These arrests ruptured Rawlings's remaining ties to Ghanaian progressives. Other socialists within the regime's own defense committees were also detained. The transition from idealistic populism to state capitalism, from democratic social activism to bureaucratic statist controls had taken only five years.'[114]

It is easy to underestimate the factors which pressure peripheral regimes with anti-capitalist features to suspend or to eliminate democratic norms. Democracy, after all, is not a set of finite legal and social principles, separate from an economic, cultural and political context. Western social democrats all too frequently separate political freedoms and individualistic civil liberties from the broader economic dimension of collective social justice, which requires ultimately the abolition of class privileges and class distinctions themselves. Moreover, newly developing, progressive peripheral states must develop security apparatuses as well as broadbased, popular support, if they are to be able to survive the blows of external and internal class enemies. The authoritarian danger occurs when the ruling party comes to view coercive and military measures as a normal and logical consequence of their exercise of state authority. Even during the initial phases of political institution-building, if strict parameters for civil discourse and political interaction are not clearly delineated for all social classes, whether they agree with the revolutionary process or not, the bludgeon will invariably take precedence over human rights. If workers cannot express themselves freely in political and organizational terms, what is the meaning or consequence of 'non-capitalist' development to them? If the concepts of human equality and participatory democracy are divested from the process of socialist construction, the inevitable political consequence is some version of state authoritarianism, not 'socialist orientation'.

4

Maurice Bishop and The Grenada Revolution

This is the true meaning of revolutionary democracy. It is a growth in the confidence in the power of ordinary people to transform their country, and thus transform themselves. It is a growth in the appreciation of people organising, deciding, creating together. It is a growth of fraternal love.

Maurice Bishop
1981

(Maurice) Bishop was one of the political leaders best liked and most respected by our people because of his talent, modesty, sincerity, revolutionary honesty and proved friendship with our country. He also enjoyed great international prestige. The news of his death deeply moved the Party leadership, and we pay heartfelt tribute to his memory. Unfortunately, the division among the Grenadian revolutionaries led to this bloody drama. No doctrine, no principle or proclaimed revolutionary position and no internal division can justify atrocious acts such as the physical elimination of Bishop and the prominent group of honest and worthy leaders who died yesterday . . . No crime can be committed in the name of revolution and freedom . . .

Cuban Communist Party and the government of Cuba
20 October 1983

The Grenadian revolution of 1979-1983 was in many respects as significant as the Haitian or Cuban revolutions. It was the first armed 'socialist revolution' to occur in a predominately Black state in the Western hemisphere. In the span of less than five years, the People's Revolutionary Government (PRG) accomplished major reforms in areas of health care, education, women's rights, and economic policy. Few critics who have assessed the revolution with any degree of objectivity have failed to be impressed with the rapid advancements registered in the social welfare of the Grenadian people. 'No examination of the Grenada revolution of 1979-83 should end on a pessimistic note,' observed historian Gordon K. Lewis. 'For there is much to be proud about.'[1]

Yet for the left and partisans of national liberation throughout the world, the causes of the implosion of the New Jewel Movement (NJM), the shocking executions of Prime Minister Maurice Bishop and other Grenadian revolutionaries, and the subsequent US invasion of the small Caribbean island in October 1983, continue to be debated. Surviving NJM leaders sympathetic to Bishop have attributed the government's destructions to the party's principal Marxist theoretician, Bernard Coard, and his supporters who comprised a majority of the party's membership. Kendrick Radix, an NJM co-founder, condemned Coard's 'Stalinist tactics' and the use of 'rumor and deceit to slander Maurice.' NJM leader George Louison argued that 'the revolution was destroyed from within,' while Bishop's press secretary Don Rojas claimed that Bishop was actually 'more Leninist' than Coard's group, and that Coard's 'call for a more Leninist organization was misused to cover up in its essence a bid for power.'

American Trotskyists were highly supportive of the Grenadian revolution, and they have essentially shared the interpretations of Radix, Louison and Rojas. Trotskyist journalist Steve Clark wrote in late 1983: 'Unlike Bishop and other NJM leaders, Coard's relations with the Grenadian workers were not based on promoting their organization, mobilization, and class consciousness, but on administrative dictates and persuasion of the gun . . . Coard's secret faction had moved from ambition and cliquism, to open treachery and betrayal of the revolution, and then to the murder of the revolutionary people and their leadership.'[2]

British partisans of the NJM have vigorously denied that Coard was a 'hard-line Stalinist' and 'ultra-leftist rival' to Bishop: 'There had been no ideological difference between Bishop and the majority of the (NJM) Central Committee . . . but a tactical problem over the organization of the Party leadership . . . Tactical difference left the orbit of the Party structures and became gaping wounds into which counter-revolutionary elements both within and outside Grenada could pour their poison . . . (Coard) has been used as the major scapegoat for everything that went wrong with the Revolution.'[3]

The Cuban Communist Party for its part embraced, in succession, sharply divergent perspectives on the disaster in Grenada. Upon first learning of Bishop's ouster from office and his house arrest, the Party expressed the view that 'rather than a substantive conflict, there appeared to be personality clashes and disputes on methods of leadership in which other subjective factors also played a role.' Cuba indicated to the NJM's Central Committee that its cooperation with Grenada 'would continue, regardless of any changes in the Party and national leadership, since this was a purely internal matter.' Following Bishop's murder and the US invasion, however, President Fidel Castro characterized Coard's bloc as 'hyenas,' 'extremists drunk on political theory,' and 'ambitious, opportunistic individuals' who had 'objectively destroyed the Revolution and opened the door to imperialistic aggression.' Parallels were drawn between the genocidal regime of Pol Pot in Kampuchea and the Coardites, the 'conscious or unconscious tools of Yankee imperialism.'[4]

There are already many studies of the Grenadian revolution, the US invasion and subsequent military occupation. This chapter therefore does not examine in any great detail the PRG's economic strategy, its international relations, or the post-invasion events in Grenada. Rather, the concerns presented here are fundamentally sociological and historical. The discussion centers on four primary issues: first, the evolution of social stratification and political culture in Grenada — the relations between the masses and the authoritarian colonial and postcolonial state, their role within production, and the cultural and social factors which structured their perceptions of society and leadership; second, the history of political and social conflict between the indigenous middle strata and landed elite on one side, and the pseudopopulist trade unionism of Eric M. Gairy on the other; third, the internal composition and evolution of the NJM, the germination of contradictions between its social theory and practice, its general public policy orientation while in control of the state apparatus; and fourth, the ideological and progamatic roots of the split within the NJM and the ultimate rupture between the revolutionary state and the Grenadian people.

The differences between Bishop and Coard cannot in the end be relegated to 'personal' or 'tactical' issues, nor should they be reduced to a simplistic equation of 'Stalinist' versus 'social democratic' or 'anti-Stalinist' versions of Marxism. My central argument is that two uneven and contradictory strains of socialism were present within the NJM, both of which were reinforced by the traditional political culture and social structure of the population. One current of Grenadian socialism was egalitarian, democratic, and Jamesian; the other was hierarchical, statist, command-oriented, placing power above the masses, and resembling in several administrative respects the rigid autocratic features of the Crown Colony and Gairy regimes.

I

The Grenadian revolution of 1979-1983 had its origins in the decline of British crown colony government, three decades before, and in the pervasiveness of socioeconomic inequality for the island's Black majority. The local economic system remained dominated, as in the nineteenth century, by a small number of wealthy estate-owners, entrepreneurs, traders and white collar professionals. In the 1950s about one hundred estates occupied half of the island's farm acreage, while over 11,000 farms (95 percent of all farms) were fewer than 10 acres in size, representing less than one third of all agricultural land. The plight of the rural peasantry and the small working class was severe. Families lived in delapidated straw, wooden and mud housing frequently without plumbing facilities, and four-fifths of these dwellings had not more than two rooms. Public education was rudimentary at best. Thousands of children commonly suffered from a variety of diseases, including yaws, hookworms, tuberculosis and gastroenteritis.

The Grenadian 'elite', comprising barely five percent of the adult population, was distinguished from the rural masses in terms of both class status and phenotypical appearance, or racial designation. Whites numbered barely one percent of the island's population, but the overwhelming majority of the elite were 'mixed' or mulattoes. The colonial state apparatus reinforced the white and coloured middle strata's economic domination in a number of respects. The Grenada Sugar Factory, for instance, was established as a public corporation in 1936 to produce and market sugar and rum. Large sugar estates were paid 25 percent more than peasant producers for their cane. As George Birzan notes: 'The peasants and workers not only did most of the hard labor for little pay but also had to pay most of the local taxes . . . Large proprietors paid little or no tax and those locals who bore the brunt of financing government expenditure were the consumers — of whom 95 per cent were peasants and laborers. Between 1944 and 1950 the gentry received $11 million [B.W.I. currency] from cocoa and $17 million for nutmegs exported; this was essentially tax-free, as estate owners who received the bulk of this $28 million paid very little income tax.'[5]

The economic and political underdevelopment of Grenada was such that it did not experience the mass labor strikes and nationalist unrest that swept across the rest of the Caribbean in the 1930s. Part of the reason for this has been attributed to T.A.Marryshow's firm belief in 'nonviolent, almost religious' demonstrations during the Depression, which expressed solidarity with regional anticolonialist struggles but failed to mobilize the poor and laborers against the local regime.[6] In the 1930s and 1940s, peasant 'proto-protest' formations emerged. The 'Su-su,' a cooperative savings network for small agriculturalists, achieved limited success. More widespread were the 'Friendly Societies,' self-help associations which loaned money to members and their families during times of illness or death. By 1947 Grenada had 99 Friendly Societies, consisting of nearly 20,000 members, with net assets of £137,357. Nevertheless, there were few other outlets for workers and peasants to express their grievances, and the local bourgeoisie was confident that it could control any potential unrest. In April 1949 the colonial regime announced several constitutional 'reforms' for Grenada, to take effect in late 1951, including a new legislature of twelve members, eight of whom would be elected by universal suffrage. The colonial Governor retained the authority to pass bills rejected by the legislature, and could veto any legislation. In effect, despite a formal measure of representative democracy, the regime remained rigidly authoritarian, with the Black majority intended to continue in a subservient, and largely powerless position.[7]

Two separate events in 1950 radically transformed the political terrain. First, a severe decline in the world cocoa prices prompted local employers to slash agricultural workers' wages, which were roughly 82 cents per day. Simultaneously, several estate-owners initiated a drive to expel poor peasants who were occupying small sections of their property illegally. These issues merged to spark an unprecedented level of anger among the Black poor. Their most charismatic spokesman was a young oilworker, Eric Matthew Gairy, who in July 1950 formed the Grenada Manual and Mental Workers Union (GMMWU). In January 1951, the owners of the La Sagesse estate harassed Gairy, and sympathetic farm workers instantly went on strike. Within several days, hundreds of other farm laborers had joined the protest. Pushed from below, Gairy called for a mass, general strike on 19 February. Plantations were looted and put to the torch; thousands of workers and peasants filled the streets of St. George's in support of 'Uncle Gairy.' In desperation, the Governor ordered the arrest of Gairy, but the action only provoked additional violence. An administrator in the colonial labor department later remarked that the strike was 'an upheaval such as has not been known within living memory. Workers who showed a disinclination to go on strike were intimidated and beaten by co-workers, by the unemployed and by the unemployables; estates were looted in broad daylight, while Management stood by unable to interfere; valuable trees were deliberately damaged; estate buildings, medical health centres, schools, and privately owned residences were burnt, rioting and bloodshed occurred . . . ' Police from Trinidad and St. Lucia were brought in to control the masses, but only the landing of British sailors and marines brought a modicum of civil peace. By mid-March, the property damage to government buildings was estimated at £18,000, and damages to the estates amounted to nearly £200,000.[8]

The aftermath of this social eruption was the polarization of classes into antagonistic camps. The local bourgeoisie, and especially the large planters, were 'on the verge of hysteria' and began to brandish firearms. In their view, the colonial regime had been lax and tardy in suppressing the rabble. A phalanx of estate owners caucused with the governor in mid-March, warning bluntly that 'unless Government is prepared to rule, we, the planters and the merchants will have to take the Government into our own hands, and we hope that you will give us the license which you have given to these communistic hooligans when we do act.'

Meanwhile, the Superintendent of Police called the strike a 'deepseated communist plot' and ordered his men to 'shoot all those who misbehaved.' One of Grenada's largest merchants, W.E. Julien, correctly termed the struggle against Gairy's followers a class struggle, 'the haves against the have-nots.'[9]

But Gairy himself was no radical. Throughout the strike he insisted that he had no intention of overthrowing the colonial regime. Released from detention, he instructed workers to 'stop the burning of the fields' and to go 'back to work.' Gradually the unrest subsided. Gairy's immediate objective was to build an electoral vehicle to challenge the island's ruling class in the 1951 elections. The Grenada People's Party (GPP) was formed from Gairy's GMMWU, recruiting hundreds of campaign organizers from the laboring and rural classes. On 10 October 1951, the GPP won a historic victory, carrying six out of eight constituencies with 60 percent of the overall vote. Running in St. George's parish, Gairy personally received a 83.5 percent endorsement. An analysis of the 1951 vote revealed both a rural/urban split, and a division based roughly on colour. Marryshow, the veteran liberal representative of the middle strata, carried the town of St. George's over the GPP candidate by a 56-44 percent margin. The GPP won over 70 percent of the electorate in strictly rural areas, but barely 50 percent in the rural villages and St. George's. The oppressed social classes, primarily Black, openly identified with Gairy as being 'for us Black people'; the mixed middle strata and upper bourgeoisie universally detested him, and Gairy's 'name became anathema' in their homes. But the regime was now forced to ask Gairy to help form Grenada's new Executive. The self-described 'messiah' of the Black proletariat and peasantry had become the nation's preeminent politician.[10]

Despite his party's nominal triumph, Gairy exercised virtually no authority, since the executive powers of the governor remained comprehensive. Moreover, four of the six GPP representatives were ideologically closer to the local bourgeoisie than to their working class and peasant constituencies, and the legislature passed few measures which improved the status of the subordinated classes. Disaffected, hundreds of GMMWU members withdrew or stopped paying union dues. In the 21 September 1954 elections, Gairy's party — renamed the Grenada United Labour Party (GULP) — won a second victory, carrying six out of eight constituencies. Actually the vote was deceptive. GULP won only 46 percent of the total vote and its success was primarily due to the failure of the anti-Gairy forces to unite around a single slate. Moreover the 1954 election actually accelerated, at several levels, the organizational decline of GULP. Gairy's GMMWU's total membership dropped from 16,000 to 7,700 by 1959. Union leaders seemed more interested in partisan politics than in labor grievances. Indeed, between 1955 and 1959 there were only five minor strikes in Grenada, and the GMMWU was involved in none. Wages were increasing somewhat, but were still abysmally low when contrasted with other British Caribbean states. In 1958 the per capita income of Grenada was only BWI $259, compared to BWI $510 in Jamaica and BWI $612 in Trinidad in 1958. New unions soon began to challenge the GMMWU. In 1956, the Commercial and Industrial Workers Union was formed, followed by the Grenada Technical and Allied Workers, the Grenada Civil Service Association, and the Grenada Union of Teachers. As GULP's base in the working class was fractured, some party leaders broke away from Gairy. L.C.J. Thomas, GULP's representative in the parishes of St. John's and St. Mark's, quarreled with Gairy and was expelled from the party. Thomas quickly established the *Torchlight* newspaper in 1955 and published anti-Gairy polemics.[11]

In the election of 24 September 1957, four organized parties and several independents ran for office. The major anti-Gairy parties were Thomas's People's Democratic Movement, and the Grenada National Party (GNP), led by barrister Herbert A. Blaize. The GNP generally represented the island's brown middle strata — the civil servants, teachers, merchants, and some skilled workers. In its 1956 document, a 'Plan for Grenada,' the party stressed the goals of 'good government,' and proposed 'the development of both the rich and the poor in Grenada.' The ability of the petty bourgeoisie to manipulate the electoral process was apparent after the voting. The GNP/PDM received 43.9 percent of the vote and four seats, while GULP's electoral base slipped to 40.2 percent and only two seats. Although Gairy was reelected, he was soon ejected from office and barred from participating in any elections for five years for disrupting a public assembly of his opponents. The GNP government under Blaize in 1957-1961 was actually a victory for the ruling class. Between 1957 and 1960, the net income of planters soared by 170 percent through legislative policies which subsidized the costs of production while workers' wages only marginally increased. By 1960 Grenada's unemployment rate had soared to 42.6 percent. Redundancy once again promoted mass migrations of the working poor from the island. 'Between 1958 and 1960,' sociologist Beverley Steel observes, '6,600 persons emigrated from Grenada, a figure higher than for any of the other British Islands of the Lesser Antilles, including Barbados, with its much higher population. In 1959 alone, 2.46 (percent) of the total population migrated.'[12]

GULP was returned to office in the 27 March 1961 elections, winning 53 percent of the popular vote. But the Colonial Office suspended Grenada's constitution in June 1962, after a commission found GULP guilty of establishing a network of clientage and illegal kickbacks known popularly as 'squandermania.' New elections were set for 12 September 1962. After a decade of parliamentary politics, the divisions between the pro and anti-Gairy forces had become extremely rigid. The middle strata and national bourgeoisie were completely convinced that GULP 'scared the foreign investors.' GNP ran an 'intensely partisan' campaign. Taxicabs were hired to shuttle voters to the polls; and according to one observer, 'feelings ran so high that children were warned not to play with children whose families were presumed to be supporting the opposition.' Neighbors who had been friends for years became estranged over the election. GULP warned that a Gairy victory would lead to 'a dishonest, dirty, worthless and good-for-nothing Government.' The British also quietly manoeuvered to defeat GULP. Over three thousand voters, including many Gairy supporters, were inexplicably dropped from the electoral register.[13] The result was a narrow GNP victory. Out of 21,000 votes cast, the GNP received 50.5 percent of the popular vote and six of ten constituency seats. Blaize became the leader of the new government, and Gairy was again ousted from power. The GNP restored its elitist policies of the 1957-61 period. No structural social or economic changes were proposed, and 'if anything, the urban bourgeoisie and rural gentry became more entrenched as their Party was now in power,' notes George Brizan. 'Gairy's defeat at the polls was a hard blow, one he found difficult to live with. While out of power he lived in virtual penury . . .'[14]

Gairy correctly attributed his electoral defeat to his failure to maintain a credible base among the workers and peasants. The GMMWU's total membership slumped to barely 3,000 by 1962. The road to power required a new level of labor militancy. The GMMWU mobilized workers in the Grenada Sugar Factory, whose managers and investors were strong GNP supporters; and it increased its organizing efforts on estates owned by GNP members. Between 1964 and 1966 the GMMWU led eighteen strikes against the GNP government over issues concerning pay increases and improved working conditions for wage employees. Gairy's opportunity finally arrived in 1967, when Grenada was given a new constitution. The new terms of Grenada's 'Associated State' status gave full control of the island's affairs — except defense and foreign policy — to an elected House of Representatives and its Premier. In a bitterly waged campaign, GULP defeated GNP by a popular vote margin of 54.5 to 45.5 percent, and won seven of ten legislative seats. Gairy defeated his GNP challenger overwhelmingly in his district, receiving 62.7 percent of the popular vote.[15]

Gairy wasted little time in establishing the foundations of a personal dictatorship. The GMMWU's pro-labor demands were promptly dropped, but the political warfare against the elite was continued. Gairy's overall strategy was not to strengthen the working class, but to create a 'new class of capitalists dependent on his patronage machine.' He extorted money from local merchants to provide perks for GULP officials and loyal trade-union leaders, while women were forced to provide sex to party and government officials in order to maintain their jobs. The civil service was gradually purged of many anti-Gairy elements. GULP members' estates were seized by the state under the pseudopopulist slogan, 'Land for the Landless,' and some farms were subdivided among the regime's friends. A few of the largest landlords, wary of the growing authority of Gairy, transferred their loyalty and financial patronage to GULP, and the government did nothing to their estates. Other plantations owned by supporters of Gairy were purchased by the state at ridiculously inflated prices. This massive mismanagement and graft had its costs, as the funds for economic infrastructure and social welfare projects dried up. 'The island's road system fell into dangerous disrepair. Medical care was inferior and expensive: doctors were scarce, and the few medical clinics unsanitary and ill-equipped. Education was an area of particularly pointed neglect. Primary school buildings deteriorated, teachers went untrained, while secondary schooling became an elite privilege. Gairy also stopped paying Grenada's dues to the University of the West Indies, so that Grenadians could no longer receive subsidized university training in the regional system.'[16] After declining slightly in the mid-1960s, unemployment rates increased to 55 percent by 1970.[17]

In the early 1970s, the Gairy government was partially transformed from being simply a corrupt and inefficient neocolonialist regime into an authoritarian police state. This transition did not occur spontaneously, nor was it ever fully consolidated. All literature was not censored; opposition parties maintained the right to meet and mobilize their supporters; legitimate channels of dissent remained. But random searches and arrests became more frequent; and to escape harassment, leaders of civil society had to express neutrality if not fealty to GULP. Legal and extralegal measures were used to paralyze the opposition. The Firearms Act of 1968, for instance, effectively rescinded all firearm permits issued to GNP members. The Emergency Powers Act of 1970 permitted Gairy's agents 'to search without warrant, limit public assemblies and confiscate literature.'[18] To the country's two major security forces, the police and the army — popularly called the 'Green Beasts' — Gairy added a private, extralegal force termed the 'Mongoose Gang.' The Premier recruited hardened criminals for this gang, men with long records of assault, burglary, and physical violence, and unleashed them against his political opponents. The Mongoose Gang was employed to suppress a nurses' strike in November 1970, as scores of nonviolent protestors were viciously beaten in the streets and arrested.

Regimes of this type make few distinctions between moderate critics and radicals bent on the total destruction of the ruling establishment. A landlord or entrepreneur who was outraged at GULP's use of terror was viewed as being 'objectively' a subversive. Consequently the small left inside the Grenadian working class and radicalized petty bourgeoisie was agreeable to form a popular front with the GNP, in order to contest the February 1972 elections. The most outstanding representative of this left tendency was Unison Whiteman, a young intellectual who had received a Master's degree in economics at Howard University in 1969. Whiteman ran as the GNP's candidate in St. David's constituency. Selwyn Strachan, a young working-class militant, ran against Gairy in St. George's Southeast constituency. But Gairy had little difficulty in winning yet another electoral mandate. GULP constantly reminded the voters that 'the GNP consisted of "Big Shots", the estate owners who were their former masters.'[19] GULP received over twenty thousand votes, 59 percent of those cast, and carried all but two constituencies. In St. George's Southeast, Gairy defeated Strachan by a 71-29 margin, and Whiteman received only 34 percent of his constituency's vote. Gairy's reelection moved forward British plans to grant Grenada complete independence with Commonwealth status.

The profound weaknesses of the Grenadian elite now became fully evident. For two decades it had waged electoral struggles against Gairy's brand of populist demogoguery. But tutored beneath the colonial regime's increasingly authoritarian rule, the GNP was incapable of combatting GULP when left to its own resources. It had no genuine roots among the workers and peasantry, and had never developed a program to advance the interests of the majority. The elite could not even claim honestly that it was 'more democratic' than the Gairyites. A.W. Singham's interviews with Grenadian 'elites' in the late 1960s revealed that 'the attitude most prevalent among members of these groups is that politics is dirty, vulgar and not respectable.' Most believed that the 'introduction of adult suffrage had been a mistake,' and a majority favored 'the return of a limited franchise based on literacy or educational qualifications. Not only were the masses castigated for illiteracy, they were said to be lacking in intelligence, gullible, easily led, and, worst of all, "they are in the majority!"' [20] The colored petty bourgeoisie's leaders were small men, capable of playing only small roles in political struggles. Thus the fulcrum of social change was passed to a new generation of young Grenadians. For the radicalized children of many elite households and for the younger laborers and farmers, Gairy's political image began to 'evoke revulsion and even hostility . . . (they) could remember only inflation, unemployment and acts of brutality, sometimes sporadic, sometimes widespread.'[21]

New oppositionist currents surfaced most strongly in St. George's.[22] Young intellectuals and professionals, mostly from middle strata families, had been profoundly influenced by the Black Power movement in the USA and the resurgence of Black militancy in neighboring Trinidad. One group of activists, led by twenty-six-year-old attorney Maurice Bishop, established Forum in 1970. Forum maintain political contacts with other Black Power advocates in the Caribbean, such as George Odlum of St. Lucia, and it held several small public demonstrations against Gairy. After the 1972 elections, these progressives created the Movement for the Advancement of Community Effort (MACE). MACE tended to emphasize the need for political education and mobilization among the St. George's electorate, and it recognized that the GNP had become hopelessly inept in challenging the Gairy regime. The key figures were Bishop and his close friend Kendrick Radix, a 28-year-old law graduate from Univeristy College, Dublin.

In October 1972 MACE merged with yet another St. George's organization, the Committee of Concerned Citizens, which represented the younger and more liberal elements of the GNP and the commercial establishment. This new formation was called the Movement for Assemblies of the People (MAP). Its general strategy proposed the abolition of the Westminster parliamentary model and the initiation of mass, popular 'assemblies,' which would exercise effective state power. Implicitly this version of bottom-up, radical democracy drew its inspiration from C.L.R. James, and from the Tanzanian example of *ujamaa vijijini*. 'We envisage a system which would have village assemblies and workers' assemblies,' Bishop later related. 'In other words, politics where you live and politics where you work . . . ' Theoretically, MAP was still quite eclectic in its political orientation. Bishop himself had a vague understanding of James's Marxism, but probably had done little serious theoretical study on his own.[23]

In rural St. David's, Unison Whiteman established the Joint Endeavour for Welfare Education and Liberation (JEWEL) in early 1972. JEWEL organized agricultural workers, and led a significant demonstration against a rural landlord in January 1973. On 11 March 1973 the two formations merged to create the New Jewel Movement (NJM). The NJM's initial manifesto was largely drafted by MAP's major intellectual, Franklyn Harvey, who had been influenced heavily by the writings of James. The NJM advocated the 'economic integration of the Caribbean 'under popular ownership and control,' and the toal 'nationalization of all foreign-owned hotels,' banks and insurance companies. The parliamentary system would be replaced by a network of popular assemblies, which would 'involve all the people in decision-making. The political system proposed by the NJM did not envision a competitive, multiparty electoral process. More importantly, the NJM perceived its role as being severely limited: it would function as a catalyst to initiate the new nonpartisan state apparatus. It implicitly rejected the Leninist concept of the vanguard party, and expressed an almost voluntaristic belief in political spontaneity. This underestimated, perhaps, the degree to which partisan electoral politics had become firmly entrenched in the country, as well as the fact that for a majority of the people the system still retained considerable legitimacy despite Gairy's despotism and corruption.

On 20 April 1973 the police executed a young militant, Jeremiah Richardson, and his family went to the NJM for help in protesting his murder. Bishop and other NJM activists organized a major demonstration in the east coast town of Grenville, the site of the killing. About five thousand villagers and farmers surrounded the small police station in Grenville, and succeeded in closing down Pearls Airport, Grenada's only air terminal, for three days. Outraged, Gairy spoke to the nation over the radio, warning that he would 'not be ruffled, or excited by any threats, any demands, or any demonstration whatsoever in the exercise of my responsibility to the State. I was born to do the job that I am doing today.' Gairy's banal platitudes could no longer diffuse the situation. On 6 May, the NJM organized a 'People's Conference on Independence', in which ten thousand Grenadians took part. The regime responded to the crisis with violence. In late May several NJM supporters were beaten by Gairy's Mongoose gang and by police officers. On 1 June, an NJM member was 'chopped up by the secret police for selling NJM newspapers.' Eight days later 'Clarence Ferguson was savagely beaten and chopped up by the Mongoose Gang; his daughter, a high school student, who was with him, was stripped naked in public.'

These vicious acts failed to check the mobilization. On 4 November, a second convention was held at Seamoon in St. Andrew's parish, which attracted another ten thousand Grenadians. The Premier was tried and convicted *in absentia* for a series of crimes ranging from simple 'incompetence' to brutality'. Gairy was given two weeks to resign; if he refused, a general strike would begin. 'When a government ceases to serve the people and instead steals from and exploits the people at every turn,' declared one NJM pamphlet, 'the people are entitled to dissolve it and replace it by any means necessary.'[24]

II

The 1973 manifesto of the NJM 'made no mention of the word "socialism",' Fitzroy Ambursley has observed.[25] Despite the influence of C.L.R. James, Nyerere's Ujamaa model and the Black Power concepts which had been widely popularized in the Caribbean in the early 1970s, the early NJM was essentially an eclectic social movement of national democratic, liberal and progressive forces. It attracted individuals who shared a common antipathy toward the Gairy regime, but disagreed over other political issues. One of the 'oldest' activists was 35-year-old Hudson Austin. A graduate of the Jamaica Institute of Science and Technology, he had majored in construction engineering. In 1958, Austin had taken a six month course at the US military base in Chaguaramas, Trinidad, and in the 1960s he served as a prison officer in Grenada. Meanwhile from the liberal professional class came Radix and Lloyd Noel, a 38-year-old barrister. Younger militants included Selwyn Strachan and Harold Strachan, who worked as a taxi driver and provided security for NJM leaders. Rural activists were led by Whiteman, Teddy Victor and Sebastian Thomas. Although Whiteman was technically NJM co-leader, the driving spirit of the movement from the beginning was barrister Maurice Bishop. Tall, physically attractive and articulate, Bishop had an 'easy manner and self confidence' which made him very popular, 'a man who found it easy to communicate with people.'[26] Although this nucleus of activists was politically immature in many respects, its political potential presented an immediate threat to the Gairy government.

On Sunday morning, 18 November, six of the NJM leaders — Bishop, Whiteman, Austin, Radix, Selwyn Strachan, and Simon Daniel — agreed to meet a group of Grenville businessmen to discuss the nature of the general strike, which was planned to begin the next day. Leaving in three automobiles, the six men were followed and harassed along the way by Gairy's police. When they arrived at the appointed meeting place, Strachan later related, 'we were confronted by plain-clothes policemen and secret police fully armed with pickaxe handles.' Secret police led by Inspector Innocent Belmar ordered his men to 'Get them dogs!' The NJM activists dodged several bullets, but were eventually cornered. Strachan recalled: 'We were beaten unconscious, fell, regained consciousness, fell again and were then dragged through the streets by the secret police into the police station. There the plain-clothes and secret policemen were ordered to shave us and to collect the blood that was flowing from our bodies. They actually threatened us to drink the blood which they collected. All three of us [Bishop, Whiteman and Strachan] were there, bleeding in the cell because they had shaved us with broken bottles and the blood continued to flow from our bodies. The other three comrades were also shaved and thrown into the cell with us. Throughout the night we were tortured by Belmar and the secret police who had taken over from the plain-clothes policemen. From time to time, Belmar would come and order us to get up and sit down, under much pain. I could recall that Comrade Austin had Comrade Bishop in his lap, bleeding profusely. The underpants Comrade Austin was wearing changed colour from white to red. It was a night of terror.'[27]

'Bloody Sunday' sent political tremors throughout Grenada. Civil and social groups that previously had little sympathy with the NJM, were forced to act. A coalition of various organizations, including the Chamber of Commerce, the Grenada Union of Teachers, the Civil Service Association and the Rotary Club, formed the 'Committee of Twenty-Two.' On 19 November the Committee issued a call for a national strike, and demanded that Gairy prosecute all Mongoose Gang members and policemen involved in the 'Bloody Sunday' incident. The Premier initiated an independent commission of inquiry into the NJM beatings, but after the strike was called off, he repudiated any concessions he had made to the Committee.

The regime's repression continued, and on 27 December NJM activist Harold Strachan was murdered by the Mongoose Gang. The Seamen and Waterfront Workers Union's (SWWU) rank and file initiated an anti-Gairy strike on 1 January 1974, leading to a national shutdown. School children, youth, taxi drivers, dockworkers, industrial laborers and others daily marched in protest through the streets of St. George's. The Technical and Allied Workers Union, which ran the telephone system, the Leeward Islands Air Transport and the water and electric power services, also went on strike. In solidarity, the Oilfield Workers Trade Union and the Seamen and Waterfront Workers' Trade Union in Trinidad started a boycott of cargo bound for Grenada. On 21 January — later known throughout the country as 'Bloody Monday' — the

Mongoose Gang and the police were sent out to smash the popular resistance. Police attacked Otway House, headquarters of the SWWU, and began to beat striking workers. Maurice Bishop's father, Rupert Bishop, was murdered by police. For several weeks, it seemed to most Grenadians that Gairy would be forced to resign. Fuel on the island ran out; civil servants and even some police officers threatened to leave work; the SWWU received £45,000 from sympathetic unions abroad to support the strike. However, SWWU officials feared the militancy of their own members, and ordered their union back to work. The British government came to Gairy's rescue with an 'independence gift' of £100,000 which was used in part to cover civil servants' wages. Britain and Canada also sent three frigates to St. George's harbor, 'ostensibly to participate in the "independence celebrations", but in reality serving as a subtle warning of imperialist support for the Gairy government.'[28] Grenada was granted full independence on 7 February 1974. But taking no chances, Gairy ordered the arrest of Maurice Bishop six hours before independence ceremonies were held, charging the NJM leader with 'illegal possession of firearms.' One hour before independence, a building owned by an NJM sympathizer was 'mysteriously' burned to the ground.'[29] Bishop was not released on bail for two days; Gairy seemed fully in command.

The failure of the NJM to force Gairy's resignation in 1973-1974 led the movement to reassess its strategy and tactics. The NJM attempted to deepen its roots within the peasantry and small working class. 'Support groups' were initiated in villages and rural constituencies, and regular public sessions were held — despite their frequent disruption by Gairy's agents. The NJM newspaper *The New Jewel,* edited by Selwyn Strachan, quickly achieved a circulation of ten thousand. New militants were recruited to the party, such as Scotilda Noel of Birch Grove in St. Andrew's, who was an organizer of banana grove workers; teenager Alister Strachan, who distributed *The New Jewel*; and Jacqueline Creft, a former MAP member, and a political science graduate of Carlton University, Ontario.

Bishop and some leaders now recognized that the NJM 'had to think about organization of the party and training and preparation of the cadres. That is, to try to build a party with the character of a vanguard party.'[30] Bishop's selection of words here is instructive. After 'Bloody Sunday,' the founders of NJM understood that some capacity for clandestine organizing and political networking required a more closely knit formation which roughly approximated a Leninist party. The party's survival required some level of security, and a more direct system of accountability by individual members to the organization as a whole. A few activists such as Teddy Victor opposed these organizational changes, and also criticized what seemed to be a shift in the political centre of gravity of the party from the countryside to St. George's. Gradually, some of the original members of the NJM were 'phased out,' and replaced by militants who were willing 'to suffer beatings up, imprisonment or even death in the cause of the fight against Gairy.'[31] Despite these modifications in its internal structure and ideological orientation, as Fitzroy Ambursley and James Dunkerley have observed, the NJM still remained 'more of a movement than a party. By 1976 the party had succeeded in securing and broadening its popular appeal . . . but [it] lacked a strategic programme and coherent internal organisation.'[32]

The Gairy government responded to the NJM challenge with more repressive laws. In February 1975 GULP Finance Minister George Hosten secured the passage of the 'Public Order Act,' which declared that any group 'intending to hold a march or demonstration anywhere in Grenada must get the approval of the Commissioner of Police.' The Commissioner had to be given 'the names and addresses of the organisers, the purpose of the march, the approximate hours when the demonstration will begin and end, and the route it will take.' The police retained the right to refuse the application; any violators of the Act could be 'arrested without warrant,' and subject to a fine of $2,000 and/or two years in jail. On 4 July 1975 the 'Newspaper Act' became law, which required all periodicals to pay an annual licence fee of $500, a bond of $900, and a cash deposit of $20,000 in order to publish. Designed to put *The New Jewel* out of business, the NJM newspaper simply went underground, and copies were circulated by party members. On 20 August 1976 Whiteman was arrested for 'distributing illegal newspapers' under provisions of the law, but charges were not filed and he was later released. Gairy stepped up the harassment against other NJM members. When Jacqueline Creft returned to Grenada in late 1977 after working briefly in Trinidad, the GULP regime blocked her applications for employment. After several jobless months, she was forced to take a position in Trinidad.[33]

The struggle against Gairy's authoritarian regime inspired the creation of other formations, which soon had a decisive role in the NJM's subsequent development. In the early 1970s, a small group called Joint Organization of Youth (JOY) had developed in

Catholic Presentation College for young men and in St. Joseph's Convent school for women. Participants in the organization, which focused on the secular implications of the reformist Second Vatican Council, included Leon 'Owusu' James and Basil 'Akee' Gehagan. Members of JOY and other Grenadian youth associations became increasingly radicalized by the anti-Gairy mass movement, and they began to study Marxist-Leninist theory. In 1974 JOY members were joined by students at Grenada Boys Secondary School to create the Organisation for Revolutionary Education and Liberation (OREL). Some of OREL's key participants included Victor 'Nazim' Burke, Liam James, Leon Cornwall, Ewart Layne, John Ventour and Chris Stroude. Although OREL functioned largely as a Marxist study group, and its members took part in the NJM's public activities, there was no direct organizational relationship between the formations. OREL's chief theoretical savant was Bernard Coard. Born in 1944, Coard was the son of an influential Grenadian civil servant. He received a B.A. degree in economics and sociology at Brandeis University in 1966, and his master's degree in comparative political economy at the University of Sussex. During his years in the UK, Coard was on the periphery of the British Communist Party. His primary political activities were directed against institutional racism in the British public schools. Coard's 1971 book, *How the West Indian Child is made Educationally Subnormal in the British School System*, was well received among Black and progressive educators. But as Tim Hector has noted, Coard's text 'took basically a Black nationalist position', and had few elements of 'a class analysis.'[34]

Coard's version of Marxism was formed principally in 1972-74, when he lectured at the Institute of International Relations at the University of the West Indies' St. Augustine campus, and in 1974-76, when he was a lecturer of government and management at the Mona campus of UWI in Jamaica. Both Coard and his wife Phyllis Evans, the daughter of a wealthy Jamaican family, became closely associated with Trevor Munroe and the Worker's Liberation League. Under Munroe's influence, Coard grounded himself in the Soviet theory of the noncapitalist path of development. During Coard's term at Mona, the League's generally hostile positions toward the governing PNP underwent a major change as previously noted. OREL's initial relationships with the NJM roughly paralleled those of Munroe's WLL vis a vis the PNP. Although OREL had fewer than two dozen members, it managed to produce a modest Marxist newspaper, unoriginally named the *Spark*.

During 1975-1976, Coard addressed OREL several times, but he does not appear to have been a formal member of the group. OREL originally criticized the NJM as a 'petty bourgeois' reformist movement. But sometime later — probably under the urging of Coard, who did not return permanently to Grenada until September, 1976 — OREL proposed a merger with the NJM. OREL insisted that the NJM transform its internal structure to reflect the Leninist norms of Munroe's party and other Marxist formations, but Bishop and the NJM refused to do so. After further discussions OREL consented to drop its preconditions, and joined the NJM. As in Guyana and Jamaica, Marxist-Leninists were now prepared to participate in a united front with revolutionary democrats.

Despite these initial tensions, most NJM members warmly accepted Coard as their party's 'theoretical powerhouse,' and the former members of OREL became the movements's most dedicated cadre. In retrospect, the frequent accusation that OREL remained a 'Clandestine group' created by Coard with the aim of dominating Bishop and other original NJM leaders is highly inaccurate.[35] OREL continued as an ideological tendency, but not as a coherent, conspiratorial faction in the NJM. The Party did not even create a Central Committee, an essential Leninist structure, until 1979. Much of the dissension in these years focused on Coard's overtly aggressive behavior, not on his ideological views. Indeed, Coard's acquaintance with Marxist scholarship left much to be desired. Coard was ever-ready to provide a 'dogmatic quotation, chiefly from Stalin,' but he curtly dismissed C.L.R. James as a 'neo-Trotskyist.'

Coard's stock inside the NJM rose rapidly less because of his theoretical acumen and moreso but because of the ideological limitations of other leaders. As Ambursley and Dunkerley put it, 'Bernard Coard was in many respects the antithesis of Bishop . . . An unkempt and plump figure, Coard had none of the ostensibly natural features of a revolutionary leader and never sought personal popularity.' Moreover, he and his wife had been absent during the NJM's difficult early years. Veterans privately accused Coard of 'wanting to grab power.' But even his harshest critics recognized that Coard was a valuable theoretician, well-trained in practical economic and educational affairs. Conversely all acknowledged that Bishop was 'not a theorist or strategist;' and none of the NJM's other leaders had any rigorous background in Marxism.[36] NJM veterans, moving toward a cadre party model, needed a Marxist like Coard; and Coard, despite his private misgivings about the petty-bourgeois orientation and social democratic tendencies of NJM leaders, needed the Party in order to assert himself in Grenadian politics.

Although the police continued to harass Party activists, and leaders were not permitted to speak over the radio, the NJM became the major opposition to Gairy's dictatorship by the mid-1970s. The NJM at this stage essentially consisted of three informally defined tendencies. One group comprised numbers of petty-bourgeois professionals, intellectuals and entrepreneurs who favored the overthrow of Gairy and the implementation of social democratic and populist reforms. Within the NJM itself, this current included educator and labor union consultant George Brizan, barrister Lloyd Noel, and former Jewel activist Teddy Victor. On the periphery of the Party, political sympathizers and allies included GNP member and merchant Norris Bain, and economist Lyden Ramdhanny, the son of a wealthy merchant and estate owner.

The second current included those like Austin, Radix and Whiteman, who were personally close to Bishop and had considerable popularity within the masses. Others within this tendency were labor activist Vincent Noel, educator Jacqueline Creft, and George Louison, a former Youth Coordinator for the Caribbean Conference of Churches. They were essentially revolutionary democrats who had come to embrace a Marxian class analysis of their society, and accepted the necessity for a type of vanguard party structure to topple the Gairy regime. Their commitment to socialist goals was bound to their belief in mass education, participation and popular mobilization. In a limited sense, they were the logical descendants of Marryshow, who had been the representative of liberal resistance to colonial authoritarianism a half century before. With a few exceptions, most of these NJM leaders were drawn from the island's elite and petty bourgeois households.

Although OREL's organizational independence was gone, its former members comprised a distinct third tendency of opinion with the NJM. It favored close fraternal ties with Guyana's PPP, Munroe's WLL and other Caribbean Marxist formations. OREL encouraged and promoted the NJM's transition from an anti-capitalist movement to a coherent vanguard party. Through Coard, and perhaps later Selwyn Strachan, former OREL members tried to guide the NJM ideologically, to prepare the Party for a two-stage revolution: a national democratic stage which would overthrow Gairy's regime, and ultimately a Marxist-Leninist stage which would establish a socialist state. OREL's membership was drawn largely from the poor and working-class families.

However, it must be emphasized that NJM members themselves were largely unaware of any potentially antagonistic divisions that might one day divide the Party. The NJM's decision-making process was achieved through consensus, votes were seldom if ever taken, and a sense of comradeship was strong. Bishop's prestige and personal popularity allowed the NJM to relate to diverse social strata. But Bishop never tried to overshadow other leaders, and encouraged a diversity of opinion within the Party. Bishop was 'perhaps the most modest' of all key NJM figures, 'and probably the number one adherent to the principle of collective leadership.'[37] The challenge of combatting the GULP regime obviously took precedence over any consideration of personal and ideological disputes.

The GNP recognized that the NJM's cooperation had become vital in its electoral struggle to remove Gairy. In the GNP's publication, Herbert Blaize proposed that the NJM join in 'united action' against GULP in the next elections. The GNP organized a small rally on 6 April 1975, and party speakers again urged the NJM 'to renounce certain aspects of their Manifesto and work together with GNP.' The NJM rejected the GNP's appeal as 'comical,' and added that it would work only with 'serious organisations' that advocated policies which will 'achieve genuine liberation. A strong, vibrant, energetic organ can easily be slowed down or even killed by close contact with a dying one.'[38] A year later, however, Bishop and other NJM leaders began to have second thoughts. GULP had lost much of its credibility, and defections from its ranks were now obvious. Former GULP minister Winston Whyte and Leslie Pierre had established the conservative United People's Party (UPP) in 1974, drawing support from a section of the petty bourgeoisie and merchants who opposed the regime. After some internal debate, the NJM agreed to form a 'People's Alliance' with the GNP and UPP to contest the November 1976 elections. It is curious that Coard was given the 'safest' constituency, the town of St. George's, for the campaign. Bishop, nominally the leader of the People's Alliance, agreed to run in St. George's Southwest, a district which GULP had carried in the 1972 election by an electoral margin of 63-37 percent. Whiteman was a candidate in St. George's Northeast, in which GULP had received 53 percent of the popular vote four years before.[39]

Under democratic procedures, the People's Alliance would have won the 1976 election, but Gairy used every tactic to guarantee GULP's reelection. Only GULP candidates were permitted to use loudspeakers at their political rallies. The Mongoose Gang was ordered to disrupt People's Alliance meetings and demonstrations. Most crucial was the gross manipulation of the electoral rolls. Bishop later estimated that 'about 10,000 voters favorable to the alliance (were removed) from the rolls, while 13,000 nonexistent voters were registered.' All election officials were government employees, accountable to Gairy. In spite of this fraud, the People's Alliance recorded nearly twenty thousand votes (48.2 percent) and won six out of fifteen legislative seats. Bishop, Coard and Whiteman defeated GULP candidates, and Bishop became the leader of the opposition.[40]

Their moral victory over Gairy was unfortunately short-lived. On the one hand, the Prime Minister totally ignored or verbally abused the legislative opposition, and political repression became more severe. Government corruption in every form — including the sexual exploitation of women government workers, financial kickbacks, and the skimming of official funds — grew worse. On the other hand, the inability to use the parliamentary system against the regime exposed the contradictions within the People's Alliance. The GNP and UPP criticized the NJM's 'domination' and 'extremism', and effective cooperation between the three parties ceased by mid-1977. Social democratic elements inside the NJM began to grumble as well. The chief architect of the People's Alliance manifesto, George Brizan, and barrister Lloyd Noel opposed the trend toward Marxism within the Party. Noel was removed from the NJM's Political Bureau, while Brizan ultimately resigned.[41]

Although Brizan would later become Chief Education Officer after the US invasion, he has correctly identified direct 'parallels' between Gairy's draconian provisions and earlier steps taken in 1951 to curtail Grenadian workers' protests. GULP's neocolonial regime in the late 1970s was a continuation or logical extension of the restrictive and hierarchial Crown Colony system. Any facade of a parliamentary process, requiring at least the formal cooperation of major parties to discuss and shape public policies had disintegrated. GULP's parasitic elite had consolidated itself as a bureaucratic bourgeois stratum, imposing crudely dictatorial controls over all aspects of public life. 'He built up a highly centralized bureaucracy and succeeded in stripping the Civil Service of all autonomy in decision-making,' observed Brizan. 'Every matter was to be dealt with in Cabinet — from the hiring of a janitor to the building of a school — and in the Cabinet, Gairy's voice was supreme and his word law.'[42] The Essential Services and Port Authority Acts passed by the government prohibited strikes in the sectors where the NJM had many followers. Pro-Gairy bosses fired NJM workers, and refused to negotiate with independent unions.

To strengthen his credentials with Washington and London, Gairy attacked his opponents as communists, and vowed to 'cooperate with the western democracies placing our future on a foundation of free enterprise.' In 1976 he made state visits to South Korea and fascist Chile. He tried to sell Grenada's offshore fishing rights to the Koreans, (a move eventually thwarted by the NJM's mobilization of Grenadian fishermen), while in Santiago he negotiated the admission of several Grenadian police for the Police Academy as well as obtaining arms from Pinochet for his 'Green Beasts.'[43] (Meanwhile, the United States continued to mobilize international support for Gairy, and in June 1977 the annual conference of the Organization of American States was scheduled in St. George's. The People's Alliance staged a peaceful demonstration of 500 or 600 led by Bishop, denouncing Gairy's violation of human rights. Police firing automatic weapons brcke up the rally, as Gairy explained to his OAS colleagues that the demonstration 'at the particular time (was) not in the best interests of the State. We're not going to wash our dirty linen in public.' One of the NJM casualties in the demonstration was seventeen-year-old activist Alister Strachan.[44]

By late 1978, something of a political stalemate existed between the NJM and the Gairy regime. NJM activist Vincent Noel, a member of the Party's Political Bureau, had established the Bank and General Workers Union, strengthening the NJM's base among urban workers. Hudson Austin, Leon Cornwall and 'Akee' Gehagan had formed a clandestine military arm of the NJM, the People's Revolutionary Army (PRA), which obtained some weapons from sympathetic police and army members. Under Coard's ideological direction, the NJM became 'a disciplined, organised, tightly-knit, security-conscious party, so that it was therefore possible in the circumstances to call on people, day and night to respond to the call, and move swiftly.'[45]

The Gairy regime stagnated economically: the island's balance of payments deficit reached EC $5.3 million for 1978, and half of the labor force was unemployed. Gairy's personal behavior seemed increasingly detached from reality, as he became increasingly preoccupied with pornography, the occult, and 'flying saucers.'[46] Yet his bizarre behavior could not obscure the GULP regime's peculiar strengths. The neo-colonial authoritarian state retained marginal support among some middle-aged and elderly farmworkers and rural people; Gairy's party controlled the electoral system so completely that a truly democratic campaign was impossible for the opposition; and the Prime Minister had the political backing of the United States, anxious to contain Cuba's influence throughout the Caribbean. Upon leaving Grenada to visit the United Nations in March 1979, Gairy ordered the political decapitation of the NJM. Police informants leaked this information to Bishop and other leaders. Radix managed to flee the island, but Vincent Noel was arrested and imprisoned.

The essential nucleus of the NJM — Bishop, Whiteman, and Coard — caucused secretly with Hudson Austin and George Louison on the morning of 12 March. They had become convinced that the masses were ready to support the NJM in an armed insurrection. Coard thought that 'a majority of Grenadians would rise up actively' against GULP's regime, and that few military personnel would try to save Gairy. At this critical moment, Bishop alone remained unconvinced. True, Gairy had given orders to assassinate six of the NJM's top leaders, and to incarcerate many others. What probably troubled Bishop was the timing of this insurrection. He had long anticipated a second period of massive social unrest, similar to 1973-74, which would create the mass popular base for the NJM's actions. Other than Vincent Noel's recent mobilization of urban workers, no comparable social protest movement had reemerged. Complicating matters was the very nature of Grenadian society, which lacked a militant, leftist tradition inside the working class. If the NJM successfully overthrew Gairy, their action would not be a genuine social revolution, but a political insurrection against a despotic and corrupt regime. In the fullest sense, the NJM would gain a mandate to expel Gairy from power, but not a national consensus to implement socialism.

Bishop reflected on the precedent of the Cuban revolution. Castro's bold example in 1953, when the Fidelistas attacked the Moncada barracks, set the stage for the guerrilla struggle which later toppled Batista. Hector states, 'Maurice fully expected the revolution to fail when they attacked. The assault on the police barracks was their "Moncada." No one was more suprised than Bishop to realize how fragile Gairy's repressive regime was.' Bishop's mental reservations were overcome by his comrades' consensus that decisive measures had to be taken. It was simply a question of 'them or us,' Bishop admitted later, 'and we didn't plan on it being us.' Bishop's indecision should not be interpreted as an indication of weakness, or lack of resolve. No leader of any popular movement can afford to be cavalier with the lives of comrades, or to jeopardize the existence of his/her organization, even under the spectre of death. But at least one participant at this pivotal discussion, Coard, never forgot Bishop's momentary vacillation.[47]

Early the next day, 13 March 1979, NJM supporters in the telephone company cut all international phone service. The main target was the True Blue army headquarters, six miles south of St. George's. Austin and two lieutenants, Cornwall and Gehagan, were in command of the PRA, which numbered all of forty-six combatants that morning. Only eighteen had firearms, including eight M-1 rifles; the others were issued home-made Molotov cocktails. Inside the barracks were about 280 soldiers. After a half hour of shooting, the entire defense force surrendered or fled. The radio station was taken, and several cabinet ministers were captured in their beds by the PRA. As news of the insurrection became known, thousands of laborers and farmers joined in. In Birchgrove about two hundred people, mostly women, marched on the local police station and ordered officers to put up the white flag. PRA members and citizens captured the Mongoose Gang and secret police agents. Women cooked hot meals for the revolutionaries, and volunteers set up roadblocks in search of weapons.

GULP leaders quickly capitulated. George Hosten, Gairy's Deputy Prime Minsiter, broadcast over the radio that all GULP supporters should 'cooperate with the new Government. They are in full control of the situation and we want to avoid bloodshed.' Only three persons were killed in the fighting on 13 March, including one accidental death. Fifty to sixty persons were arrested, and more than half were released on the same day.[48] The uprising was even popularly supported by erstwhile NJM critics and elements of the local bourgeoisie. George Brizan affirms that the revolution was led by the NJM 'and sanctioned by the thousands who rallied to its banner.' The insurrection was immediately applauded by the Grenada Chamber of Commerce as 'a glorious opportunity to build something new and different in the Caribbean.' The uprising was successful, in part, because the central concern which motivated the people was democratic rights. In order to appeal to all social classes, socialism and class struggle were never mentioned. In one radio broadcast on 13 March, the Party declared: 'all democratic freedoms, including freedom of elections, religious and political opinion, will be fully restored to the people. The personal safety and property of individuals will be protected . . . (Gairy's supporters) will not be injured in any way. Their homes, their families, and their jobs are completely safe, so long as they do not offer violence to our government . . . The benefit of the revolution will be given to everyone regardless of political opinion or which political party they support.'[49]

The People's Revolutionary Government (PRG) established in March 1979 appeared to represent a continuation rather than a break with the People's Alliance strategy. The PRG immediately promised to move to 'free and fair elections', and Sir Paul Scoon, the Governor General appointed under Gairy, was retained as Grenada's representative to the Queen. Only nine NJM members initially belonged to the fourteen member PRG cabinet announced on 16 March: Bishop, Prime Minister; Coard, Minister of Finance, Trade and Industry; Whiteman, Minister of Agriculture, Tourism and Fisheries; Selwyn Strachan, Minister of Communications Works and Labor; Radix, Minister for Legal Affairs; Lloyd Noel, Deputy Minister for Legal Affairs; Louison, Minister of Education, Youth and Social Affairs; Vincent Noel and Hudson Austin. Other government posts were given to GNP leader and entrepreneur Norris Bain, and to Sydney Ambrose, a teacher and an unsuccessful People's Alliance candidate in the 1976 elections. Lyden Ramdhanny was selected as Minister of Tourism. The initial 'People's Laws,' a series of popular decrees, were in keeping with the principle of a broad class alliance. All pension rights for Grenadian civil servants were guaranteed. The jurisdiction of all legal magistrates courts were preserved. No political parties were officially outlawed.

Even on the sensitive issue of foreign policy, the PRG voiced no criticisms of the United States in the first weeks and only noted that it would 'stand against racism, especially as practiced in South Africa and [white-ruled] Zimbabwe.' The PRG was soon recognized by most nations, including Trinidad, Great Britain, Canada, Guyana, Barbados and Jamaica. What was not fully comprehended by some of the PRG's supporters in the Grenadian bourgeoisie was that the NJM, not the PRG, was rapidly consolidating hegemonic position within the domestic reconstruction process. The PRA replaced the island's police force, and was given the authority to arrest and interrogate citizens. In early April, People's Laws No.17 and No.21 established the policy of preventive detention for any persons attempting to 'subvert' or 'sabotage' the government. 'Persons detained under this law would be allowed no bail; the writ of habeas corpus would not lie in the case of any person denied bail by or under this law, and the Supreme Court . . . had no jurisdiction to grant such bail.'[50]

The political significance of the Grenadian revolution in the Caribbean — despite the island's small size of 133 square miles, and a population of less than 110,000 — was immediately profound. As Ambursely observed, the armed seizure of power 'represented the highest level of class struggle attained in the English-speaking Caribbean since the tumultuous slave uprisings of the seventeenth and eighteenth centuries.' Theoretically, it seemed to validate the theory of non-capitalist development or 'socialist orientation' for the Caribbean, by including within the PRG prominent representatives of the Grenadian elite. The first 'official' history of the revolution, published in 1980, stressed this central point: 'to adopt an overtly Marxist-Leninist path . . . is to court alienation and take a deliberately long route to national liberation.'[51] The obvious historical and political inclination was to assert direct parallels between the Cuban and Grenadian revolutions. Castro himself terms the Grenadian insurrection 'a successful Moncada'; Bishop stated that 'Cuba laid the basis for Grenada . . . ' In November 1979 Selwyn Strachan also predicted: 'Our course of development will be more or less the same as the Cuban revolution. There may be one or two minor differences, but nothing dramatic. And that, of course, will go for almost every country in the Caribbean, because we have [all] been underdeveloped by the imperialist world.'[52] The principal critic of the Cubans inside the NJM, interestingly enough, was Coard, who had 'imbibed the unofficial criticisms that the Soviet leadership has levelled against the Castro regime.'[53]

Some historical parallels were obvious. Batista and Gairy were despotic leaders; their authoritarian Bonapartist regimes were parasitic, riddled with corruption, and highly unpopular. In both societies, the electoral systems had become widely discredited, and broad sectors of the petty bourgeoisie and even some national bourgeoisie were anxious for some major type of political change. The progressive forces of both islands were led by charismatic figures, Castro and Bishop, yet the revolutionary process had created a core of individual leaders and lieutenants who were articulate and popular among the masses. But nevertheless, the discontinuities were far more profound. The Cuban proletariat had been receptive to the socialist policies of Castro, precisely because of its rich history of class struggle and industrial organization. Even under Batista, half the Cuban labor force belonged to unions, and the Communist Party's political prestige and ideological influence were extensive. Unemployment was a chronic problem in Cuba prior to the 1959 revolution, but it never reached the levels obtained under the Gairy regime in the 1970s.[54] The Grenadian working class was small and had absolutely no tradition of Marxism. Castro could appeal to the revolutionary, national demoractic tradition of Marti, in presenting the 1959 revolution as a logical culmination of a nearly century-long process. Bishop and the NJM had no similar frame of reference within the political culture of Grenada, beyond the anti-colonial liberalism of Marryshow.

The entire English-speaking Caribbean also retained a profound identity with the Westminster system, even in states such as Guyana, where the democratic mechanisms had atrophied and a bureaucratic bourgeois stratum dominated society. The Grenadian masses endorsed the 1979 revolution as the only legitimate means to overturn GULP's dictatorship, but it is much less certain that they had ever transcended their traditional commitment to the formal processes of representative democracy and partisan political elections. The spontaneous collapse of the Gairy regime could not be equated, in short, with a demand for a dictatorship of the proletariat, or any popular endorsement for a socialist reorganization of society. As Rosa Luxemburg observed: 'The socialist system of society should be, and can only be, an historical product, born out of the school of its own experiences, born in the course of its realization, as a result of the developments of living history . . . The whole mass of the people must take part in it. Otherwise, socialism will be decreed from behind a few official desks by a dozen intellectuals.'[55]

Neither Bishop nor the NJM militants seem to have considered another aspect of the Cuban revolution which should have had immediate relevance to Grenada. The defeat of the Batista dictatorship marked the end of one phase of the struggle for national liberation, and only placed the possibility for a transition to socialism on the national agenda. The early history of socialist Cuba was marked by numerous political cleavages within the 26 July Movement, and major tensions between Fidelistas, the Communists, and radicals in the Directorio Revolucionario. Communist leader Aníbal Escalante would be purged twice, in 1962 and in 1968; and when the 'new' Communist Party of Cuba was finally established in 1965, only a small minority of the members of its central committee had been Marxist-Leninists before 1959.[56] Political schisms and the development of internal party factions are an integral feature of post-revolutionary societies, both capitalist and socialist. Perhaps the NJM had convinced itself that such fissures would never take place inside Grenada.

III

Although Maurice Bishop was the charismatic, symbolic link between the PRG, the NJM and the Grenadian masses, Bernard Coard must rightfully be considered the chief architect of the revolution's political economy of 1979-1983. Speaking for the PRG in September 1979, Coard observed that the new government had numerous tasks, including the 'stabilization of the economy,' the liquidation of 'the massive debts we had inherited,' the abolition of public corruption, 'victimisation and sexual abuse and exploitation of women in society.' Well down the list of priorities was the scheduling of 'free and fair elections.'[57] Following the thesis of 'socialist orientation' to a precise degree, Coard projected the general course of the social reconstruction process. As Minister of Finance, Coard emphasized: 'we are developing our economy on the *mixed economy model*. Our economy as a mixed economy will comprise the state sector, the private sector and the cooperative sector. The dominant sector will be the state sector, which will lead the development process.'[58]

Other priorities for Grenada's socialist orientation strategy included the promotion of socialist values and consciousness within cultural, political, social and gender relations; the 'expansion of mass participation in and control of the state administration and the state economic enterprises;' 'the development of appropriate planning techniques and organizational methods to raise productive forces;' and the 'abolition of imperialism's political domination.'[59] Bishop raised no substantial criticisms of this agenda, and was in fact pivotal in popularizing its underlying theory to the masses. In mid-1983, Bishop explained that the NJM's 'concrete alliance to fight the 1976 elections . . . continues to help us today in pursuing a policy of alliances with sections of the upper petty bourgeoisie in our country, and even the bourgeoisie, as part of our overall policy of socialist orientation.'[60]

From the outset the NJM was determined to scrap the Westminster parliamentary system. For Coard, the NJM represented 'a reaction to and repudiation of the old-style rum-and-corned beef politics, the politics of bribery and corruption . . . a process that consciously sought to divide the people into two warring camps, the "ins" and the "outs." ' Bishop viewed the parliamentary process with equal repugnance. The Westminster system promoted 'political tribalism,' and had been used by the CIA 'to get some of the parliamentarians to use the medium of parliament . . . to destabilize the country. Masterminded by their American puppeteers, they raise bogus concerns about the economy, they spread vicious propaganda . . . and seek to make the people lose faith and confidence in their revolutionary government . . . '[61]

Since the NJM was effectively in command of the state apparatus, Grenada became a *de facto* one party state, and the old 'bourgeois' parties had no institutional means to articulate grievances. In July 1979 the GNP attempted to hold public meetings in Grenville and Sauteurs. NJM supporters disrupted these gatherings, shouting 'We want Bishop!' Blaize condemned these demonstrators as 'ragamuffins,' but to his dismay, the GNP soon disintegrated as a coherent political force. The GNP had failed to build a meaningful protest movement against Gairy's regime in the 1970s, and its checkered legacy in power perhaps merited its demise. However, Bishop perceived the 'attempts to revive Herbert Blaize and his GNP' as part of imperialism's 'attempts to build a popular base' for counterrevolution. If the GNP was permitted to exist, it could 'exploit genuine objective grievances of the masses,' and retard the revolution. Although this was undoubtedly Blaize's aim, the GNP's previous history had condemned it to obscurity, and the PRG never officially banned the party.[62]

Before seizing state power, the NJM had created local parish branches to reach the population. These structures became Parish Councils, which permitted village and rural residents to discuss state policies and problems with PRG leaders and other officials. Within two years, a system of 18 smaller Zonal Councils was created, which encouraged political debate and participation at local levels. Through these councils and the mass organizations (such as the trade unions, the National Youth Organisation and National Women's Organisation), issues were discussed and resolutions on major concerns were adopted. Theoretically, this was a system of revolutionary, grassroots democracy. Through the local Zonal Council or within one of many mass formations, workers and farmers could freely express their opinions. Representatives from the Zonal and Parish Councils and the mass organizations were sent to a National Conference of Delegates, which made recommendations on the national budget or other critical matters. Local NJM members' resolutions and suggestions would filter directly to the Party's Central Committee, which was chaired by Bishop. The PRG's official view was that this system was infinitely superior to the discredited electoral structure: 'Parliament has moved out of town into the communities . . . Political power has been taken out of the hands of a few privileged people and turned over to thousands of men, women and youth.'[63]

But the NJM's version of mass participatory democracy contained many serious flaws. 'The principle of accountability is fundamental in building a new people's democracy,' declared Coard. But for the Finance Minister, and most other NJM leaders, 'accountability' meant that PRG representatives should directly report on 'everything which affects the people' at local assemblies. But accountability also requires the ability to recall or remove officials who are responsible for unpopular public policies. Agendas of Parish and Zonal Council meetings were frequently set in advance, and no institutional mechanism existed to ensure that local decisions would be acted upon by those in power. The Councils' executive committees were chosen by the NJM, and not democratically elected by the participants. The NJM did not seriously consider the question of 'minority rights' in establishing these Councils. The network of Councils tended to frustrate many honest and sincere Grenadians who had hoped to find some legitimate outlet for their opinions. Finally, the political system as developed by the NJM could only be termed 'democratic' if a high level of mass participation was maintained, and if the national leadership was intimately involved in all local discussions.

But the NJM itself was much too small to carry out this level of intense mobilization for a protracted period. In 1983, the NJM's total membership, including candidate or non-voting members, was still only three hundred. Considering their fulltime responsibilities in the PRG and mass organizations like the trade unions, key leaders were simply unable to devote much extra energy or time to regular public meetings. The NJM's newspaper, the *Free West Indian,* repeatedly urged citizens to take part in Council gatherings: 'This type of democracy brings added responsibility . . . it means doing the utmost at your workplace and then shedding your working clothes and going to a meeting . . . ' For several years, about half of all adults in the country attended weekly meetings. But by 1982-1983 participation began to decline: not a single NJM Central Committee member attended even one Zonal Council meeting in the last eighteen months of the revolution.[64]

The PRG's economic policies were almost entirely shaped by Coard. As the Finance Minister admitted in 1982, he was the NJM's 'only hatchetman . . . everyone was depending on him for everything especially in the area of the economy.'[65] Coard's first objectives were to 'cut recurrent expenditure as far as possible, channeling the saved money into capital development projects,' and to increase worker productivity in the public sector. Toward this end, Coard and Deputy Finance Minister Lyden Ramdhanny developed an efficient planning apparatus, and eliminated the corruption and administrative backwardness left by Gairy. The NJM disavowed any intention to launch major nationalisations, but used legal and political methods to promote the 'class conscious development of the working class.' People's Law 46 protected the right to strike, and People's Law 62 allowed unions to buy and lease property. Under NJM labor leader Vincent Noel's direction, the Bank and General Workers' Union (BGWU) expanded from 100 to over 3,000 workers in banks, restaurants, hotels, banana box factories, and in other small firms. Total trade-union membership in Grenada soared from 30 to 80 percent of the wage labor force. Stronger unions meant that the working class was empowered to obtain long overdue wage increases. In 1981, according to Coard, 'the wages on average based on wage contracts in both the public and private sector rose 17.5 per cent.' Grenada's per capita income under the PRG rose from US $450 in 1978 to US $870 in 1983.[66]

This did not mean that the PRG acceded to all wage demands, or that its relations with every union were harmonious. Coard believed in strict fiscal management and labor productivity, and the heads of several major unions were politically antagonistic to the government. The conservative United People's Party had supporters in the Technical and Allied Workers' Union (TAWU), and leaders of the Public Workers' Union (PWU) and the Grenada Teachers' Union (GUT) pressed the PRG with unrealistic wage demands. All three unions asked for a 90 percent salary increase in late 1980, which was subsequently cut to an 'irreducible minimum' of 37.5 percent for 1981 and 25 percent in 1982. Coard took an extremely hard line, offering increases of 12.5 percent in 1981, and 5 percent in both 1982 and 1983. In January 1981, leaders of TAWU, PWU and GUT ordered union members to stage a massive 'sick out' to paralyze the government. Coard and many other PRG leaders believed that the strike was 'part of a plan by certain unpatriotic and counter-revolutionary elements.' Coard openly attacked the PWU for its 'sheer selfishness and avarice.' In March, the PRG fired one recalcitrant civil servant, suspended ten more, and distributed 'warnings' to seventy others. The majority of the employees were sympathetic with the government, and did not join the 'sick out.' In fairness, however, these unions had received no salary increases since 1973 and inflation had seriously eroded the buying power of rank-and-file members. Bishop recognized that coercive measures would be counterproductive, and in April, 1981, he held twenty-three meetings in factories, union halls and banks to listen to employees' grievances. An agreement was finally reached which set wage increases at 17.3 percent in 1981, 10 percent in 1982, and 12.5 percent in 1983.[67]

Throughout the PRG's tenure, Coard identified himself as having the most rigid attitudes towards workers' responsibilities for discipline and productivity. For example, speaking before the BGWU on 5 February 1982, Coard defined workers' democracy as 'the right of every single worker . . . to have the financial Statement of Accounts of the enterprise in which they work.' Labor should have a role to play in electing representatives to set on corporate boards, Coard said, but he emphasized their more general responsibility 'to stop corruption and waste and increase efficiency in the workplace.' To reinforce the work ethic, the Finance Minister advocated a system of profit-sharing 'for those who have worked hard to increase production.' Constantly critical of state employees, Coard demanded that they cultivate 'correct attitudes to work, punctuality, discipline, training, care of equipment, proper use of supplies, (and) proper use of time . . . '[68]

The PRG's rural economic schemes were characterized by pragmatism and careful planning. Coard recognized that Grenada's economic dependency on the West could not be broken unless overall agricultural production was increased and made more efficient, and this also required a reduction in the share of traditional export goods. Before the revolution, almost three-fourths of the Grenadian diet consisted of imported foods. Only 8,000 Grenadians worked full-time as farmers, and roughly one-third of the arable land was not under regular cultivation. A similar situation existed in fishing. Grenadians purchased several million dollars' worth of Canadian salted cod each year. 'In a country blessed with an abundance of every tropical fruit imaginable, the most common fruit drink (was) imported Florida orange juice.'[69] To move toward agricultural self sufficiency, the PRG developed policies to strengthen small farmers, while expanding domestic consumption of local produce. The Ministry of Agriculture in 1981 alone allocated EC $4.6 million in assistance for the purchase of tools, seeds, equipment, and for farmers' credit. In April 1980 the National Cooperative Development Agency (NACDA) was formed to sponsor rural cooperatives on unused properties. NACDA staff members regularly visited cooperatives and provided technical advice, and within two years, the NACDA disbursed over EC $600,000 to twenty-three cooperatives. By mid-1983 thirty-seven cooperatives had been started.

Overall, the rural cooperatives were a mixed success. Low wages kept many young people away, and ten cooperatives had to be shut down for various reasons. To sustain its rural development program, the PRG solicited aid from many foreign governments. In early 1980, for example, the Nigerian government gave the PRG EC $110,000 for the improvement of roads. In August 1981 George Louison, then serving as Agricultural Minister, secured the backing of the Canadian government for a 'Cocoa Rehabilitation Project,' which involved the replanting of 10,000 acres of cocoa fields at a cost of EC $20 million. During Coard's 1981 trip to the Soviet Union, he obtained a gift of twenty jeeps, 20 irrigation pumps, 10 tractors, 12 trucks and six bulldozers. Cuba gave the PRG ten fishing boats between August 1979 and March 1982, and trained forty Grenadian fishermen. In late 1981 Louison obtained 270 metric tons of fertilizer from the United Nations Food and Agriculture Organization, which was used to increase vegetable production. And in early December 1982, India gave the PRG a power tiller, and Cuba donated another 23 tractors, twelve ploughs, 18 planters and other agricultural equipment valued at EC $2 million. Gradually, the island became less dependent on external food sources. Grenada's fishing industry expanded so quickly that by early 1982 the PRG had become a net exporter of saltfish, selling Dominica 25,000 pounds of fish that year.[70]

To protect the rights of rural laborers, the NJM established the Agricultural and General Workers Union (AGWU) in late 1979, under the leadership of Fitzroy Bain. The AGWU initially had 1,000 members, including laborers on government-owned estates, privately-held farms, and road repair crews. Within two years the AGWU had grown to 2,300 members, and the union aggressively defended its members interests. In September 1981 the AGWU struck successfully on eight privately-owned estates over the right for paid holidays. In 1980, the PRG established the Grenada Farms Corporation (GFC), which managed and developed the twenty-five estates that had been acquired by Gairy's regime. The AGWU obtained a profit-sharing program at GFC estates, and soon extended their demand for similar plans at private estates. Throughout these and other types of programs, the PRG successfully reduced unemployment, especially for women and young people. Overall unemployment dropped from 49 percent in 1979 to about 10 percent by late 1983.'[71]

While increasing the organizational capacity of the urban and rural proletariat, the PRG simultaneously attempted to maintain good relations with the local bourgeoisie. Several initial decisions were made to inspire 'business confidence.' The PRG did not withdraw from the East Caribbean Currency Authority; Grenada had no central bank, and the state had limited ability to borrow substantial amounts from abroad to finance social welfare projects. The PRG had to depend upon the private sector's cooperation to create many jobs, and this would only occur if incentives were provided. Thus The National Development Bank loaned EC $740,000 to 191 private-sector projects in 1981 to stimulate small business. Nevertheless, private-sector investment declined that year by one fourth. The PRG's response was to apply the classic 'carrot and stick' approach to the problem. In early 1982, Coard announced that the basic business tax rate of 50 percent was to be hiked to 55 percent. However, if manufacturing, construction and hotel firms expanded existing facilities, or initiated a 'new business activity,' they would be granted a rebate which would reduce the effective tax rate to 40 percent. 'In other words,' Coard warned the private sector bluntly, 'for those who sit on their behinds and do nothing about reinvestment, the tax has gone up . . . ' The National Development Bank's loans to private sector projects were increased substantially to EC $1.5 million in 1982. As a result, private sector investment and company tax revenues increased.[72] A revealing instance of this pragmatic approach toward the Grenadian bourgeoisie was the government's response to a 1979 labor protest at the local Coca Cola bottling plant. When the local owner refused to come to terms with workers, the PRG took charge of the plant and rehired dissident employees. However, the PRG did not nationalize the plant. Minister of Labour, Selwyn Strachan, observed: 'It was not a question of us taking full control of the factory . . . although the factory has been run by government, the ownership still remains in [private] hands . . . All we are concerned about now is getting the industrial matter settled.' For over two years the PRG ran the factory, but in early 1982 an agreement was reached with the owner, and all funds acquired from production were returned to him.'⁷³

Perhaps Coard's greatest achievement as Finance Minister was his adroit manipulation of international financial institutions. Under Coard, Grenada's debt service ratio declined to 3.7 percent of export earnings, one of the world's lowest rates. The World Bank subsequently issued a favourable study on Grenada's management in mid-1982; and in August, 1983, the IMF authorized a stand-by loan to the PRG of £14.1 million. Coard soon acquired a reputation in international financial circles as a model of prudent caution. As one international banker who worked with the Finance Ministry put it: 'affable and approachable, Coard was intellectually and operationally head and shoulders above his colleagues from the other islands in the Eastern Caribbean. . . . Coard was always willing to meet the IMF more than half way. He also knew the way to get money quickly and efficiently out of the international lending agencies. While some of the other financial ministers would rant and rave about the bureaucracy of the lending banks, Coard saved his energies to understand the system and make it work for Grenada.'⁷⁴ Rivalling Coard in sophisticated economic diplomacy was Ramdhanny, who in late March 1982 led a Grenada Chamber of Commerce delegation to lobby the US Congress on the Reagan Administration's Caribbean Basic Initiative. Ramdhanny explained that the PRG did not oppose 'joint ventures between foreign private interests and local private interests, and between foreign private interests' and the government.'⁷⁵

The centerpiece of the PRG's economic development strategy was the Point Salines airport project. First conceived by the British, and later advocated by the Gairy regime, the NJM recognized that a major international airport was essential to increase tourism to the island. Bishop also viewed the airport project 'as a symbol of what a small poor Third World developing country can do to bring about its own development in the face of pressure from imperialism.' In September 1979, the PRG requested funding for the airport from a number of international agencies and nations, including the United States. Cuba quickly offered to provide at least 250 construction workers and technicians, 85 pieces of heavy equipment for airport construction, and donated 4,000 tons of cement and 1,500 tons of steel. Iraq promised $5.4 million to the PRG in late 1979, part of which was to be used for the airport. Libya, Algeria and Syria pledged $27 million by February 1980. Venezuela provided a gift of 10,000 barrels of diesel fuel for the project. The European

Economic Community (EEC) gave over $2 million despite US attempts to block EEC funding. The US government rejected an IMF report which endorsed the PRG's claim that the project was 'critical to the economic development of the island.' State Department and Pentagon officials claimed that the international airport 'might serve as a a staging area and refueling stop for Cuban troops on the way to Africa or South America, and another Soviet base in the Western hemisphere capable of servicing Soviet Bombers . . .' American attacks simply reinforced the PRG's commitment to the project, which captured the enthusiastic support of the Grenadian people. Thousands of citizens purchased 'airport bonds' worth EC $850,000 to help pay for the construction costs by the beginning of 1982.[76]

The PRG's general policy of a 'strategic alliance' between the national bourgeoisie, middle strata, workers and farmers, despite its constructive achievements, was inherently unstable over the long run. For generations, the estate owners and small factory owners had become well-to-do by exploiting subordinated classes: reducing small landowners to the status of farm laborers, keeping wages low, avoiding taxes, and so forth. The Grenadian elite accumulated capital at the expense of the state sector, and sought to reduce state intervention into its affairs, except where it added to its potential profits. The international airport would greatly expand tourism, and thus was in the interests of most of the local elite. But the NJM's sponsorship of new unions, particularly the BGWU and the AGWU, its policy of profit-sharing on GFC estates, and its agricultural cooperatives were viewed as radical and disturbing developments. Laborers who had come to anticipate higher wages, better working conditions and a generous share of the profits might one day make the leap to total worker control. In fact, in early 1983, the NJM took the 'confidential' decision to absorb another 6,000 acres of land under the GFC and to create 36 new state farms. The next step was to win the peasantry to socialism by expanding cooperatives and strengthening the Peasants' and Farmers' Unions 'as the organ for carrying out the tasks of the Party.' The only impediments which slowed the pace of development of collectivization were the lack of sufficient NJM cadre and the still conservative cultural and social values of many rural working people.[77]

Equally perturbing to the national bourgeoisie was the rapid growth of the state sector, and what appeared to be embryonic moves toward expropriation. By raising substantial funds abroad, the PRG's capital spending increased from EC $16 million in 1979 to EC $101.5 million in 1982. Overall capital spending for the PRG in 1980-82 amounted to almost EC $237 million, a figure which, Coard declared, 'completely overshadows the tiny amounts spent on capital projects during all of Gairy's 25 year dictatorship.' However, the PRG had also seized all of Gairy's hotels and nightclubs without compensation, and nationalized the telephone and electric power companies. When the Canadian Imperial Bank of Commerce made plans to depart, the PRG took over the facility, renaming it the National Commercial Bank. The PRG promised to compensate the owner of the Point Salines property when the airport was under construction, but no payments were ever made. In early 1983 the PRG seized several estates which were termed 'idle land', and in several instances no compensation was given. When the NJM introduced political education courses into the trade unions also in early 1983, the national bourgeoisie probably perceived that its economic prerogatives were going to go the way of Lenin's 'state' in *State and Revolution* — that is, 'withering away.' Its political options were limited by the disintegration of the UPP and GNP, and the absence of a parliamentary system. Local capitalists kept their funds in private banks and through various illegal conduits much of the national savings were transferred out of the country. A few entrepreneurs even resorted to types of economic sabotage. The Grenadian bourgeoisie recognized that it had lost state power, perhaps irrevocably, and that its relations with the PRG were degenerating beyond repair. The NJM's Central Committee also reached this conclusion in July 1983: 'The alliance with the bourgeoisie to create a national economy has become more complex and must be re-examined.'[78]

IV

The Grenadian revolution received its highest praises abroad for its humanistic social welfare and cultural policies. As Coard came to be viewed as the revolution's technocrat and theoretician, Bishop was the revolution's spiritual and popular guide. No NJM leader could motivate the masses nearly as well; none was as deeply loved by non-Party members. Bishop's intimate knowledge of Grenada's social history allowed him to place the NJM within its 'tradition of resistance,' from the Fedon uprising of 1795 through the years of anticolonial agitation and the eloquent leadership of T.A. Marryshow. His flowing rhetoric gave the people a sense of their own latent capacity to struggle and to transform their environment.

'When a conscious, determined people rises as a united body and cries "enough", injustice, tyranny, and exploitation are doomed,' Bishop stated in November 1981. 'Thus begins a new and glorious chapter in the history of man: the construction of a just and equal society by the poor, for the poor, and with the poor . . . From the very inception of our party, the NJM, we have been guided by the clear understanding that the struggle against the dictatorship was not an end in itself, but a necessary precondition for the infinitely larger struggle of building that new and just society.'[79] Bishop, and to some extent Unison Whiteman and George Louison, personified the popular will, the bond between the revolutionary state and the masses. Bishop was a 'Marxist humanist,' and the PRG's social welfare agenda was rooted firmly in a humanistic perspective.[80]

The problems of pre-revolutionary health-care in Grenada were similar to those of other underdeveloped and neocolonial states. Infant mortality in 1976 was 27.6 per thousand live births; there were only twenty-three physicians in the country, and dentistry was virtually nonexistent. In June 1979, a twelve-person medical team arrived from Cuba, including an orthopedic surgeon, three dentists, and three pediatricians. All services by the Cubans were free to the public. In December 1979 an eye clinic staffed by a Cuban surgeon was opened in St. George's general hospital. Ten months later, the PRG announced that all public dental and medical care was to be without charge. Doctors retained the right to treat patients privately for a fee, but they could not do so in public hospitals or state-owned clinics. By early 1982, the PRG had nearly doubled the number of physicians in Grenada, had established at least one major health center in every parish, and twenty-eight small medical stations across the island. Fourteen percent of the PRG's 1982-1983 budget was allocated to health-care.[81]

Housing was another major priority of the PRG. In late 1979 Coard announced the initiation of four major housing schemes entailing expenditure of over EC $7 million. The first program, designed for civil servants, was projected to cost EC $3 million over a five-year period. The second scheme, focusing on 'the poorest and lowest paid workers in our country,' permitted poor laborers to receive home improvement loans up to EC $1,000, of which one third was an outright grant, and the balance was to be repaid interest-free in ten years. Workers earning EC $150 to $250 per month could also borrow $1,000, but had to repay the entire amount of the interest-free loan. Furthermore, Coard added that the government would begin construction of low income housing under the supervision of a National Housing Authority. The housing program was one of the most popular measures of the PRG. Between January 1980 and February 1982 about 1,600 Grenadian families benefitted from the loans, mostly estate workers, road laborers and the poor. Household life also was improved by government measures to expand electrification and plumbing facilities. Between 1979-1983 electricity output in Grenada increased 40 percent, and the number of homes with indoor toilets increased 50 percent. Again, foreign assistance provided an additional boost, as the Venezuelan government gave Grenada one hundred prefabricated wooden houses in August 1982. The following year, the Sandino Housing Plant was started, which had a projected output of five hundred prefabricated houses per year.[82]

Probably the most striking social reforms were accomplished in education, which comprised 22 percent of the PRG's 1982-1983 budget. For Bishop, 'the worst crime that colonialism' had committed in Grenada was its 'educational system . . . The colonial masters recognized very early on that if you get a subject people to think like they do, to forget their own history and their own culture, to develop a system of education that is going to have relevance to our outward needs and be almost irrelevant to our internal needs, then they have already won the job of keeping us in perpetual domination and exploitation. Our educational process, therefore, was used mainly as a tool of the ruling elite.'[83] Under Gairy, the educational system still suffered: only thirty percent of all primary school teachers had any college training, and less than one in ten secondary-level instructors had professional training. Only eleven percent of all youth of secondary school-age even attended schools in 1978. Under the supervision of Louison, and after August 1981, Jacqueline Creft, the Centre for Popular Education (CPE) was initiated to combat illiteracy, with the long term goal of providing all Grenadian adults with a minimal sixth grade level education. The first phase of CPE, beginning in late July 1980, established village committees led by volunteer teachers, which met once a week. Throughout this process, Bishop emphasized the profoundly political character of education for the oppressed. 'If we are to end unemployment and poor housing, we will have to increase our levels of production by working harder, using better, more scientific methods of production, and using higher forms of technology. To teach a brother or sister to read and write is a deeply rewarding task, it is a revolutionary duty for those who know how to voluntarily place their knowledge at the service of those who do not.' By

February 1981, the first phase of the CPE drew to a close as a popular success. CPE's 'Phase Two,' initiated in March 1982, provided a post-literacy curriculum including courses in Grenadian history, English, mathematics, geography and the natural sciences.[84]

Other important components of Grenada's educational offensive included the National In-Service Teacher Education Programme (NISTEP) and the Community School Day Programms (CSDP). Started in November 1980, NISTEP was designed to improve the skills of 612 untrained teachers within a three-year period, and to standarize the nation's school curriculum. One day each week, teachers left the classroom for training, creating a direct link between classroom theory and direct practice. 'Teachers are understanding that education should be a part of the process of developing a free and just society,' the Prime Minister remarked in October 1981. 'Whom should education service? It should serve the process of transformation from a colonial territory to a liberated, self-reliant nation.' CSDP scheduled regular dates at all schools when community people were invited into the classroom to 'teach what they know.' CSDP-supported Community School Councils also functioned as parent-teacher associations. All education, for the first time in Grenadian history, was free. The PRG built a new secondary school, and in 1981 started an assistance fund of EC $60,000 to cover the cost of uniforms and textbooks for the children of poor families. Cuba promptly offered Grenadians scholarships for technical and university-level studies in medicine, engineering, dentistry, architecture, veterinary medicine and other fields. Between 1978 and 1983, the number of Grenadians being educated abroad on scholarships soared from 3 to 330.[85]

The NJM's approach toward women's rights was generally progressive, but in some respects was compromised by its tendency to rely on hierarchical and command-oriented measures. Males were disproportionately represented on the Party's Political Bureau and Central Committee. By contrast, the PRG had a number of women working as permanent secretaries of ministries, including Gloria Payne-Banfield, Ministry of Planning; Faye Rapier, Ministry of Legal Affairs; and Dorcas Braveboy, Ministry of Health. Program directors included Valerie Cornwall, National Coordinator of the CPE; Yvonne James, Health Planner in the Ministry of Health; Regina Taylor, General Secretary of the Agency for Rural Transformation; Bridget Horsford, manager of the Agro-Industrial Plant; Jane Belfon, Director of Tourism; and Joan Ross, Program

Director for 'Television Free Grenada.' In the important post of ambassador to the Organization of American States was an articulate diplomat, Dessima Williams.

Undoubtedly the two most influential women in the PRG were Phyllis Coard and Jacqueline Creft. First appointed Deputy Secretary in the Department of Information and Culture, in August 1980 Coard was named Secretary for Women's Affairs in the Ministry of Education, Youth and Social Affairs. With the development of the National Women's Organization (NWO), Coard was elected president — although Hector insists that other more popular women leaders may have been pressured not to contest the election against her. The NWO started its own newspaper, and by early 1982 its membership reached 6,500, organized in 155 local units. By mid-1983, however, the NWO was rapidly losing members. At the July 1983 NJM Central Committee sessions, Phyllis Coard bitterly blamed the NWO's problems on women harboring 'petty-bourgeois' traits, who were 'unaccustomed to working on their own.' No one apparently questioned Coard's responsibility for the NWO's difficulties. Creft was in many ways the opposite of Phyllis Coard, an intelligent and sensitive educator who perceived socialism as a protracted process, involving mass participation and decision-making at every level. After the revolution, Bishop separated from his wife Angela and began living with Creft; the couple had a son, Vladimir, in 1981. In August 1982 a new Ministry of Women's Affairs was initiated, for which Creft and Coard were named Minister and Secretary respectively.'[86]

Upon assuming power, the PRG immediately halted Gairy's policies of 'sex-ploitation,' the granting of public jobs in exchange for sexual intercourse. Despite the opposition of many private employers and estate owners, the PRG issued the 'Maternity Leave Law' which went into effect on 5 October 1980. The law gave all pregnant employees three months maternity leave with the right to return to their jobs. For workers with 18 months or more time with a single employer, the law required that two of the three months' leave must be at full salary. Employers were not permitted to dismiss pregnant women, and violations of the law were punishable by a fine of EC $1,000 or six months in jail. The state required that all women employees in government jobs receive 'equal pay for equal work,' and it upgraded salaries for women workers. Although the PRG's efforts to improve the socioeconomic and political role of women in Grenadian life were important, it was the self-conscious activism of women themselves that began to transform gender relations. Supported by the revolutionary process, Grenadian women began 'moving into non-traditional occupations such as carpentry, plumbing, fisheries, and agricultural cooperatives.'[87]

Grenadian youth also benefitted from the revolution. The NJM had always viewed the mobilization of youth as a 'major priority,' and before Gairy's removal, it had recruited about forty young supporters to its youth wing. Once in power, the Party founded the National Youth Organization (NYO), chaired by a young protege of Coard's, Leon Cornwall. Growing rapidly at first, by late 1981 it had more than 7,000 members. NYO volunteers accounted for almost two-thirds of all CPE literacy workers. About 800 youth participated in summer camps in 1981, which included a variety of educational and sports programs. A 'Young Pioneer' organization designed for younger people, aged 9 to 15, was started in January 1980 in St. Andrew's Parish, and quickly spread throughout the island. Directed by the NJM, the 'Young Pioneers' was designed to reinforce the ideological support for 'defending the Revolution' among young people. But the NYO lacked sufficient cadre for extensive development, and by the beginning of 1983 some Party leaders had become deeply dissatisfied with its lack of progress. NJM Central Committee member Tan Bartholemew privately complained in August, 1983, for example, that NYO 'stood for "Not Yet Organised." '[88]

The relations between Grenada's religious leaders and the NJM were rather strained for several reasons. The majority of Grenadians were Roman Catholics, although the island also included a number of Anglicans, Methodists, Presbyterians, Baptists, and members of other denominations. Grenada Catholic Bishop Patrick Webster had denounced Gairy's 'Bloody Sunday' incident, and was replaced by a conservative priest, Bishop Sydney Charles of Trinidad. Although many young Catholics were supporters of the NJM, the Catholic hierarchy and many other Christian ministers were caught off-guard by Gairy's overthrow, and feared the socialist-orientation of the new government. In his 21 October 1979 pastoral letter to Grenadian Catholics, Bishop Charles pledged the church's 'loyalty, support and co-operation' to the PRG, noting that it approved of 'Government programmes which aim at developing the whole man and every man in society without discrimination . . . ' But Bishop Charles also voiced criticisms of the PRG's 'suppression of freedom,' which he predicted was 'certain to lead to restlessness and rebellion.'[89]

Other clergy soon voiced further complaints. Leaders of the

Conference of Churches in Grenada (CCG) expressed stern displeasure with the weapons instruction given to Pioneer youth. Clergy warned that 'exposing children to the handling of guns' would not only 'affect their young minds adversely,' but also 'undermine children's respect for authority in the home and at school.' In early 1980, the PRG learned of a plot by several Catholic priests to 'use Grenada as a test-bed for church agitation in a "Marxist-oriented" society.' Confronting Bishop Charles with this evidence of religious destabilization, he quickly 'disowned' the plan. Informing the public about the covert strategies of reactionary Catholics, the Prime Minister emphasized that the PRG would always 'guarantee our fullest, continued cooperation with the church in all areas which will bring social and material benefits to our people . . . We have not in the past attempted to tell the church how to conduct its religious activities and we have absolutely no intention of doing so in the future.' But Bishop also added, 'we are not prepared to allow the church or elements within the church to carve out a new, political role for themselves,' or to 'engage in counterrevolutionary activities against the interests of the people.' After this incident, most clergy were slightly more reluctant to issue unconditional criticisms of the PRG. The Reverend Gerald Hutchinson, head of Grenada's Presbyterian Church, admitted in March 1980, 'at least 70 percent' of the population supported the socialist government. 'There can be no doubt that (Prime Minister Bishop) has massive support clean across the country and including all age groups.'[90]

V

The attitude of Washington toward the PRG was overtly hostile from the beginning. The NJM's accession to power occurred precisely at a moment when US political and economic interests in the Caribbean and Central America were on the defensive. In Nicaragua, a bloody social revolution which had taken the lives of over 40,000 was entering its final phase. The Carter administration desperately tried to bolster the dictatorial Somoza regime, and used its proxies to provide military and economic support. In May 1978, the Inter-American Development Bank gave $32 million to Somoza; the Israelis dispatched a military unit to design a more effective air defense system; and in early 1979, the United States used its leverage over the IMF to secure $65 million for the regime. Such assistance was too little and too late: the Sandinista Front for

National Liberation toppled Somoza in July 1979. That same month, the social democratic Labour Party won the elections in St. Lucia. The new Deputy Prime Minister of St. Lucia, George Odlum, was an old political ally of Bishop's. In St. Vincent, the radical petty bourgeoisie and militant workers were being mobilized by Dr. Ralph Gonsalves through the socialist Youlou Liberation Movement. And in Antigua Bishop's close personal friend Tim Hector had created a new leftist party, the Antigua Caribbean Liberation movement.[91]

Although direct US investments in the region were substantial — over $2 billion in the Caribbean and $3.65 billion in Central America — the major consideration which motivated Washington was 'geopolitical.' Both Democratic and Republican administrations remained committed to the isolation of revolutionary Cuba, and to stopping the growth of socialist and Marxist parties by any means necessary. When the PRG established cordial political and economic relations with Cuba, a destabilization campaign was immediately initiated against Grenada. The State department warned travel agents to inform Caribbean-bound tourists that Grenada was now an 'unsafe destination.' US newspapers editorialized that the island was becoming 'a training ground for terrorists.' In an overt display of force, the Pentagon conducted major naval exercises in the Caribbean in November, 1980. These were followed by even larger naval exercises in 1981 and 1983.[92]

The NJM anticipated US hostility to their government, but it refused to repudiate its political principles in the face of American intimidation. In the weeks following the revolution, Gairy – as bizarre as always – even met with Ku Klux Klan leaders to plot 'the best strategy for a mercenary attack' against Grenada.[93] Perhaps the first act of internal destabilization occurred on 6 May 1979, when two major fires were set within two hours of each other, the first at a hotel outside St. George's, and the second in a three-storey building in the center of the city. On 14 October, the PRG arrested twenty counterrevolutionaries who had arms and ammunition in their possession and were alleged to be plotting to assassinate government leaders. The principal organizers of the group were former NJM activist Teddy Victor, UPP leader Winston Whyte, and several Rastafarians who opposed the PRG from an 'anarchistic' position. Another sixteen persons involved in the antigovernment group were arrested on 2 November. The key contact between local counterrevolutionaries and the CIA appears to have been a former Howard University professor, Stanley Cyrus. The

PRG was reluctant to employ coercive measures at this point, and most of these men were released from custody in early 1980.

However, in February 1980, a small faction of former NJM members, led by Kenneth and Kennedy Budlhall attempted to provoke unrest by using ultra-left tactics. The Budlhalls and their followers seized control of a privately-held estate, and 'claiming to be more revolutionary than the Revolution, began to organize the mass cultivation of marijuana.'[94] Viewing this unauthorized move as a direct challenge to its policy of alliances with the national bourgeoisie, the PRG evicted the Budlhalls, but also set up a commission to resolve workers' legitimate grievances against the estate owner. When this ploy failed, the Budlhalls then initiated a conspiracy to assassinate NJM leaders. Despite the PRG's efforts to check such terrorism, disaster struck suddenly on 19 June 1980, when a bomb exploded at a rally at Queens Park in St. George's. The explosive device had been placed directly under the speakers' platform, where five major cabinet ministers were seated. The full blast was deflected by the concrete platform into the crowd of several thousand people, injuring nearly one hundred and killing three young women. One man who was involved in the bombing, disaffected NJM member, Strachan Philip, was killed by police later that day. Philip's home contained 'a massive arsenal, including pistols, rifles and sub-machine guns, plus two thousand rounds of ammunition, detonators and fuse wire, and an illustrated manual showing how to construct a time bomb of the type used at Queen's Park.' The next day, twenty thousand Grenadians marched through St. George's led by Bishop, expressing both their grief and solidarity with the PRG. Bishop declared, 'what is happening in Grenada is really part of a regional plan that imperialism has devised for dealing with progressive forces and revolutionary processes . . . '[94]

Although the United States government and internal dissidents had failed to remove the PRG's leaders, they succeeded in creating an environment that was intolerant of any political criticism. Justifiably concerned about Bishop's personal safety, PRA units were stationed around his home every night. The PRA was well aware of previous media tactics by the CIA to destabilize progressive governments, from *El Mercurio* under Allende in Chile to the Jamaican *Daily Gleaner* during Manley's tenure. With the demise of the GNP and UPP, the island's major newspaper, the *Torchlight*, quickly became the mouthpiece of anti-PRG sentiment. Owned partially by the Trinidad *Express*, the twice-weekly publication was 'consistently anti-socialist and anti-Cuban.' When the *Torchlight* published 'photographs of Bishop's security personnel and details, with maps, of all security installations,' a majority of NJM leaders demanded that the newspaper be shut down. Privately, Bishop argued against the closure. However, while he was overseas on a state visit, the NJM decided to act without his consent. On 13 October 1979 Hudson Austin announced the closing of the *Torchlight* due to its publication of 'vicious lies' and its role in provoking 'the maximum amount of confusion and unrest in the country.' On 26 October 1979, the PRG stated that no aliens would be permitted to publish a newspaper in Grenada, and that 'no Grenadian may hold more than 4 percent of the paid up capital of a Company that is a proprietor, printer or publisher of a newspaper.'[96] The *Free West Indian* declared that the *Torchlight* had tried 'to undermine the government.'[97]

Given this *fait accompli*, Bishop could not repudiate the PRG's actions. Regrettably, he also denounced the *Torchlight* for its record of 'deceitfulness and hypocrisy,' a publication managed by 'jokers' and 'stooges' who were in the 'back pockets' of US imperialism. Freedom of the press is never absolute, and certainly never within capitalist states, but by eliminating the *Torchlight*, the PRG did nothing to bolster the government's national security, and it increased the political fears of the national bourgeoisie and middle strata. With some credibility, opposition leaders could characterize the PRG's censorship as a revival of Gairy's policies towards the press. The *Torchlight* controversy also showed that the majority of the NJM Central Committee were quite confident in overriding Bishop's objections.[98]

The destabilization campaign continued. On 18 September 1980 an anti-PRG pamphlet was distributed at several places in the country entitled 'Getting to Know You: From Out of Slumber to Reality.' The Underground flyer attacked the PRG as 'a dictatorial regime,' and characterized the Prime Minister as being 'baptised, christened, conformed and married to comrade Leader Brezhnev and Castro. You can brainwash some people some of the time but you cannot brainwash all of the people all of the time.' A second pamphlet, distributed two months later in Grenville, was addressed specifically to Bishop: 'We know that anyone who opposes you is a CIA, a capitalist, an imperialist, a reactionary, a counter-revolutionary, a petty bourgeoisie, a destabiliser, an exploiter or an opportunist.' The flyer predicted that Bishop would be tried and published for his 'past and present sins and crimes against the people.'⁹⁹ On 17 November 1980, four young men were executed by unknown assailants in St. Patrick's Parish, and a young militiaman was horribly murdered. The soldier had been shot nineteen times, his eyes cut out and his torso ripped by a bayonet. In mid-January 1981, yet another protest flyer was widely circulated, announcing the creation of the 'Grenada National Party for Reconstruction and Liberation.' Similar to the previous pamphlets, the document claimed that 'the Spectre of Communism is haunting the Caribbean.' The new 'party' stated that Manley's electoral defeat in 1980 made Grenada 'the official headquarters for espionage by the Soviets in the Caribbean . . . Bishop's thoughts, words and deeds, expressed and implied, are politically calculated to serve his [Soviet] masters.' The secret group asked that funds for the party be forwarded to the anti-PRG publication, the *Trinidad Express*.¹⁰⁰

Any state that is besieged will take necessary measures to defend itself. The PRG was unwilling to reallocate major funds from social welfare and economic programs to defense. The government's 1982-83 budget, for instance, gave only six percent to the police and military. However, cabinet members were usually assigned bodyguards at public forums. Security personnel from the German Democratic Republic advised Party and government members on techniques to minimize risk. Cuba committed twenty-seven permanent and one dozen temporary military advisers to the PRA. Cuba, North Korea, and the Soviet Union signed secret protocols with the PRG, providing machine guns, seond-hand anti-aircraft guns, anti-tank weapons, and thousands of rifles. After the 1983 invasion, the US would claim that these secret agreements indicated that 'a large-scale Soviet base was being constructed in Grenada.' Such assertions were fantasies or outright distortions. Given US diplomatic pressure and naval operations in the Caribbean, the PRG had every reason to believe that the US would invade Grenada, and it took steps to ensure a modest defense. The weapons it actually obtained were minimal, given the military capacity of the US.¹⁰¹

The realistic sense of vulnerability placed greater responsibilities on the PRA and the voluntary People's Militia, which in turn gradually gave the military a more prominent role within the revolution. Militia drills became more frequent, and PRG leaders applauded their contributions to the state. 'A Revolution which has the support of the people but which cannot defend itself very soon would be no revolution at all,' Coard declared at one 1981 public rally. 'Therefore comrades, the people and the material means to defend the people are indispensable and interconnected in the process of the Revolution.' The leader of the PRA, General Hudson Austin, was a member of the NJM Central Committee, but was considered at best 'nonideological.' However, Austin was probably the most 'popular' military leader, widely viewed as 'a man who could get things done,' according to Hector. Austin vigorously promoted the campaign for mass military vigilance, although in rather crude terms. At one rally, Austin predicted that an American invasion could occur 'at any moment . . . We must be ready to kill . . . to wipe them out, we must be ready to use them as manure for the bananas and nutmegs!'[102]

The NJM Central Committee, and particularly PRA Major Leon Cornwall, Lt. Colonel Liam James, Lt. Colonel Ewart Layne, and other former OREL members, advocated strict policies to repress any signs of subversive or counterrevolutionary activity. After the Queen's Park bombing, their demand for 'revolutionary manners' became an obsession for security. According to Kendrick Radix, the PRG authorized the formal interrogation of about three thousand Grenadians between 1979 and 1983. To appreciate this figure, one should consider that it represented one amongst every thirty-five Grenadians. In practical terms, this meant that everyone knew someone — a neighbor, co-worker, or relative — who had been questioned by the police or militia. At least 300 persons were imprisoned, the majority for only a matter of hours or, at most, days. But others suspected of conspiracies or crime against the state weren't so fortunate. At least one hundred persons were confined to tiny prison cells without formal charges or hearings for two years or more. The PRG did not make a clear distinction between criminals like the Budhlalls and critics who simply opposed the government but had committed no specific acts of violence. Several political prisoners were also subjected to beatings. Although the PRA and militia guards committed no systemic beatings on the scale of severity of the Mongoose gang, a few officers, and notably Leon Cornwall, were guilty of unjustified acts of cruelty.

Bishop and other PRG leaders did not tolerate such violence, to their credit, yet their concern for state security sometimes superseded their humanistic values. Hector relates that Bishop was ashamed of Cornwall's odious behavior, but could not publicly reprimand him. Instead, Cornwall was appointed ambassador to Cuba, and was sent out of the country. Bishop tried to balance the necessity for security with his commitment to Marxist humanism, but had difficulty doing so. In his last official interview with Afro-

American journalists, Bishop discussed the charges of human rights violations in Grenada: 'After the revolution when you are attempting to consolidate, there has to be a certain measure of dislocation . . . the choices are open to any revolutionaries following a revolution . . . and they are always the same. You can line people up and shoot them down in the streets. We didn't like that option so we didn't use it. You can *pretend* they all escaped into the bush and that you shot them down in the bush. We didn't like that either . . . or, you lock them up! . . . *You must remember,* Grenadians now have the right to get houses repaired, free milk, free education. However it was a disruptive violent minority that is willing to use violence to try to stop that. *They have to be crushed.* That's the only way to insure your revolution.'[103]

Washington's shrill accusations that Grenada was becoming a 'police state' increased with the suppression of another newspaper, the *Grenadian Voice,* in June 1981. The most prominent figures behind the newspaper were Lloyd Noel, who served briefly as the PRG's Acting Attorney General, Leslie Pierre, and journalist Alister Hughes. In 1980 Noel resigned from the PRG, and subsequently agreed to represent accused terrorist Kenneth Budlhall in his trial in connection with the Queen's Park bombing. In May 1981, a State Department official meeting with Radix in Barbados casually mentioned that Grenada 'was shortly to see the publication of a new newspaper.' Several weeks later the *Grenadian Voice* appeared. The newspaper attacked the *Free West Indian* as a publication which promoted freedom 'only for certain sections' of the population, and criticized the PRG for failing 'to keep its promise of 'early, free and fair elections.'' ' The *Grenadian Voice* was careful not to call for any direct confrontation against the state, and did not promote political violence. However, the PRG closed the newspaper after its first edition, stating that its shareholders were 'big exploiters who are claiming that their voice is the voice of the Grenadian people.' Following this act, the Trinidad *Express* carried a strong editorial denouncing the PRG, and urging all other Caribbean states 'to isolate the Grenada Government.' When the paper was banned, Noel went to London and in several public gatherings attacked the PRG's suppression of 'freedom of the press.' On 11 July Noel and two investors in the newspaper, barrister Tillman Thomas and businessman Stanley Roberts, were placed in detention on charges that they were 'agents of the CIA and are involved in counter-revolutionary activity in Grenada.'[104]

Most of the international left in solidarity with the NJM

applauded the banning of the *Grenadian Voice*. Author Chris Searle, for example, described the newspaper as 'a classic example of CIA manipulation of local reaction . . . it was yet another demonstration to the people of the duplicity of these particular standard-bearers of the local bourgeoisie, posing as patriots, ÿet seeking to turn back everything that the mass of the people had won for themselves . . . '[105]

Most NJM members believed that the US was involved in the planning, financing and distribution of the newspaper. Otherwise, it would be difficult to explain how thousands of free copies of the *Grenadian Voice* were promptly distributed to Grenadian communities abroad. It was clearly an attempt to create another *La Prensa* or *El Mercurio*. Bishop outlined the destabilization tactics which may have occurred had the newspaper been permitted: 'You might see them try to graduate from the free press to a political organization, a political party . . . [then] to come through a Chamber of Commerce and try to put out some damaging statement; you might see them use their economic base to try to get shortages or to lay off people or to try to close down businesses. You might see them try to use the banks in a particular way. These are all kinds of tricks that are possible, all stages, all elements on the total road to the overthrow of the Grenadian revolution.'[106] Of course, another scenario was possible. Given the closure of the *Torchlight* in 1979, it was highly doubtful that the PRG would have permitted any other opposition paper. The banning of the *Grenadian Voice* would have jeopardized the PRG's extensive financial negotiations with Western European countries, undermined the strategic class alliance between the Grenadian government and the local capitalist class, and provided part of the political pretext to justify US armed intervention.

Any social revolution which had to its credit the remarkable economic and social achievements of the PRG had more to lose by imprisoning Noel and banning the *Grenadian Voice* than it gained by following a policy of selective repression. When the state-owned *Free West Indian* denounced the *Voice's* nominal owners as 'parasites', 'power-hungry vagabonds', 'pawns and sycophants,' it made few new converts.[107] The Roman Catholic hierarchy was angered by the arrest of Noel, who had served as president of the St. John's Catholic Church Council. St. John's Catholics petitioned Bishop to release Noel. Bishop refused, but he surely sensed within his own Party a growing intolerance, a siege mentality which resorted to blunt bureaucratic edicts rather than mass mobilization.

Within the NJM Central Committee, Bishop argued against the prosecution of the so-called 'Gang of 26,' the investors and supporters of the *Grenadian Voice*, but was overruled. Two years later, Phyllis Coard would cite this as evidence of the Prime Minister's 'Idealism' and 'failure to face up to hard decisions.' Bishop accepted his Party's decisions as binding on all members, and suppressed any residual doubts. Less than one week after the newspaper was closed, Bishop declared before a mass rally in Queen's park: 'The paper is illegal . . . When the revolution speaks, it must be heard, listened to. Whatever the revolution decrees, it must be obeyed; when the revolution commands, it must be carried out; when the revolution talks, no parasite must bark in their corner.'[108]

This was the 'socialist' rhetoric of a Forbes Burnham, or perhaps more accurately, that of Bernard Coard, and not the genuine language of Maurice Bishop. As Rosa Luxemburg had pointed out long before: ' . . . without unrestricted freedom of press and assembly, without a free struggle of opinion, life dies out in every public institution, becomes a mere semblance of life, in which only the bureaucracy remains as the active element. Public life gradually falls asleep, a few dozen party leaders of inexhaustible energy and boundless experience direct and rule.'[109] So long as the national bourgeoisie or its political representatives take no *overt* actions or incite violence against the working class or the state, freedom of expression should be the rule rather than the exception. Denied this access to public debate, critics of a regime are far more likely to resort to violent conspiracies and sabotage. But there is an even more important reason to encourage ideological pluralism and free discussion. To outlaw all political discourse outside a ruling party can create a powerful tendency to stifle debate within the party's cadre and leadership. Without democracy, democratic centralism becomes the rationale for authoritarianism. A rupture can occur between the dominant tendency of a party and the working class which it claims to represent. The party's leadership then must place the masses under 'revolutionary manners.' It was Bishop's tragedy that 'during the years the NJM was preparing itself for the exercise of power [he] advocated, or permitted, lines of action, which contributed to the strengthening of a narrow ideological outlook in the party.'[110] He never anticipated that this growing political intolerance could be turned against him, or the people.

The NJM's internal organization and leadership had changed considerably during the decade 1973-1983. What had once represented a social democratic tendency within the Party no longer existed. George Brizan had become a school principal, and dropped out of active political life; Teddy Victor and Lloyd Noel were held in detention. Party leaders closest to Bishop personally and politically tended to hold government administrative posts, or were the leaders of mass workers' formations. As their official responsibilities increased, the level of energy and work they gave to the NJM declined. Vincent Noel, head of the BGWU, was described by Bishop as 'the most outstanding leader of the working class'; but to Coard, Liam James and other OREL members, Noel's actual contributions toward building the Party itself were minimal. Agricultural and General Workers' Union head, Fitzroy Bain, was termed by Bishop 'the leader of the rural working class'; yet his detractors on the NJM Central Committee privately detected 'petty bourgeois' influences in his political behaviour.

The subsequent political split within the NJM, which culminated in the murder of Bishop and his supporters, is usually characterized as between the Leninist 'radicals' vs. 'pragmatists led by Bishop.' But this generalization overlooks several points. The one PRG minister who was most prominently identified with policies favorable to local capitalists, and who was noted for strict labor discipline and productivity, was Coard. The PRG's Finance Minister insisted upon a gradualistic and pragmatic relationship with capital. Selwyn Strachan, another 'radical', had vetoed workers' demands for state-owned factories, in his capacity as Minister of Labor. What actually distinguished the two factions were their conflicting definitions of 'socialism', and their profound difference over the relationship between the Party and the masses. Hector emphasizes this point: what was at stake was 'whether as in Bishop's view the mass organizations of workers, students, farmers, women and youth would be the centers of power, or whether, as in Coard's view, the Party and its Central Committee would be the center of power.'[111]

For Bishop, Radix and the NJM's founders, socialism meant the self-conscious development and empowerment of workers and farmers. The Party's original manifesto of 1973 stressed this anti-elitist perspective: 'No small group of persons, regardless of how intelligent or educated or wealthy they are, have the right to sit down together in a small room and proclaim themselves the new Messiahs . . . Leadership must not mean the creation of Masters. Leadership instead should regard itself as the servants of the people, and must aim at . . . destroying the whole class relationship in our society.'[112] This faction of the NJM can be identified with the classic traditions of egalitarian socialism and left moralism: a belief in constant mass mobilization; unitary, direct democracy without the encumbrance of traditional bourgeois parties; the use of persuasion and appeals to collective welfare; and advocacy for the equalization of material wealth. As in other societies which have developed mass egalitarian socialist movements, Grenadian socialists in this tradition believed that effective power resided in the masses, and that the PRG was simply the 'public servant' through which popular needs and demands were expressed.

Thus the evolution of the 'charismatic leadership' of Bishop was neither accidental, nor ancillary to the process of socialist construction, from the perspective of these NJM members. The charismatic leader is the living symbol, the historically necessary link between the state and the people. In a small society such as Grenada, the questions of democratic political style and egalitarian, informal procedures on the part of such leaders becomes absolutely critical. The *Free West Indian's* description of Creft provides only one example of this element in the revolution: 'Her style is as casual as her clothes — blue jeans, cotton top, sandals . . . Always on the go and totally at ease wherever she goes, whatever she does, she's well known as simply "Jackie" to public servants and the masses, teachers and pupils alike. Whether she's padding around in her office, answering the phone, taking part in a committee or Cabinet meeting . . . hurrying along the streets and hailing the folks she knows, her manner is down-to-earth . . . Jackie's role is to provide the means to help create the new personality — youth, woman, man — to form the new society.'[113] Bishop was much the same. The Prime Minister normally worked up to fourteen hours a day, yet occasionally he 'would call in saying he couldn't attend an NJM meeting, but would instead be playing cards with the fellows,' Hector recalled. 'The masses loved him, not just because of his personal sacrifices to the struggle, but because of his human style.' In a limited historical sense, Bishop, Creft and their associates were Grenada's 'Levellers,' advocates of egalitarian radicalism and democratic social justice.[114] What they did not comprehend was that the narrow structure of the NJM and its refusal to permit political pluralism undermined and would eventually negate the revolution's egalitarian and humanistic orientation.

Bernard Coard and those NJM cadre closest to him perceived the revolutionary process differently. True, they could be moved to passionate rhetoric, and their sacrifices were no less meaningful toward the goal of social transformation. Yet they tended to view the problems of the revolution from the tradition of statist socialism: emphasis on individual incentives to promote productivity; the pursuit of central planning and an all-inclusive economic program for society; a hierarchical system of decision-making; a firm conviction that all power should reside within the party organization. When such men and women are placed above mass organizations, as in the case of Phyllis Coard, they frequently falter. And through their statist version of Marxism-Leninism, they consequently attribute their problems not to their own subjective inadequacies, but to the 'backward', 'underdevloped' and 'petty bourgeois nature of society.'

Neither the Coards, Strachan, nor the other leading figures who had belonged to OREL actively sought personal popularity. Like Gbedemah and Botsio in the CPP, these NJM leaders frequently promoted the populist image of Bishop as the personification of the revolutionary state. But there was a degree of opportunism in their behavior, since they were privately critical of Bishop's charismatic, informal style. Socialism to them basically meant social engineering, state planning, and public conformity to each phase of their interpretation of the 'socialist orientation' model. The vanguard, Leninist party, steeled by its protracted struggles against Gairyism and US imperialism, would lift the masses of Grenadian working people from their poverty and backwardness, toward the ultimate aim of a socialist society. In all this, there was something akin to a Leninist *noblesse oblige* at work, an unquestioned faith in the power of dogma, a belief that small Grenada could adhere to a preordained model of social transformation.

The statist socialist tendency of the NJM felt acutely besieged by internal and external enemies, in part because it really had little confidence in the capacity of the Grenadian masses to handle their own affairs without supervision. Coard, more than any other PRG leader, constantly complained about being overburdened with policy decisions and various political tasks. 'I don't know when last the comrades in the Ministry of Finance and Planning slept,' Coard commented in a 'Radio Free Grenada' interview in February 1983. He attributed this willingness for self-sacrifice to 'sheer revolutionary enthusiasm,' which was not entirely the whole truth. One primary factor at work was the NJM's crucial decision not to expand the Party's membersip, and its failure to bring larger numbers of non-NJM people into the administrative process. But to do this meant, to Coard and his followers, the possible 'deterioration of the Party into a social democratic Party and hence the degeneration of the Revolution.' To ensure ideological purity within the left meritocracy, NJM cadre were forced to accept a rigorous schedule. They were expected to leave work on Friday afternoons, 'go into a rural retreat, read and study some text by Stalin, and sleep on the hard ground overnight.' If one complained, 'you were attacked as petty bourgeois.' All-night study marathons such as these left little time for one's children or spouse, 'no recreation, no personal life' outside of the Party. It was not long before many Grenadian working people began making a rough distinction between the PRG and the NJM. The PRG was Bishop, Whiteman, Creft, Louison, and other popular leaders who had initiated humanistic social welfare, educational and cultural programs; the NJM was the country's sole official party which operated rather like an evangelical cult. Few outside the small party knew who sat on its Central Committee; fewer still understood that the NJM was actually in complete command of the state apparatus. As far as most Grenadians knew, the PRG was 'their government,' and Bishop was 'their leader.' Coard, widely recognized for his organizational genius and theoretical acumen, was nevertheless 'heartily disliked, if tolerated' by the general public.[115] If Bishop can be said to represent the 'Leveller heritage,' Coard could be judged a latter-day Cromwell, a revolutionary statist who favored order more than egalitarianism.

In the wake of the revolution's collapse, the Coardites have been held in wide contempt for their decision to preempt the leadership of Bishop, and to place the government's chief representative under arrest. But simply to excoriate the NJM's majority faction does not help us to comprehend why they acted as they did. Any state which perceives itself under constant siege must organize itself for war; a high degree of efficiency and ideological commitment among its principal leaders is absolutely vital. One disturbing feature of the Bishop tendency, from the perspective of the Coardites, was its refusal to engage in theoretical study. Whiteman, Louison, and Radix had acquired the 'language' of Marxism, but little actual content. Creft bluntly refused to attend morning ideological sessions, which were frequently scheduled before six a.m. NJM cadre responded that to facilitate Creft's hectic schedule the morning meetings would be moved to her home. Even then, Creft refused to leave her bedroom to engage in group discussions. The Coard faction probably feared that the revolution was being 'stalled' at the national democratic stage, and would fail to develop further towards socialism. If this occurred, a reactionary restoration of Gairyism was still a distinct possibility. For the sake of building the social revolution, they may have concluded that some of the key

NJM representatives within the PRG would have to be removed. Their political motivation was never for personal power — their actions were determined by what they believed, however distortedly, was truly in the best interests of Grenada's working people.

In April 1981, the NJM Central Committee established criteria for 'higher standards of personal discipline' for members and a more intense effort to combat 'petty bourgeois' traits within the Party. Rapidly the internal workings of the Party became more dogmatic and hierarchical. Coard and his supporters insisted that these changes within the Party were in keeping with 'Leninism.' Members of the Central Committee began to be selected solely by Coard, rather than elected by the membership, no NJM Party Congress was ever called. Beginning in 1982, the Coard faction increased its criticism of 'dead-weight' leaders on the Central Committee who gave too much attention to the government and 'participated little' in the NJM's internal affairs. Vincent Noel was forced off the Central Committee; Jacqueline Creft actually resigned from the Party, but was permitted to keep her government posts. Coard then circulated complaints against Radix, demanding his removal from the Central Committee on the grounds of 'neglect of state functions.' A diabetic, Radix admitted that his health problems had created difficulties in his work. But he also responded that 'a certain polarization was taking place, that there were certain factions that were developing in the party.' Bishop's attitude toward these internal conflicts was curiously shortsighted. He respected Coard's administrative skills, and recognized that the former OREL cadre deserved representation on the NJM's Central Committee. Bishop did not want to 'break up the "unity" of the movement, and as a result, tolerated grave problems,' Hector states. Creft constantly complained about the NJM's authoritarianism and increasing isolation and alienation from the masses. Yet 'Maurice refused to listen to her . . . he did not take her criticisms seriously.' Bishop attempted to 'stay above factions and mediated differences, refusing to engage in political maneuvering of any kind.' When close friends voiced concerns about the dogmatism of many Party members, Bishop responded characteristically: 'Ah well, that's *their* thing. It's harmless, and it's not me.'[116]

The Party's crisis deepened in October 1982 when Coard announced his resignation from the Central Committee and Political Bureau. His stated reason was that he was 'excessively overworked,' and that his presence had retarded 'the development of other comrades in the Committee.' Bishop was privately relieved: when first told of Coard's decision, 'Maurice's attitude was "he can go to hell as far as I'm concerned".' The OREL faction used Coard's temporary departure to justify a review of any others who had failed to maintain 'Leninist standards and functioning.' Radix was immediately charged with 'deep seated individualism' and a 'petty bourgeois opportunist attitude to criticism,' and was forced to resign. Others who were attacked included Fitzroy Bain and Whiteman. Several additional OREL members were added to the Central Committee, and the decision was made not to tell most NJM militants of Coard's resignation. In retrospect, the political groundwork for the October 1983 putsch was now set. A majority of Central Committee members and PRA officers favored Coard's political views — Liam James, Ewart Layne, Selwyn Strachan, Chris De Riggs, John 'Chalky' Ventour, Ian St. Bernard, Phyllis Coard, and others. By appearing to retreat, Coard placed himself 'in a good position to re-enter the arena when matters went awry, as he warned they might.'[117]

In late 1982-1983 the schism widened between the egalitarian and statist factions of the NJM around several issues. Two years before, the Party had joined the Socialist International (SI), and in July, 1981, a social democratic regional conference was held in St. George's. Coard had no objection to the SI affiliation, and perceived that it would indirectly assist Grenada's economic and political connections with Western Europe. Bishop was no social democrat, although Coardites may have winced at the Prime Minister's public statements praising the SI for playing 'a positive role in the struggle for world peace, for disarmament . . . and for the peaceful and progressive development of all peoples.' However, Whiteman had represented the NJM in Spain during the negotiations which led to the Party's acceptance into SI, and it was not difficult for some to perceive the Foreign Minister as a dangerously 'social democratic' influence.

This impression was reinforced in early 1983, when Whiteman urged a moratorium on anti-US polemics on behalf of the PRG. Whiteman and Bishop had concluded that Grenada's airport and tourist traffic would depend heavily on the US market, and that some kind of civil relationship had to exist with the Reagan administration. During Bishop's May-June 1983 visit to the United States, he met briefly with Reagan foreign-policy aides. Bishop met subsequently with Trinidadian Prime Minister George Chambers, and reportedly agreed to 'consider a sharply accelerated programme of

Maurice Bishop and the Grenada Revolution 255

elections.' Chambers also urged Bishop to capitalise on his Washington discussions by sharply reducing the Cuban and Soviet presence once the airport was opened.[118] When the NJM Central Committee reviewed Bishop's negotiations in mid-July, several criticisms surfaced immediately. The PRG had recently formed a constitutional commission, headed by Trinidadian attorney Allan Alexander, which projected national elections sometime in 1985. And although the proposed elections were not designed to undermine the NJM's 'vanguard position,' Bishop's statements to Chambers seemed to indicate some sort of 'sell-out.' The Prime Minister's discussions with Reagan administration officials had also been conducted 'without prior reference and without guidance' from the Central Committee.[119] Bishop's ad hoc negotiations disturbed Coard's allies, some of whom had become convinced that Bishop was 'swollen with power and grasping for "one man leadership."'[120]

The Coard faction had maneuvered against Bishop for at least one year, but had failed to establish a suitable pretext to remove him from authority. At the July 1983 sessions, it laid the foundations for its final assault by grossly exaggerating the failures and problems of the revolution. The CPE, NISTEP and the mass organizations were said to be 'suffering from bureaucratic and leadership inefficiency'; the economy was rapidly deteriorating; public rallies were 'poorly attended'; and the NJM had failed to respond to the crisis due to the absence of 'firm leadership on a Leninist path.' An emergency meeting of the NJM Central Committee in late August repeated most of these criticisms, and new warnings were added. 'We are seeing the beginning of the disintegration of the party,' declared Liam James. Austin reported 'widespread dissatisfaction and demoralisation' among PRA members; and Minister of Health Chris De Riggs observed that 'the heart of the crisis is the Central Committee.' Gradually the noose was tightened, yet Bishop could not feel it.[121]

Bishop's faction readily admitted that the revolution was plagued with difficulties, but suggested that the majority of the Central Committee members were distorting the real situation. At the 15-17 September 1983 Central Committee meeting, Bishop argued that increased contact with the masses, 'visits to communities to meet people at an informal level', were essential. Louison and Whiteman concurred. But it was Liam James who first shifted the debate by attacking Bishop personally. 'The fundamental problem is the quality of leadership . . . provided by Comrade Maurice Bishop,' who lacked 'a Leninist level of organisation and discipline' and 'brilliance in strategy and tactics.' Other Coardites promptly agreed. Phyllis Coard bitterly predicted that the NJM would 'fall apart' within 'five or six months,' and that prominent 'petit bourgeois elements' in the Party refused to engaged in self-criticism. She condemned Bishop's 'idealism' and his refusal to admit mistakes. Fitzroy Bain attempted to defend Bishop, cautioning against 'overhasty decisions.' But Bishop's proponents were stunned when James proposed a 'joint leadership' structure, making Bernard Coard co-chairperson with Bishop. Coard would be in charge of the Party's Political Bureau and Organising Committee, would direct NJM strategy and tactics, and the ideological development of Party members; Bishop was to remain Prime Minister, would supervise the structure of 'popular democracy,' and would 'direct work among the masses.' The theoretical justification for the scheme was gleaned from 'the example of the Soviet army,' according to Ewart Layne, in which 'the concept of Political Commissar and Military Leadership had developed and worked.' De Riggs also proposed that Austin be removed from the leadership of the PRA and replaced by Leon Cornwall, who would also direct the police force.

Bishop may have been somewhat naive, but he was not blind. The Coard faction's proposition was utterly transparent. According to the socialist orientation scheme, the vanguard party commanded the state, and the central Committee dictated policy to the party. Coard and his coterie of supporters would for all practical purposes control the state. Bishop's real role would be essentially that of public relations. James's resolution also signalled a final assault on the founders and the early members of the NJM. Radix and Vincent Noel had been purged from the Central Committee; now Whiteman was charged with 'representing the right wing within the Party.' The motion to replace Austin was defeated, but James's resolution for the duumvirate passed with nine votes. Austin and Bishop abstained, while Whiteman and Louison voted against the motion. On 25 September, a meeting of 48 full members of the NJM adopted the duumvirate proposal. Bishop declared at this meeting that he would 'use the criticism positively and march along with the entire party to build a Marxist-Leninist party that can lead the people to socialism and communism.' Bishop vowed 'to erode his petit bourgeois traits,' and he warmly embraced Coard.[122] The 'crisis' seemed resolved to most NJM members, but in reality, it was only simmering to a climax. Bishop knew he had been outmaneuvered. But he was responsible, far more than Coard, for his predicament. He had condoned the silencing of non-NJM political opposition, the detention of political prisoners, and the elevation of OREL-trained sectarians into the Central Committee. In a matter of months, Whiteman and Louison would probably be removed from the Central Committee, and the Party's intolerance of internal political pluralism would increase.

Bishop's dilemma was a familiar one in Marxist politics. His closest supporters had been caught almost completely by surprise by the events of August-September 1983. Lyden Ramdhanny would later attribute the crisis to 'a plain thirst for power'; Bishop's secretary Don Rojas would call the confrontation a product of 'blind mechanical obedience to the dictates of a faction that had maneuvered behind the backs of the party to replace the leadership tested by a decade of struggle.' Radix would later attribute most of the NJM's shortcomings to Coard, claiming: 'Coard is 95 percent genius and 5 percent insane. And the 5 percent took over.'[123] But these retrospective insights do not reveal the whole story. The elimination of the pre-1979 NJM 'right wing,' consisting of Brizan, Lloyd Noel and others, had permitted the subsequent redefinition of 'right opportunism' to include Bishop, Whiteman, Creft and their supporters. OREL members had not received appointments to the Central Committee by 'behind the back' maneuvers, but had been elevated primarily through hard work and dedication. Bishop had never called for the broad expansion of the NJM, and popular leaders of farmers', and labour, and women's organizations were not dominant in Party's policy making positions. Instead of addressing these contradictions, he had ignored them. He was left with only two alternatives: accept the decision of the NJM, which in effect was a vote of 'no confidence' in his leadership, or to go over the head of the Party by appealing directly to the masses.

Tradition and logic were at odds here. As Castro explained later: 'When a group of conspirators is a minority there is greater room for action. But what happened in Grenada was that the Coard grouping had a majority against Bishop. This was apparently clean, and even legally in accord with democratic norms. It is necessary to accept such a decision, even when one realizes it is an error or a grave development.'[124] Traditionally, NJM decisions were binding on all members, and Bishop had never questioned the Central Committee's right to determine policy. But the logic of the situation called for him to place his case before the masses. If the Grenadian working people were truly the final political arbitrators, the crisis would easily be resolved in Bishop's favor. Unless, of course, the

Party refused to accept the central principle of popular, revolutionary democracy — that the will of the people was preemininent.

On 26 September, Bishop, Whiteman and Rojas left Grenada to join Louison in Hungary for talks on further economic assistance. During the two-week trip, which included stops in Czechoslovakia and Cuba, the Coard faction learned through Bishop's bodyguard that the Prime Minister had not accepted the duumvirate proposal. The Party's leaders were also fearful that Bishop had divulged the NJM's internal crisis to Castro. During Bishop's absence, Coard bolstered his position by giving PRA members hefty pay increases. Soldiers were informed that Bishop had opposed their wage hikes, and that Coard had approved them. Upon Bishop's return, he informed Strachan that he wanted the Central Committee to review 'certain points' of the joint leadership decision. Perhaps deliberately, Strachan gave Coardites a 'distorted and exaggerated' report of Bishop's position, which greatly added to their sense of paranoia. The Central Committee caucused without Bishop on 10 October, and refused to reexamine the duumvirate ruling. Within twenty-four hours, a rumour was circulated in St. George's that the Coards, Strachan and Cornwall were planning to murder the Prime Minister.

On the basis of this rumor, the Coard faction took extreme measures. At 1:00 a.m. on the morning of 12 October, Major Keith Roberts polled all security personnel who were not known as Bishop supporters. They were told that Bishop had rebelled against the Central Committee, and that 'they were to defend the working class as a whole and not the life of any individual leaders.' Six hours later, the Coardites brought together all NJM full members, candidate members and applicants inside the PRA, about 58 people. Informed that Bishop was refusing to adhere to NJM dictates, the loyal soldiers signed a statement which called on the party leadership 'to expel from the party's ranks all elements who do not submit to, uphold and implement in practice the decision of the Central Committee . . . ' Later that day, the Central Committee ousted Louison from his position as Minister of Agriculture. On 13 October, before a full NJM meeting of 300 people, Bishop was vehemently denounced: members condemned their former leader as a 'right opportunist,' and demanded that he be arrested and courtmartialed. Bishop was not expelled from the NJM, but was removed as Prime Minister and placed under strict house arrest. Coard was at last fully in command; reportedly he declared, 'Blow them up before they do it to us.'[125] Apocryphal perhaps, but

Coard's mood at this moment was hardly charitable. Coard's dogmatic version of Marxism-Leninism had led him to an authoritarianism no less rigid and elitist than Cromwell's hatred for the Levellers.[126] The clever calculations of the Coard faction failed to include one element. The revolution was less than five years old, and despite the tremendous strides taken in political education, the Grenadian working class did not possess 'Marxist-Leninist consciousness.' The humanistic and social welfare reforms nevertheless had popularized the view that the PRG 'belonged' to the people; the obscure Marxist machinations of the Coardites were seen as an irrelevant or perhaps regrettable by-product of what was an overall healthy and positive experience. Bishop was the personal and symbolic connection between the masses and the state, a 'symbol of national pride.' As George Lamming noted, within the context of Grenadian 'political culture', to arrest Bishop was to arrest 'the revolution itself.'[127] On 12 October, a group of Bishop supporters in St. David's seized guns from the militia armoury to defend him. Their disarmed leader was murdered, and was summarily denounced as a 'Gairyite' and 'criminal.' On Friday, 14 October, Strachan went to the *Free West Indian* office to announce Bishop's removal from office, and the workers literally chased him off the premises. Coard was forced to make another temporary, tactical retreat, resigning his PRG post 'in order to put a stop to the vicious rumor that he has been attempting to replace Comrade Maurice Bishop as Prime Minister.' The following day, Radix organized a rally of about 300 people in St. George's Market Square to denounce Bishop's arrest. Radix was soon arrested and placed in Richmond Hill prison. On the eighteenth, at least 500 protestors rallied in Grenville, and smaller demonstrations occurred in Gouyave and Sauteurs. Students marched on Pearls airport and managed to close the facility for several hours. In the streets, the schools, the factories, hour by hour, a popular movement erupted: 'No Bishop, no revo!'[128]

Progressives throughout the Caribbean and the world were stunned by Bishop's arrest. From the UK, C.L.R. James sent a telegram to Coard and the NJM Political Bureau, stressing that Bishop's detention was 'an issue of importance not only to Grenada but the whole of the Caribbean, [which] must be solved through the mass of the population, unions and the Party . . . Primary is the safety of Bishop, for himself and the general public.'[129] Rupert Roopnarine of Guyana's working People's Alliance and Michael Als of the Trinidadian People's Popular Movement attempted to negotiate between the factions. Louison held several lengthy and fruitless meetings with Coard. One exchange between the two men summarizes the fundamental differences between the two groups. Louison patiently explained to Coard: 'the people are going to continue to manifest their disapproval . . . What are you going to do? How will you respond? Coard's contemptuous reply was nothing short of elitist and authoritarian: 'Well, the people can march, they can demonstrate, and we won't stop them. But they'll get tired. Gairy let them march and demonstrate almost daily for two months in 1973 and 1974. The same happened in Trinidad in 1970. The masses will get tired, and life will return to normal. And we will continue the revolutionary process on a more Marxist, more Leninist footing.' Ramdhanny, Whiteman, Louison and Norris Bain resigned from the PRG, and began to organize Bishop's supporters. Creft was placed under house arrest with Bishop, and Louison was quickly imprisoned.[130]

'Bloody Wednesday' — 19 October 1983 — represents a crucial date in Caribbean political history. Despite numerous eyewitness accounts and secondary research, the actual sequence of the day's events, and the political motives and decisions of key participants, still remain unclear. About 15,000 Grenadians from all corners of the island assembled early that morning in St. George's Market Square. Every store and office was closed, as workers struck in solidarity with Bishop. Anti-PRG elements were also evident among the crowd. Former GNP members and others who may have been agents provocateurs held signs: 'America we love you!' 'We don't want Communism.' and 'C for Coard, C for Communism, C for Corruption.'[131] Three or four thousand people led by Whiteman proceeded to march toward Bishop's residence. One hundred or more PRA guards briefly kept the masses back, but a group of teenagers managed to outflank the soldiers and enter the house. Bishop and Creft had been stripped to their undergarments and strapped to two beds. Once unbound, Creft appeared alert, but Bishop was not. Tears flooded his face, as he cried: 'The masses. The masses.'

Bishop and Creft were taken downhill into town, and with little difficulty the people took over Fort Rupert, a small army installation. Vincent Noel and PRA major Einstein Louison distributed weapons to adults who had received militia training. Evidently, some of those who obtained weapons, according to Einstein Louison, were 'counter-revolutionary civilians.' Nevertheless, the general mood was festive, as the news of Bishop's liberation spread.

One observer noted: '... it was party time. The little cafes and rum shops had opened and were jammed, doing even better business than during Carnival ... beer and soda were being sold and consumed everywhere as we waited for Maurice to appear ... The mood was joyous, but amazingly calm considering the importance of this occasion.'[132] The general consensus was that the people had won. Creft asked that 'people stay around,' because if a PRA detachment was sent, 'then they won't shoot.' Trinidadian Merle Hodge, who was with Creft and Bishop at morning, commented later: 'With the whole country coming down to town to support Maurice, you wouldn't think that it would enter anybody's head to try and take power in the face of all that. Because you'd be fighting the whole nation.'[133]

Several PRA officers, including Lt. Lester Redhead, came to Fort Rupert unarmed to initiate fresh negotiations, but Noel and Whiteman refused to compromise. After they departed, the Coard faction concluded that force was the only means left to restore the status quo. In effect, they consciously made the decision to 'fight the whole nation', and to impose their pristine vision of socialism upon the people at the point of an AK-47. About one o'clock, a troop carrier and two Soviet-built armoured cars descended on the fort. There is conflicting evidence whether the PRA or the crowd fired first, but the fact that heavily-armed soldiers were sent indicates that the Coard faction was fully prepared to crush all resistance. After the firing began, Bishop ordered his supporters to surrender. But in only minutes, several PRA soldiers were killed and wounded, and over one hundred civilians were killed, including many children. Vincent Noel also died in the brief battle. The PRA cleared the fort, except for Bishop, Creft, Whiteman, Fitzroy Bain and Norris Bain. Lt. Redhead pulled his revolver and shot the unarmed Bishop through the head. The rest were executed with machine guns.

Two hours later, Austin coldly declared over Radio Free Grenada: 'Today our People's Revolutionary Army has gained victory over the right opportunists and reactionary forces ... the friends of imperialism were crushed. [Bishop] and his petty bourgeois and upper bourgeois friends had deserted the working class and working people of Grenada.' The creation of the Revolutionary Military Council (RMC) was announced, chaired by Austin, with Layne and James serving as vice chairs, which would have full legislative and executive authority. A four-day curfew was imposed, during which 'anyone found our of doors will be shot.' All schools, churches and workplaces were closed 'until further notice.' As Akinyele Sadiq, an international worker at Radio Free Grenada put it: 'As far as we were concerned, this was a right-wing military coup . . . The entire nation was now under "house arrest," with the army free to round-up anyone they distrusted.'[134]

The theory of socialist orientation had been Coard's *passepartout*. Grenadian social realities and the workers unfortunately had not conformed to the theory; hence coercion was used to mold society into proper alignment with theory. Austin was placed in nominal command of the RMC, because he was one of the few putschists who had any personal popularity. James directed the RMC's political department, and another Coard protege, Nazim Burke, drafted the regime's 'emergency economic programme.' Coard receded into the shadows, but was very much in touch with every major decision. The general strategy was to restore, if possible, some modest level of public confidence in the left 'Bonapartist' regime, while at the same time ruthlessly identifying and eliminating any prominent critics. A new civilian cabinet was scheduled to be formed within two weeks, and the RMC promised that both local and foreign private investments would be 'encouraged much more positively' than before. 'All social classes and interests in our country' would be represented in the new government. To restore confidence inside the military, another pay increase was ordered. Secretly, however, the regime was simultaneously preparing a plan to bring 'various areas of private property under Martial Law,' and it anticipated problems of sabotage and disruption from various quarters. A number of Grenadian businessmen, journalist Alister Hughes, Einstein Louison and various 'counter-revolutionaries' were imprisoned. Radix and George Louison were denied food and water for several days. Ian St. Bernard, an RMC member, informed both men 'that they were to be executed and a "shot while in crossfire" story concocted.' What saved Radix perhaps was his lapse into a diabetic coma; prison authorities reluctantly allowed him to be transported to a hospital.[135]

Up to its final hours, the RMC failed to recognize what Castro and other leftists understood all too well: ' . . . the Coard grouping could not sustain itself after having killed Bishop. The revolution had committed suicide.'[136] At the maximum, barely two percent of the Grenadian people supported the RMC regime. After 'Bloody Wednesday' and a nationwide curfew, the people had been 'traumatized back into an oppressor-loving condition.'[137] Washington finally had the opportunity and the means it needed to crush the aborted Grenada revolution. With a token Caribbean force including Barbadian and Jamaican troops, 1,900 US Marines and Rangers landed on the morning of 25 October. Within three days, over 6,000 US troops were ashore on Grenada; or as Catherine Sunshine noted, 'the equivalent of a 14-million-man army occupying the United States.'[138] The fact that this armed invasion had absolutely no validity in international law did not perturb the Reagan administration.[139] But the sad reality remains that Reagan could not have exercised the military power to destroy the NJM without the fatal split within the Party's leadership. The absence of real political pluralism, an unencumbered press, legal rights for all nonviolent oppostions, and a truly broad-based and democratic party were the root causes for the NJM's implosion. These factors, more than any ideological or personal feuds between Bishop and Coard, led to the destruction of the revolution.

VII

The US invasion and occupation of Grenada has been well documented. But a brief comment on the restoration of the neocolonial model on the island should be made. First, a 'free press' was reestablished, as Leslie Pierre quickly revived the *Grenadian Voice*, with financial, editorial and technical assistance from several rightwing Caribbean newspapers, including the Trinidadian *Express*. When leftists tried to start the *Indies Times* several months later, however, the regime's Ministry of Information closed the paper.[140] On 10 November 1983, Grenada's governor-general Paul Scoon authorized a series of authoritarian decrees authorizing 'warrantless arrests,' press censorship, and bans on public meetings. Within three weeks of the invasion, US Army Intelligence had jailed or detained 1,200 people.[141] The reestablishment of 'democracy' also required a new relationship between labor and management. According to one British labor delegation visiting Grenada in 1984: 'Trade unionists have suffered from detention, harassment, dismissal and persecution . . . Specific actions against trade unions have included the looting of offices, the requisitioning of essential transport, the detention of trade union leaders, the harassment and persecution of executive members . . . the dissemination of antiunion propaganda, [attempts] by American-trained and backed Grenadians to remove elected union officers and take over some unions . . . the torture of some trade unionists while under detention and arbitrary searches of union offices and members' homes by US intelligence personnel.' Approximately 3500 NJM supporters and sympathizers were fired from their jobs or 'purged' from the civil service.[142]

Virtually all social welfare and educational projects of the PRG were destroyed, and state-owned enterprises were closed. The social consequences were predictable. By mid-1985, Grenadian unemployment reached 40 percent, almost all economic development was at a 'standstill', and prostitution and crime flourished.[143] The repression of the left continued long after US military personnel were removed. Members of the RMC and the Coards were tortured — Bernard Coard himself was first administered 'a severe beating on a US warship' prior to his imprisonment.[144] In late 1985, the Council on Hemispheric Relations, a human rights group, observed that conditions in Grenada 'are among the worst in the English-speaking Caribbean . . . reliable accounts are circulating of prisoners being beaten, denied medical attention, and confined for long periods without being able to see lawyers.'[145]

Still the Reagan administration was not prepared to restore Gairy's dictatorship on the Grenadian people, because it preferred to employ more subtle means. The strategy that was eventually adopted was to create a 'centrist' united front of anti-GULP and anti-NJM constituencies, thus weakening the potential base of the left. A new electoral system had to be established as well, 'democratic' in appearance, yet rigid enough to guarantee a victory for its local clients. The pro-US political formation which was created, the 'New National Party' (NNP), was a coalition consisting of Blaize's GNP, Francis Alexis's conservative Grenada Democratic Movement, and liberal-to-social democratic elements led by George Brizan. The electoral process was designed to intimidate leftists from participating in the voting, or to exclude pro-NJM constituencies entirely. The final voting list had 48,000 registered voters, 16,000 *less* than the electorate of 1976. Voter registrars demanded the photographing and fingerprinting of every adult — a procedure which made thousands of Grenadians unwilling to vote. Finally, the Reagan White House and the Republican Party directly aided the NNP's campaign. Former Reagan aide, Morton C. Blackwell, who was also involved previously in the spring 1984 El Salvador elections, and other Republican operatives, helped to coordinate the NNP's activities. The National Republican Institute for International Affairs allotted $20,000 to a Grenada business group with ties to the NNP. The AFL-CIO's Free Trade Union Institute channeled

$80,000 into Grenada to promote what was termed 'a program of public discussions on the future of the country.' The head of the extreme rightist 'accuracy in Media' group, Philip Nicolaides, raised funds from US conservatives to finance the NNP. Not surprisingly, the NNP carried majorities in 14 out of 15 districts in the voting on 3 December 1984. The reliable and pliable Blaize was once again Prime Minister. However, within less than a year, a bitter fractional struggle threatened to divide the NNP. Labor Minister Alexis narrowly defeated Brizan for the post of NNP deputy leader. The on-going battle over the division of the spoils compromised the NNP's ability to govern.'[146]

The implosion of the Grenada revolution sparked a major division in the Caribbean left which will be debated and analyzed for years to come. Obviously, the dissension was most bitter within Grenada itself. In May 1984, the remnants of Bishop's faction, led by Radix, Louison and Ramdhanny, created the Maurice Bishop Patriotic Movement (MBPM). In its initial manifesto, the MBPM upheld the PRG's former programs, pledged 'to continue the struggle to bring bread, peace and justice to the poor and working people,' and attacked the 'bankruptcy of those who exercise temporary authority and their allies.'[147] After some hesitation, the MBPM ran 13 candidates in the 1984 elections. The new movement was thoroughly crushed in the voting. Several factors were involved. Some Grenadians who were sympathetic with the MBPM voted for Blaize's NNP, simply to keep Gairy out of office. Other former NJM militants observed critically that only 3 out of 13 candidates for the MBPM had belonged to the Party.

Moreover the pro-Coard NJM still exists, despite the fact that its leaders are imprisoned. In September, 1984, the NJM circulated a public statement, declaring that it would not participate in elections which 'can neither be fair nor free.' Jailed NJM leader Leon Cornwall later outlined the Party's immediate tasks: 'The revolutionary movement . . . must find ways to rapidly reorganise and rebuild itself . . . The necessity of building a broad anti-imperialist front which involves all genuine patriots and progressive-minded persons is a vital one.' Cornwall's document, which was secretly transported from prison and published in London, admitted the NJM's 'grave errors', but expressed confidence that the 'broadest possible antiimperialist front' could be established. To date, the MBPM has refused to have any dealings with its former NJM comrades, and rejects any united front with the 'Coard clique.' Rojas's rejoinder argued: 'Deliberate crimes against the entire world revolutionary process must never be allowed to be explained away as "errors." The Coardites' uncontrollable ambition for power led them to a counterrevolutionary coup that offered up the revolution to Washington on a platter . . . by their actions in October 1983, they have no claim to be revolutionaries.'[148]

Debate on the Caribbean left began even before the US invasion. In general, the parties with fraternal connections to the Soviet Union expressed disappointment and even outrage at Bishop's death, but made no direct criticisms of the RMC regime before the invasion. Trevor Munroe had visited Grenada in September 1983, and had approved the duumvirate scheme. Monroe's WPJ was still inclined to view Bishop as a Grenadian-version of Michael Manley, and it boldly praised the actions of the Coardites. Munroe not only questioned 'whether Bishop had actually been exectued,' but later attacked the Cubans for 'facilitating the US invasion through its public criticisms' of the RMC. Others substantially agreeing with Munroe were Renwick Rose, head of the Vincentian United People's Movement, and the Trinidadian People's Popular Movement. Jagan's PPP expressed its 'deep sense of grief and loss at the death of Maurice Bishop and his colleagues,' but was silent about the RMC itself. Most Communists did not want to take any action which indirectly would help to justify US intervention.

The opposite approach was taken by the Trotskyist Socialist Revolution Group of Martinique and Guadeloupe, which demonstrated against both the 19 October massacre and the subsequent invasion. The independent Marxist left and social democrats were also much more critical of the RMC than the Communists. Hector's Antigua Caribbean Liberation Movement, for instance, claimed that Strachan was a CIA agent, whose part was 'to foment the leadership struggle into a clear political division.' Trinidad's Oilfields Workers Trade Union strongly deplored Bishop's murder, insisting that 'freedom was first hi-jacked by the Butchers of St. George's and this laid the foundation for the invasion of foreign troops.' The Working People's Alliance of Guyana argued that 'Bishop as revolutionary leader of free Grenada was a shield protecting Grenada and the entire Caribbean.' And Michael Manley termed the executions 'a squalid betrayal of the hopes of the ordinary people of our region.' Radicals and reformists alike mourned Bishop's demise, but to an extent, they sometimes tended to 'personalize' the NJM conflict as a simplistic struggle between the 'good' Bishop and the 'bad' Coard. The Trotskyists and also Hector drew direct parallels between Coard's coup and the 1968 Escalante affair in Cuba. In both cases, this obscured the complexity of the Grenada situation.[149]

As the left bickered, the Caribbean right scrambled to take full advantage of the new repressive political environment. The region's most dangerous demagogue, Jamaican Prime Minister Edward Seaga, promptly devalued the Jamaica dollar by 43.5 percent, and announced a general election on 15 December 1983. The JLP ran a fiercely anticommunist campaign which applauded the invasion. Manley's PNP denounced the 'bogus elections' and refused to participate, noting that 100,000 registered voters who had either migrated from the country or died were still on the voters' rolls, and another 120,000 new unregistered voters would be effectively disfranchised. Consequently, the 'constitutional coup' left the entire bourgeois democratic apparatus in the hands of an increasingly despotic and desperate national bourgeoisie, and moved Jamaica closer to an unambiguously authoritarian regime on the Chilean mode.

In Barbados, Prime Minister Tom Adams attacked the Caribbean Conference of Churches, an ecumenical group which had condemned the invasion, and expelled the progressive Guyanese editor of *Caribbean Contact,* Rickey Singh, from the island. Singh's expulsion 'signaled clearly that dissent — even dissent unconnected with any political part or movement — is to come under increasing repression.'[150] In Dominica, the regime of Eugenia Charles ratified a 'State Security Act' and a 'Treason Act' which 'impose harsh punishments (including death by hanging) for a series of vaguely worded offenses, including "forming an intention to overthrow the state." ' In St. Vincent, Marxist leader Renwick Rose was prosecuted by the state 'for possession of several Soviet magazines.' In St. Vincent's 25 July 1984 elections, an 'anticommunist and pro-business' party led by James Mitchell was elected, although the major party which lost was even further to the right; the percentage of the United People's Movement's vote plummetted from 15 percent in the 1979 elections to only 3 percent.[151] And in Antigua, the reactionary Antigua Labour Party swept all sixteen seats and carried 71 percent of the popular vote in the 17 April 1984 elections. Hector's ACLM refused to participate in the elections, when the united front of all local, anti-government parties fell apart. Journalist Milton Benjamin grimly observed that a 'rightist tide' had descended across the Caribbean, a series of 'repressive campaigns' which vitiated democracy.'[152]

What fundamental lessons can be gleaned from the Grenadian

experience? George Lamming has attributed the tragedy of the Grenadian revolution to a 'persistent legacy' of colonialism, 'the negation of identity and the multilation of self.' Colonialism had fostered not merely economic and political underdevelopment, but 'a psychology of dependence which has crippled the imagination and makes it inoperative in moments of crisis.' 'The colonial legacy is deep and pervasive; and it had afflicted the political Left, no less than the Right . . . Bishop, Kenrick Radix, George Louison, Bernard Coard, Unison Whiteman, were the first men of their generation who had attempted to make a decisive break, a fundamental departure from the old colonial legacy, and who had the power to consolidate that break. But there was no history within their own political culture which they could follow . . . There was no precedent, no example which they could use as a guide to action in their own crisis. They were naked, abandoned by their English-speaking neighbors, and confronted always by a hostile environment. But they were not wholly without resources which might have redeemed the situation. They had acquired an experience of their own during the years of struggle. They had a concrete knowledge of the people and the political culture of Grendada which existed long before 1979. And I would like to think that they were men who were not without imaginations.' The NJM's tragic 'failure of imagination,' Lamming insists, led it to separate acts of brutality from their inevitable consequences.[153]

Lamming's insight elevates the question of political culture from the abstract realm of 'super-structure' to the very center of a socialist strategy for the Caribbean. The Westminster system has been a method of consolidating authoritarian, neocolonialist regimes, but its legitimacy is deeply engrained in much of the region's political culture. Freedom of the press and speech, trade unions, laws against racial discrimination and women's oppression, and other reforms were the historical products of collective, popular struggles against the colonial and postcolonial state. Had Bishop and Coard seized the progressive kernels from the trappings of bourgeois democratic structures, and developed an 'imaginative' synthesis with new institutions of revolutionary democracy, the PRG could have acquired an even greater base among working people.

The Grenadian revolution's demise also provides additional clarity on the tensions between egalitarian and statist versions of socialism. Egalitarian socialists are often influenced by left libertarian, voluntaristic and populist notions of social change. Frequently, the egalitarians conclude that political history is basically made by the spontaneous, self-motion of the masses; that once oppressed people are brought to full self-consciousness, they will inevitably pave the way toward social class liberation and proletarian democracy. The purest representative of this argument in the Caribbean remains C.L.R. James, who stated in one 1985 interview: 'Democracy means government by the people. The people will find out ways and means of expressing themselves and the technical basis for a complete democracy . . . the means of communication, means of information today are such that it is impossible to believe that as time goes on it does not mean greater and greater communication between people, which means, ultimately a democratic system of some sort.'[154]

This adherence to revolutionary spontaneity, if advanced abstractly, seriously underestimates the contradictions which exist within political cultures of working people: e.g., the traditional religious hostility to the 'atheism' of Marxism, the petty-bourgeois entrepreneurialism and consumerism which is constantly projected by the capitalist-owned media, the materialistic sociocultural values which are antithetical to progressive social change. Each progressive step forward by working people has historically required more advanced levels of organization, which in turn help to create a more class conscious proletariat, and new arenas for struggle. Each major political advance which has restricted the prerogatives of capital and the power of the state in peripheral capitalist-colonial regimes has been won through the conscious, planned intervention of activists who have developed programs, organizations, tactics and longterm strategies in the broad context of mass struggle.

The populist current within egalitarian socialism has produced charismatic leaders, who serve as symbolic 'mediators' between the party, the state and the masses. In his post-coup critique, Louison argued that one 'fundamental issue which was violated in its extreme in Grenada is the recognition of the role of a key figure in national democratic revolutions, [which] require a strong leader who is popular among the masses and who is able to help build that process, and any attempt to remove that strong person . . . can spell disaster.'[155] Messianic, populist-style leaders have been familiar figures throughout Caribbean political history, but there is absolutely no guarantee that their promulgation will promote national democratic revolutions. In a *limited* sense, therefore, the Coardites may have been right: Bishop's personal charisma and populist style probably did not assist the development of an explicitly Marxist political culture. Bishop was too heavily personified as 'the revolution,' and his downfall surely meant the immediate disintegration of the regime's legitimacy. But in concrete terms, Louison's analysis still remains correct, when the actual level of political development and class consciousness of Grenada's working class and agroproletariat is considered.

Conversely, statist-oriented Marxist-Leninists are subject to dogmatism in theory, intolerance in questions of cultural and political pluralism, and all too frequently, a tendency toward economism. Such political rigidity and ideological dogmatism was constantly criticised by Lenin himself, if not by those who currently identify with his political legacy. 'History as a whole,' Lenin observed, 'is always richer in content, more varied, more multiform, more lively and ingenious than is imagined by even the best of parties.'[156] Nevertheless, the rigid statist socialist tries to impose social order in close approximation with social theory. Inevitably, the dialectic of abstract theory and practice begins to break down. The political power of the new revolutionary bureaucratic stratum is exercised above the mass organizations, and authority finally may be concentrated in the hands of a few ideologues. Specifically, this process has been acclaimed as 'democratic centralism,' but in practice it is utterly alien to the actual historical writings and political practice of Lenin. Clive Thomas has criticized the NJM for 'vanguardism,' which directly contributes to 'a certain type of depoliticization of the people and a rise of authoritarianism . . . When one reads the [Central Committee] record, one sees for example such ridiculous statements as "the position of Central Committee and of the masses of workers do not always coincide, because in many instances we have the advantage of science." It shows how divorced a small vanguard group had become from the very people and situations they were seeking to represent.'[157] Had the United States invasion and military occupation not taken place, the RMC would have been a left Bonapartist, authoritarian state, not unlike Nkrumah's regime in 1962-66, at odds with virtually every social class on the island. Even with massive economic and military assistance from external regimes, its popular legitimacy would have been nearly nonexistent.

Any socialist ruling party in peripheral societies must embody a creative synthesis of statism and egalitarianism, maintaining organic links with the masses, and encouraging structures of independent, autonomous authority exercised by working people, which permit close accountability of the government and the ruling party. A socialist ruling party should reflect the broadest possible range of constituencies within a society, permit all democratic criticism, and allow effective channels of nonviolent opposition to exist. Historically, Marxist parties in the periphery have repeatedly failed to recognize the dangers of attempting to impose abstract structures and policies upon the proletariat. Georg Lukacs's observations in 1924 are still relevant: 'The vanguard party of the proletariat can only fulfill its destiny if it is always a step in front of the struggling masses, to show them the way. But only *one* step in front so that it always remains leader of *their* struggle . . . For it is of the essence of history always to create the *new*, which cannot be forecast by an infallible theory . . . Therefore, all dogmatism in theory and all sclerosis in organisation are disastrous for the party.'[158]

Could the collapse of the revolution have been avoided, given the composition of the NJM, the errors and shortcomings of the regime, and the hostile political climate fostered by imperialism? Friends of Bishop insist that the Prime Minister did not realise the gravity of his situation until September 1983. But on balance, for such an astute politician, this seems unlikely. One must recognize that Bishop indirectly contributed to the Party's dogmatism and lack of political pluralism in critical respects. Indeed, viewed from the perspective of Caribbean revolutionary history, Bishop shared some of the same flaws of the great Toussaint. Nearly a half century ago, James observed that Toussaint's 'error was his neglect of his own people. They did not understand what he was doing or where he was going. He took no trouble to explain. It was dangerous to explain, but still more dangerous not to explain . . . (Toussaint) went his tortuous way, overconfident that he had only to speak and the masses would follow.'

This judgement may appear curious and erroneous when applied to Bishop, who was so warm, so open-hearted in his relations with the Grenadian masses. And yet, on the decisive questions of the deteriorating relations between factions inside the NJM, and the growing contradictions between the Party and the state, he was as taciturn and 'shut up within himself' as Toussaint. Perhaps Bishop was also 'too confident' in his powers of persuasion, and deliberately selected to minimize or to ignore the repeated warning of Creft, Hector and others. He opposed unnecessary censorship, but did little to halt it; he deplored the use of physical violence against the regime's critics, but did not effectively censure his comrades' criminal behavior; he advocated close and cordial links with the masses, but did nothing as the NJM drifted toward sectarianism and dogmatism; he recognized his pivotal role as the PRG's charismatic spokesperson, and assumed that not even the NJM's most dogmatic elements would possibly consider his physical elimination. But Bishop was tragically incorrect, as was Toussaint.

The implosion of the Grenadian revolution represents a major setback in the ongoing Caribbean revolution. But its collapse should not permit us to reject its concrete achievements, or to retreat into Caribbean Fabianism. The errors of the NJM were not the direct result of democratic centralism, but of its sectarian and hierarchical implementation. Social democracy in the periphery has resulted either in social, economic and political stasis, or deterioration into Bonapartist, authoritarian states. The task of Marxist parties is to lead the masses, building multiclass alliances, while never divorcing themselves or their programs from the actual level of political culture and social consciousness of the working class. Marxist theory 'is not a dogma,' Lenin reminded an earlier generation of sectarian leftists, 'but a guide to action . . . A vanguard performs its tasks as a vanguard only when it is able to avoid being isolated from the mass of the people it leads and is able to lead the whole mass forward. Without an alliance with non-Communists in the most diverse sphere of activity there can be no question of any successful communist construction.'[159]

Notes

Chapter 1

1. Robert William Fogel and Stanley L.Engerman, *Time on the Cross: The Economics of American Negro Slavery*, Boston 1974, 17-19.
2. Bernard Braudel, *Capitalism and Material Life, 1400-1800*, New York 1973, pp. 156-158
3. Maurice Dobb, *Studies in the Development of Capitalism*, New York 1963, p. 208.
4. Andre Gunder Frank, *World Accumulation, 1492-1789*, New York 1978, 42-43.
5. David M. Davidson, 'Negro Slave Control and Resistance in Colonial Mexico, 1519-1650,' in Richard Price, ed., *Maroon Societies: Rebel Slave Communities in the Americas*, Baltimore 1979, pp. 82-103.
6. David Brion Davis, *The Problem of Slavery in Western Culture*, Ithaca, New York 1966, pp. 234, 240, 253, 286; and Robert C. Twombly and Robert H. Moore, 'Black Puritan: The Negro in Seventeenth-Century Massachusetts,' *William and Mary Quarterly*, vol. 34, April 1967, pp. 224-242.
7. Basil Davidson, *The African Slave Trade: Precolonial History, 1450-1850*, Boston 1961, p. 154.
8. Walter Rodney, 'The Impact of the Slave Trade on West Africa,' in Roland Oliver, ed., *The Middle Age of African History*, London 1967, pp.37-39.
9. Beverley Steele, 'Grenada, An Island State, Its History and Its People,' *Caribbean Quarterly*, vol. 20, March 1974, p. 9.
10. Latin American Bureau, ed., *Grenada: Whose Freedom?* London 1984, p. 17; and EPICA Task Force, *Grenada: The Peaceful Revolution*, Washington, D.C. 1982, p. 13.
11. Eric Williams, *Captialism and Slavery*, New York 1966, p. 114.
12. Eric Williams, *From Columbus to Castro: The History of the Caribbean 1492-1969*, New York 1970, p. 151.
13. Steele, 'Grenada, An Island State,' p. 11; and Bridget Brereton, *A History of Modern Trinidad, 1783-1962*, London 1981, pp. 13-14, 22.
14. EPICA, *Grenada: The Peaceful Revolution*, pp. 18-19.
15. Eugene D. Genovese, *From Rebellion to Revolution: Afro-American Slave Revolts in the Making of the New World*, New York 1979, pp. 107-109.
16. C.L.R. James, *The Black Jacobins: Toussaint L'Ouverture and the San Domingo Revolution*, New York 1963, p. 279.
17. *Ibid.*, pp. 257, 264.
18. Ralph Korngold, *Citizen Toussaint*, New York 1944, pp. 184-186, 205, 210; and *Ibid.*, p. 242.
19. Alex Dupuy, 'Class formation and undervelopment in nineteenth-century Haiti,' *Race and Class*, vol. 24, Summer 1982, pp. 17-31; and Frank Moya Pons, 'The Land Question in Haiti and Santo Domingo: The Sociopolitical Context of the Transition from Slavery to Free Labor, 1801-1843,' in Manuel Moreno Fraginals,

Frank Moya Pons, and Stanley L. Engerman, eds., *Between Slavery and Free Labor: The Spanish-Speaking Caribbean in the Nineteenth Century*, Baltimore 1985, pp. 181-182.

20. Genovese, *From Rebellion to Revolution*, pp. 48-49.

21. Clive Y. Thomas, *The Rise of the Authoritarian State in Peripheral Societies*, New York 1984, pp. 18-19.

22. Williams, *Capitalism and Slavery*, p. 153; Steele, 'Grenada, An Island State,' p. 13; and M.G. Smith, *Stratification in Grenada*, Berkeley 1965, p. 10.

23. Mário C. Vázquez, 'Immigration and Mestizaje in Nineteenth-Century Peru,' and Magnus Morner, 'Historical Research on Race Relations in Latin America During the National Period,' in Magnus Morner, ed., *Race and Class in Latin America*, New York 1970, pp. 73-95, 199-230.

24. Reynold A. Burrowes, *The Wild Coast: An Account of Politics in Guyana*, Cambridge, Massachusetts 1984, pp. 4-5.

25. EPICA, *Grenada: The Peaceful Revolution*, p. 25.

26. Smith, *Stratification in Grenada*, p.12.

27. Thomas, *The Rise of the Authoritarian State in Peripheral Societies*, pp. 21.

28. Ivar Oxaal, 'The Intellectual Background to the Democratic Revolution in Trinidad,' in Wendell Bell, ed., *The Democratic Revolution in the West Indies*, Cambridge, Massachusetts 1967, pp. 23-24; and C.L.R. James, *Beyond a Boundary*, New York 1983, pp. 38-39.

29. Burrowes, the Wild Coast, p. 60; and Thomas, *The Rise of the Authoritarian State in Peripheral Societies*, pp. 21-22.

30. James, *Beyond a Boundary*, pp. 55-59.

31. Smith, *Stratification in Grenada*, pp. 92-94, 186-188.

32. Prominent Caribbean exiles and expatriates of the late nineteenth century also included Jóse Martí and Daniel DeLeon. Martí, born in Havana in 1853, became the central figure of the Cuban independence movement, yet spent most of his adult life in exile. From 1870 to 1878 he lived variously in France, Spain, Guatemala and Mexico, before settling down, from 1881 until 1895, in the United States. 'Of the seventy-four volumes of his collected writings, seventeen discuss life in the land of his exile.' (See Ramon Eduardo Ruiz, *Cuba: The Making of a Revolution*, New York 1968, p. 62.) DeLeon was born in Curaçao in 1852 and at the age of fourteen left for Europe. After teaching at Columbia University in New York, he joined the Socialist Labor Party in 1890 and almost immediately became its leader and dominant theorist. A prickly sectarian, he was nonetheless admired for his brilliant and erudite polemics; Lenin is supposed to have regarded him 'as the only one who had added anything to socialist thought since Marx.' (See David Herreshoff, *The Origins of American Marxism: From the Transcendalists to DeLeon*, New York 1973, pp. 108-116; and John P. Diggins, The American Left in the Twentieth Century, New York 1973, p. 66.)

33. Robert A. Hill, ed., *The Marcus Garvey and Universal Negro Improvement Association Papers, volume 1*, Berkely 1983, pp. 111-112, 194.

34. EPICA, *Grenada: The Peaceful Revolution*, pp. 27-28.

35. Smith, *Stratification in Grenada*, p. 14; and Simon Rottenberg, 'Labor Relations in an Underveloped Economy,' *Caribbean Quarterly*, vol. 4, January 1955, pp. 53-54.

36. Steele, 'Grenada, An Island State,' pp. 30-31.

37. Herreshoff, *The Origins of American Marxism*, p. 108; Hill, ed., *The Marcus Garvey and Universal Negro Improvement Association Papers*, volume 1, p. 527; Oxaal, 'The Intellectual Background to the Democratic Revolution in Trinidad,' p.

26; and C.L.R. James, *At the Rendezvous of Victory*, London 1984, p. 227.

38. Samir Amin, *Unequal Development: An Essay on the Social Formations of Peripheral Capitalism*, New York 1976, pp. 328-329.

39. Josephine F. Milburn, *British Business and Ghanaian Independence*, Hanover New Hampshire 1977, p. 5; and Tony Killick, 'Mining,' in Walter Birmingham, I. Neustadt, and E.N. Omaboe, eds., *A Study of Contemporary Ghana: volume 1, The Economy of Ghana*, London 1966, p. 270.

40. Samir Amin, *Neo-Colonialism in West Africa*, New York 1973, pp. 42-43.

41. Bereket H. Selassie, *The Executive in African Governments*, London 1974, pp. 129-130.

42. David Martin and Phyllis Johnson, *The Struggle for Zimbabwe*, New York 1981, pp. 52-54.

43. Nicola Swainson, *The Development of Corporate Capitalism in Kenya, 1918-77*, Berkeley 1980, pp. 34-38, 176.

44. *Ibid.*, pp. 59-61.

45. Kwame Nkrumah, *Neo-Colonialism: The Last Stage of Imperialism*, New York 1980, pp. 127-136, 162-166.

46. Amin, *Unequal Development*, pp. 330-331.

47. John Riddell, 'Trade Unionism in Africa as a Factor in National Building,' *Civilisations*, vol. 12, 1962, pp. 28-36.

48. David E. Apter, *Ghana in Transition*, New York 1963, p. 5; Dennis Austin, *Politics in Ghana, 1946-1960*, London 1964, p. 72; and Milburn, *British Business and Ghanaian Independence*, p. 8.

49. Ibrahima B. Kaké, 'The Impact of Afro-Americans on French-Speaking Black Africans, 1919-1945,' in Joseph E. Harris, ed., *Global Dimensions of the African Diaspora*, Washington, D.C. 1982, pp. 198-199.

50. Martin and Johnson, *The Struggle for Zimbabwe*, pp. 56-57; and Allen Isaacman and Barbara Isaacman, *Mozambique: From Colonialism to Revolution, 1900-1982*, Boulder, Colorado 1983, pp. 51-52.

51. Milburn, *British Business and Ghanaian Independence*, p. 8.

52. Kwame Nkrumah, *Africa Must Unite*, New York 1970, pp. 28-35.

53. Milburn, *British Business and Ghanaian Independence*, pp. 69, 75-79, 81-82, 90-92.

54. Martin and Johnson, *The Struggle for Zimbabwe*, pp. 49-50.

55. R.I. Rotberg, *The Rise of Nationalism in Central Africa*, Cambridge, Massachusetts 1966, p. 86.

56. See Ronald H. Chilcote, *Protest and Resistance in Angola and Brazil*, Berkeley 1972.

57. Bernard Makhosezwe Magubane, *The Political Economy of Race and Class in South Africa*, New York 1979, pp. 280-286.

58. Wagu Ananaba, *The Trade Union Movement in Africa: Promise and Performance*, New York 1979, pp. 2-3, 37, 41, 51, 61; and Y.M. Ivanov, *Agrarian Reforms and Hired Labour in Africa*, Moscow 1979, p. 70.

59. Robert E. Dowse, *Modernization in Ghana and the U.S.S.R.*, London 1969, p. 29.

60. D. Kimble, *A Political History of Ghana, 1850-1928*, Oxford 1963, p. 150.

61. See J.C. Casely-Hayford, *Ethiopia Unbound*, London 1911.

62. Manning Marable, 'A Black School in South Africa,' *Negro History Bulletin*, vol. 37, June/July 1974, pp. 258-261.

63. Martin and Johnson, *The Struggle for Zimbabwe*, p. 64.

64. Magubane, *The Political Economy of Race and Class in South Africa*, p. 273.

65. James Africanus B. Horton, 'Letters on the Political Condition of the Gold Coast' (1870), in Henry S. Wilson, ed., *Origins of West African Nationalism*, London 1969, pp. 202-203.
66. Manning Marable, 'Booker T. Washington and African Nationalism,' *Phylon*, vol. 35, December 1974, pp. 398-406.
67. Austin, *Politics in Ghana, 1948-1960*, p. 10.
68. Amin, *Unequal Development*, p. 340.
69. R.W. July, *The Origins of Modern African Thought*, London 1964, p. 407.
70. Martin and Johnson, *The Struggle for Zimbabwe, pp. 64-65*.
71. M.M. Bober, *Karl Marx's Interpretation of History*, New York 1965, pp. 69-70; and Shlomo Avineri, ed., *Karl Marx on Colonialism and Modernization*, Garden City, New York 1969, p. 454.
72. Philip S. Foner, *Organized Labor and the Black Worker, 1619-1981*, New York 1981, p. 12.
73. Albert Fried, ed., *Socialism in America*, Garden City, New York, 1970, p. 387. Debs biographer Ray Ginger observes that Debs 'found pleasure' in telling 'Negro dialect stories,' despite his public commitment to racial equality. However, at the Socialist Party convention of 1903, Debs opposed a resolution which called for a 'special fight for the rights of Negroes.' Debs declared that such resolutions were not needed by Blacks, 'and they serve to increase rather than diminish the necessity for explanation . . . We have nothing special to offer the Negro, and we cannot make separate appeals to all the races . . . ' See Ray Ginger, *Eugene V. Debs: A Biography*, New York 1962, pp. 231, 277.
74. David Herreshoff, *The Origins of American Marxism*, New York 1970, pp. 159, 168-169.
75. *Ibid.*, pp. 169; Fried, ed., *Socialism in America*, p. 386; and Milton Cantor, *The Divided Left: American Radicalism, 1900-1975*, New York 1978, p. 14.
76. Foner, *Organized Labor and the Black Worker, 1619-1981*, p. 119.
77. See W.E.B. Du Bois, 'Close Ranks,' *Crisis*, vol. 16, July 1918, p. 111.
78. Perry Anderson, *Considerations on Western Marxism*, London 1976, p. 35.
79. Edward Hyams, *The Millennium Postponed: Socialism From Sir Thomas More to Mao Tse-Tung*, New York 1973, pp. 115, 126, 129,
80. Sheldon B. Liss, *Marxist Thought in Latin America*, Berkeley, 1984, pp. 33, 39, 73, 127, 191, 206-207; and Juan Eugencio Corradi, 'Argentina,' in Ronald Chilcote and Joel Edelstein, eds., *Latin America; The Struggle with Dependency and Beyond*, Cambridge, Massachusetts 1974, pp. 309-407.
81. Anderson, *Considerations on Western Marxism*, p. 11.
82. See V.I. Lenin, 'Two Tactics of Social-Democracy,' pp. 50-147, and 'The State and Revolution,' ppl 263-348, in Institute of Marxism-Leninism, ed., *Lenin: Selected Works*, Moscow 1977; and 'What is to be Done?' in Robert C. Tucker, ed., *The Lenin Anthology*, New York 1975, pp. 12-114.
83. See V.I. Lenin, 'The Right of Nations to Self-Determination,' in Tucker, ed., *The Lenin Anthology*, pp. 153-180.
84. See V.I. Lenin, 'Imperialism, the Highest Stage of Capitalism,' in Institute of Marxism-Leninism, ed., *Lenin: Selected Works*, pp. 169-262.
85. Quintin Hoare and Geoffrey Nowell Smith, ed., *Selections from the Prison Notebooks of Antonio Gramsci*, New York 1971, p. 238.
86. V.I. Lenin, 'Report on the Commission on the National and the Colonial Questions,' 26 July 1920, in Institute of Marxism-Leninism, ed., *Lenin: Selected Works*, pp. 596-600.
87. R.A. Ulyanovsky, et al., *Fighters For National Liberation*, Moscow 1983, pp.

60-61; Jon Halliday, 'The North Korean Enigma,' in Gordon White, Robin Murray, and Christine White, eds., *Revolutionary Socialist Development in the Third World*, Lexington, Kentucky 1983, pp. 114-154; and Nikhil Roy, 'Fifty Years of Indian Socialism,' *Frontier* (Calcutta), vol. 18, 31 August 1985, pp. 6-8, 10.

88. Milene Charles, *The Soviet Union and Africa: The History of the Involvement*, Lanham, Maryland 1980, pp. 6, 9, 20-21, 156-157, 168; and Harvey Klehr, *The Heyday of American Communism*, New York 1984, p. 325.

89. Claude McKay, *A Long Way from Home*, New York 1947, pp. 175, 180.

90. Klehr, *The Heyday of American Communism*, pp. 324, 328; Theodore G. Vincent, *Black Power and the Garvey Movement*, San Francisco 1972, pp. 81-83; Hill, ed., *The Marcus Garvey and Universal Negro Improvement Association Papers*, vol. 1, p. 256; and Sterling D. Spero and Abram L. Harris, *The Black Worker: The Negro and the Labor Movement*, New York 1968, p. 423.

91. H.J. Simons and R.E. Simons, *Class and Color in South Africa, 1850-1950*, Baltimore 1969, pp. 261, 263.

92. Magubane, *The Political Economy of Race and Class in South Africa*, p. 283.

93. Ken Luckhardt and Brenda Wall, *Organize or Starve! The History of the South African Congress of Trade Unions*, New York 1980, p. 49.

94. Klehr, *The Heyday of American Communism*, pp. 324-326.

95. Charles, *The Soviet Union and Africa*, pp. 19, 21.

96. Klehr, *The Heyday of American Communism*, pp. 330-331; and *Ibid*., pp. 25-26.

97. Luckhardt and Wall, *Organize or Starve!* pp. 51, 54; and Charles, *The Soviet Union and Africa*, pp. 32-33.

98. Klehr, *The Heyday of American Communism*, pp. 17, 334, 348; and George Padmore, 'The Bankruptcy of Negro Leadership' (1931), in Theodore Vincent, ed., *Voices of a Black Nation: Political Journalism in the Harlem Renaissance*, San Francisco 1973, pp. 184-189. Du Bois's attitude toward American Communists throughout the 1920s and 1930s was generally negative. The theory of 'class struggle' did not apply to Afro-American conditions, Du Bois observed in 1921, because 'the colored group is not yet divided into capitalists and laborers.' The Comintern's commitment to colonial liberation and anti-racism was positive; however, Black Americans could not 'assume on the part of unlettered and suppressed masses of white workers, a clearness of thought, a sense of human brotherhood, that is sadly lacking in most educated classes.' In any event, Du Bois curtly declared, he was 'not prepared to dogmatize with Marx and Lenin' or to 'join a revolution which we do not at present understand.' See W.E.B. Du Bois, 'The Negro and Radical Thought,' *Crisis*, vol. 22, July 1921, pp. 102-104; and Du Bois, 'The Class Struggle,' *Crisis*, vol. 22, August 1921, pp. 151-152.

99. Simons and Simons, *Class and Color in South Africa*, pp. 401-402, 429.

100. Kake, 'The Impact of Afro-Americans on French-Speaking Black Africans, 1919-1945,' pp. 206-208.

101. Klehr, *The Heyday of American Communism*, p.340; and James, *At the Rendezvous of Victory*, pp. 227-228, 258.

102. George Padmore, 'Race Relations: Soviet and British,' *Crisis*, vol. 50, November 1943, pp. 345-348; and Oxaal, 'The Intellectual Background to the Democratic Revolution in Trinidad,' pp. 33-35. This was also a period when the major theoretical works by Pan-Africanists in the British sphere of influence acquired a harshly anti-Communist tone. Several examples would include James's *World Revolution* (1937), which 'became a kind of Bible of Trotskyism'; James's *A History of Negro Revolt* (1938); and Padmore's *How Britain Rules Africa* (1936).

103. Irene L. Gendzier, *Frantz Fanon: A Critical Study*, New York 1973, pp. 39-41.

104. James, *At the Rendezvous of Victory*, p. 259.

105. Aimé Césaire, *Discourse on Colonialism*, New York 1972, pp. 69-71.

106. Aguibou Y. Yansané, *Decolinization in West African States with French Colonial Legacy*, Cambridge, Massachusetts 1984, pp. 31, 50-51, 139, 239; and John Cartwright, *Political Leadership in Africa*, New York 1983, p. 102.

107. Césaire, *Discourse on Colonialism*, p. 70; and David Caute, *Frantz Fanon*, New York 1970, p. 61.

108. Ulyanovsky, et. al., eds., *Fighters For National Liberation*, pp. 60-61.

109. Marguerite J. Fisher, 'New Concepts of Democracy in Southern Asia,' *Western Political Quarterly*, vol. 15, December 1962, pp. 626-636.

110. Gordon H. Torrey and John F. Devlin, 'Arab Socialism,' *Journal of International Affairs*, vol. 19 (1965), pp. 47-53. It should be noted that Communists' relations with Baathists have not always been particularly fraternal. After the Baath Party seized power in Iraq in 1968, the Iraqi CP voted to cooperate with the government 'in a national front on the basis of equality and the preservation of all participants of their ideological, political, and organisational independence.' In 1973, the Baathists and Iraqi CP created a 'National Progressive Front' which called for democratic elections, renounced 'capitalism as a road of development,' and advocated an anti-imperialist foreign policy. Nevertheless, the Baathist regime continued to obstruct the Iraqi CP's activities, and repressed mass social movements which it did not directly control. After the Iraqi CP voiced substantial criticism of the regime in 1978, the Baathists unleashed a wave of terror. Communists were 'discharged from their jobs, arrested, and tortured,' and the Marxist press was closed. See Hamid Majid Mussa, 'Tempered in the Crucible of Battles – Iraqi Communist Party,' *World Marxist Review*, vol. 27, April 1984, pp. 128-131.

111. Thomas, *The Rise of the Authoritarian State in Peripheral Societies*, p. 33.

112. Robert H. Bates, *Markets and States in Tropical Africa; The Political Basis of Agricultural Policies*, Berkeley 1981, pp. 12-13.

113. Swainson, *The Development of Corporate Capitalism in Kenya*, pp. 112-113.

114. *Ibid.*, p. 99.

115. Nkrumah, *Neo-Colonialism: The Last Stage of Capitalism*, pp. 61-62; James O'Connor, 'The Meaning of Economic Imperialism,' in Rhodes, ed., *Imperialism and Underdevelopment*, pp. 132-133; and Amin, *Unequal Development*, p. 210.

116. Swainson, *The Development of Corporate Capitalism in Kenya*, p. 110.

117. Philip Reno, 'Aluminium Profits and Caribbean People,' in Rhodes, ed., *Imperialism and Underdevelopment*, p. 84.

118. Malcolm Cross, *Urbanization and Urban Growth in the Caribbean*, Cambridge 1979, pp. 33, 39-40.

119. See A. Segal, ed., *1975 Population Policies in the Caribbean*, Lexington, Massachusetts 1975.

120. Cross *Urbanization and Urban Growth in the Caribbean*, p. 51; and Raymond A. Mack, 'Race, Class, and Power in Barbados,' in Bell, ed., *The Democratic Revolution in the West Indies*, pp. 140-164.

121. Peter C.W. Gutkind, 'The Poor in Urban Africa: A Prologue to Modernization, Conflict, and the Unfinished Revolution,' in Warner Bloomberg, Jr., and Henry J. Schmandt, eds., *Power, Poverty, and Urban Policy*, Beverly Hills, California 1968, pp. 355-396; and Amin, *Unequal Development*, p. 241.

122. Thomas J. Spinner, Jr., *A Political and Social History of Guyana, 1945-1983*, Boulder, Colorado 1984, p. 23; and C.H. Allen, 'Union-Party Relationships in

Francophone West Africa: A Critique of "Téléguidage" Interpretations,' in Richard Sandbrook and Robin Cohen, eds., *The Development of an African Working Class: Studies in Class Formation and Action*, Toronto 1975, pp. 99-125. Also see A. Lewis, *Labour in the West Indies*, London 1977.

123. Ivar Oxaal, *Black Intellectuals and the Dilemmas of Race and Class in Trinidad*, Cambridge, Massachusetts 1982, p. 91.

124. William Minter, *Portuguese Africa and the West*, New York 1972, pp. 21, 35.

125. Oxaal, *Black Intellectuals and the Dilemmas of Race and Class in Trindidad*, p. 89.

126. John Iliffe, 'The Creation of Group Consciousness Among the Dockworkers of Dar es Salaam, 1929-50,' in Richard Sandbrook and Robin Cohen, eds., *The Development of an African Working Class: Studies in Class Formation and Action*, Toronto 1975, pp. 49-72

127. Oxaal, *Black Intellectuals and the Dilemmas of Race and Class in Trinidad*, p. 151.

128. Spinner, *A Political and Social History of Guyana, 1945-1983*, p. 37.

129. Cartwright, *Political Leadership in Africa*, p. 134

130. Martin and Johnson, *The Struggle for Zimbabwe*, p. 202.

131. Swainson, *The Development of Corporate Capitalism in Kenya*, p. 177

132. Martin and Johnson, *The Struggle for Zimbabwe*, p. 203.

133. Oxaal, *Black Intellectuals and the Dilemmas of Race and Class in Trinidad*, p. 73.

134. Spinner, *A Political and Social History of Guyana, 1945-1983*, pp. 24, 29.

135. Reynold Burrowes, *The Wild Coast: An Account of Politics in Guyana*, Cambridge, Massachusetts 1984, pp. 35-36. By 1955, Burnham would publicly declare: 'Ours is not a communist party nor is the party affiliated to any communist organisation outside or inside the country . . . we will not and cannot permit persons who consider an international reputation for being communists more important than the success of our struggle to thereby slow up our movement and weaken it.'

136. Spinner, *A Political and Social History of Guyana, 1945-1983*, p. 30.

137. Oxaal, *Black Intellectuals and the Dilemma of Race and Class in Trinidad*, pp. 137-139; and Winston Mahabir, *In and Out of Politics*, Port of Spain 1978, pp. 139-140.

138. A.R. Zollberg, 'Ivory Coast,' in J.S. Coleman and C.G. Rosberg, eds., *Political Parties and National Integration in Tropical Africa*, Berkeley 1964, p. 87; and Cartwright, *Political Leadership in Africa*, p. 114.

139. Kenneth J. King, ed., *Pan-Africanism From Within*, London 1973, p. 219; Martin and Johnson, *The Struggle for Zimbabwe*, p. 71; and Oleg Ignatyev, *Secret Weapon in African*, Moscow 1977, pp. 34, 67.

140. W. Howard Wriggins, *The Ruler's Imperative: Strategies for Political Survival in Asia and Africa*, New York 1969, p. 22.

141. Cross, *Urbanization and Urban Growth in the Caribbean*, p. 110.

142. Yansané, *Decolonization in West African States with French Colonial Legacy*, pp. 140-142.

143. *Ibid.*, p. 239.

144. Oxaal, *Black Intellectuals and the Dilemmas of Race and Class in Trinidad*, pp. 116, 154-156, 165-168, 172.

145. Spinner, *A Political and Social History of Guyana, 1945-1983*, pp. 39, 41, 45, 56-60. Also see Cheddi Jagan, *The West on Trial: The Fight for Guyana's Freedom*, East Berlin 1972; Raymond T. Smith, *British Guiana*, London 1962; and Roy Arthur Glasgow, *Guyana: Race and Politics among Africans and East Indians*, The Hague

1970.

146. *Ibid.*, pp. 72, 79; and Burrowes, *The Wild Coast*, p. 129.

147. Walter Rodney, 'The Politicization of Race in Guyana,' *Third World Socialists*, vol. 1, Autumn 1983, pp. 42-44.

148. Ibid

149. Frantz Fanon. *The Wretched of the Earth*, New York 1968, pp. 149, 156-158.

150. Hamza Alavi, 'The State in Post-Colonial Societies – Pakistan and Bangladesh,' *New Left Review* 74, July-August 1972, pp. 59-81.

151. John S. Saul, *The State and Revolution in Eastern Africa*, New York 1979, p. 158.

152. Micheala von Freyhold, 'The Workers and the Nizers,' quoted in *Ibid.*, p. 188.

153. Bereket H. Selassie, *The Executive in African Governments*, London 1974, pp. 49-51.

154. *Ibid.*, pp. 64, 140.

155. Sékou Touré, *Toward Full Re-Africanisation*, Paris 1959, pp. 53, 55.

156. Julius Nyerere, *Freedom and Unity*, Oxford 1967, p. 312.

157. Ali A. Mazrui and Michael Tidy, *Nationalism and New States in Africa*, London 1984, p. 227.

158. Ogingo Odinga, *Not Yet Uhuru*, London 1967, pp. 302-303.

159. Catherine A. Sunshine, *The Caribbean: Survival, Struggle and Sovereignty*, Washington, D.C. 1985, pp. 109-110.

160. Wogu Ananaba, *The Trade Union Movement in Africa*, New York 1979, pp.10, 31, 38, 46, 63, 74; Ignatyev, *Secret Weapon in Africa*, pp. 36-38; and Fred Halliday and Maxine Molyneux, *The Ethiopian Revolution*, London 1981, pp. 81-82.

161. Stewart Smith, *U.S. Neocolonialism in Africa*, New York 1974, pp. 144-145.

162. Sunshine, *The Caribbean*, pp. 112-113.

163. See Kwame Nkrumah, *Dark Days in Ghana*, New York 1968.

164. Saul, *The State and Revolution in Eastern African*, p. 396.

165. Olusegun Obasanjo, *My Command: An Account of the Nigerian Civil War, 1967-70*, London 1980, pp. 5, 174.

166. A.A. Afrifa, *The Ghana Coup*, London 1967, pp. 99, 107-112.

167. Odinga, *Not Yet Uhuru*, pp. 249-250, 254.

168. Swainson, *The Development of Corporate Capitalism in Kenya*, pp. 184-185.

169. Abdul Mohamed Babu, *African Socialism or Socialist Africa?* London 1981, p. 35.

170. 'The Dakar Colloquium on African Socialism,' (December 1962), in Martin Minogue and Judith Molloy, eds., *African Aims and Attitudes*, London 1974, pp. 167-169.

171. Oxaal, *Black Intellectuals and the Dilemmas of Race and Class in Trinidad*, pp. 125-126, 129-136.
The debate about 'socialism' in Trinidad became even more muddled in 1964, when Capildeo announced that the 'new ideology' of the opposition DLP would be democratic socialism.' (p.175).

172. Idi Amin, 'Policy Statements', and I.K. Acheampong, 'Interview,' in Minogue and Molloy, eds., *African Aims and Attitudes*, pp. 352, 366.

173. 'African Socialism in Kenya,' (1965), in *Ibid.*, pp. 129-141.

174. Swainson, *The Development of Corporate Capitalism in Kenya*, pp. 183-186, 195, 286; and Odinga, *Not Yet Uhuru*, p. 302.

175. V.I. Lenin, ' "Left-Wing" Childishness and the Petty-Bourgeois Mentality,'

in Institute of Marxism-Leninism, ed., *Lenin: Selected Works*, p. 448-449.
   176. Mahmoud Hussein, *Class Conflict in Egypt*, New York 1977, pp. 64-65, 89-90, 129, 135, 161.
   177. Gendzier, *Frantz Fanon*, pp. 165-166.
   178. Ulyanovsky, et al., eds., *Fighters for National Liberation, pp. 97-98, 170, 174.*
   179. Charles, *The Soviet Union and Africa*, p. 70.
   180. Charles, *The Soviet Union and Africa*, p. 121; and Martin and Johnson, *The Struggle for Zimbabwe*, pp. 87-88, 146, 266.
   181. Immediately after Guinea gained independence, Toure requested US military assistance. The US did not even answer Toure's request. Four months after the American rejection, the first group of Soviet-made armored cars and arms docked at Conakry, along with an eighteen member Czech mission. See Charles, *The Soviet Union and Africa*, pp. 56, 91-92, 101.
   182. Amin, *Neo-Colonialism in West Africa*, pp. 85-86.
   183. Karen Brutents, *National Liberation Revolutions Today,* vol. 2, Moscow, 1977, pp. 67, 75.
Somalia had secretly expressed 'a desire for improved relations' with the US in 1976, but was rebuffed by the Ford administration. The Carter and Reagan administrations reacted differently. The US sent Somalia $65 million in 'nonlethal' military assistance – e.g., trucks, radar equipment – in fiscal years 1980-82. In mid-1982, the US sent the Siad regime 24 armored personnel carriers, antitank guns, and large supplies of arms and ammunition. The Reagan administrations also promised an additional $40 million in military hardware. See Donald K. Peterson, 'Somalia and the United States, 1977-1983: The New Relationship,' in Gerald J. Bender, James S. Coleman and Richard L. Sklar, eds., *African Crisis Areas and US Foreign Policy*, Berkeley 1985, pp. 194-204.
   184. Mahmood Mamdani, *Imperialism and Fascism in Uganda*, Trenton, New Jersey 1984, pp. 26-28, 62-64, 75; and Charles, *The Soviet Union and Africa*, p. 105. John Saul's comments on both Obote's 'Move to the Left' in 1969-70, and the political continuity between Obote and Idi Amin, are indeed persuasive: 'Obote was no socialist . . . nor was the "Move to the Left" a particularly deep-cutting left initiative, demanding . . . only marginal readjustments on the part of international capital and the domestic private sector, and in certain respects even further servicing the latter's interests . . . Amin's attack on the Asian community seems to have been designed, as much as anything, for populist purposes, similar to those which inspired the "Move to the Left". Like the latter, the expulsion was aimed at broadening Amin's popular constituency and thereby further consolidating his position . . . Amin, like Obote, was not one to mobilize the populace in any very fundamental way. Like Obote, too, he was prepared (albeit in a much more ruthless and paranoid manner) to subordinate his search for populist legitimacy to the forging of a narrower, well-trusted consituency and the use of force.
Saul, *The State and Revolution in Eastern Africa*, pp. 376, 381.
   185. Cartwright, *Political Leadership in Africa*, p. 249; and Mamdani, *Imperialism and Fascism in Africa*, pp. 79-86.
   186. Mamdani, *Imperialism and Fascism in Africa*, pp. 68-75, 107.
   187. Lenin, 'Imperialism, the Highest Stage of Capitalism,' pp. 240-242.

Chapter 2

1. Akwasi A. Afrifa, *The Ghana Coup: 24th February 1966*, London 1966, pp. 32-37; and Kwame Nkrumah, *Dark Days in Ghana*, pp. 21-22. Other sources discussing the 1966 coup include B. Fitch and M. Oppenheimer, *Ghana: The End of an Illusion*, New York 1966; and Dennis Austin, *Politicians and Soldiers in Ghana, 1966-1972*, London 1975.
2. Robert Pinkey, *Ghana Under Military Rule, 1966-1969*, London 1972, p. 8; and Apter, *Ghana in Transition*, p. 217.
3. Nkrumah, *Dark Days in Ghana*, p. 28.
4. Austin, *Politics in Ghana*, p. 420.
5. Afrifa, *The Ghana Coup*, p. 98.
6. W. Scott Thompson, *Ghana's Foreign Policy, 1957-1966: Diplomacy, Ideology and the New State*, Princeton 1969, p. 412; Pinkney, *Ghana Under Military Rule*, pp. 10, 38-39, 129; and Austin, *Politics in Ghana*, pp. 115, 167, 224, 268, 406-407, 412.
7. Thompson, *Ghana's Foreign Policy*, p. 19; and Nkrumah, *Dark Days in Ghana*, pp. 11, 16-17.
8. Nkrumah, *Dark Days in Ghana*, pp. 113, 116, 119; and Ministry of Information, ed., *The Rebirth of Ghana*, Accra 1966. The Chairman of the NLC was Lieutenant General Joseph A. Ankrah, who had served as Nkrumah's Deputy Chief of Defense. Ankrah was largely a figurehead, and had not been party to the actual planning of the coup. The real leaders were two Ewes who had gone to the same Presbyterian school. John W.K. Harley, Commissioner of Police, and Kotoka; the third leader was Afrifa, an Ashanti. Other NLC members included Bawa A. Yakubu, Deputy Police Commissioner; Albert K. Ocran, colonel in command of the arm's first brigade; Assistant Police Commissioner John E.O. Nunoo; and Deputy Police Commissioner Anthony K. Deku, head of the Ghana Branch of Interpol and the Criminal Investigations Department.
9. Ukandi G. Damachi, 'The Internal Dynamics of Trade Unions in Ghana,' in Richard Sandbrook and Robin Cohen, eds., *The Development of an African Working Class: Studies in Class Formation and Action*, Toronto 1975, pp. 179-184; and Pinkney, *Ghana Under Military Rule*, pp. 34-35.
10. Damachi, 'The Internal Dynamics of Trade Unions in Ghana,' p. 189; and Austin, *Politics in Ghana*, pp. 174-175. Tettegah had spent ten days in Israel in early 1957, and was impressed with the Israeli Histadrut. Indeed, even when Nkrumah's foreign policies became pro-Arab, Tettegah 'was still prepared to stand by his former mentors.' See Thompson, *Ghana's Foreign Policy*, p. 47.
11. Afrifa, *The Ghana Coup*, pp. 121-123, 144.
12. Austin, *Politics in Ghana*, p. 420; Pinkney, *Ghana Under Military Rule*, p. 37; and C.L.R. James, *Nkrumah and the Ghana Revolution*, Westport, Connecticut 1977, p. 164.
13. Thompson, *Ghana's Foreign Policy*, p. 14; and King, ed., *Pan-Africanism From Within*, pp. 222-223, 238.
14. Thompson, *Ghana's Foreign Policy*, p. 186.
15. 'Nkrumah, The Great Internationalist,' *Black World*, vol. 21, July 1972, p. 21; Basil Davidson, *Black Star: A View of the Life and Times of Kwame Nkrumah*, New York 1974, p. 13; and Afrifa, *The Ghana Coup*, p. 121.
16. C.L.R. James, 'Kwame Nkrumah: Founder of African Emancipation,' *Black World*, vol. 21, July 1972, p. 4.
17. Bankole Timothy, *Kwame Nkrumah: His Rise to Power*, London 1955, p. 33.
18. Stanley Weir, 'Revolutionary artist,' and George Rawick, 'Personal notes,'

Urgent Tasks, Number 12 summer 1981, pp. 87-89, 118-121. The Shachtmanite Workers Party had about 600 members, located mostly in heavy industry. Its newspaper, *Labor Action,* reached tens of thousands of workers during the war years. The Party was one of the few left political formations in the US to oppose the war after 1941, and argued for a 'Third Camp,' and 'independent socialist alternative to both Washington and the Kremlin.'

19. James, 'Kwame Nkrumah: Founder of African Emancipation,' p. 5.
20. J.R. Johnson [C.L.R. James], 'Why Negroes Should Oppose the War,' in Fred Stanton, ed., *Fighting Racism in World War II,* New York 1980, pp. 28-40; and James and Grace Lee Boggs, 'A Critical Reminiscence,' *Urgent Tasks,* vol. 12, Summer 1981, pp. 86-87.
21. James, *At the Rendezvous of Victory,* pp. 173, 258.
22. Kwame Nkrumah, *Ghana: The Autobiography of Kwame Nkrumah,* Edinburgh 1957, p. 52.
23. W.E.B. Du Bois, *The World and Africa,* New York 1965, p. 292.
24. Nkrumah, *Ghana: The Autobiography of Kwame Nkrumah,* p. 53.
25. James, *At the Rendezvous of Victory,* p. 173; Austin, *Politics in Ghana,* p. 268; *Ibid.,* pp. 55, 60; and Kwame Nkrumah, *Revolutionary Path,* New York 1973, pp. 47-50.

Nkrumah later argued that the Circle 'did not rule out the use of armed force' to achieve decolonization, but 'clearly stated that it was to be used only as a last resort.' (p. 47) Nevertheless, the Circle statement, despite several rhetoric commitments to socialism, was much closer to the spirit and practice of Mohandas Gandhi than to that of Lenin.

26. King, ed., *Pan-Africanism From Within,* pp. 262-263.
27. Austin, *Politics in Ghana,* pp. 53-54; Nkrumah, *Ghana: The Autobiography of Kwame Nkrumah,* pp. 62-63; and *Ibid.,* pp. 261, 263.

Makonnen's 'suspicions' may have been correct. When Nkrumah was first arrested by four policemen in early March, 1948, they discovered an unsigned Communist Party membership card in his possession. Nkrumah claimed that the card 'had been given' to him in London before and he 'had long since forgotten' about it. Nkrumah, *Ghana: The Autobiography of Kwame Nkrumah,* p. 79.

28. Davidson, *Black Star,* pp. 64, 66; Austin, *Politics in Ghana,* p. 73; and Apter, *Ghana in Transition,* p. 169.
29. Apter, *Ghana in Transition,* pp. 170, 175-185; and Nkrumah, *Revolutionary Path,* pp. 55, 72, 87.
30. Nkrumah, *Ghana: The Autobiography of Kwame Nkrumah,* pp. 100-103; Austin, *Politics in Ghana,* p. 81; and Davidson, *Black Star,* pp. 67-68.
31. Nkrumah, *Ghana: The Autobiography of Kwame Nkrumah,* pp. 105-108.
32. James, *Nkrumah and the Ghana Revolution,* pp. 103-104.
33. Davidson, *Black Star.* p. 71.
34. Timothy, *Kwame Nkrumah,* pp. 69, 78, 83, 178; and T. Peter Omari, *Kwame Nkrumah: The Anatomy of an African Dictatorhip,* New York 1970, p. 38.
35. James, *Nkrumah and the Ghana Revolution,* pp. 133, 136; Davidson, *Black Star,* pp. 77-78; and Austin, Politics in Ghana, p. 89.
36. Nkrumah, *Ghana: The Autobiography of Kwame Nkrumah,* pp. 120-121.
37. Chinweizu, *The West and the Rest of Us, p. 139.*
38. James, *Nkrumah and the Ghana Revolution,* p. 139.
39. Austin, *Politics in Ghana,* pp. 73, 139, 233, 353, 384.
40. Nkrumah, *Ghana: The Autobiography of Kwame Nkrumah,* pp. 128-129.
41. Chinweizu, *The West and the Rest of Us,* pp. 135-136; Nkrumah, *Revolu-*

tionary Path, p. 71; and Apter, *Ghana in Transition*, p. 173.
  42. George V. Plekhanov, *Fundamental Problems of Marxism*, New York 1975, pp. 168-171.
  43. Timothy, *Kwame Nkrumah*, p. 111, Austin, *Politics in Ghana*, pp. 84-85, 114-115, 120, 129, 268; and Apter, *Ghana in Transition*, p. 172.
  44. Quoted in Saul, *The State and Revolution in Eastern Africa*, pp. 177-178.
  45. James, *Nkrumah and the Ghana Revolution*, pp. 141-142, 146; Apter; *Ghana in Transition*, pp. 200-201; Austin, *Politics in Ghana*, pp. 140-141; Dowse, *Modernization in Ghana and the USSR*, p. 14; and Nkrumah, *Revolutionary Path*, pp. 58-71.
  46. Erica Power, *Private Secretary (Female)/Gold Coast*, New York, 1984, p. 92. Power was Nkrumah's personal secretary from 1955 until 1966. This incident was small, but symbolic of the theatrical elements surrounding Nkrumahism. Any party or social movement whose leaders 'rewrite' history or events, even in minor ways, may acquire the capacity to move to higher and more dangerous levels of public dishonesty.
  47. Davidson, *Black Star*, pp. 85, 89.
  48. James, *At the Rendezvous of Victory*, p. 175.
  49. Davidson, *Black Star*, pp. 85, 92.
  50. Austin, *Politics in Ghana*, p. 150.
  51. Nkrumah, *Africa Must Unite*, pp. 87-88.
  52. Chinweizu, *The West and the Rest of Us*, pp. 164-165.
  53. James, *Nkrumah and the Ghana Revolution*, pp. 157-158.
  54. James, *At the Rendezvous of Victory*, p. 258.
  55. Thompson, *Ghana's Foreign Policy*, pp. 8, 29-30, 107.
  56. Padmore, *Pan-Africanism or Communism*, pp. 352-356.
Padmore's call for an African version of the Marshall Plan completely severed any residual claims he may have had to Marxism. Du Bois was frankly shocked by Padmore's position, terming his views 'dangerous thinking.' If Padmore could not comprehend the corporate impetus behind US 'foreign aid', George Marshall certainly did. In urging Congress to rebuild Western Europe as a bulwark against Communism, Marshall stated, 'the paramount question before us . . . can be stated in business terms. Without a new aid program there would a sharp drop in American exports.' See William Appleman Williams, *The Tragedy of American Diplomacy*, New York 1962, pp. 269-271.
  57. *Ibid*, pp. 217, 225-226, 269, 319-323.
  58. Du Bois, *The World and Africa*, p. 293.
  59. Gerald Horne, *Black and Red: W.E.B. Du Bois and the Afro-American Response to the Cold War, 1944-1963*, Albany, New York 1986, pp. 339-340.
  60. George Padmore to W.E.B. Du Bois, 3 December 1954; and Du Bois to Padmore 10 December 1954, in Herbert Aptheker, ed., *The Correspondence of W.E.B. Du Bois*, vol 3 Amherst, Massachusetts 1978, pp. 373-375.
  61. Amin, *Neo-Colonialism in Africa*, p. 48.
  62. Josephine F. Milburn, *British Business and Ghanaian Independence*, Hanover, New Hampshire 1977, pp. 79-80, 90-91.
  'Africanization' in transitional stage between late colonial rule and independence becomes a major concern of the would-be African elite, who are its prime beneficiaries. The parallels with 'equal opportunity' in the U.S. vis-a-vis the Afro-American petty bourgeoisie are especially striking. See Fred G. Burke and Peter L. French, 'Bureaucracy and Africanization,' in Fred W. Riggs, eds., *Frontiers of Development Administration*, Durham, North Carolina 1971, pp. 538-555.
  63. Tony Killick, 'Mining,' and Killick, 'The Monetary and Financial Systems,' in

Walter Birmingham, I. Neustadt, and E.N. Omaboe, eds., *A Study of Contemporary Ghana: vol. 1, The Economy of Ghana*, London 1966, pp. 255, 297-298.
64. Austin, *Politics in Ghana*, p. 162.
65. *Ibid.*, p. 166.
66. Davidson, *Black Star*, p. 127.
67. Austin, *Politics in Ghana*, p. 168; and Apter, *Ghana in Transition*, pp. 206, 225, 230.
68. Austin, *Politics in Ghana*, p. 170; Padmore, *Pan-Africanism or Communism*, p. 319; and Thompson, *Ghana's Foreign Policy*, p. 14.
69. Austin, *Politics in Ghana*, pp. 181, 184-187, 232-234; and Padmore, *Pan-Africanism or Communism*, p. 319.
70. Davidson, *Black Star*, p. 136.
71. Nkrumah, *Revolutionary Path*, p. 116; Austin, *Politics in Ghana*, pp. 230-245, 252, 282; and Apter, *Ghana in Transition*, pp. 300-301.
72. Davidson, *Black Star*, pp. 109, 137-138, 143, 147.
73. Omari, *Kwame Nkrumah*, pp. 60-61.
74. *Ibid.*, p. 2.
75. Austin, *Politics in Ghana*, pp. 267-268; Nkrumah, *Revolutionary Path*, pp. 117-118; and Dowse, *Modernization in Ghana and the USSR*, pp. 23, 29.
76. Nkrumah, *Revolutionary Path*, p.119; Austin, *Politics in Ghana*, pp. 332, 334.
77. Austin, *Politics in Ghana*, pp. 340-353.
78. Timothy, *Kwame Nkrumah*, p. 179; Nkrumah, *Ghana: The Autobiography of Kwame Nkrumah*, p. 43; Austin, *Politics in Ghana*, pp. 103, 182; Thompson, *Ghana's Foreign Policy*, pp. 18, 49, 182; and Manning Marable, 'The Fall of Kwame Nkrumah,' *Urgent Tasks*, number 12, Summer 1981, p. 43.
79. Nkrumah, *Revolutionary Path*, p. 120.
80. Timothy, *Kwame Nkrumah*, pp. 188-189.
81. Nkrumah, *Revolutionary Path*, pp. 126, 135.
82. See Kwame Nkrumah to W.E.B. Du Bois, 18 June 1960; Du Bois to Nkrumah, 10 October 1960; Du Bois to Nkrumah, 4 January 1961; Nkrumah to Du Bois, 23 January 1961, Du Bois to Nkrumah, 30 November 1961; Nkrumah to Du Bois, 4 December 1961; Du Bois to Sékou Touré, 16 January 1962; and Nkrumah to Du Bois, 9 June 1962, in Aptheker, ed., *The Correspondence of W.E.B. Du Bois*, vol. 3, pp. 443-444, 446-447, 456-459. Du Bois died at the age of 95 in Ghana on 27 August 1963 and was given a state funeral.
83. King, ed., *Pan-Africanism From Within*, p. 114; and Thompson, *Ghana's Foreign Policy*, pp. 91, 149.
84. Thompson, *Ghana's Foreign Policy*, p. 46.
Israeli exports of diamonds increased from $5 million in 1950 to $130 million by 1960. Most of these diamonds were shipped from apartheid South Africa. The Israeli weapons were shipped via West Germany to the Portuguese regime, and used against African nationalist movements rhetorically supported by Nkrumah. See Minter, *Portuguese Africa and the West*, p. 136; and Cruse, *The Crisis of the Negro Intellectual*, p. 487.
85. W.E.B. Du Bois, 'Letters from Du Bois,' *Crisis*, vol. 17, February 1919, pp. 163-164; and Horne, *Red and Black*, pp. 142, 283-284.
86. King, ed., *Pan-Africanism From Within*, pp. 144, 166, 198, 216-217, 235.
87. Thompson, *Ghana's Foreign Policy*, pp. 14, 46-47.
88. *Ibid.*, pp. 46, 48; King, ed., *Pan-Africanism From Within*, p. 235; and Nkrumah, *Africa Must Unite*, pp. 113-114.
A careful reading of *Africa Must Unite* reveals not a single mention of Israel,

Palestine, or any commentary on matters sensitive to Israel.

89. Thompson, *Ghana's Foreign Policy*, p. 119; King, ed., *Pan-Africanism From Within*, pp. 215-216; and Kwame Nkrumah, *Challenge of the Congo*, New York 1967, p. 14. Nkrumah does not state Avriel's role in his historic meeting with Lumumba, nor does he discuss his mentor Padmore's support for Kasavubu before 1960.

90. Thompson, *Ghana's Foreign Policy*, pp. 49, 223; and King, ed., *Pan-Africanism From Within*, p. 217. Makonnen was the first to sense something amiss about Roberto. 'From my friends in the post office I had learnt that Holden had a number of American millionaire friends (I had these letters photographed) . . . I went to Kwame and said I felt that Holden should be arrested.' (p. 217). Roberto had the facility of being in rather strange places. For example, he appeared at the bedside of Frantz Fanon when the latter was dying of leukemia in Washington, DC in December 1961. See Gendzier, *Frantz Fanon*, p. 232.

91. Austin, *Politics in Ghana*, pp. 103, 384-385; and Davidson, *Black Star*, pp. 169-170.

92. W. Howard Wriggins, *The Ruler's Imperative: Strategies for Political Survival in Asia and Africa*, New York 1969, p. 162.

93. Omari, *Kwame Nkrumah*, pp. 50-53, 55, Henry L. Bretton, *The Rise and Fall of Kwame Nkrumah: A Study of Personal Rule in Africa*, New York 1966, p. 48; and Austin, *Politics in Ghana*, pp. 31, 242, 380-384.

94. J.B. Danquah, 'Christmas message to the Nation,' 20 December 1959, in Minogue and Molloy, eds., *African Aims and Attitudes*, p. 29.

95. Bretton, *The Rise and Fall of Kwame Nkrumah*, pp. 50-51; Apter, *Ghana in Transition*, p. 335, Omari, *Kwame Nkrumah*, p. 64; and King, ed., *Pan Africanism from Within*, p. 236.

96. Thompson, *Ghana's Foreign Policy*, p. 13.

97. Davidson, *Black Star*, pp. 179, 210.

98. James, *At the Rendezvous of Victory*, pp. 178-179, Omari, *Kwame Nkrumah*, pp. 84-85; Apter, *Ghana in Transition*, p. 287; Austin, *Politics in Ghana*, pp. 383, 405; and Thompson, *Ghana's Foreign Policy*, p. 112.

99. James, *At the Rendezvous of Victory*, p. 178.

100. Kwame Nkrumah, exerpt from 'All-African Regional Conference of ICFTU,' January 1957, reprinted in Minogue and Molloy, *African Aims and Attitudes*, p. 25.

101. Richard D. Jeffries, 'Populist Tendencies in the Ghanaian Trade Union Movement,' in Sandbrook and Cohen, eds., *The Development of an African Working Class*, p. 263; Tony Killick, 'Labor: A General Survey,' in Birmingham, Neustadt, and Omaboe, eds., *A Study of Contemporary Ghana*, vol. 1, pp. 142-143, 146-147; and Ananaba, *The Trade Union Movement in Africa;* pp. 9-12. The urban population in Ghana grew rapidly and was increasingly central to national politics. The total population in towns with more than 5,000 inhabitants was 1.6 million in 1960, 23 percent of the entire country. Accra had 338,000 inhabitants, Kumasi, 181,000 and Sekondi-Takoradi 76,000. The size of Ghana's wage labour force, moreover, was quite substantial by African standards. In 1960, there were nearly one million non-agricultural workers in Ghana, including 48,000 mineworkers, 89,000 construction workers, 68,000 transportation workers, 169,000 service workers, and almost one quarter million industrial workers. See Amin, *Neocolonialism in Africa*, pp. 46, 68.

102. James, *Nkrumah and the Ghana Revolution*, pp. 8, 163, 171-177.

Notes   287

103. Davidson, *Black Star*, pp. 180, 211.
104. Nkrumah, *Revolutionary Path*, p. 205.
105. *Ibid.*, pp. 151-159.
106. Omari, *Kwame Nkrumah*, pp. 86-89.
107. Davidson, *Black Star*, p. 175.
108. Jeffries, 'Populist Tendencies in the Ghanaian Trade Union Movement,' p. 267.
109. St. Clair Drake and L.C. Lacy, 'Government Versus the Unions: The Sekondi-Takoradi Strike, 1961,' in G. Carter, eds., *Politics in Africa*, New York 1966, pp. 68, 99; and Omari, *Kwame Nkrumah*, p. 90. Sekondi-Takoradi exploded for several other reasons. It had a relatively small petty bourgeois strata locally; 90 percent of the earnings in the city came from wage labor, a much higher rate than in Accra (67 percent) or Kumasi (22 percent). Unemployment was at least 12 percent in 1961.
110. Austin, *Politics in Ghana*, p. 35; Owusu, *Kwame Nkrumah*, pp. 88, 91-92.
111. Omari, *Kwami Nkrumah*, pp. 92-93.
112. *Ibid.*, p. 93; and Austin, *Politics in Ghana*, pp. 405-407.
113. Amin, *Neo-Colonialism in Africa*, p. 244.
114. Baako's metaphysical definition of Nkrumahist socialism was 'a non-atheistic philosophy' which is 'modelled or adapted to suit the conditions and circumstances of Africa . . . Nkrumaism is not a religion, but it preaches and seeks to implement all that true religion teaches. I can safely therefore describe Nkrumaism as applied religion . . . It seeks to realise its socialist aims amid the legacies of colonialism and yet, in the process, never sacrificing its African character and heritage.' See Omari, *Kwame Nkrumah*, pp. 194-195.
115. *Ibid.*, p. 120; and Apter, *Ghana in Transition*, pp. 325-326.
116. Thomspon, *Ghana's Foreign Policy*, pp. 48, 155, 165-175, 195, 258, 284-286.
117. Killick, 'Mining' and 'The Monetary and Financial System,' in Birmingham, Neustadt, and Omaboe, eds., *A Study of Contemporary Ghana: volume I*, pp. 251, 264, 294-296; and Amin, *Neo-Colonialism in Africa*, p. 246.
118. Bretton, *The Rise and Fall of Kwame Nkrumah*, p. 106.
119. Omari, *Kwame Nkrumah*, p. 95; and Davidson, *Black Star*, p. 185.
120. James, *At the Rendezvous of Victory*, pp. 179-180; and James, *Nkrumah and the Ghana Revolution*, pp. 10-11, 183.
121. Apter, *Ghana in Transition*, p. 77; Thompson, *Ghana's Foreign Policy*, pp. 21, 23, 272, 293; Davidson, *Black Star*, pp. 185-186; and Bretton, *The Rise and Fall of Kwame Nkrumah*, pp. 110-111.
122. Karl Marx, *The Eighteenth Brumaire of Louis Bonaparte*, New York 1963, pp. 121, 133.
123. Gramsci, *Prison Notebooks*, pp. 227-228.
124. Bretton, *The Rise and Fall of Kwame Nkrumah*, p. 34.
125. Timothy, *Kwame Nkrumah*, p. 136; Nkrumah, *Ghana: The Autobiography of Kwame Nkrumah*, pp. 100, 221-222; Nkrumah, *Africa Must Unite*, pp. 54, 72-73; and James, *At the Rendezvous of Victory*, p. 179.
126. Nkrumah, *Revolutionary Path*, pp. 394-413; and Omari, *Kwame Nkrumah*, p. 112.
127. Thompson, *Ghana's Foreign Policy*, pp. 275-276; King, ed., *Pan-Africanism From Within*, pp. 223, 245-253; and Amin, *Neo-Colonialism in West Africa*, p. 245.
Makonnen adds: 'there were only a handful of socialists in Ghana – the socialist boys, or the Socialist Six, as people used to call us.' The 'Socialist Six' were *Evening News* editor Eric Heymann, Cecil Forde and T. Baffoe of the *Ghanaian Times*, CPP

ideological secretary K. Akwei, Finance Minister Kwesi Amoaka-Atta, and Makonnen.
128. Thompson, *Ghana's Foreign Policy*, pp. 332-333.
129. *Ibid.*, pp. 24-43, 307, 328, 333, 350, 353, 386-387.
130. Amin, *Neo-Colonialism in West Africa*, p. 249.
131. Malcolm X, *The Autobiography of Malcolm X*, New York 1973, pp. 354-360.
132. Leslie A. Lacy, 'African Responses to Malcolm X,' in LeRoi Jones and Larry Neal, eds., *Black Fire*, New York 1968, pp. 32-38; and Lacy, 'Malcolm X in Ghana,' in John Henrik Clarke, ed., *Malcolm X: The Man and His Times*, New York 1969, pp. 217-225.
133. Basil Davidson places the constituency favoring Nkrumah's policies at a slightly higher percentage: 'My own opinion . . . is that an honest referendum would have still yielded much the same result as general elections in the 1950s: a decisive but not overwhelming majority in a poll of about three-fifths of the electorate. As it was, the CPP became Ghana's only political party by the assistance of electoral fraud.' *Black Star*, p. 193.
134. Omari, *Kwame Nkrumah*, pp. 109, 114.
135. Ministry of Information, ed., *The Rebirth of Ghana*, pp. 6-18.
136. Afrifa, *The Ghana Coup*, pp. 114-115, 122.
There is considerable evidence that Nkrumah planned to eliminate his potential rivals in the military during 1966. Three weeks before the coup, Nkrumah spoke before the National Assembly on the problem of coups d'etat in Africa. 'The duty of the armed forces is to defend and support the Civil Government, and not to overthrow it . . . it has no political mandate and its duty is not to seek a political mandate . . . The substitute of a military regime or dictatorship is no solution to the neo-colonialist problem.' Nkrumah, *Revolutionary Path*, pp. 370-371.
137. Maxwell Owusu, *Uses and Abuses of Political Power: A Case Study of Continuity and Change in the Politics of Ghana*, Chicago 1970, pp. 243-244.
138. Nkrumah, *Dark Days in Ghana*, pp. 97-101; Pinkney, *Ghana Under Military Rule*, p. 140; and Yaw Agyeman-Badu and Kwaku Osei-Hwedie, *The Political Economy of Instability: Colonial Legacy, Inequality and Political Instability in Ghana*, Lawrenceville, Virginia 1982, p. 25.
139. Pinkney, *Ghana Under Military Rule*, pp. 132-135; Omari, *Kwame Nkrumah*, pp. 170-173; and 'Ghana: After Nkrumah,' *Africa Confidential*, vol. 13, no. 10 (1972), p. 5.
140. 'Appiah's Return,' *Africa Confidential*, vol. 11, no.1 (1970), p. 5; 'Ghana: Busia on the Offensive,' *Africa Confidential*, vol. 12, no. 19 (1971), p. 5; 'Ghana I: The Acheampong Regime,' vol. 14, no. 7 (1973), p. 2; and Pinkney, *Ghana Under Military Rule*, p. 150.
141. 'Ghana I: The Acheampong Regime,' p. 2; 'Ghana' The Search for Union Government,' *Africa Confidential*, vol. 18, no.3 (1977), pp. 6-7) and Davidson, *Black Star*, pp. 205-206.
The NRC regime was also pagued with problems. Ghana's national consumer price index (1963-100) rose to 1,729 by mid-1977. The military regime devalued its currency by 139 percent; food shortages became acute, and 'the economy was in complete disarray.' After a series of strikes by teachers, factory workers, taxi drivers, nurses and laborers, the regime was toppled. See Agyeman-Badu and Osei-Hwedie, *The Political Economy of Instability*, pp. 22-23, 38.
142. Nkrumah, *Revolutionary Path*, pp. 369-370, 390, 391, 393, 438-445, 470, 511. In *Class Struggle in Africa*, Nkrumah observed: 'every form of political power, whether parliamentary, multiparty, one party of open military dictatorship, reflects

the interest of a certain class or classes in society . . . The highest point of political action, when a revolution attains its excellence, is when the proletariat – comprising workers and peasants – under the leadership of a vanguard party the principles and motivations of which are based on scientific socialism, succeeds in overthrowing all other classes.' *Struggle in Africa*, New York 1970, pp. 17, 80.

143. Ulyanovsky, et al., eds., *Fighters for National Liberation*, pp. 156-157. Soviet scholars also insist that during 1961-66, Nkrumah was repeatedly warned that his regime was committing grave errors: '[Nkrumah] did not notice the growth of the bureaucratic bourgeoisie and did not wish to see the general corruption in the country . . . that the genuine revolutionary enthusiasm of the period of the struggle for independence had given way to ponderous official pomposity and to impetuous eulogies to the 'osagyefo,' the leader and teacher, and that all this testified to the degeneration of power and its isolation from the people.' Though undoubtedly an intelligent man and experienced politician, Nkrumah missed all this . . . What is more, he was frequently told this by Marxist-Leninists. Messages to Nkrumah from leaders of the socialist states constantly pointed to these unfavorable processes within the country, but to no avail. Nkrumah did not realise the danger threatening him when he was in power, and he did not grasp the whole diversity of reasons which caused his defeat, after he had lost power.' (pp. 154-155).

144. Amin, *Neo-Colonialism in West Africa*, pp. 247, 249.

145. James, *At the Rendezvous of Victory*, p. 178.

Chapter 3

1. Barry Munslow, 'Is Socialism Possible on the Periphery?' *Monthly Review*, vol. 35, May 1983, pp. 25-26.

2. Michael Harrington, *Socialism*, New York 1972, pp. 269, 287-288.

3. Fred Halliday and Maxine Molyneux, *The Ethiopian Revolution*, London 1981, pp. 269-270.

4. Liss, *Marxist Thought in Latin America*, pp. 242, 252-256; and Hugh Thomas, *The Cuban Revolution*, New York 1977, pp. 56, 298, 340.

5. Marta Harnecker, *Cuba: Dictatorship or Democracy? How People's Power Works* Westport, Conn. 1980, pp. xix-xx; and Thomas, *The Cuban Revolution*, pp. 677-678, 683.

6. Richard Handyside, ed., *Revolution in Guinea: Selected Texts by Amilcar Cabral*, New York 1969, pp. 58-62; and Manning Marable, 'The Road toward effective African Liberation: The Cases of Ghana and Guinea-Bissau,' in John W. Forje, ed., *Third World Development and the Myth of International Cooperation*, Lund, Sweden 1984, pp. 190-209.

7. Regis Debray, *The Chilean Revolution: Conversations with Allende*, New York 1971, pp. 30, 33, 71, 127.

8. Ralph Miliband, *Class Power and State Power: Political Essays*, London 1983, pp. 73, 83-84.

9. I. Andreyev, *The Non-Capitalist Way: Soviet Experience and the Liberated Countries*, Moscow 1977, p. 26.

10. Fitzroy Ambursley and Robin Cohen, 'Crisis in the Caribbean: Internal Transformations and External Constraints,' in Ambursley and Cohen, eds., *Crisis in the Caribbean*, New York 1983, pp. 6-7.

11. C.Y. Thomas, 'The "Non-Capitalist Path" as Theory and Practice of Decolonization and Socialist Transformation,' *Latin American Perspectives*, vol. 5, Spring 1978, pp. 10-28.

12. Karen N. Brutents, *National Liberation Revolutions Today: Some Questions of Theory*, vol. 1, Moscow 1977, pp. 148-149, 283.

13. *Ibid.*, pp. 213-214, 238, 239, 243, 249, 261, 265. Brutents was aware that anti-imperialist united fronts could shatter over the issue of democratic rights: 'In order to set up and consolidate anti-imperialist coalitions, it is exceptionally important that they should take shape and act on a democratic basis, so that their functioning should lead to a strengthening of ties and solidarity between those involved. Any attempt to ignore the interests of one's allies or infringement of their legitimate rights tends to harm the development of the liberation struggle . . . Any drive against democratic freedoms . . . [is] aimed against the masses . . . (pp. 213-214). Also see V. Chirkin and Y. Yudin, *A Socialised Oriented State*, Moscow 1978.

14. Anatoly Dinkevich, 'Principles and Problems of Socialist Orientation in the Countries of Africa and Asia,' quoted in Halliday and Molyneux, *The Ethiopian Revolution*, p. 277.

15. Luis E. Aguilar, 'Cuba and the Latin American Communist Parties: Traditional Politics and Guerrilla Warfare,' in Barry B. Levine, ed., *The New Cuban Presence in the Caribbean*, Boulder, Colorado 1983, pp. 107-121; and Karen N. Brutents, *National Liberation Revolutions Today*, vol. 2, Moscow 1977, p. 9.

16. Halliday and Molyneux, *The Ethiopian Revolution*, pp. 277-279.

17. Brutents, *National Liberation Revolutions Today*, vol. 2, pp. 23, 51.

18. Halliday and Molyneux, *The Ethiopian Revolution*, p. 274; and Ambursley and Cohen, 'Crisis in the Caribbean,' p. 8.

19. Spinner, *A Political and Social History of Guyana*, 1945-1983, p. 148.

20. Most researchers describe the PNP as a social democratic party. The PNP's founder, Norman Manley, was profoundly influenced by Fabian socialism and the British Labour Party; his son Michael is currently a vice president of the Socialist International. But Ambrusley insists that the PNP 'cannot be described as an authentic social-democratic party . . . Whereas social democracy is essentially a product of the labour bureaucracy, the PNP does not have such an "organic" relationship to the working class. The NWU was set up by the PNP to suppress the militant and radical leadership of the TUC and to consolidate bourgeois hegemony over the Jamaican labour movement.' (See Fitzroy Ambursely, 'Jamaica: From Michael Manley to Edward Seaga,' in Ambursely and Cohen, eds., *Crisis in the Caribbean*, p. 90. Certainly the party is not a *European* social democratic formation in its distinct historical roots and social class evolution. But within the conditions of colonialism and neocolonialism, it has indeed played a *functional* role akin to post-World War II European social democratic parties. It maintains a partnership with fractions of national and multinational capital, and until 1974, cordial relations with the US; it retards labor mobilization, and keeps the political discourse without safe boundaries.

21. Carl Stones, *Democracy and Clientelism in Jamaica*, New Brunswick, New Jersey 1980, p. 122.

22. *Ibid.*, p. 97.

23. *Ibid.*, pp. 117-118.

24. Ambursely, 'Jamaica: From Michael Manley to Edward Seaga,' p. 77.

25. Stone, *Democracy and Clientelism in Jamaica*, pp. 151-153; and *Ibid.*, pp. 81, 89-90.

26. Barry Floyd, *Jamaica: An Island Microcosm*, New York 1979, p. 148. Stone, Democracy and Clientelism in Jamaica, p. 162; and Ambursely, 'Jamaica: From Michael Manley to Edward Seaga,' pp. 82-83.

27. Like Manley, Echeverría made his political reputation as an anti-Communist, while serving as Interior Minister in the 1960s. Also like Manley, Echeverría's domestic programs were designed to 'rejuvenate the system'; his activist foreign policy was used to win over 'liberal and leftist intellectuals' in Mexico. Neither endorsed massive expropriations from the national bourgeoisie, nor were they willing to go beyond incremental, statist reforms which would not emancipate their respective working classes. See Alan Riding, *Distant Neighbors: A Portrait of the Mexicans*, New York 1986, pp. 86, 88, 100.

28. Jenny Pearce, *Under the Eagle: US Intervention in Central America and the Caribbean*, Boston 1982, pp. 96-97.

29. Stone, *Democracy and Clientelism in Jamaica*, pp. 135, 165; and Ambursley, 'Jamaica: From Michael Manley to Edward Seaga,' p. 89.

30. Stone, *Democracy and Clientelism in Jamaica*, pp. 122, 153, 169, 173.

31. *Ibid.*, pp. 176-177; and Norman P. Girvan, *Prospects for Jamaica's Political Economy*, Kingston 1986, p. 9.

32. Girvan, *Prospects for Jamaica's Political Economy*, p. 9

33. Stone, *Democracy and Clientelism in Jamaica*, pp. 176-177.

34. Anthony P. Maingot, 'Cuba and the Commonwealth Caribbean: Playing the Cuban Card,' in Levine, ed., *The New Cuban Presence in the Caribbean*, p. 24.

35. Stone, *Democracy and Clientelism in Jamaica*, p. 176; and Ambursley, 'Jamaica: From Michael Manley to Edward Seaga,' p. 89.

36. Pearce, *Under the Eagle*, pp. 153, 160, 164.

37. Ambursley, 'Jamaica: From Michael Manley to Edward Seaga,' p. 85; and Sunshine, *The Caribbean*, p. 118.

38. Sunshine, *The Caribbean*, pp. 121, 123, 152.

39. Ambursley, 'Jamaica: From Michael Manley to Edward Seaga,' pp. 93-94; *Ibid.*, pp. 152-155; and 'Jamaica Goes for Growth,' *Latin American Monitor*, vol. 3, May 1986, p. 291.

40. Ambursley, 'Jamaica: From Michael Manley to Edward Seaga,' p. 102.

41. Stone, *Democracy and Clientelism in Jamaica*, pp. 186-187. In a November 1977 opinion poll, Stone determined that 44 percent of all respondents were favorable to democratic socialism, 25 percent were unfavorable, and 31 had no opinion. Fifteen percent endorsed Communism, 52 percent were unfavorable, and 33 percent expressed no opinion. Fifty two percent of all democratic socialists opposed Communism, while only 30 percent endorsed it.

42. At the 1984 PNP conference, one of the party's major 'centrist' leaders openly predicted to me that Jamaica would eventually develop a third major party to the left of the PNP. The two principle forces creating this entity would be the WPJ and the left wing of the PNP, led by Duncan.

43. Girvan, *Prospects for Jamaica's Political Economy*, pp. 10, 12.

44. Sunshine, *The Caribbean*, p. 156.

45. Spinner, *A Political and Social History of Guyana, 1945-1983*, p. 122.

46. *Ibid.*, p. 126; and Burrowes, *The Wild Coast; An Account of Politics in Guyana*, p. 198.

47. Clive Y. Thomas, 'State Capitalism in Guyana: An Assessment of Burnham's Co-operative Socialist Republic,' in Ambursley and Cohen, eds., *Crisis in the Caribbean*, p. 29; and Spinner, A Political and Social History of Guyana, 1945-1983, p. 136.

48. Burrowes, *The Wild Coast*, p. 250; and Spinner, *A Political and Social History of Guyana*, 1945-1983, p. 141.
49. Julian Mayfield, 'Political Refugees and the Politics of Guyana,' *Black Scholar*, vol. 4., July-August 1973, pp. 33-35; and Marvin X, 'A Conversation with Forbes Burnham,' *Black Scholar*, vol. 4, February 1973, pp. 24-31.
50. Latin America Bureau, ed., *Guyana: Fraudulent Revolution*, London 1984, pp. 53-56. The PPP refused to take its 'share' of parliamentary seats after the 1973 election, declaring a policy of 'noncooperation.' An opposition group statement declared that 'the National Assembly has been reduced by the minority PNC regime into a farce and merely serves to rubber-stamp edicts.' Burrowes, *The Wild Coast*, p. 275.
51. Spinner, *A Political and Social History of Guyana, 1945-1983*, pp. 148-149, 161.
52. Burrowes, *The Wild Coast*, p. 309. Chandisingh also charged: 'The PPP nurtured at that stage an almost pathological fear of being rendered irrelevant in a Guyana being led toward socialism by the PNC. Even the attempt to analyze, to work out socialist policies and tactics based on sound political judgement began to give way to sheer obstruction motivated by jealousy and malice . . . ' Chandisingh was named principal of the PNC's Cuffy Ideological Institute, and became a member of the party's Central Committee.
53. Spinner, *A Political and Social History of Guyana, 1945-1983*, pp. 162-163.
54. Latin America Bureau, ed., *Guyana: Fraudulent Revolution*, p. 55.
55. Spinner, *A Political and Social History of Guyana, 1945-1983*, pp. 169-170.
56. Thomas, 'State Capitalism in Guyana,' pp. 34-35.
57. Spinner. *A Political and Social History of Guyana*, 1945-1983, p. 157.
58. Essentially a Maoist, Benn withdrew from the WPA two years after it was formed. As Communist China's policies shifted to the right after Mao's death and the elimination of the 'Gang of Four,' Benn's small group also gravitated toward conservatism. In 1978 it formed a coalition with the People's Democratic Movement, led by Llewellyn John, Burnham's former minister of home affairs, and the Liberator Party, controlled by representatives of the East Indian national bourgeoisie. The newly united formation, the Vanguard for Liberation and Democracy, attacked the PNC generally from the right.
59. Spinner, *A Political and Social History of Guyana, 1945-1983*, p. 157.
60. Rodney's close intellectual kinship with James was expressed in his essay on 'The African Revolution.' Rodney observed: 'For nearly forty years, C.L.R. James has been interested in the development of political consciousness among African people and in their strivings towards grasping control of their lives . . . It will be found that anyone confining himself to the supposedly pure academic understanding of Africa will in fact fall short of the objective, because of lack of commitment and failure to relate theory to practice. The value of James's contribution to the African Revolution and to an appreciation of it stems precisely from the blend of committed scholarship and activism.' See Rodney, 'The African Revolution,' *Urgent Tasks*, no. 12, Summer 1981, pp. 5-13.
61. Trevor A. Campbell, 'The Making of an Organic Intellectual: Walter Rodney,' *Latin American Perspectives*, vol. 8, Winter 1981, pp. 49-63.
62. James Petras, 'A Death in Guyana has meaning for Third World,' *Latin American Perspectives*, vol. 8, Winter 1981, pp. 47-48.
63. Burrowes, *The Wild Coast*, pp. 304, 309.
64. Pearce, *Under the Eagle*, p. 158; and 'Guyana: The Faces Behind the Masks,' *Covert Action Information Bulletin*, no.10, August-September 1980, p. 20.

65. Spinner, *A Political and Social History of Guyana, 1945-1983*, pp. 185-186.
66. George Lamming, 'Foreword,' in Walter Rodney, *A History of the Guyanese Working People, 1881-1905*, Baltimore 1981, pp. xvii-xxv. One week after Rodney's assassination, the World Bank and the IMF 'proudly announced a special joint funding package totaling 100-plus million dollars and support for a multi-billion dollar hydropower aluminium smelter [in Guyana]. These events [were] heralded by the *Washington Post* as "good news for the Caribbean." ' See 'Guyana: The Faces Behind the Masks,' p. 25.
67. Ministry of Information, ed., *Forbes Burnham Speaks of Human Rights*, Georgetown, 1980, pp. 17-18.
68. Spinner, *A Political and Social History of Guyana, 1945-1983*, p. 211; and 'Guyana: Policy Switch Proceeds,' *Latin American Monitor*, vol. 3, May 1986, p. 297. Hoyte's selection as president was something of a surprise. Hamilton Green, vice president for production, was the second most powerful PNC leader after Burnham. One year before Burnham's death, Thomas Spinner observed that 'Green wielded considerable power . . . and would be next in line if Burnham were to [die].' (p. 200).
69. C.L.R. James, *Walter Rodney and the Question of Power*, London 1983, pp. 6, 8-10. James adds that Rodney was confronting an 'insurrectionary situation,' but he acted too prematurely. He failed to wait for an 'upheaval of the population . . . There was a danger that Burnham would strike, but I do not believe that, with the people there, Burnham could have put them in jail, and so on. On the contrary, maybe any attempt of his to act impatiently might have unloosed the upheaval, because it was there.' (p. 12).
70. Lenin, ' "Left-Wing" Communism — An Infantile Disorder,' pp. 517-518, 541.
71. *Latin American Regional Reports: Caribbean*, 25 September 1981, pp. 4-5; and 30 October 1981, pp. 3-4.
72. Spinner. *A Political and Social History of Guyana, 1945-1983*, p. 210.
73. Thomas, 'State Capitalism in Guyana,' p. 46. Other sources on Burnham and Guyanese politics include: UK Parliamentary Human Rights Group, *Something to Remember: Guyana 1980 Elections*, London 1981; Harold Lutchman, *From Colony to Cooperative Republic*, Rio Piedras, Puerto Rico, 1976; Cheddi Jagan, 'The Role of the Opposition in Guyana,' *Caribbean Review*, vol. 7, October-December 1978, pp. 37-41; Thomas J. Spinner, 'Emperor Burnham has lost his Clothes,' *Caribbean Review*, vol. 9, Fall 1980, pp. 4-9: Bonham C. Richardson, 'Guyana's "Green Revolution",' *Caribbean Quarterly*, vol. 18, March 1972, pp. 14-13; Bishwaishwar Ramsaroop, 'The Opposition in Guyana — A Response,' *Caribbean Quarterly*, vol. 8, Spring 1979, pp. 28-31; Leo A. Despres, *Cultural Pluralism and Nationalist Politics in British Guiana*, Chicago 1967; Robert H. Manley, *Guyana Emergent: The Post-Independence Struggle for Nondependent Development*, Cambridge, Massachusetts 1979; Paul Singh, *Guyana: Socialism in a Plural Society*, London 1972; and J.E. Greene, *Race versus Politics in Guyana: Political Cleavages and Political Mobilisation in the 1968 General Election*, Kingston 1974.
74. Yansané, *Decolonization in West African States with French Colonial Legacy*. pp. 144-145.
75. E.J. Berg and J. Butler, 'Trade Unions,' in J.S. Coleman and C.G. Rosberg, eds., *Political Parties and National Integration in Tropical Africa*, Berkeley 1964, pp. 366-369.
76. Cartwright, *Political Leadership in Africa*, p. 205.
77. Martin Meredith, *The First Dance of Freedom: Black Africa in the Post-War Era*, New York 1984, p. 334.

78. Ladipo Adamolekun, *Sékou Touré's Guinea*, London 1976, pp. 140-141.
79. Olatunde Odetola, *Military Regimes and Development: A Comparative Analysis in African Societies*, London 1982, p. 148.
80. See Diallo Alpha Abdoulaye, *La Verité du Ministre*, Paris 1985.
81. Yansané, *Decolonization in West African States with French Colonial Legacy*, pp. 145-146; and Cartwright, *Political Leadership in Africa*, pp. 207-208. Technically, Guinea was not a one party state until 1978, when the PDG declared itself a party-state. The Republic of Guinea became the People's Republic of Guinea.
82. Amin, *Neo-Colonialism in West Africa*, p. 237.
83. Cartwright, *Political Leadership in Africa*, pp. 203-204. Between 1959 and 1961, the investissement humain programme constructed one hospital, one maternity clinic, twenty two infirmaries, five 'village improvements,' 127 'administrative office buildings,' 413 'administrative housing' units, and 1,253 'Party Headquarters.' (p. 204).
84. Yansané, *Decolonization in West African States with French Colonial Legacy*, pp. 159-161.
85. Helen Ware, 'Female and Male Life-Cycles,' in Christine Oppong, ed., *Female and Male in West Africa*, London 1983, pp. 12-16. Touré himself claimed to have had fifty children, although he only married twice.
86. Amin, *Neo-Colonialism in West Africa*, pp. 90, 94; and see Claude Rivière, *Guinea: The Mobilisation of a People*, Ithaca, New York 1977.
87. Quoted in Brutents, *National Liberation Revolutions Today*, vol. 2, p. 71.
88. Sékou Touré, 'The Permanent Struggle,' *Black Scholar*, vol. 2, March 1971, pp. 3-9.
89. Yansané, *Decolonization in West African States with French Colonial Legacy*, p. 199.
90. Brutents, *National Liberation Revolutions Today*, vol. 2, pp. 35-36, 44.
91. Nikolai Kosukhin, *Revolutionary Democracy in Africa*, Moscow 1985, pp. 144, 148.
92. Aaron Segal, 'Cuba and Africa: Military and Technical Assistance,' in Levine, ed., *The New Cuban Presence in the Caribbean*, p. 134; and Brutents, *National Liberation Revolutions Today*, vol. 2, pp. 78, 186-187. Segal estimates that the Cubans had 350 military and fifty civilian personnel in Guinea in 1979.
93. Pearce, *Under the Eagle*, pp. 95, 96; and Yansané, *Decolonization in West African States with French Colonial Legacy*, p. 184.
94. Segal, 'Cuba and Africa,' p. 136.
95. Basil Davidson, 'No fist is big enough to hide the sky: building Guinea-Bissau and Cape Verde,' *Race and Class*, vol. 23, Summer 1981, p. 62.
96. Eric Pace, 'Ahmed Sékou Touré, a Radical Hero,' *New York Times*, 28 March 1984.
97. Studies which discuss Sékou Touré include Ladipo Adamolekun, *Sékou Touré's Guinea*, London 1976; Alpha Diawara, *Guinée: La Marche du Peuple*, Dakar 1968, Victor Du Bois, 'The Independence Movement in Guinea: A Study in African Nationalism,' Ph.D. Dissertation, Princeton University, 1962; Ruth Schacter Morgenthau, *Political Parties in French-Speaking West Africa*, Oxford 1964; R.W. Johnson, 'The PDG and the Mamou "deviation",' in C. Allen and R.W. Johnson, eds., *African Perspectives*, Cambridge 1970; and R.W. Johnson, 'Politics in Guinea to the Emergence of the PDG, 1945-1953,' B. Phil. thesis, Oxford University, 1967.
98. Befekadu Zegeye, 'On the Nature of "Leftist Juntas",' *Monthly Review*, vol.

31, July-August 1979, pp. 51-61.
Zegeye also makes another crucial observation about 'left juntas' – their capacity for organized terror equals the worst imperialist regime: 'Military governments, indeed, are notorious for their overt acts of oppression and terror. They commit political crimes few civilian governments would risk. And on the left, groups embracing a broad range of oppositional strategies have this in common: they have found military governments . . . always ready to fight. The juntas' willingness to do battle openly and by any means necessary has killed many a leftist insurrection in its infancy . . .' (pp. 58-59).

99. For instance, see John Markakis and Nega Ayele, *Class and Revolution in Ethiopia*, Nottingham 1978. Fairly uncritical works on the Ethiopia revolution include David and Marina Ottaway, *Ethiopia, Empire in Revolution*, New York 1978; and Raul Valdéz Vivó, *Ethiopia's Revolution*, New York 1978.

100. Fred Halliday and Maxine Molyneux note that the social revolution occurred 'in a country still dominated by pre-capitalist social and political institutions and with only the briefest overall experience of colonial rule. State and society diverged from the normal colonial and post colonial models.' Halliday and Molyneux, *The Ethiopian Revolution*, p. 14.

101. The Acheampong-Akuffo regimes of 1972-1979 were a disaster for nearly everyone except military officers and the Ghanaian national bourgeoisie. Olatunde Odetola notes: 'during Acheampong's rule the Ghanaian economy had been plundered by both the army and the civilian businessmen and his rule represented a textbook case of mismanagement. Between 1975 and 1978 the trade deficit had increased, money supply was completely out of control, inflation between 1976 and 1977 reached triple figures. The productive sector of the economy had been starved of foreign exchange, and of spare parts and raw materials; and cocoa had been neglected . . . During 1976-77 the money supply had risen by 45 percent, and by 65 percent in 1977-78.' Odetola, *Military Regimes and Development*, p. 136.

102. Jan Pieterse, 'Rawlings and the 1979 revolt in Ghana,' *Race and Class*, vol. 23, Spring 1982, p. 253.

103. Odetola, *Military Regimes and Development*, p. 72; and *Ibid.*, pp. 251-273.

104. Kwarteng Mensah, 'The December intervention and the current situation in Ghana,' *Race and Class*, vol. 24, Summer 1982, pp. 71-78.

105. *Ibid.*, pp. 72, 73, 77.

106. 'Ghana: Scribes Inside'; and 'Ghana: The Survival Stakes,' *Africa Confidential*, vol. 24, nos. 16 and 17, 1983.

107. A Chief lieutenant of the late Prime Minister Busia, J. Manu, was also among those arrested. See 'Ghana: The Survival Stakes'; and 'Ghana: Rebound,' *Africa Confidential*, vol. 26, no. 16, 1985.

108. 'Ghana: The Survival Stakes.'

109. 'Ghana: Ideological departures,' *Africa Confidential*, vol. 25, no.12, 1984.

110. One of the few remaining Ghanaian leaders identified as a 'leftist' was Kodjo Tsikata, Rawlings's 'special adviser on security matters.' Tsikata was made a full member of the PNDC in mid-1985. See 'Ghana: Cuba, Tsikata,' *Africa Confidential*, vol. 24, no. 24, 1983; and 'Ghana: Rebound.'

111. 'Soviets to aid Ghana,' *Baltimore Sun*, 22 August 1984.

112. Clifford D. May, 'Newly Stable Ghana Begins Showing Signs of Prosperity,' *New York Times*, 25 November 1984. Also see Jay Mallin, 'Ghana will return to civilian status,' *Washington Times*, 5 July 1984.

113. 'Ghana: Seeds of Revolt,' *Africa Confidential*, vol. 26, no.2, 1985.
The IMF had made further loans to Ghana conditional only on the appointment of

'sensible people' in charge of all production. Ghana responded by dissolving its management collectives; full time 'managing directors' were given 'full responsibility and direct personal accountability for the day-to-day management of their enterprises.' So much for workers' control. See 'Ghana: All the Committees,' *Africa Confidential*, vol. 25, no. 25, 1984.
   114. Lasisi Alao, 'Rawlings confronts his workers,' *Guardian*, 21 May 1986. Plots and conspiracies against the regime continue. In April 1986, for example, nine more people were sentenced to death for organizing against Rawlings. See 'Ghanaian Convictions,' *Africa News*, no. 26, 16 June 1986, p. 16.

Chapter 4

   1. Quoted in Catherine A. Sunshine, *The Caribbean: Survival, Struggle and Sovereignty*, Washington, D.C. 1985, p. 96.
   2. Bryce Marcus and Michael Taber, eds., *Maurcie Bishop Speaks: The Grenada Revolution*, 1979-83, New York 1983, pp. xxviii-xxxiii, xxxviii-xxxix.
   3. Bernard Coard, *Revolutionary Grenada: A Big and Popular School*, London 1985, pp. 3-4.
   4. Editorial de Ciencias Sociales, *Grenada: The World Against the Crime*, Havana 1983, pp. 10, 238, 239, 242.
   5. A.W. Singham, *The Hero and the Crowd in a Colonial Polity*, New Haven, Connecticut 1968, pp. 45, 74; and George Brizan, *Grenada, Island of Conflict: From Amerindians to People's Revolution, 1498-1979*, London 1984, pp. 229-230, 239-241.
   6. Singham, *The Hero and the Crowd in a Colonial Polity*, pp. 150-151.
   7. Brizan, *Grenada, Island of Conflict*, pp. 234, 237, 320.
   8. Chris Searle, *Grenada: The Struggle Against Destabilization*, London 1983, p. 7; EPICA, *Grenada: The Peaceful Revolution*, p. 37; and *Ibid.*, pp. 246-247.
   9. Brizan, *Grenada, Island of Conflict*, pp. 247-248.
   10. *Ibid.*, p. 320; Singham, *The Hero and the Crowd in a Colonial Polity*, pp. 87-88, 170-171; and Smith, *Stratification in Grenada*, pp. 13-14.
   11. Singham, *The Hero and the Crowd in a Colonial Polity*, pp. 62, 175, 185-186, 293; and Brizan, *Grenada, Island of Conflict*, p. 272.
   12. Singham, *The Hero and the Crowd in a Colonial Polity*, pp. 194-195, 261; EPICA, *Grenada: The Peaceful Revolution*, p. 37; and Steele, 'Grenada, An Island State,' p. 32.
   13. Singham, *The Hero and the Crowd in a Colonial Polity*, pp. 197, 270-278. The Colonial administration admitted before the election that it was 'powerless' to correct errors in the electoral rolls, and blamed the problem on the 'carelessness' of electoral supervisors. It cannot be shown that the disfranchised voters would have made a difference in the 1962 election. But Singham notes that 'there are grounds for believing that Gairy was probably more damaged by this than the GNP was.' (pp. 274-275).
   14. Bruzan, *Grenada, Island of Conflict*, pp. 325, 329.
   15. Singham, *The Hero and the Crowd in a Colonial Polity*, p. 185; and *Ibid.*, pp. 274, 276, 326-328.
   16. EPICA, *Grenada: The Peaceful Revolution*, pp. 42-44.
   17. Searle, *Grenada: The Struggle Against Destabilization*, p. 14.
   18. *Ibid.*, p. 16; and Arnaldo Hutchinson, 'The Long Road to Freedom,' in Marcus and Taber, eds., *Maurice Bishop Speaks*, p.8.
   19. EPICA, *Grenada: The Peaceful Revolution*, p. 45.

20. Singham, *The Hero and the Crowd in a Colonial Polity*, pp. 196, 263.
21. Brizan, *Grenada, Island of Conflict*, p. 332.
22. With the notable exception of GNP leader H. Blaize's Carricou constituency, the town of St. George's had been the center of anti-Gairy political sentiment for over twenty years. In the seven elections between 1951 and 1972, GULP constituency candidates ran well behind the party's national percentage of votes. In all national elections during this period, GULP received a national average of 52 percent of all votes cast; in St. George's, the average was 36.2 percent. Even in the election of 1972, in which the GULP candidate in St. George's defeated the GNP for the first time, the margin was merely 21 votes, or 50.4 percent of all votes cast. See Brizan, *Grenada, Island of Conflict*, pp. 359-364.
23. W.R. Jacobs and R.I. Jacobs, *Grenada: The Route to Revolution*, Havana 1980, p. 76; and Hugh O'Shaughnessy, *Grenada: Revolution, Invasion and Aftermath*, London 1984, p. 44.

O'Shaughnessy asserts that C.L.R. James's Marxism had 'a lasting influence on Bishop.' But Bishop's close friend Tim Hector, leader of the Antigua Caribbean Liberation Movement, states that Bishop was neither a 'social democrat' nor a 'Leninist . . . he was not an ideologically "hard" (person).' Hector adds that Bishop probably never studied James's writings beyond the *Black Jacobins*. Author's interviews with Tim Hector, Kingston, Jamaica, 20-22 September 1984.
24. Searle, *Grenada: The Struggle Against Destabilization*, pp. 17-18; and Brizan, *Grenada: Island of Conflict*, p. 337.
25. Fitzroy Amursley, 'Grenada: The New Jewel Revolution,' in Ambursley and Cohen, eds., *Crisis in the Caribbean*, p. 201.
26. Searle, *Grenada: the Struggle Against Destabilization*, p. 22; O'Shaughnessy, *Grenada: Revolution, Invasion and Aftermath*, pp. 43, 51; and Alister Hughes, 'Grenada,' *Caribbean Monthly Bulletin*, vol 13, April 1979, p. 10.
27. Searle, *Grenada: The Struggle Against Destabilization*, p. 21.
28. *Ibid.*, pp. 22-23; 'Grenada,' *Caribbean Monthly Bulletin*, vol. 8, January 1974, p. 2; and EPICA, *Grenada: The Peaceful Revolution*, p. 47. Grenada's SWWU officials had been trained by the 'American Institute for Free Labor Development,' a CIA-financed organization.
29. 'Grenada,' *Caribbean Monthly Bulletin*, vol. 8, February 1974, p. 19.
30. Latin America Bureau, ed., *Grenada: Whose Freedom?*, pp. 26-16; Searle.
31. O'Shaughnessy, *Grenada: Revolution, Invasion and Aftermath*, p. 51.
32. Latin American Bureau, ed., *Grenada: Whose Freedom?*, p. 27.
33. Alister Hughes, 'Grenada,' *Caribbean Monthly Bulletin*, vol. 9, Feburary 1975, p. 7; Hughes, 'Grenada,' *Caribbean Monthly Bulletin*, vol. 9, August 1975, p. 9; Hughes, 'Grenada,' *Caribbean Monthly Bulletin*, vol. 10, August-September 1976, p. 46; and 'Jacqueline Creft — First Woman in Cabinet,' *Free West Indian*, 5 December 1981, in Tony Martin, ed., *In Nobody's Backyard: The Grenada Revolution in its Own Words*, vol. 1, Dover, Massachusetts 1983, pp. 178-181.
34. Author's interviews with Tim Hector, 20-22 September 1984.
35. Alister Hughes, 'Grenada, '*Caribbean Monthly Bulletin*, vol. 13, April 1979, p. 9; Ambursley, 'Jamaica: From Michael Manley to Edward Seaga,' p. 83; Leonor Kuser, 'Bernard Coard's "Creeping Coup"; Interview with New Jewel Leader Kendrick Radix.' *Intercontinental Press/Inprecor*, vol. 22, 30 April 1984, pp. 253-256; and 'The Grenada Crisis,' published in *The International Book Fair of Radical, Black and Third World Books* pamphlet, London November 1983, pp. 10-11. The 'Grenada Crisis' notes: 'the OREL activists [were] bent on implementing a Soviet model of government on the Grenadian people.'

36. Author's interviews with Tim Hector, 20-22 September 1984; Latin American Bureau, ed., *Grenada: Whose Freedom?* p. 56; and Anthony Payne, Paul Sutton and Tony Thorndike, *Grenada: Revolution and Invasion*, New York 1984, p. 121.

37. Marcus and Taber, eds., *Maurcie Bishop Speaks*, p. xxxiv.

38. Alister Hughes, 'Grenada,' *Caribbean Monthly Bulletin*, vol. 9, April 1975, p. 6.

39. Brizan, *Grenada, Island of Conflict*, pp. 364-365. Within the People's Alliance slate, the UPP was alloted two candidates, the GNP had five, and the NJM received seven.

40. Sources on the 1976 election in Grenada include Shirley Brathwaite, 'Reflections on the Pending Elections in Grenada,' *Bulletin of Eastern Caribbean Affairs*, vol. 2, October 1976, pp. 15-17; and Patrick Emmanuel, 'The Grenada General Elections 1976,' *Bulletin of Eastern Caribbean Affairs*, vol. 2, January 1977, pp. 1-3.

41. Marcus and Taber, ed., *Maurice Bishop Speaks*, p. 18; and Payne, Sutton and Thorndike, *Grenada: Revolution and Invasion*, p. 15.

42. Brizan, *Grenada, Island of Conflict*, pp. 346, 348. In early 1984 Brizan established the New Democratic Party, which reflected the social democratic trend of the NJM's early development. Brizan advocated 'some of the most positive features of PRG rule in the areas of housing, health and education,' minus the 'leftists rhetoric.' In Caribbean political terms, Brizan roughly represented Grenada's version of Manley's PNP, or perhaps more accurately, the Jamaican party's centrist tendency, See Payne, Sutton and Thorndike, *Grenada: Revolution and Invasion*, p. 193.

43. Latin America Bureau, ed., *Grenada: Whose Freedom?*, p. 29; EPICA, *Grenada: the Peaceful Revolution*, p. 49; and Searle, *Grenada: The Struggle Against Destabilization*, p. 25.

44. Alister Hughes, 'Grenada,' *Caribbean Monthly Bulletin*, vol. 11, July-August 1977, p. 2; Hughes, 'Grenada,' *Caribbean Monthly Bulletin*, vol. 11, September 1977, p. 16; and Searle, *Grenada: The Struggle Against Destabilization*, p. 27.

45. EPICA, *Grenada: The Peaceful Revolution*, p. 54.

46. O'Shaughnessy, *Grenada: Revolution, Invasion and Aftermath*, p. 75.

Gairy's regime promoted a parasitic expansion of the state apparatus at the expense of the economy. Between 1965 and 1978, for example the percentage of the gross domestic product taken by government services increased from 11.8 percent to 21.9 percent. The percentages for the same years, respectively, in agriculture, fisheries and forestry fell from 38.8 percent to 32.2 percent; manufacturing, 3.2 percent down to 2.7 percent; and construction, 8.9 percent to 2.5 percent. The cost of living increased almost 300 percent between 1970 and 1977, and the real gross domestic product (in 1970 prices) declined in Grenada from EC $60 million in 1970 to $28 million in 1977. See Ambursley, 'Grenada: the New Jewel Movement,' pp. 194-195.

47. Author's interviews with Tim Hector, 20-22 September 1984.

Most interpretations of the Grenada revolution do not critically explore the immediate factors contributing to the decision to resort to armed force, beyond mentioning Gairy's order to imprison and execute NJM leaders. For example, Anthony Payne, Paul Sutton and Tony Thorndike observe: 'It was by this time quite clear that parliamentary democracy in a deeply corrupt political system could not defeat Gairy and that force was the only answer.' This assertion appears invalid for several reasons. First, Radix probably would not have fled the island if the NJM's Central Committee had concluded that an armed uprising was 'the only answer.' Hector's statements to the author are also reinforced by evidence obtained from

Louison. One of the most serious charges raised by Coard's bloc against Bishop in September 1983 was that the Prime Minister 'had been against the seizure of power on 13 March 1979.' See Payne, Sutton and Thorndike, *Grenada: Revolution and Invasion*, pp. 16, 120.

48. EPICA, *Grenada: The Peaceful Revolution*, p. 55; and Alister Hughes, 'Grenada,' *Caribbean Monthly Bulletin*, vol. 13, April 1979, pp. 6, 9.

49. Brizan, *Grenada, Island of Conflict*, p. 348; Ambursley, 'Grenada: The New Jewel Revolution,' p. 203; and Marcus and Taber, eds., *Marcus Bishop Speaks*, p. 25.

50. Alister Hughes, 'Grenada,' *Caribbean Monthly Bulletin*, vol. 13, April 1979, pp. 10-11, 14; and Brizan, *Grenada, Island of Conflict*, p. 350.

51. Ambursley, 'Grenada: The New Jewel Revolution,' p. 191; and Jacobs and Jacobs, *Grenada: the Route to Revolution*, p. 35.

52. Maurice Bishop, 'Imperialism is not invincible,' speech given at Nonaligned Nations Conference, Havana, 6 September 1979, in Marcus and Taber, eds., *Maurice Bishop Speaks*, pp. 49, 55; and Payne, Sutton and Thorndike, *Grenada: Revolution and Invasion*, p. 221.

53. The NJM's leading critic of Cuban Communism was Coard. Ambursley explains, 'Coard was somewhat fanatical in his political allegiance to Moscow and carefully studied the latest writings of Soviet scholars on socialist orientation in the Third World.' Some of the Soviets' criticisms of Cuba 'concern the ultraleftist errors made by the Cubans in domestic and foreign policy during the 1960s, the complaint that Cuba was an inefficient recipient of Soviet aid, the purge of pro-Soviet cadres from the Cuban Communist Party in 1968 and reservations about Fidel Castro's personal domination of government and party organs. Coard was determined that Grenada would not repeat these mistakes and "deviations" and he always insisted that the NJM maintain its autonomy from the Cuban leadership.' See Fitzroy Ambursley, 'The Grenadian Revolution, 1979-1983: The Political Economy of an Attempt at Revolutionary Transformation in a Caribbean Mini-State,' Ph.D. dissertation, University of Warwick, 1985.

54. Thomas, *The Cuban Revolution*, pp. 393-396. During the 1950s, about one out of ten Cuban workers was permanently jobless, and one quarter of the labour force was employed less than half the year.

55. Rosa Luxemburg, *The Russian Revolution*, Ann Arbor, Michigan 1970, pp. 70-71.

56. Thomas, *The Cuban Revolution*, pp. 601, 677-678. No veteran Marxists were selected for the 'new' Cuban Communist Party's politburo or secretariat in 1965. About one fifth of the central committee consisted of 'old' Communists.

57. Alister Hughes, 'Grenada,' *Caribbean Monthly Bulletin*, vol. 13, August-September 1979, pp. 21-22.

58. Ambursley, 'Grenada: The New Jewel Revolution,' pp. 203-204.

59. Payne, Sutton and Thorndike, *Grenada: Revolution and Invasion*, p. 215.

60. Searle, *Grenada: The Struggle Against Destabilization*, p. 125.

61. *Ibid.*, p. 127; and Payne, Sutton and Thorndike, *Grenada: Revolution and Invasion*, p. 19.

62. Marcus and Taber, eds., *Maurice Bishop Speaks*, p. 112; and Alister Hughes 'Grenada,' *Caribbean Monthly Bulletin*, vol. 13, August-September 1979, pp. 17-19. The PRG's representatives shared the view that the parliamentary process was divisive, counterproductive, or irrelevant. George Louison observed in May 1981: 'the masses have far more important things to do, like providing enough food and shelter for everybody, to be detracted and divided by elections.' See Payne, Sutton

and Thorndike, *Grenada: Revolution and Invasion*, p. 39. This position was faulty on at least two grounds. The Grenadian people had supported the NJM's insurrection against Gairy precisely because the GULP regime had violated the most elementary democratic procedures. GULP 'stole' the 1976 election through massive corruption, and hence it had ceased to be viewed as 'legitimate.' the NJM could have developed a system of elections which closely paralleled the Westminster model, while maintaining its parish and zonal councils in some form. There is no doubt that the NJM would have received an overwhelming electoral mandate, and could have continued to exert its hegemonic authority over the state. Second, some type of parliamentary election probably would have helped the PRG's relations with western European countries. Nicaragua's 1984 elections illustrated one possible model within the socialist orientation strategy.

63. Payne, Sutton and Thorndike, *Grenada: Revolution and Invasion*, p. 37.

64. Latin America Bureau, ed., *Grenada: Whose Freedom?*, p. 58; *Ibid.*, p. 124. Ambursley, 'The Grenadian Revolution, 1979-1983,' pp. 145-146; and 'Building a New Democracy,' *Free West Indian*, 13 March 1981, and 'Accounting to People Vital,' *Free West Indian*, 17 October 1981, in Martin, ed., *In Nobody's Backyard*, pp. 58-62.

65. Payne, Sutton and Thorndike, *Grenada: Revolution and Invasion*, p. 109.

66. Alister Hughes, 'Grenada,' *Caribbean Monthly Bulletin*, vol. 13, May 1979, p. 13; Coard, *Revolutionary Grenada: A Big and Popular School*, p. 41; and *Ibid.*, p. 24.

67. Searle, *Grenada: The Struggle Against Destabilization*, p. 90; Alister Hughes, 'Grenada,' *Caribbean Monthly Bulletin*, vol. 15, May 1981, p. 20; EPICA, *Grenada: The Peaceful Revolution*, p. 104; Payne, Sutton and Thorndike, *Grenada: Revolution and Invasion*, p. 31; and 'PRG Fires Public Worker,' *Free West Indian*, 7 March 1981, in Martin, ed., *In Nobody's Backyard*, pp. 194-97.

68. Alister Hughes, 'Grenada,' *Caribbean Monthly Bulletin*, vol. 16, February 1982, pp. 23-24; and Hughes, 'Grenada,' *Caribbean Monthly Bulletin*, vol. 17, January-February 1983, p. 4.

69. EPICA, *Grenada: The Peaceful Revolution*, p. 78.

70. Ambursley, 'Grenada: The New Jewel Revolution,' pp. 205-206; *Ibid.*, p. 79; Alister Hughes, 'Grenada,' *Caribbean Monthly Bulletin*, vol. 14, March-April 1980, p. 42; Hughes, 'Grenada,' *Caribbean Monthly Bulletin*, vol. 15, September 1981, p. 25; Hughes, 'Grenada,' *Caribbean Monthly Bulletin*, vol. 15, October 1981, p. 29; Hughes, 'Grenada,' *Caribbean Monthly Bulletin*, vol. 16, March 1982, pp. 31, 34; and Hughes, 'Grenada, '*Caribbean Monthly Bulletin*, vol. 16, November-December 1982, pp. 15-16.

71. Ambursley, 'Grenada: The New Jewel Revolution,' p. 205; EPICA, *Grenada The Peaceful Revolution*, p. 105; and Payne, Sutton and Thorndike, *Grenada: Revolution and Invasion*, p. 23.

72. Alister Hughes, 'Grenada,' *Caribbean Monthly Bulletin*, vol. 16, March 1982, p. 13; and Payne, Sutton and Thorndike, *Grenada: Revolution and Invasion*, p. 22. Private sector investment fell most sharply in the first three years of the revolution. From 1978 to 1981, private investment declined from EC $7.9 million to EC $2 million, and its share of the GDP fell from 7.7 percent to only 1.2 percent. See Ambursley. 'The Grenadian Revolution, 1979-1983,' p. 218.

73. Ambursley, 'The Grenadian Revolution, 1979-1983,' pp. 199-200.

74. O'Shaughnessy, *Grenada: Revolution, Invasion and Aftermath*, pp. 86-87; and Payne, Sutton and Thorndike, *Grenada: Revolution and Invasion*, pp. 24-25.

75. Alister Hughes, 'Grenada,' *Caribbean Monthly Bulletin*, vol. 16, April 1982, pp. 32-33.

76. Kwando M. Kinshasa, 'Prime Minister Maurice Bishop: Before the Storm,' *Black Scholar*, vol. 15, January-February 1984, p. 42: EPICA, *Grenada: The Peaceful Revolution*, pp. 69-70; Alister Hughes, 'Grenada,' *Caribbean Monthly Bulletin*, vol. 13, December 1979, pp. 12-13; Hughes, 'Grenada', *Caribbean Monthly Bulletin*, vol. 14, March-April 1980, p. 29; and Latin America Bureau, ed., *Grenada: Whose Freedom?*, p. 42.

The funds obtained from Libya and Iraq were far short of the total amounts promised. In late 1983 the Soviet Union was considering the PRG's request for EC $15 million to complete airport construction.

77. Payne, Sutton and Thorndike, *Grenada: Revolution and Invasion*, p. 110.
78. Ambursley, 'Grenada: The New Jewel Revolution,' p. 204; *Ibid.*, pp. 24-25, 111; and Ambursley, 'The Grenadian Revolution, 1979-1983,' pp. 197-198, 223.
79. Marcus and Taber, eds., *Maurice Bishop Speaks*, pp. 227, 241.
80. Author's interviews with Tim Hector, 20-22 September 1984.
81. Alister Hughes, 'Grenada,' *Caribbean Monthly Bulletin*, vol. 13, June-July 1979, pp. 19-20; Hughes, 'Grenada,' *Caribbean Monthly Bulletin*, vol. 14, January-February 1980, p. 24; EPICA, *Grenada: The Peaceful Revolution*, p. 86; and Payne, Sutton, and Thorndike, eds., *Grenada: Revolution and Invasion*, p. 26.
82. Alister Hughes, 'Grenada,' *Caribbean Monthly Bulletin*, vol. 13, December 1979, pp. 13-14, Hughes, 'Grenada,' *Caribbean Monthly Bulletin*, vol. 16, March 1982, p. 31; Hughes, *Caribbean Monthly Bulletin*, vol. 16, August 1982, p. 2; and Marcus and Taber, eds., *Maurice Bishop Speaks*, p. xxiii.
83. Marcus and Taber, eds., *Maurice Bishop Speaks*, p. 42; and Payne, Sutton and Thorndike, eds., *Grenada: Revolution and Invasion*, p. 26.
84. Marcus and Taber, eds., *Maurice Bishop Speaks*, pp. 120-121, 123; Searle, *Grenada: The Struggle Against Destabilization*, p. 81; and EPICA, *Grenada: The Peaceful Revolution*, p. 83.
85. EPICA, *Grenada: The Peaceful Revolution*, pp. 84-85; Marcus and Taber, eds., *Maurice Bishop Speaks*, p. 220; and Alister Hughes, 'Grenada,' *Caribbean Monthly Bulletin*, vol. 17, July-August 1983, p. 34.
86. Author's interviews with Tim Hector, 20-22 September 1984; EPICA. *Grenada: The Peaceful Revolution*, p. 99; Alister Hughes, 'Grenada,' *Caribbean Monthly Bulletin*, vol. 16, September 1982, p. 5; and Payne, Sutton, and Thorndike, *Grenada: Revolution and Invasion*, p. 112.

If Bernard Coard fancied himself as the 'Lenin' of Grenada's revolution, Phyllis Coard could be depicted as the revolution's 'Zinoviev' – vain, egotistic, elitist, and dogmatic. Hector states that Coard was certainly a strong feminist, and well grounded in Marxist-Leninist theory. But she retained something of her upper class, Jamaican background, and was probably 'the least popular leader' in the PRG. Phyllis Coard and Creft were never close, personally or politically.

87. EPICA, *Grenada: The Peaceful Revolution*, pp. 98-99, 115; Alister Hughes, 'Grenada,' *Caribbean Monthly Bulletin*, vol. 14, November-December 1980, p. 12.
88. Marcus and Taber, eds., *Maurice Bishop Speaks*, p. 21; EPICA, eds., *Grenada: The Peaceful Revolution*, p. 101; Alister Hughes, 'Grenada,' *Caribbean Monthly Bulletin*, vol. 14, January-February 1980, p. 21; and Payne, Sutton and Thorndike, *Grenada: Revolution and Invasion*, p. 118.
89. EPICA, *Grenada: The Peaceful Revolution*, pp. 107-108; and Alister Hughes, 'Grenada,' *Caribbean Monthly Bulletin*, vol. 13, October-November 1979, p. 45.
90. Searle, *Grenada: The Struggle Against Destabilization*, pp. 71-73; Marcus and Taber, eds., *Maurice Bishop Speaks*, p. 68; Alister Hughes, 'Grenada,' *Caribbean Monthly Bulletin*, vol. 14, March-April 1980, pp. 32-33; and Hughes, 'Grenada,' *Caribbean Monthly Bulletin*, vol. 15, January-February 1981, p. 20.

91. Noam Chomsky and Edward S. Herman, *The Washington Connection and Third World Fascism: The Political Economy of Human Rights*, volume 1, Boston 1979, pp. 291-292; Jenny Pearce, *Under the Eagle: US Intervention in Central America and the Caribbean*, Boston 1982, p. 123, 125, 127; Payne, Sutton and Thorndike, *Grenada: Revolution and Invasion*, p. 92; Paget Henry, *Peripheral Capitalism and Underdevelopment in Antigua*, New Brunswick, New Jersey 1985, pp. 192-193; and Anthony P. Maingot, 'Cuba and the Commonwealth Caribbean,' in Barry B. Levine, ed., *The New Cuban Presence in the Caribbean*, Boulder, Colorador 1983, pp. 36-37.

92. 'Ocean Venture 81,' held in August 1981, was the largest US naval exercise since the end of World War II. Involving more than 120,000 men and 250 ships, the official scenario prepared US troops to invade a hostile Caribbean island group called 'Amber and the Amberines.' The choice of 'Amber' was not accidental; a site near the Point Salines airport, then under construction, is called 'Amber.' Follow-up naval exercises took place in November 1981 and in March 1983, when US ships were placed only six miles from the Grenadian coast.

93. Searle, *Grenada: The Struggle Against Destabilization*, p. 36.

94. EPICA, *Grenada: The Peaceful Revolution*, pp. 66-67; Alister Hughes, 'Grenada,' *Caribbean Monthly Bulletin*, vol. 13, October-November 1979, p. 48; and *Ibid.*, p. 40.

95. Marcus and Taber, eds., *Maurice Bishop Speaks*, pp. 113-115; and EPICA, *Grenada: The Peaceful Revolution*, p. 68.

96. Alister Hughes, 'Grenada,' *Caribbean Monthly Bulletin*, vol. 13, November 1979, p. 42; and Payne, Sutton and Thorndike, *Grenada: Revolution and Invasion*, pp. 40, 120.

97. 'Out The Torchlight,' *Free West Indian*, 20 October 1979, in Martin, ed., *In Nobody's Backyard*, pp. 96-98.

98. Marcus and Taber, eds., *Maurice Bishop Speaks*, pp. 156-157.
After his election in 1961, Gairy took control of the state-owned *Citizen's Weekly* newspaper, and transformed it to promulgate GULP's objectives. Renamed '*The Star*,' the paper promoted a strongly anti-GNP line. See Singham, *The Hero and the Crowd in a Colonial Polity*, p. 293.

99. Alister Hughes, 'Grenada,' *Caribbean Monthly Bulletin*, vol. 14, September-October 1980, p. 11; and Hughes, 'Grenada,' *Caribbean Monthly Bulletin*, vol. 14, November-December 1980, p. 3.

100. Searle, *Grenada: The Struggle Against Destabilization*, p. 41; and Alister Hughes, 'Grenada,' *Caribbean Monthly Bulletin*, vol. 15, October 1981, p. 26.

101. Payne, Sutton and Thorndike, *Grenada: Revolution and Invasion*, pp. 26, 39, 84-85.

102. *Ibid.*, p. 38; Author's interviews with Tim Hector, 20-22 September 1984; and Alister Hughes, 'Grenada,' *Caribbean Monthly Bulletin*, vol. 17, March-April 1983, pp. 11-12.

103. Payne, Sutton and Thorndike, *Grenada: Revolution and Invasion*, pp. 39-40; Author's interviews with Tim Hector, 20-22 September 1984; and Kinshasa, 'Prime Minister Maurice Bishop: Before the Storm,' p. 59.

104. Searle, *Grenada: The Struggle Against Destabilization*, pp. 48-52; Alister Hughes, 'Grenada,' *Caribbean Monthly Bulletin*, vol. 15, August 1981, pp. 1-5, 12.

105. Searle, *Grenada: The Struggle Against Destabilization*, pp. 49-50.

106. Marcus and Taber, eds., *Maurice Bishop Speaks*, p. 161.

107. 'Press Freedom: For Whom?' *Free West Indian*, 20 June 1981, in Martin, ed., *In Nobody's Backyard*, pp. 98-99. The PRG did not outlaw all criticism in the media. The *Free West Indian* published letters which were very critical of government policy.

Time, Newsweek and the London *Times* were also available in Grenada during the PRG's term.

108. Payne, Sutton and Thorndike, *Grenada: Revolution and Invasion*, pp. 119-120; Marcus and Taber, eds., *Maurice Bishop Speaks*, p. 164; and Alister Hughes, 'Grenada,' *Caribbean Monthly Bulletin*, vol. 16, July 1982, p. 14.

109. Luxemburg, *The Russian Revolution*, pp. 71-72.

110. O'Shaughnessy, *Grenada: Revolution, Invasion and Aftermath*, p. 103.

Tim Hector explains the dilemma somewhat differently, using Jamesian political logic: 'Bishop sought consensus with the Stalinist tendency represented by Coard . . . that consensus was not wrong, [but] it lasted too long. Therein lies Maurice Bishop's tragic flaw.'

111. Marcus and Taber, eds., *Maurice Bishop Speaks*, pp. 150-151; Payne, Sutton and Thorndike, *Grenada: Revolution and Invasion*, p. 105; and Author's interviews with Tim Hector, 20-22 September 1984.

112. 'Manifesto of the New Jewel Movement,' 1973, in Martin, ed., *In Nobody's Backyard*, pp. 41-42.

113. 'Jacqueline Creft — First Woman in Cabinet,' *Free West Indian*, 5 December 1981, in *Ibid.*, pp. 178-181.

114. Author's interviews with Tim Hector, 20-22 September 1984.

Members of the NJM recognized their links to the earlier revolutionary tradition of the Levellers. The *Free West Indian* observed on 13 March 1981: ' . . . there were people like the Levellers and the Diggers who thought that democracy was much more than the right to vote. It should be, they thought, a system through which each citizen actively participated in all the decisions affecting his life. The Grenadian experience did not happen by accident; it was shaped by the way in which the Revolution came into being . . . In a real democracy, like the one being built in Grenada, the most important role rests with the people. It means that the participation of every man, woman and child is decisive.'

115. Payne, Sutton and Thorndike, *Grenada: Revolution and Invasion*, p. 109; *Ibid.*; and Coard, *Revolutionary Grenada: A Big and Popular School*, pp. 34-35.

116. Kuser, 'Bernard Coard's "Creeping Coup," ' p. 253; and Author's interviews with Tim Hector 20-22 September 1984.

In November 1982 Hector confronted his old friend with his own reservations about the NJM, and the discussion degenerated into a shouting match. 'We must have a steeled, ideologically-advanced vanguard party, not a mass-based party,' Bishop argued. Given the omnipresent 'threat of [US] militarism, unity was necessary among leaders of the NJM.' Hector replied tartly and accurately, 'Your "vanguard" isn't s — ! It's ideologically confused, and despised by the masses.' Bishop broke off the debate, arguing perhaps to convince himself: 'Our revolution is not going to get bogged down in any ism or schism. The people are the driving force of this Revolution.' Hector's long association with Bishop was at an end. 'Bishop was actually much further to the left than Coard or anybody else,' Hector later reflected. 'But a true left is that which learns from and is led by the masses. The greatest failure of Bishop was his assumption that his critics inside the NJM possessed his own morality . . . that disagreements between individuals could be resolved peacefully and constructively.'

117. Author's interviews with Tim Hector, 20-22 September 1984; Payne, Sutton and Thorndike, *Grenada: Revolution and Invasion*, pp. 109-110; and Latin America Bureau, ed., *Grenada: Whose Freedom?*, p. 58.

118. Marcus and Taber, eds., *Maurice Bishop Speaks*, p. 216; and Payne, Sutton and Thorndike, *Grenada; Revolution and Invasion*, pp. 116-117.

119. Payne, Sutton and Thorndike, *Grenada: Revolution and Invasion*, pp. 36,

116-117; and 'Three Named to Commission,' *Free West Indian*, 11 June 1983, in Martin, ed., *In Nobody's Backyard*, pp. 65, 67.
The PRG's constitutional commission included Alexander, Jamaican Marxist Richard Hart, who was then Grenada's Attorney General, and attorney Ashley Taylor. The commission reviewed the constitutions from various nations, including Tanzania's. The general goal was to permit some form of direct participation by all sectors of Grenadian society, yet to maintain NJM political hegemony over the state apparatus.

120. Catherine Sunshine and Philip Wheaton, *Death of a Revolution: An Analysis of the Grenada Tragedy and the U.S. Invasion*, Washington, D.C. 1983, pp. 6. 10.

121. Payne, Sutton and Thorndike, *Grenada: Revolution and Invasion*, pp. 111-115.

122. *Ibid.*, pp. 119-128; Latin American Bureau, ed., *Grenada: Whose Freedom?*, pp. 59-60, 69-70; O'Shaughnessy, *Grenada: Revolution, Invasion and Aftermath*, pp. 114-119; and Marcus and Taber, eds., *Maurice Bishop Speaks*, pp. xxi-xxxiii.

123. *Guardian*, 16 November 1983; Don Rojas, 'Don't defend the Coard gang; Defend Bishop's legacy instead,' *Guardian*, 27 March 1985; and Johatan Bennett, 'Insiders, records and supporters tell of a revolution in disarray,' *Guardian*, 30 November 1983.
The testimony of George Louison on 1 November 1983 is particularly important, because it illustrates that most of Bishop's allies did not anticipate a power struggle: 'It was all very rapid. In a sense there was no notice. We always thought that we had one of the most united parties [that could] reach consensus on almost every issue . . . Therefore, [when] the issue of joint leadership . . . arose, and there was opposition to it by some comrades, we never thought at the time that it could have led to such a conflict.' *Guardian*, 30 November 1983.

124. 'A Talk with Fidel Castro,' *Intercontinental Press/Inprecor*, vol. 22, 30 April 1984, p. 248.

125. Payne, Sutton and Thorndike, *Grenada: Revolution and Invasion*, pp. 128-131; O'Shaughnessy, *Grenada: Revolution, Invasion and Aftermath*, pp. 123-127; and Latin America Bureau, *Grenada: Whose Freedom?*, pp. 71-73.

126. C.L.R. James reminds us of Cromwell's famous statement about the Leveller Party: 'either we deal with these people or they are going to deal with us.' James, *Modern Politics*, p. 15.

127. George Lamming, 'Lamming's Challenge to Barbadians,' *Caribbean Contact*, vol. 11, December 1983, pp. 9. 12.

128. Akinyele Sadiq, 'Blow by Blow: ' Personal Account of the Ravaging of the Revo,' *Black Scholar*, vol. 15, January-February 1984, pp. 9-12; Payne, Sutton and Thorndike, *Grenada: Revolution and Invasion*, pp. 130-132.

129. 'The Grenada Crisis,' p. 11.

130. Steve Wattenmaker, 'Behind the revolution's overthrow: interview with New Jewel leader Don Rojas,' *Intercontinental Press/Inprecor*, vol. 21, 26 December 1983, p. 761; and Payne, Sutton and Thorndike, *Grenada: Revolution and Invasion*, pp. 132-133.

131. Wattenmaker, 'Behind the revolution's overthrow,' p. 763; Alister Hughes, 'Grenada,' *Caribbean Monthly Bulletin*, vol. 17, September-October 1983, p. 43; and Sadiq, 'Blow by Blow,' p. 12.

132. Sadiq, 'Blow by Blow,' pp. 14, 17; and Payne, Sutton and Thorndike, *Grenada: Revolution and Invasion*, p. 134.

133. Payne, Sutton and Thorndike, *Grenada: Revolution and Invasion*, p. 135.

134. Sadiq, 'Blow by Blow,' pp. 14-16; *Ibid.*, pp. 134-137; O'Shaughnessy, *Grenada: Revolution, Invasion and Aftermath*, pp. 134-141; and Latin America

Bureau, ed., *Grenada: Whose Freedom?*, pp. 75-77.
135. Sadiq, 'Blow by Blow,' p. 17; and Payne, Sutton and Thorndike, *Grenada Revolution and Invasion*, pp. 136-141.
136. 'A Talk with Fidel Castro,' p. 248.
137. Sadiq, 'Blow by Blow,' p. 20; and Wattenmaker, 'Behind the revolution's overthrow,' pp. 762-763. Rojas claims that after Bloody Wednesday 'there was such serious demoralization within the armed forces that a mutiny would have broken out in a matter of days . . . The regime would have been left without friends, without neighbors, and most fundamentally without a people.'
138. Sunshine, *The Caribbean*, p. 128.
139. Sunshine and Wheaton, *Death of a Revolution*, pp. 12-14.
140. John Steel, 'Grenada's Free Press,' *Disweek* [Belize], 2 December 1983; Mohammed Oliver, 'Grenadian paper harassed by government,' *Militant*, 18 May 1984; and Seth Mydans, 'On Grenada, Sounding Off Again in Print,' *New York Times*, 5 January 1984.
141. Robert Costa, ' "Political Police" go into action,' *Guardian*, 23 November 1983.
142. Cathy Sunshine, ' "Rescue Mission" or Occupation?' *Guardian*, 6 June 1984.
143. Milton Benjamin, 'US pullout coincides with Coard trial,' *Guardian*, 12 June 1985.
144. Payne, Sutton and Thorndike, *Grenada: Revolution and Invasion*, p. 185.
145. 'Grenada Placed High on List of Human Rights Violators,' *New York Times*, 31 December 1985.
146. Cathy Sunshine, 'How the US New Right engineered the elections,' *Guardian*, 26 December 1984; Mark Allen, ' "Free" election in Grenada,' *Daily World*, 26 December 1984; Joseph B. Treaster, 'Grenada Politician: After Exile, New Incarnation?' *New York Times*, 26 July 1984; Treaster, 'A Centrist in Grenada,' *New York Times*, 5 December 1984; Sunshine, ' "Rescue Mission or Occupation?"'; and 'NNP in-fighting surfaces,' *Jamaican Weekly Gleaner*, 23 December 1985.
147. Keith Jeremiah, 'New Party Carries on Bishop's Work,' *Guardian*, 11 July 1984; 'Grenadians Start New Party Names After Maurice Bishop,' *New York Times*, 29 May 1984; Norman Faria, 'Spirit of Bishop lives in Grenada,' and 'New Grenada party aims to restore gains,' *Daily World*, 17 July 1984.
148. Caribbean Labour Solidarity and NJM (UK) Support Group, ed., *The Grenada Elections*, London 1985; and Rojas, 'Don't defend the Coard gang; Defend Bishop's legacy instead.'
149. O'Shaughnessy, *Grenada: Revolution, Invasion and Aftermath*, pp. 146-147; Ernest Hatch, 'Left debates Grenada Events: From Jamaica to Trinidad,' *Intercontinental Press/Inprecor*, vol. 22, 2 April 1984, pp. 169-171; Payne, Sutton, and Thorndike, *Grenada: Revolution and Invasion*, p. 129; Sunshine, *The Caribbean*, p. 201; and Author's interviews with Tim Hector, 20-22 September 1984.
150. Sunshine, *The Caribbean*, pp. 154, 200; Latin America Bureau, ed., *Grenada: Whose Freedom?*, p. 99; 'The Struggle for Democratic Socialism in Jamaica,' *Third World Socialists*, vol. 1, Summer 1984, pp. 38–41; and Sunshine and Wheaton, *Death of a Revolution*, pp. 25-26.
151. Sunshine, *The Caribbean*, 200; and Cathy Sunshine, 'Winds of change stir tropical isles,' *Guardian*, 22 August 1984.
152. Milton Benjamin, 'Rightist tide swamps another Caribbean nation,' *Guardian*, 9 May 1984.
153. Lamming, 'Lamming's Challenge to Barbadians.'
154. 'Conversation with C.L.R. James,' in Jan Hillegas, ed., *C.L.R. James:*

Every Cook Can Govern, and What is Happening Every Day: 1985 Conversations, Jackson, Mississippi 1986, pp. 25-26.

155. Jonathan Bennett, 'Insiders records and supporters tell of a revolution in disarray,' *Guardian*, 30 November 1983.

156. Lenin, 'Left Wing Communism,' in Institute of Marxism-Leninism, eds., *Lenin: Selected Works,* Moscow 1977, p. 570.

157. Sunshine, *The Caribbean*, p. 202.

158. Georg Lukacs, *Lenin: A Study on the Unity of His Thought,* Cambridge, Massachusetts 1971, pp. 30, 35-36. Lukacs continues: 'It is through struggle that the new element must be recognized and consciously brought to light from its first embryonic appearance. In no sense is it the party's role to impose any kind of abstract, cleverly devised tactics upon the masses. On the contrary, it must continuously learn from their struggle and their conduct of it. . . . If it fails to do this it will sabotage developments which it has not understood and therefore not mastered.'

159. Lenin, 'Left Wing Communism,' p. 551.

Index

Abdoulaye, Diallo Alpha, 184
Abrahams, Peter, 95
Acheampong, I. K., 78, 146–7, 189–90, 194
Achebe, Chinua, 88
Adamafio, Tawia, 119, 120, 126, 130–6, 138, 144
Adams, Grantley, 57, 71
Adams, Tom, 267
Addams, Jane, 34
Addison, Kodwo, 140
Adjei, Ako, 94–5, 97–9, 119–20, 122, 132–6, 144
Adjei, Mike, 192
Adu, A. L., 109
Aflaq, Michel, 47
Afrifa, Akwasi A., 76, 88–9, 92–3, 144–5, 190
Ahidjo, Ahmadou, 56
Ahwoi, 194
Akata-Pore, Alolga, 191, 193–4
Akrasi-Sarpong, Yaw, 193
Akuffo, Frederick, 189–90, 194
Alavi, Hamza, 67
Alexander, Allan, 255
Alexander, H. T., 144
Alexis, Francis, 264–5

Allende, Salvador, 153, 242
Als, Michael, 259
Alves, Bain, 18
Ambrose, Sydney, 222
Ambursley, Fitzroy, 154, 158, 169, 210, 213, 215
Amegbe, G. K., 105
Ametowobla, Rev. F. R., 115
Amin, Idi, 1, 10, 74, 78, 85–7
Amin, Samir, 21–2, 24, 51, 133, 135, 142, 148, 184–5
Amoako-Atta, Kwesi, 90, 147
Amponsah, R. R., 90, 105, 118, 123–4
Anderson, Perry, 34–5
Andreyev, I., 154
Ankrah, Joseph, 144
Apaloo, M. K., 116–7, 124
Apithy, Souron Migan, 46
Appiah, Joe, 96, 118, 123, 132, 149
Arden-Clarke, Sir Charles, 108, 110
Arkhurst, F. S., 91
Armah, Kwesi, 90
Armattoe, R.E.G., 111
Assad, Hafez, 158
Atim, Chris Bukari, 191–4
Atta, William Ofori, 98

Austin, Dennis, 89
Austin, Hudson, 210–1, 216, 219–22, 243, 245, 255–6, 261–2
Autra, Ray, 54
Avriel, Ehud, 122–3, 134
Awolowo, Chief, 62
Azikiwe, Nnamdi, 56–7, 62, 97, 104, 141

Baako, Kofi, 90, 100–1, 130, 133, 142
Badu, Kofi, 147
Bain, Fitzroy, 230, 249, 254, 256, 261
Bain, Norris, 216, 222, 260–1
Banda, Hastings, 1, 57, 121, 141
Barrow, Errol, 54, 57
Barry, Diawadou, 183
Bartholomew, Tan, 239
Barwah, Maj.-Gen., 89
Basner, H.M., 137, 142–3
Bates, Robert H., 48
Batista, Fulgencio, 151, 220, 223–4
Batsaa, Kofi, 115, 133
Belfon, Jane, 237
Bell, Eric, 167–8
Belmar, Innocent, 210–1
Ben Bella, Ahmed, 82
Benjamin, Milton, 267
Benn, Brindley, 177
Berg, E.J., 183
Berger, Victor, 33
Bettelheim, Charles, 159
Bhagwan, Moses, 177–8
Biney, Pobee, 102, 131
Bing, Geoffrey, 137, 147
Bishop, Angela, 238
Bishop, Maurice, x, 10, 179, 197–9, 208–12, 215, 217–27, 229, 232, 234–8, 240–63
Bishop, Rupert, 212
Bishop, Vladimir, 238
Blackwell, Morton C., 264
Blaize, Herbert A., 204, 217, 226, 264–5
Blatchford, Robert, 35
Blyden, Edward Wilmot, 17
Boateng, Kwaku, 90, 134

Bognor, Joseph, 136
Bokassa, Jean-Bedel, 1
Bossman, Kofi Aduma, 91, 104
Botchway, Kwesi, 193–4
Botsio, Kojo, 96, 98, 100–1, 105, 113–4, 117, 122, 126, 129–32, 135, 138, 147–8, 251
Boumedienne, Houari, 158
Braimah, J. A., 115
Braudel, Fernand, 3
Braveboy, Dorcas, 237
Brezhnev, Leonid, 88, 243
Briggs, Cyril V., 117, 40–1
Brizan, George, 200, 205, 216, 218–9, 221, 249, 257, 264–5
Brown, Egbert Ethelred, 18
Brown, Irving, 72
Brown, Sydney, 114
Brutents, Karen, 155–8, 186
Budlhall, Kennedy, 242, 245
Budlhall, Kenneth, 242, 245–6
Bukharin, N., 150
Burke, Nazim, 262
Burke, Victor, 214
Burnham, Forbes, 2, 55, 57–8, 64–5, 111, 158, 170–83, 185, 248
Burns, Sir Alan, 27
Burrowes, Reynold, 171, 178
Busia, K.A., 78, 91, 107, 109, 115–9, 138, 145–7, 149, 192
Bustamante, Alexander, 51–2, 54, 57, 162
Butler, J., 183
Butler, T. U. 'Buzz', 19, 51, 64

Cabral, Amilcar, x, 93, 152–3
Camar, B., 61
Campbell, Trevor A., 178
Capildeo, Rudranath, 63
Carmichael, Stokely, 186
Carter, Jimmy, 167–8, 178, 240
Carter, Martin, 65, 178
Cartwright, John, 59, 183–4
Casely-Hayford, J. E., 29–31
Castro, Fidel, 151–2, 157, 164, 167, 171, 174, 179, 193, 199, 220, 223–

4, 243, 257, 262
Césaire, Aimé, 2, 45–7
Chambers, George, 254–5
Chandisingh, Ranji, 175
Charles, Eugenia, 267
Charles, Sydney, 239–40
Chase, Ashton, 65
Chilembwe, John, 27, 30
Chinweizu, 103, 108
Christophe, Lieut., 10
Cipriani, Arthur, 18, 20, 51, 64
Clark, Steve, 198
Cleland, S. H. K., 104
Clemenceau, Georges, 31
Cliff, Tony, 159
Coard, Bernard, 198–9, 214–6, 219–23, 225, 227–32, 234–5, 244, 248–62, 264–6, 268
Coard, Phyllis, 214, 238, 248, 251, 254, 256, 264
Cohen, Robin, 154, 158
Columbus, Christopher, 6
Coombs, Allen George, 51
Cornwall, Leon, 214, 219, 221; 245, 256, 258, 265
Cornwall, Valerie, 237
Crabbe, Coffie, 134–6
Creasy, Gerald, 99
Creft, Jacqueline, x, 212–3, 216, 236, 238, 250, 252–3, 257, 260–1, 271
Critchlow, Hubert Nathaniel, 18
Cromwell, Oliver, 252, 259

D'Aguiar, Peter, 171
Dake, Mawuse, 193–4
Damas, Leon, 45
Damua, Rev. Kwabena, 191, 194
Daniel, Simon, 210
Danquah, J. B., 98–100, 102–4, 106–7, 109, 115, 117, 119, 125, 132, 141, 149
Davidson, Basil, 101, 107, 124–6, 129, 135, 137, 187
Dayan, Moshe, 122
Debray, Régis, 153
Debs, Eugene V., 32–4

De Leon, Daniel, 33–4
Deller, Charles, 103
De Riggs, Chris, 254–6
Dessalines, General, 9–10
Dia, Mamadou, 56
Diagne, Blaise, 30–1
Diallo, Sayfaulaye, 61
Diallo, Yacine, 46
Dinkevich, Anatoly, 157
Djan, Boake, 194
Djilas, Milovan, 159
Domingo, W. A., 17, 19
Donovan, William Galway, 18
Drake, St Clair, 132
Dube, John Langalibalele, 29–31, 43
Du Bois, W.E.B., xii, 31, 34, 43, 96, 112–2, 121
Duncan, D. K., 164–5, 167–70
Dunkerley, James, 213, 215
Dupuy, Alex, 10
Dwemoh-Kesse, Kwame, 194
Dzewu, Dzenkle, 100–1, 113–5, 138

Echeverría, Jose Estaban, 36
Echeverría, Luis, 164
Edun, Ayube, 51
Edusei, Krobo, 90, 100–1, 105, 113–4, 117–8, 122, 129, 132
Eiseman, Lisa, xi
Engels, Friedrich, 32, 154
Escalante, Anibal, 152, 224, 266
Evans, Phyllis, see Coard, Phyllis

Fanon, Frantz, x, 47, 66, 68, 82–3, 148
Farnana, Paul Panda, 44
Fedon, Julien, 7, 234
Ferguson, Clarence, 209
Fitz-Gerald, Sir Patrick, 137, 140
Fletcher, Benjamin Harrison, 33
Foner, Philip S., 33
Ford, Gerald, 165
Ford, James, 42
Forde, Cecil, 114
Frank, Andre Guner, 4
Fried, Albert, 33

Gandhi, Mahatma, 47, 58
Gairy, Eric M., 1, 199, 201–7, 209–14, 216–24, 226, 228, 231–2, 234, 236, 238–9, 241, 243, 260, 265
Garvey, Marcus, 17–8, 40, 44, 95, 122
Gbedemah, Komla, 99–102, 104–6, 113–4, 116–7, 120, 122, 126, 129–34, 136, 138, 145–7, 251
Gehagan, Basil, 214, 219, 221
Genovese, Eugene, 7, 11
Girvan, Norman, 166, 170
Goldstein, Melanie, xi
Gomes, Albert, 54
Gonsalves, Ralph, 241
Gordon, Max, 43
Gramsci, Antonio, 38, 138
Grant, A.G., 98
Guèye, Lamine, 31, 46
Gumede, Archie, 43

Halliday, Fred, 158
Hardy, Keir, 35
Harley, John, 144
Harvey, Franklyn, 208
Haywood, Harry, 40, 44
Hector, Tim, 214, 220, 238, 241, 245, 249–50, 253, 266–7, 271
Hersant, Robert, 73
Hertzog J.B.M., 28
Hillquit, Morris, 33
Hodge, Merle, 261
Home, Ninian, 7
Horne, Gerald, 121
Horsford, Bridget, 237
Horton, James Africanus, 30
Hosten, George, 213, 221
Houphouet-Boigny, Felix, 2, 10, 46, 59, 61, 141, 187
Howard, Sir John, 137
Hoyte, Desmond, 180
Huang Hua, 142
Hughes, Alister, 246, 262
Hughes, Victor, 7
Hunton, Alphaeus, 121
Hutchinson, Gerald, 240
Hutton-Mills, Tommy, 117, 123

Hyndman, H. M., 35

Ikoku, Sam G., 137
Iliffe, John, 155
Ivanov, Y. M., 29

Jacha, Aaaron, 31
Jackson, Sir Robert, 137
Jagan, Cheddi, 54–5, 57–8, 64–5, 111, 114, 158, 170, 173–5, 177, 180, 182, 266
Jagan, Janet, 54–5, 64
James, C. L. R., x–xii, 1, 9–10, 15–7, 20, 44–5, 58–9, 78, 92–6, 101, 103–4, 108–9, 126–9, 132, 136, 139, 149, 173, 177, 180–1, 208, 210, 215, 259, 271
James, Liam, 214, 245, 249, 254–6, 261–2, 269
James, Yvonne, 237
Jeffries, Richard D., 131
Johnson, Charles, 168
Johnson, J. C. de Graft, 114
Johnson, Phyllis, 84
Jones, Rev. Jim, 176

Kadalie, Clements, 28
Kaké, Ibrahima B., 25
Karikari, Kwame, 193–5
Kasavubu, Joseph, 66, 123
Kaunda, Kenneth, 57–8, 121
Kawawa, Rashidi, 54
Keita, Fodeba, 183
Keita, Madeira, 54
Kenyatta, Jomo, 2, 40, 44–5, 56, 70–1, 77, 83, 95
Kessie, Cobina, 103, 115
King, Sydney (see also Kwayana), 55, 65
Koana, Ohene, 178
Kole, Mate, 114
Korsah, Arku, 136
Kosukhin, Nikolai, 187
Kotoka, Emmanuel K., 88, 92, 144
Kouyate Garan, Tiemoko, 44, 46
Kouyate, Seydou, 77

Index   311

Kruschev, N., 134
Kwashie, Tetteh, 21
Kwayana, Eusi (*see also* King, Sydney), 177
Kwei, Joachim A., 191, 194
Kyem, K. G., 114

Lachmansingh, J. H., 65
Lacy, L. C., 132, 142
Lamming, George, 179, 259, 268
Lamptey, Kwesi, 90, 113–5, 123
La Vallette, Jean Pierre, 7
Layne, Ewart, 214, 245, 254, 256, 261
Lee, Grace, 94
Lenin, V. I., 36–9, 80, 87, 104, 154, 181, 234, 270, 272
Leopold II of Belgium, 20
Lewis, Gordon K., 197
Lewis, W. Arthur, 136
Limann, Hilla, 190–1
Liss, Sheldon B., 36
Louison, Einstein, 260, 262
Louison, George, 198, 216, 220, 222, 230, 235–6, 252, 255–6, 260, 262, 265, 268–70
L'Ouverture, Moise, 8–9
L'Ouverture, Toussaint, 8–11, 80, 271–2
Lukács, Georg, 271
Lumumba, Patrice, 123, 134

Macaulay, Herbert, 31
Macpherson, Sir John, 62
Magubane, Bernard, 28, 30
Mahabir, Winston, 59
Makabeni, Gana, 43
Makonnen, Ras, 92–3, 95, 97–8, 121–2, 125, 140, 142
Malcolm X, 142
Manley, Michael, 158–9, 162, 164–70, 172, 179, 182, 187, 242, 244, 266–7
Manley, Norman, 54, 57–8, 71, 162
Margai, Milton, 57
Maríatequi, José Carlos, 36
Marryshow, Theophilus Albert, 18–9, 200, 202, 216, 224, 234

Marshall, Alfred, 4
Martí, José, 10, 158, 224
Martin, David, 84
Marvin X, 173
Marx, Karl, 32, 34, 47, 137, 154–5
Mayfield, Julian, 173
Mazrui, Ali, 70
Mboya, Tom, 56, 58, 72
KcKay, Claude, 41
Mensah, Kwarteng, 191
Mikoyan, Anastas, 93
Miliband, Ralph, 153
Miller, Paul, 164
Mitchell, James, 267
Mockey, Jean-Baptiste, 59
Molyneux, Maxine, 158
Montet, Marius, 46
Moussiyko, Evgeni, 86
Mugabe, Robert, 57–60, 84
Munroe, Trevor, 164–5, 167, 214–6, 266
Murray, Roger, 106
Mutesa, Edward, 63

Napoleon Bonaparte, 10
Narayan, Jayaprakash, 47
Nartey, E. S., 114
Nasser, Col., 82–3, 122, 134, 160
Ndebugre, John, 193–4
Nehru, Pandit, 78
Nelson, Cecil, 167
Nguoabi, Marien, 158
Niang, Habib, 138
Nicolaides, Philip, 265
Nii Kwabena Bonne III, 98, 104
Nikoe, Ashie, 96, 101, 114–5, 123
Nimeiri, Jafaar al, 83–4
Nkomo, Joshua, 54, 59–60, 84, 121
Nkrumah, Kojo, 114
Nkrumah, Kwame, x, 26, 59, 72, 74, 76, 83, 88–149, 156, 158, 161, 173, 183, 186, 188, 191–4, 270
Nkumbula, Harry, 121
Noel, Lloyd, 210, 216, 222, 246–7, 249, 257
Noel, Scotilda, 212

Noel, Vincent, x, 216, 218–20, 222, 228, 249, 253, 256, 260–1
Nunoo-Mensah, Joseph, 191
Nurse, Malcolm (*see also* George Padmore), 18, 20
Nyemetei, H. P., 114–5
Nyerere, Julius, 2, 57–8, 60, 70, 87, 121, 141, 156, 158, 174, 210

Obafemi, Chief, 58
Obasanjo, Olusegun, 75
Obote, Milton, 63, 74, 78
Ocran, Turkson, 114–5
Odetola, Olatunde, 183
Odinga, Oginga, 56–7, 70–1, 76–7, 80, 83
Odlum, George, 208, 241
Ollennu, Nii Ama, 104
Olympio, Sylvanus, 74
Otu, Michael, 92
Ovington, Mary White, 34
Owusu, Victor, 90, 105, 118–9, 132, 192
Oxaal, Ivar, 52, 64, 78

Padmore, George (*see also* Malcolm Nurse), 42, 44–5, 58–9, 92, 94–7, 104–113, 115–6, 119–23, 134
Patterson, P.J., 106, 169
Pavlovich, Mikhail, 40
Payne, Clement, 51
Payne-Banfield, Gloria, 237
Pearleman, Moshe, 122
Petras, James, 178
Philip, Strachan, 242
Pierre, Leslie, 217, 246, 263
Pieterse, Jan, 190
Pinochet, General, 219
Plange, Kwesi, 101, 106
Plekhanov, George, 105
Poku, Bediako, 100
Pol Pot, 199
Popov-Lenskii, I. L., 40
Potekhin, Ivan I., 42, 83
Prosser, Gabriel, 11
Provencal, H. S. T., 134

Quaison-Sackey, Alex, 90

Radionov, Georgi, 134
Radix, Kendrick, 198, 208, 210, 216, 220, 222, 245–6, 249, 252–4, 256–7, 259, 262, 265, 268
Ramdhanny, Lyden, 216, 222, 228, 232, 257, 260, 265
Rapier, Faye, 237
Rawlings, Jerry, 160, 188–95
Reagan, Ronald, 168, 188, 195, 254–5, 263-4
Redhead, Lester, 261
Reindorf, C.C., 29
Renner, Awooner, 96, 113
Reno, Philip, 50
Renwick, C. F. P., 18
Richards, Alfred, 18
Richards, Alonzo, 33
Richardson, Jeremiah, 209
Rivière, Claude, 185
Roberto, Holden, 60, 72, 123
Roberts, Keith, 258
Roberts, Stanley, 246
Robertson, James, 64
Rodney, Walter, 5, 10, 65–6, 163, 177–82
Rodrigues, Carlos Rafael, 152
Rojas, Don, 198, 257–7, 265
Roopnarine, Rupert, 259
Roosevelt, Franklin D., 78
Rose, Renwick, 266–7
Ross, Joan, 237
Rottenberg, Simon, 19
Roux, Eddie, 43
Russell, Charles Edward, 34

Sadat, Anwar, 82
Sadiq, Akinyele, 262
St. Bernard, Ian, 254, 262
Saint-Just, 88
Samkange, Rev. Thomas, 31
Sandino, 153
Savage, Alfred, 64
Schachtman, Max, 94, 159
Scheck, Saki, 100–1, 105, 113–5

Schlueter, Hermann, 33
Scoon, Sir Paul, 222, 263
Seaga, Edward, 168–70, 267
Searle, Chris, 247
Seko, Mobutu Sese, 1
Selassie, Bereket, 69
Selassie, Haile, 81, 121
Senghor, Léopold Sédar, 2, 10, 45, 47, 56–7, 77, 141, 148, 156
Sharpe, Samuel, 11
Siad Barre, Mohammed, 84, 158
Silkin, Sam, 179
Sims, R. T., 33
Singh, Rickey, 267
Singham, A. W., 207
Sissoko, Dabo, 46
Sithole, Ndabaningi, 60
Smith, Gregory, 179
Smith, Ian, 84
Smith, M. G., 16–7
Smith, Mary, xi
Smith, Randolhp, 18
Smith, Stewart, 72
Somoza, 240–1
Spears, Edward, 137, 145
Spinner, Thomas J., 55, 171, 180
Stalin, J., 40, 63, 81, 154, 215, 252
Steel, Beverley, 204
Stevens, Siaka, 54
Stokes, Rose Pastor, 41
Stone, Carl, 162–3, 167, 169
Strachan, Alister, 212, 219
Strachan, Harold, 210–1
Strachan, Selwyn, 207, 210–2, 216, 222–3, 231, 249, 251, 254, 258–9, 266
Stroude, Chris, 214
Sunshine, Catherine, 73, 263
Swainson, Nicola, 23, 49, 79
Swaniker, J. G., 114

Tamakloe, Ben, 103
Taylor, Kurankyi, 114, 118
Taylor, Regina, 237
Tettegah, John, 72, 91, 115, 122, 124, 127, 134, 141

Thomas, C. Y., 154–5
Thomas, Clive, 48, 172, 176–7, 182, 270
Thomas, L. C. J., 203–4
Thomas, Tillman, 246
Thomas, Sebastian, 210
Thompson, W. Scott, 141
Tidy, Michael, 70
Timothy, Bankole, 102, 105
Tiptip, Ole, 76–7
Todman, Terrence, 179
Touré, Mamouna, 187
Touré, Sékou, 2, 47, 54, 61–2, 70, 84, 120, 141, 156, 158, 182–8
Trotsky, L., 40, 104
Tshombe, Moise, 1, 66
Tsiboe, John, 103
Tsiboe, Nancy, 124
Tsikata, Fui, 193, 195
Tsvetaev, D., 86
Turner, Nat, 11

Ventour, John, 214, 254
Vesey, Demark, 11
Victor, Teddy, 210, 213, 216, 241, 249
von Freyhold, Michaela, 68

Wallace, George, 142
Wallace, Henry, 58
Walling, William English, 84
Ware, Helen, 185
Washington, Booker T., 30
Webster, Patrick, 239
Welbeck, Nathaniel, 101, 125
Westmaas, Rory, 65
Weydemeyer, Joseph, 32
Whiteman, Unison, x, 207–8, 210–1, 213, 220, 235, 252, 254–8, 261, 268
Whittingham, Peter, 165
Whyte, Winston, 217, 241
Williams, Dessima, 238
Williams, Eric, 6, 55, 57, 59, 63, 77–8
Williams, Henry Sylvester, 17, 20
Wong, Clinton, 55
Woode, Anthony, 102, 114–5
Wriggins, W. Howard, 124

Yakubu, Bawa Andani, 144
Yansane, Aguibou, 61–2, 185
Yearwood, James B., 18

Zegeye, Befekadu, 188–9
Zuma, A. B., 43
Zusmanovich, B., 42

Printed and bound by CPI Group (UK) Ltd, Croydon, CR0 4YY
22/03/2026
02076205-0008